HARD CANDY

Also by Barbara Condos
Beautifully Kept

HARD CANDY

Barbara Condos

B
C755

WILLIAM MORROW AND COMPANY, INC.
New York

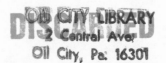

Library of Congress Cataloging-in-Publication Data

Condos, Barbara.
   Hard candy / Barbara Condos.
   p.   cm.
   ISBN 0-688-04477-8
   1. Caplin, Hymie, 1901?–1949.   2. Boxing—United
States—Managers—Biography.   3. Condos, Barbara.
I. Title.
GV1132.C26C66 1988
338.4'77968'3092—dc19
[B]   88-1391
                                                CIP

Printed in the United States of America

First Edition

1   2   3   4   5   6   7   8   9   10

BOOK DESIGN BY CONRAD CARLOCK

For my family.
And those friends who became family.

Contents

Prologue: Foreign Relations, Naples 1958   13

BOOK ONE: Lifelines   **21**

Doing Time   23
All That Jazz   31
A Friend of the Family   47
History Lessons   67
False Starts   83
The Sweetheart of Sigmund Freud   101
Night Flights   111
The Thing About Dying   129

BOOK TWO: Love and Kisses   **153**

Marriage, and Other Pleasures of the Flesh   155
Wife No. 2   179
Easy Come . . .   203

. . . Easy Go   215
Teresa   225
Serious Considerations   249
Daily Bread   259

BOOK THREE: Transitions in a Spaced Age   273

Changes of Heart   275

BOOK FOUR: Mixed Tense   317

Tale of Three Cities   319
A Matter of Blood   349
Sisters   371

BOOK FIVE: A Case of Mistaken Identity   393

Something Borrowed, Something Blue   395
Epilogue: Return to the Ring—New York 1987   423

The pain passes, but the beauty remains.

—Pierre Auguste Renoir
as an aging artist

Prologue

Foreign Relations,
Naples 1958

The terrace of the California Ristorante sits one step above the Via Santa Lucia, giving us a ringside seat onto the Naples street scene from our table. Important, if you want to keep your eye on your car, which Count Vittorio absolutely does. Even so well situated, he can see only one side of the car, and to do that, he has to get up from his chair. He rises and resettles at least once a minute, never breaking the pace of his patter, rapid Italian to the waiter, with a running replay in English. The waiter is patient with us.

"I order one special for you with onions and green peppers," says Vittorio.

"I hate green pepper," says Melodye.

"Okay, I stop the green peppers." Vittorio adjusts the order.

"What about sausage and meatballs?" Melodye is not easy to please.

"I don't think they serve pizza that way, but I ask them," says Vittorio.

"They serve it that way in New York," Melodye challenges.

"But maybe not here." Vittorio meets her challenge, then retreats. "*Ecco, bambina,* it will be as you like."

Chalking that round up for my stepdaughter, I wonder how my own scorecard reads. There is Vittorio's leg, for instance, pretending innocence as it presses mine under the table. I pretend ignorance. That's not the answer. Twice he placed his hand conversationally on my thigh since driving from Pompeii, always as if to draw my attention to something special. We are both aware of the game, and my young *married lady* edge is slipping. And there is still Sorrento to get through before Capri.

Vittorio's leg is suddenly away, following the rest of him to the street, where he stands screaming Italian oaths at a band of kids trying to lift a fixture from his car. He returns smiling and complaining of how it's always like this in Naples and how those monsters would steal anything unprotected, the car itself if they could, but he was too quick for them, and let's order wine to settle our stomachs after our ride.

This sidewalk restaurant seems to me very much like every other sidewalk restaurant in Italy. Somehow familiar. A few tables away an old man sits with a small boy. The old man seems familiar, too. The small boy, one of Count Vittorio's dreaded street urchins, is unkempt, hostile, and sly. The old man is offering him an ice cream. It seems to me the offer is conditional. He wants the boy to clean his hands first with a napkin and some water. The kid refuses; the man takes away the ice cream and offers it again, the same condition. The kid hesitates, then refuses again. The man, half-affectionately, slaps the boy on his head. The kid, as if by reflex, slaps the man back, and they look hard at each other. Other tables are watching them, too, in a kind of awe.

"You know who is that man?" Vittorio whispers.

"No, who?"

"He is from America. He is a big mafioso from America; his name is Luciano."

"Lucky Luciano?"

"*Si, bella,* your country sent him back to Italy to wait to

14

die. He comes here every afternoon til seven o'clock, and then he must return to stay in his house until morning."

Lucky Luciano. I have stopped listening to Vittorio. I'm rushing through one of those moments when the things of your life seem to collide. Back to as it was before high heels and silk stockings, pre penny loafers and pleated skirts. Back past those parked cars where I flirted with my virginity to the songs of Frank Sinatra, back before my first corsage, before V day, Victory girls, and Victory bonds. All the way back to Stanley Loeb, eight years old, wearing glasses, pointing his finger, and laughing, while I scrambled on bloodied knees to gather my books from the pavement. He'd tripped me. Stanley Loeb, who had a crush on me since kindergarten, shouting, "Don't cry for your *daddy*, he can't hear you, he's in jail . . . he's a jailbird . . . a crook, everyone knows that, he's got two million dollars buried in your backyard, and they put him in the can 'cause he's such a big crook . . . ."

Other kids, other friends, had watched. Those same kids who used to follow my father through the neighborhood streets like puppies, waiting for treats, the hard candy and bubble gum he always seemed to find for them in his pocket. He explained how the crystal candy actually grew on strings. And how we should be careful not to crack our teeth. Playing games, pointing out the finer points of marbles, stickball, and street hockey, my father was a party. He created events, potato roasts in the vacant lots, scattered among the neat rows of Forest Hills homes, July fireworks, explaining about safety, fall tulip-planting festivals, teaching us how bulbs grow to flowers. He'd pal with the boys and flirt with the girls. He was the handsomest daddy in the neighborhood with the prettiest wife and the best-dressed little house.

No more. The ladies of the newly formed Hadassah snubbed my mother out of the organization. They whispered about us when we passed. We, the too well favored, were now fallen, and some were just a little pleased by it. I remember my older brother, Melvin, and I listening to our favorite radio show, *The Shadow*, about Lamont Cranston, who could become invisible and solve crimes. After each show, after the final "Who knows what evil lurks in the hearts of men? . . . The Shadow knows!," Cranston would tell about some infamous criminal brought to justice. One night he talked about my father. We turned him off quickly and sat looking at each other, knowing that around every radio in Forest Hills, kids were listening to those words. We thought about school the next day.

The next day Stanley Loeb tripped me. Getting to my feet and holding tight to my books, I ran the rest of the way home, trying to figure out a way not to go back to school. But I went, and came home, and listened to adult talk I didn't quite understand, about the no-good fixed judge and the appeals that failed and how much the lawyers would cost and whether the fighters would remain loyal and still consider my father their manager. That way there would be a little money, but not much, and we'd have to watch it.

I also watched my mother grow frail and ill. One day I found her kneeling on the floor of my father's closet, crying bitterly into his clothes, hugging and kissing those clothes and crying. I sneaked away before she saw me.

Sing Sing was a short trip from New York, but later, when my father was transferred to Auburn prison, it took ten hours to get there. Prison doors slammed shut behind us as prison guards watched with detachment the hungry embrace of convict and family. Embarrassed by the lack of privacy, embarrassed by the desperation of my father's touch, the glass that separated us, after greeting time was over, I hated those guards. Yet I begged to be taken to see him. He would harry my mother, not knowing how ill she was, and ask what she was doing for him: Had she spoken to this one or that one? What about Jim Farley, what about Burt Stand, what about the new appeal? Then, when my mother could no longer come, and with his face tense and worried, he would ask me of her condition. Did the X-ray treatments help; what did the latest biopsy show; could her disease be somehow related to something she had caught from him, the gonorrhea he had once brought home from Havana, where his first champion, Al Singer, had out-danced Cuban Kid Chocolate in a ring no bigger than a postage stamp? Could it be that? Had something started growing in her then? Was it his fault? And when did you see her last, Babsie, and how was she looking? And be a big girl, Babsie, write and tell me everything. But I didn't know everything.

And then I knew even less. Whispers filled the house. And finally Mother was lying in a room at Memorial Hospital that I never saw. The logistics involved in dragging children into the city to visit her was avoided by those tense, terrified persons concerned with us. But one winter day we went. And found Daddy there, accompanied by two businesslike detectives. He was waiting in the entrance lobby of the hospital. They'd allowed him out of prison to say goodbye to his Rosie. People said things: "Isn't it nice they let your father come to your mom because she's sick?" and "Be good children," and "Wait till after your daddy sees her and we'll take you up." And "Don't make noise; this is a hospital." We waited, and we were quiet. Then Father was in the lobby, again flanked by the detectives, trying to smile as he embraced us, his face wet, his eyes dead. And then came a choice: "Barbara, your mother wants to see you, she has something to say to you . . . but if you see her, you can't ride downtown with your daddy to the Tombs; there just isn't enough time for both." The Tombs was what they called the jail where my father was to stay overnight on his way back to the penitentiary. I hadn't seen my mother in five months, but I hadn't seen my father for a year. And how I wanted to ride again in a car with him, to cuddle, to hold and smell him, maybe even sit in his lap. "We'll bring you back to see your mom on Saturday if you want." So I rode with my daddy down to the Tombs. I rode with him, and my mother died two days later. There was never a Saturday.

After that I was to visit my father a little more often. Mostly we went on weekends, we visitors from the wider world, waiting on lines for okays to be given and gates to slide back. We waited with other visitors, who twisted handkerchiefs, adjusted glasses, and looked at their watches but not at one another. Only once do I remember seeing another child, but I never learned who he was or whom he belonged to. We didn't talk.

Prologue

It had taken political angling to get my father transferred from Auburn, one of the worst of New York State's penitentiaries, to Comstock, a "reform" prison, where the rules were more humane and inmate trustees could even work on the outside. There my father lived in a little firehouse attached to the prison, just outside the main gate. At Comstock prison two places supplied beds for visitors. One was Queenie's, a dingy restaurant-bar with mean little rooms upstairs. At night the locals, mostly guards, dropped by for beer, darts, or pinball. Sometimes my brother and I and whoever brought us joined their games. Everyone aware of why we were there. Next door the rooming house operated by Queenie's sister was more comfortable. It even had curtains on its windows and clean towels in its rooms. Queenie's sister offered these comforts to compensate for the crazy old lady she kept locked up there. That old lady, probably their mother, moaned all day and sang all night. I would lie in the dark listening to her twisted lyric "Way down upon the Swanee River . . . that's where I slept last night," sung over and over.

But some mixed joys were to be found at Comstock. Visiting hours were no longer the only access we had to Father. We could wave at him in the morning, from across the road, while he tended the little garden of the firehouse, just outside the prison wall. Sometimes I could sneak across and get a quick kiss, usually more possible in the evening, after the sun had set and before the lights were turned on. The guards, a better sort than those at the maximum security prisons, might have known about it but pretended not to. My father, aware of who was on duty, would signal us, and then either my brother or I would carefully and quietly approach the side of the firehouse out of range of the guards and get our kiss. We vied for these turns, arguing about who had gone last. Sometimes we had a bonus. Daddy knew what the food was like at Queenie's, and he worried over it. When he could, he would smuggle us a bowl of homemade pasta topped with the pure Mafia five-hour tomato sauce he and Uncle Charlie, the other trustee who worked the firehouse, grew and cooked for themselves.

Finessing it past the guards to the rooming house, we ate it in the dark, listening to the crazy old mother's serenade.

Another bowl of spaghetti confronts me while I stare at Luciano and the boy. Saying, "Excuse me," to Melodye and Vittorio, I rise and walk to their table.

"Hello, Uncle Charlie." I greet him, standing nervously, half wishing I hadn't done it and had stayed put with my phony count. Charles "Lucky" Luciano turns and looks at me guardedly. "It's me, Barbara." I continue, "Hymie Caplin's daughter Babsie . . . do you remember?" The eyes relax and lead the face into a smile.

"Yes, of course." He grabs my hand and calls for a chair. "Just look," he says, "how big and beautiful you are. You got a lot of Hymie in you. How is your pop?" He sits me down, holding my hand as if I were a memory he wants to secure.

"He's dead," I say.

Charlie averts his eyes, reaches for the wine. And after a moment asks, "Of what?"

"Cancer."

"When?"

"When I was sixteen, about five years after he got out."

Charlie pours us some wine. "You kids were always on his mind." He grips my hand tighter. "I got him Lou Salica, the lightweight." Luciano says, "Your pop turned him into a champ. Everybody loved your pop, you know that." I know. His hand is still tight around mine. "You know he was an honest man, don't you? . . . The best in the business, he got a bum rap, he was railroaded, you should know that, those lousy Tammany chiselers . . . you were just a kid then, but that's how it was . . . don't let nobody tell you different." He lets go of my hand, pats my cheek, and keeps talking. "You really look a lot like him. So did your brother, what's his name?"

"Melvin."

"Yeah, Pal Mel your pop called him, a good-looking little guy, too. How is he, what's he doing now?"

Here we go. "He's dead, too," I say. Charlie looks at me carefully and asks what happened. I tell him Hodgkin's disease, like my mother.

Prologue

"My God," says Charlie "Lucky" Luciano, "my God." We sit quiet then, and I notice that the rest of the California Ristorante seems quiet, too.

Vittorio's face is staring at me in disbelief from across the terrace, his mouth actually hanging open. Melodye tries for my attention. "I am married now," I say to help the moment pass. Uncle Charlie manages a smile and pours me a second glass of wine. He asks about the lucky guy who grabbed me off and is he with me now and do I need anything and is he treating me right?

"He isn't a wise guy, is he?"

Charlie is glad when I say, "No."

And is he treating me with enough respect?

"Sure, of course."

"Well, if he don't," he tells me, grabbing my hand again, "just remember you got family, you know what I'm saying." I know and suddenly want away from this conversation. I want to be on the road to Sorrento, talking about Etruscan ruins, or in Anacapri, seeing the beautiful San Michele. I don't move. He asks more things, and as I answer, the day becomes evening. I signal Melodye to come over and be introduced, deciding to leave Count Vittorio where he is. Melodye offers her best parochial-school manners and says all the correct things. Talented child of theatrical experience, she picks up her cues.

Finally the kissing good-byes are over, and we return to our table. Vittorio has paid the bill, so we slip out of the restaurant, aware of sudden celebrity. The ride to Sorrento is strangely quiet. Melodye, secretly savoring the twists and turns of the ancient cliff road, asks some few, quiet questions about Uncle Charlie. I reply briefly and Vittorio never puts his hand on my thigh again. Nevertheless, I decide to save the sweetness of San Michele for the future. Surely I will pass this way again.

BOOK ONE

Lifelines

Doing Time

My mother had come home from the hospital again, and we were going.

The trip was always an ordeal, a vigil to be lived through because it had to be. Eight hours of trying to stay still and not drive her crazy. Against doctor's orders, she would go, at this point taking only me along, not that I was a comfort, but I was reliable. I could be counted on to contain childish crankiness and control my behavior. She would stare out the window and make small sounds of pain. And I would try to spot red barns or cows or anything exotic to focus on, keeping my discoveries to myself.

I did a lot of numbering, too. Telephone poles became tedious, and I missed too many. Then how much time should I let lapse before going again to the end of the car and pressing squirts of stale water into a conical cup? En route I'd number my steps to see if they stayed the same. Games to hold my attention. I'd decide the next person to walk the car would be a woman; if I was right, it meant good luck. Chancy, with conductors on the move. When I was right, I would cherish the luck, which I was stockpiling for my future. Sometimes someone would talk to me, but I tried to avoid that as it upset her.

"Stop tapping your shoes, Babsie; be careful or I'll take all my troubles out on you." I knew she would. How fiercely she'd shaken me when I put on the wrong shoes that morning. I'd heard her say the brown but put on my new black pumps anyway, to be pretty for Daddy. I took it in hurt silence. The important thing was the going.

So the tapping stopped, and the counting continued. My mother's hands, clenched on her lap, looked old and dry. When had that happened? Where had the plump fingers with their red tips gone? All her skin had gone funny. I knew that under her clothing her body held strange hard spots and squares of burnt patches and that the scarf on her neck covered the bandage she still wore over the cut they made that wouldn't heal. But her face was pretty, and passing men looked at her. She looked at no one.

"Bring me some water, Babsie." That was good. I moved quickly then, not counting and using two cups for extra firmness. I carried the water back with pride, proud she picked me to go with her. "Don't tell your auntie H. if she calls, Babsie, but we're going in the morning." Lying in darkness, I'd visualized Comstock prison and the half town that surrounded it.

In the bleak November morning we passed through the almost elegant streets of Forest Hills Gardens without luggage, or laughter. We boarded our bus, rode our subway, found our train, and tunneled to the top of New York City. There we rumbled above streets crowded with tenements stuffed with life. I wondered how many people lived in our swaying car.

Twenty-three, I decided. A hard guess based on two walks for water and nothing more. I was too low in my seat to count heads. If I were right, it would mean a great load of luck, and if wrong, well, I wouldn't lose much. My mother had closed her eyes, the quick-vanishing scenes of fields and farms wearying her.

Then a factory town. Dirty windows sent back the image of our train as we lumbered past. A yard full of broken-down railroad cars came and went, slowly. Twenty-three people in my car? I needed to know before we stopped and the count changed. Moving carefully to my knees, I peeked over the back of the seat. Six, nine, ten, twelve, "Babsie, sit down and stay down." A boy two rows back heard her and laughed at me. Hot-faced, I slid back down. Later, when she asked for more water, I wondered if she was making it up to me.

Nearing our station, I began to lay in wait for it. This stop everyone knew as a prison stop with its miserly platform and meager protection. One final count to the end of the car, avoiding eyes along the way. The conductor, polite and businesslike, handed us down. She stumbled.

"Mommy!"

"I'm all right, Babsie."

"Your stocking's torn."

"It will have to do. There's no store to buy more even if I wanted."

She struggled against herself, took my arm, and moved me along. Something left its funny taste in my mouth. I thought of Bandit, our prison-bred bird with black markings. Lots of prisoners raised canaries. We had buried Bandit in a kitchen match box which seemed too small to fit till she got him in. "He must have caught a draft," she'd said. I think her heart had broken when she lost the battle of electric pad and bulb-heated cage. I hadn't realized she loved him, too. Oh, I'd see him jump on her finger and take a biscuit from her lips, but those were tricks he did for all of us. "Don't feed Bandit apple, Babsie; apple gives him diarrhea."

Her hand was tight on my arm as we crossed the bridge to where Bandit was born. "Let me get my breath," she said, so we stopped, and I tried not to look down through the metal mesh to the water below. "We'll take two rooms at Queenie's," she said as we reached the other side. Her coughs, she explained, would keep me awake. It was too late for visiting hours.

The rooming house fed us cold turkey under hot gravy in honor of Thanksgiving. She didn't eat much but made me finish it all. They were having stuffed capon at home, a present from our old butcher.

"Don't be afraid, Babsie," she said as she left me in the ugly room with its iron cot and stained walls. "I'm right next door." Her room had a real bed, which I would have happily shared. It passed my mind that she preferred to sleep alone. Later in the night I heard coughing from her side of the wall. It was the kind of place where sound carries.

The morning broke sharp and sunny. Rushing through breakfast, we rushed again, too early, to wait for our time. The whole world became my father's face. She and I shared in this. We stared, unable to make talk, still holding on to the hug and kiss the law allowed before walking to our separate sides of the glass partition, to sit inches apart but touch no more.

He spoke of her trip, should she have made it, if she had the doctor's okay. She nodded. He decided to believe her. But kept looking at her hands pressed against the glass and her shadowed eyes and the corner of surgical stuff sticking out from under her scarf.

"Did Babsie have her breakfast?" he asked.

"Ham and eggs," she answered, with a smile, the first I'd seen in months, "not very kosher, but that's what they had, except for cornflakes."

"Oh, my God, Rosie, don't let the kid eat anything they fry over there! She's better off with cornflakes."

"I wanted her to eat something hot," she said.

"Listen, Rosie, they use cheap stuff over there, they get it from here, the guards sell it off. Rancid oil, spoiled food. Everyone knows it." He sighed and tried to smile. "Don't be upset, but be careful."

I wondered if she was worrying about the Thanksgiving gravy because she asked if he'd had turkey. He said that Thanksgiving was the only decent meal they got. We all were quiet again.

"Hymie, I spoke to Willie like you wrote, but he says there's almost nothing left from the purses after the promoters are through."

"He's lying."

"Well, that's what he says." She looked at her hands and took them off the glass. "He says he can't make the deals you used to make."

26

"He's stealing."

"The fighters"—she kept looking down, causing a black curl to fall out of place—"the fighters all want to work; they're willing to take less to help you. Allie gave a nice interview to Red Smith before his last bout. All about wanting to fight for you. I'd have sent it up, but they don't allow, well, you know. But it was nice. Only Willie says the promoters—" He grimaced and signaled her to stop.

"Why," he said in a funny voice, "why do you think Willie's never come to see me since Sing Sing? Because he's a guilty crumb-bum ashamed to look me in the eye." He spoke fast and artificially soft. He wanted to yell. My mother's eyes shot to the guard by the barrier. He kept going. "He's a penny ante weasel with no gratitude."

"Hymie, don't."

"A trainer I made him, 'cause we were kids together. Why, he couldn't hold a job sweeping up at Stillman's. He's not even a good stickman, he's lousy handling cuts. A boy could bleed to death with him in his corner." My father took a breath. "Listen, Rosie, make sure he gets a real stickman for Allie's next fight. Allie's a bleeder."

"Allie's a good boy," she said quietly.

"They're all good boys," he agreed. Then, looking at me: "Ah, Babsie, come on and smile for your daddy. Frowning makes lines. Tell me about school. Your report card says you're always late. Try and control it, it's a bad habit. And remember to sit straight. Look how you're slumping, no good, it cramps your breathing. Remember, Babsie, in this world the thing you gotta do is breathe. In and out. Almost everything else is a matter of choice. Are you pitching in at home? You're my good girl, and I'm counting on you."

I sat as straight as I could.

"She drew naked people, I had to slap her," my mother told him.

"Nah, Rosie, you shouldn't slap her for something like that. She's not a kid to slap. Talk to her, don't slap."

"I slapped. Where does she learn such stuff?"

"Where *did* you learn it?" he asked.

I didn't have to answer because a terrible sound blasted the room. It meant morning visit was over. "See you at three," he called as he followed the line of men through the narrow metal door.

I hated walking with the herd of other visitors. Outside the gate I pretended to fix my shoe so they could pass us by. Strangely Mother allowed me to take a long time doing it.

The afternoon visit, before the train ride home, was a cruel affair. We were led through the double steel doors precisely at three, and we waited. I watched the minute hand above the narrow door where the inmates enter. We'd already cleared the visitors' checkpoint with its minisearch.

"Is it all right if my little girl gives her father a candy bar?"

"Where did she get it?"

"At Queenie's, just now."

He stared at my fifteen-cent Hershey bar, blew into its slip-away wrapper, and felt it up and down. "I really should crack it," he said. Cracking would spoil it.

"Okay," he said at last, "you can leave it with me, and I'll give it to him after we pass him back out."

I hated that a guard could play God with a candy bar.

"Thank you," said my mother.

The guard accepted her appreciation. Keys clanked, metal scraped, and the narrow door opened to let in the gray-clothed men. One by one.

"Look at my beautiful little girl," Daddy said to the man with the gun; it was habit. "Look at my beautiful little girl," he'd say to friends met on our strolls, to Good Humor men selling us ice cream, to ticket takers at the circus. The guard looked and even tried to smile. "Look at my beautiful Babsie," Daddy said to the other caged men he passed as we walked our parallel ways to where we would sit.

"Keep it moving," the guard called.

My mother was walking unevenly, her hand to her breast. I saw her waver, then grab at a chair. My father watched her in horror. His quickly stretched hand hit the glass barrier. "Help Mommy," he said. I already was. She started to cough, then got it under control and sat down facing the barricade. "She can die at any second," my brother had said, but that was before they let her leave the hospital.

She smiled at my standing father and gestured me into my chair. "Something got stuck in my throat," she told him.

"Don't talk, Rosie." He leaned to the glass and made the sound of a kiss against it. By now he was the only man on his side not seated. He realized that and sat down hard. His shoulders, always held so straight, suddenly sagged. I'd never seen him cry before. It lasted only a moment, but it was enough.

The wind had come up strong, and we had to push our way against it, toward the station.

Only the rumbles and squeaks of the train broke the silence of our travel. My mother stared into the blackness, and I wished myself back asleep, but I couldn't get comfortable. I was worried about my skirt riding up.

"How would you like to go to the dining car?" she suddenly asked. What a wonderful question. I always wanted to go to the dining car. Ever since I was very little and we'd all gone to Florida, I had longed for dining cars. Our family, the fighters, and their families, we'd eaten in the dining car, and what jokes and games and card tricks. Singing, too. But on these trips we always brought sandwiches from home or bought them on the way back.

"Yes," I said.

"Let's go then," she said, and got clumsily to her feet. I walked close behind. The hard part was passing between the cars.

A black waiter in a starched white jacket seated us. He did it elegantly.

"I want the child to have some soup," she said. "Make sure it's hot." They had tomato or chicken noodle. I disliked chicken noodle, and she remembered. She ordered tomato for me and a glass of wine for herself. It was the only drink I ever saw her take except for the High Holidays.

I fixed my skirt so the prickly fabric of the seat wouldn't touch my nakedness. And arranging my napkin with great care across my lap, I sat very straight and very still. It would have been perfect but for the throbbing of my head, her soft, constant cough, and my father miles behind us.

The soup arrived so hot it burned my mouth. I dropped

my spoon too quickly on the cloth, where it made a red smudge. Instead of a reprimand, she asked me if I'd like a sip of her wine. I'd tasted wine before at Passover feasts, when Father, a cloth napkin on his head, had sung to us in Hebrew. When he paused, everyone tasted wine. This wasn't as sweet, but I swallowed, said thank you, and offered it back to her carefully, by the stem. Miracles were not for comment. Then I drank my soup slowly, making sure not to overload the spoon. When we finished, she paid the waiter and even left a dollar tip.

After we reached the safety of our seats, she touched me. First her hand on my forehead, then her lips. "You're very hot," she said, and I nodded. She made me bundle up, using my coat as a pillow and hers as a blanket. She watched me as we rumbled toward the city.

"You must have caught a draft," she said.

A year later I stretched my nine winters tiptoe by her coffin and stroked her cheek, something I'd never dared to do while she was alive. She was so shy of public touching.

All That Jazz

The thing of it was to seem like everyone else. But it was not a thing easily allowed. Especially not by Auntie H., Mother's Broadway-wise sister, pulled weekly off her slick turf to worry over moneys and papers in weedy Forest Hills.

"I really need this," she'd mutter between puffs of her Lucky Strike, "especially just after my poor Rosie. Where's your father's family, those ingrates? A few months of you kids was too much for them in their big houses. They were ready to stick you in an institution." They were? "And what," she'd continue, "do I know about kids anyway?"

She didn't. Since show business, she'd spent most days at the bridge club, playing gin, telling jokes, and waiting for "Almost Uncle" Eddie to arrive for his daily "rubber" before they took "a customer" to dinner.

"Don't think I'm bad for his business," she'd say, crossing the best legs on Central Park South. "I'm a helluva sport who knows how to jazz up a dull dinner. You think he's my meal ticket for nothing?"

"Rosie? I can't take your kids," she used to say back

when things were good. "Hymie has spoiled them rotten." Adversity hadn't lent us charm. But still, it seemed we were of some value.

"Look at them," she'd insist to the newest set of Daddy's lawyers, lining us up for their inspection. "Look at Baby Janice."

She shoved my sister forward. Janice promptly started to cry. Janice cried better than Margaret O'Brien. My brother and I lay in awe of her powers. "Get us some good pictures," said the lawyers. Auntie H. did.

"Smile, pretty little girl," urged the man behind the tripod. I turned up the corners of my mouth. Later, shuffling through those old scattered prints, I will think of a midget Mona Lisa, but then there was no room for thoughts, only for Auntie H., scowling.

"I really got lucky with this idiot," Auntie H. now proclaimed skyward. "On him I spent good money. Listen," she scolded directly, "I told you, I want these kids sweet, but sad, sad, get it?" My brother cringed, Baby Janice's eyes closed, and I dropped my corners.

"No good!" she critiqued. "Some time of it you kids are giving me. My whole Saturday. Stop making faces." She rushed in to rub rouge on my lips, straighten my barrettes, Janice's pinafore, and Melvin's tie. "Now," she commanded. Janice widened her four-year-old eyes, Melvin straightened tall, and I lifted the corners of my lips just a touch. The photographer snapped and snapped, and it was over.

"Be nice to Eddie at dinner," she warned as usual, ushering us toward her hotel. "Eat what he orders and no arguments. He gave up a customer for you kids."

The pictures may have helped because they let Daddy out the following year, carrying two new canaries and wearing a gray cap. He threw the cap in the garbage as soon as he got to our kitchen. Still, it remained hard to seem like others. At a certain year my brother decided to become a finger snapper and went on Saturdays to sit at the 3 Deuces and other Fifty-second Street dives to snap, in what he hoped was proper rhythm, while listening to music he had

no natural feeling for. All for Zeta Beta Tau. My brother,
who loved Bach, was lusting after girls who loitered around
fraternity boys, who listened to jazz. It had taken years to
get there.

"I just watch the bass player and snap to him," he said,
pleased with his ploy. "And I nod my head a lot. That way
nobody can tell. In fact, some black guy who was snapping
just like me asked me if I wanted to go to the Savoy with
him. Then they tossed him out. Said he was a jazz fairy."
What nobody could tell was that Melvin was dying. Hard,
even for me, to imagine this handsome six-foot sixteen-
year-old dying. But he was. And he knew it. The same
disease he'd seen kill his mother, only slower. But no one
spoke of it. Instead, my father boiled beef in milk bottles
and made him drink its bloody broth and dragged him to
clinics for miracles of medicine. Sometimes I went, too.

Between clinics Melvin laughed at P. G. Wodehouse and
Evelyn Waugh, argued politics with whoever would listen,
and picked on or protected me as the mood took him. All
the while he longed just to be one of the boys. He already
was one of certain boys, but those who wore glasses or had
refugee accents or scrawny shoulders: the intellectuals. But
it was the boys with Greek letters on their sweaters and girls
on their arms Melvin longed for. He didn't want to die a
virgin. So he let Davey copy his math and lent book reports
to Richie, combed his hair in a Sinatra swirl, and snapped
his fingers with religious fervor till it happened.

"Davey's done it," he told me one afternoon as he
poured the last of the milk into himself. "Davey, the guy
who's been admiring my deltoids. Well, he's proposing me
as a pledgie at tonight's meeting."

That admired neck development was due to masses of
lymph nodes pushing out the muscle. Thinking Davey's
misconception funny, he accepted the compliment as it led
to important talk of biceps and pectorals and girls. No more
sitting around with guitar fumblers learning the "Interna-
tionale." Big things were coming. But after a month of
joyously carrying their books, running their errands, and
being butt to their jokes, he was blackballed. It took only
one Zeta to do it. Those were the rules.

I was quiet as he sat on his bed, his head drooping over his inflated neck, and told me how it happened. He'd run, he said, all the way from the lunchroom to the gym lockers to pick up the notebook forgotten by a brother, and when he got back, breathing hard and waiting for his token of approval, Howie, the guy in charge of pledgies, told him, "You won't have to do that anymore, Mel. You've been blackballed." I watched him take down the big felt letters he'd tacked to his wall and fold them neatly into his drawer. I'd have flushed them down the toilet.

His old pal Alfred came by to console him. Brushing greasy hair off a mammoth forehead, Alfred said, "You're too smart for them anyway." My brother said being smart meant shit, and what hurt was not knowing what he'd done wrong. "Maybe," suggested Alfred, "they caught you whistling Mozart."

I thought that was funny, and Melvin told me to go away. But I stayed and listened as he worried about which Zeta had done him in. "It must have been Richie. Richie always said I was too slow."

"What does it matter who?" said Alfred.

"It matters," said my brother. I silently agreed. On further thought he decided it was Lenny. Lenny always called him "piker" when he didn't join their after-school pool game. Mel didn't have the money to lose, but he put in his time watching. Money was so tight then I'd pasted cardboard into the soles of my Capezio ballerinas to make them last. "Go to my pocket," my father would say, but mostly there was nothing there.

I knew Melvin didn't sleep that night because I heard music from his room. Rachmaninoff. Pushing into my pillow, I warned myself to stop thinking about him.

On the third day my father noticed. "What's bothering your brother?" he asked me in private. "He's acting funny."

"Ask *him*."

"I did," my father said, "but he just says it's nothing."

I shrugged and said maybe it *was* nothing. He told me not to be a smart aleck and walked away. Then he realized Melvin wasn't wearing his pledge button and knew.

"Did you tell him?" my brother asked on our way to

school. I said no, I hadn't; but he didn't believe me, and somehow I felt guilty anyway.

The fraternity boys in their little huddle avoided him in the lunchroom. Only Lenny in his Jerry Lewis voice, complete with spasm, called out, "Here comes Melvin!" and they laughed.

A week passed that way, and I was almost relieved when treatments kept him home a few days. On the second morning Mel was in bed, my father told me he'd meet me after school. I saw him as soon as I came out, his double-breasted Linton tweed, his cigar, his hat tilted back on his head. And his presence somehow embarrassed me. He was a great flirt, and I knew my girl friends thought him cute. He'd invented nicknames for them. Blond, blue-eyed Janet was Little Nell, he'd read himself some Dickens up the river; Beverly, whose breasts were enormous for any age, he dubbed Big Bertha, after the cannon. And told her jokes about the brassiere mob, known for their "holdups." There were no jokes today. "Where are they?" he asked. "Those Boy Scouts from that club?"

"I don't see them," I answered.

"Where can we find them?"

"I don't know," I said.

He gave me a stop-playing-games look. "They," I said at last, "must have walked to the village, " meaning Continental Avenue, where almost everyone walked.

"Let's go," he said.

They weren't in front of Penn Drug, and they weren't in the T-Bone Diner. "They might be playing pool." I was finally being helpful. We found the narrow entrance that led down to Forest Hills' one poolroom, between our Woolworth and our flower shop. I'd never been there. Girls didn't go.

"You'll have to come in with me," he said, "so I grab the right bum."

"Daddy, please don't make it worse." Did he intend to beat up Richie Levin? Could he?

I walked my ballerinas behind him, down the stairs, and into the low-ceilinged room. It was mostly empty, but two tables were crowded with kids. My torn sole caught on a rubber mat. He waited as I adjusted it and looked around. "That table there," I said.

"Come and introduce me to the main guy."

"He's the big one," I said, pointing out Richie. I didn't want to go any further. By now people had noticed us.

"Wait here then," he said, and walked toward their table. I waited in the darkest corner nearest the door and listened to the sound of cues hitting balls or rattling beads on strings. I watched as he interrupted their game. My father singled Richie out and was leading him, gently, by the arm back to where I stood. "You want *me* with you, buddy?" called a frat brother, pointing his cue like a gun.

"No," said Richie. "We'll be by the stairs."

"I'm coming with you," said his buddy, who turned out to be Lenny, the Laugh King, and followed along.

My father sat down midway up the steps. So did Richie. Lenny stood, leaning against the banister, rubbing his fingers along his cue. I waited on the bottom step, wishing it all over or never begun.

"Listen, pal," my father said, giving Richie one of his better smiles and ignoring Lenny altogether, "this is going to hurt me more than you." No laugh for this familiar joke.

"Listen," he went on, "I want to talk to you about my boy, but first promise you'll never tell him we had this talk. Okay?" Neither boy responded. "It's important," my father said, "that he doesn't know." He waited then, and finally Richie said all right.

"I know you all got together and put the kibosh on him, and the kid's taking it hard. In normal circumstances I'd never come to you," he said, no longer trying to smile, "but it's not normal circumstances." My father was having a bad time, and my standing there wasn't helping.

"Ah, shit," interrupted Lenny. "Blackball is blackball, and that's it."

"Don't talk like that in front of my little girl."

They both turned to observe the little girl, who was now standing with her meager chest out as far as it would go.

"As I said," he went on, "there are things you don't know that might mean something. Lemme ask you, was it for a real reason or just something petty?"

"What's the difference?" said Lenny, still tapping away with his stick.

"The difference," my father said, "is if it's something serious, then I'll stop now."

"All it has to be," said Lenny, "is some guy just doesn't want him around."

"Is that what it was?" They both nodded, and my father slipped his hat farther back. "It's not my nature to plead," he said, "but that's what I'm doing." He reached to his pocket. "Babsie, be a good girl, and get me a cigar, you know, Primadora." I knew he was supposed to cut down on smoking, but I took the dollar and walked the few doors to Penn Drug. Kids were still there, the same who were usually late to class and always ready to cut. "Hey, Barbara," called my second best friend, Ruth, whose brother played drums and who was just old enough and tough enough for my father to dislike. "What's up?"

"Nothing much," I said. Later, cigar in hand, I left. My father was standing by the pool hall door alone.

"I had a hot chocolate with the change, Daddy."

"That's all right," he said.

"Here's your cigar." He took it and let it roll between his fingers. Then he put it in his breast pocket.

"What did they say, Daddy?" I asked as we passed by the Forest Hills Tennis Stadium. Forest Hills, my geology teacher had taught only that day, was where great forests once grew from terminal moraine.

"About what, Babsie?"

"About blackballing Melvin."

"They said they would reconsider it at their next meeting."

"Do you think they'll take him back?"

"Yes," he said.

"Why?"

"Because I told them he was dying."

"But why?"

"Because it's true," he said, "and because he wants that Mickey Mouse fraternity." Dying.

"Did you belong to a club when you were a kid?" I asked. I wanted him to talk about when he was a kid. I wanted him to tell about swimming the East River and the fights between the Irish and the Italians and how his older brothers protected the Jewish blocks and maybe even get to the good part of how he met my mother.

He said, "Hold my hand, Babsie. I don't feel so good."

A full week had passed since the day of the poolroom and each afternoon I'd ask Melvin, "What's new?"

"Nothing," he'd say.

What was taking so long? Would they let him back in, or had they just said that to be rid of my father? Then I saw him walking along with Richie and other assorted Zetas. Those Zetas no longer looked so good to me.

"Well?" I said as he fumbled through the icebox, finding things to eat; when he could taste, he stuffed himself. "Well?" I repeated.

"They asked me back," he said with a crooked smile.

"Are you going back?"

"Oh, I don't know," he said. "They won't tell me who dropped the blackball."

"C'mon," I said. "You know you want to."

So, snapping our fingers and bopping our feet, we danced around and unfolded his Greek letters and tacked them up again, and he ran and fetched and groveled all the way to Hell Night.

"What happens on Hell Night, Mel?"

"I'm not quite sure, but after that you get your pin."

"Hell Night," my friend Ruth assured me, in her most knowing manner, "ain't called Hell Night for nothing. They put them through all kinds of jazz."

Did my father understand about Hell Night? I decided not to find out. After all, Hell Night was months way. My father had enough on his mind, like the blood in his urine, and how to arrange fights without a license, and who would care for us if he had to go to the hospital. Who would take care of us was the old problem when our father was away.

"What about the kids? Who'll take care of the kids?" had echoed about the house for months before my mother made her final trip to Memorial Hospital. It would have been too much for Auntie H. alone. Teresa, the sweet Polish girl who'd come to help our mother, and whose whole life changed because of it, had seen us through as best as she could. But she was now pregnant, and her husband wanted her home with her newborn. A wartime job meant he could afford that luxury. "We'll have to divide you kids up and send you to your father's brothers." Auntie H. had finally made up her mind.

Baby Janice had been sent to Uncle Ed and Aunt Martha, Melvin to Uncle Al and Aunt Lily, and I went to Uncle Harry and Aunt Sadie. Uncle Harry, handsomest of my father's handsome brothers, had been hooked by the ugliest of uglies. Mean as she was miserly, Aunt Sadie gave shabby shelter.

I slept in what I remember as an attic and frequently ate either before or after her family, as convenienced her. "There's no room at the table," she explained at those times to Uncle Harry, who turned his head away from as many domestic discussions as possible.

I didn't write my father the months I was there. What was there an eight-year-old could say? Following their daughter to school along the winding ways of Jamaica Estates, I was terrified to lose sight of her and be lost forever. My cousin didn't want me tagging along with her friends. So I struggled in solitude and sang myself to sleep with oldies, Gay Nineties songs my father had taught me. And I never said a word I didn't have to.

"She's become secretive like her mother," said Sadie. So I became. Writing poems about clouds and snow, I cried over *Jane Eyre*, those parts I understood, and prophesied terrible things for the hosts of my exile. One day Aunt Sadie said Teresa, baby and all, was to come back to look after us and I could go home.

"I think she has a fever," Uncle Harry said. "Let's call a doctor."

"House visits are expensive," Aunt Sadie told him. "She'll get over it." So the last week I lay in bed and counted days.

"You get skinny," said Teresa, as she unbuttoned my coat and unpacked my refugee bundles, which was a job as

I wouldn't stop hugging her. Who cared about "skinny"? I was home, and I didn't have to see Aunt Sadie anymore. I never spoke to Sadie again, not even at the funeral.

Two words were seldom spoken in our household. One was "cancer," and the other "prison." "When Daddy was away" or "the disease your mommy had" was said often. It became a way of dating our life: "before Mommy got sick" and "after Daddy got out." Later variations appeared: "around when Mel was in St. Vincent's" and "while Daddy was in the hospital."

"Is your father still in the hospital, Barbara?"

"Yes, Miss McCauley, that's why I didn't hand in the history assignment. It takes so long to get there by subway."

"It's all right, Barbara, you can make it up. I know you understand the work."

"Thank you, Miss McCauley." I took advantage of being "a case."

"How come you're excused from gym?" asked Jane Jones, my best friend.

"I explained that I get dizzy lately, and they said it was okay."

My friend Jane was in some kind of love with Melvin, but he never acknowledged her. Too bad, because she was fascinated by his dying. "Hang around with her," he'd say, sounding like my father, "and you'll wind up no good." Jane, who'd let some boys see her breasts, was his idea of a scarlet woman, and she and I had a history of misdemeanors, years of "Jane made me." She'd been placed in the gifted children's class two years before, and I never overcame the psychological edge. The two of us plotting away always made him angry. Hard for Melvin not to feel angry at a sister stuffed with health and steeped in sin. But I knew he could be bought. *Things* had become important to us. Things we didn't have, things other kids flaunted. And quite by accident I found a way to get "things." Things to camouflage pain. I became a shoplifter.

We'd gone, Jane and I, to Christmas-shop in Manhattan. Twenty-five dollars of baby-sitting money waiting to be splurged. When I was younger, my brother would take me to Macy's and help me select what I could pay for. Now I wanted to spend my money privately in stores like Bonwit Teller. The secrecy was for Robert.

I faced constant family fights over Belgian-born Robert. Neither my brother nor my father could stand him. He was notorious, the local bad boy and an accomplished pool shark. My brother bore him particular resentment as in order to meet me, Robert had offered to teach Mel the finer points of the game. It was a short-lived arrangement. Once he had my attention, Robert had no more time for Mel. "Don't let me see that Frenchie hanging around," said my father. So I didn't let him see, which meant secrets. Most of my Christmas money was reserved for Robert. But Bonwit's was more than I bargained for.

"Everything's too expensive here," Jane said, pushing me out the doors, where the Santas asked for dimes and carols rang out over public-address systems. Somewhere down Fifth Avenue, I realized I still held a seventy-five-dollar cigarette lighter right in my hand. "I'll give it to Robert," I said, delighted.

"A seventy-five-dollar lighter!" Jane was more practical than I. "Why not return it for cash." We huddled and worked out how to do it. "Put it in here," she said, removing a two-dollar hairband from its Bonwit's bag.

"It's not wrapped," I said.

"It won't matter," said she, and walked me back up the avenue to Bonwit's service counter to wait our turn.

"What's wrong with this?" asked the woman with the glasses on a ribbon.

"I don't know," I said, "but my father doesn't want it."

"Where's the receipt?"

"I lost it."

"Okay," she said, "just give me your name and address." I did. "And when you bought it?" She wrote down December 5, 1947, and I signed where she pointed. "Cash or credit?" she asked. She counted it out.

"You shouldn't have given your real name," Jane said as we subwayed home. We decided to remember that next time. Next time was the next Saturday. Within two weeks we had a blooming business and money. Money for "things": new ballerinas and burgers and, best of all, taxis. How nice to bribe my brother with jazz albums, the better to amuse those Zetas. We hit Saks for a compact, Best and Company for a music box, and De Pinna's for a wallet. De Pinna's only gave credit. But that was fine; we used it on gifts, selected at leisure. Christmas was a great success.

In the new year we took Jane's neighbor Trudy into the syndicate. She was the alternate returner, and we split with her, fifty-fifty, when she did. Then her cousin joined us. By spring, we'd formed a nice ring of boosters. "Remember," said Trudy's cousin, "anything over one hundred dollars is grand larceny." Trudy's cousin came from a family of lawyers.

Jane came from a family of philosophers. "Everyone steals one way or another," she said. I agreed.

"Where did you get that skirt?" My father noticed. I told him Jane gave it to me. "Nice," he said. It was Bergdorf's best.

"You will be the most chic girl at the dance," said Robert as I pirouetted before him, allowing my taffeta to twirl and my New Look petticoats to peek. "The noveau riche of Forest Hills, what do they know about style?" Robert adjusted his French cuffs and smiled. On silk-shod legs and satin sandals, making sure not to trip over the worn patch on the third step, I paraded my contraband out of our house, which was starting to crumble: Wood broke through the carpet-covered stairs, sun split the lining of the brocade drapes, and the chandelier under which Robert had waited was missing most of its crystals. Still, it looked good from the outside, I reassured myself, and that was what counted.

"Just like a queen," said Teresa, watching him hand me camellias for my wrist.

"What do you let Robert do to you?" Jane asked me in private, after informing my brother and two other Zeta pledgies that she believed in free love.

"Well," I answered carefully, "I don't let him go all the way. Only almost."

"What's almost?"

"Almost" wasn't the poking or grabbing of other boys, but something more mysterious. Robert's family didn't own a car, so our trysting spot was the remote end of the Long Island Railroad waiting room, around the bend, where only occasionally snoring drunks were a threat to our privacy. Polite men, they never awakened. After school we'd wind up wedged in a dark telephone booth, Robert on his knees, his head beneath my Bergdorf pleats pushing past my purloined panties. It was hard to tell this even to Jane. No other girl in our group reported such action. Melvin was right: I was becoming a scarlet woman.

The day Jane and I were caught was bright and sunny. My conscience was clear on that Saturday subway ride to the city. I had retired two weeks before and was along only for the ride. My father had told me too many get-away-with-it stories with bad endings. "Enough is enough," I'd stated.

Jane grudgingly gave in to me. "Let's just look at some dresses," she said as we strolled into Saks Fifth to sight-see. I watched Jane select similar styles and allow herself to be shown to a dressing room. I waited outside. Finished was finished.

Jane left the dressing room, satisfied and smirking. She handed back her bunch of garments, saying she hadn't found what she was looking for. Noticing her bunch was two dresses short, I looked to the Lord & Taylor's shopping bag on her arm. It was about to burst. Don't, oh, God of retired thieves, let it burst before we get to the street. I was too angry to speak, so we descended in silence. Behind us on the elevator some middle-aged women were saying words I should have paid attention to. Vaguely I overheard something like "Perhaps they'll return it and we won't have to—" But I was too angry to listen to them either. As we pushed through the second set of doors onto Forty-ninth Street, a heavy hand fell upon my shoulder, and one of the women said, "You girls better come with us."

The service cars were full of personnel leaving. I knew they all knew. Once in the security office, we found ourselves facing Jane's saleswoman and a tall man who needed only hat and beard to become Uncle Sam. They separated us into little rooms; they would talk to Jane first.

Reform schools danced in my brain. Bonita Granville being prodded into line with drably dressed institution girls who worked in laundries to earn gruel. I avoided the real memories of Sing Sing, Auburn, and Comstock. They didn't send kids to those places. But then Jane had lifted two expensive dresses, at least seventy dollars each. Grand larceny. Would it be right to let Jane, my partner in so much successful crime, carry grand larceny alone? One dress apiece brought the act back to petty. I thought I could make out the muffled sounds of voices and Jane crying. Then they came for me.

"Well," said the Uncle Sam man, "you know you're in trouble, don't you?" All thoughts of protesting disappeared. Tears watered my eyes and overflowed down my cheeks.

"I never—" I sobbed.

"We know," said Uncle Sam, "it's the first time, but this is a serious matter."

First time, I thought, how smart of Jane, and never again if they would only show mercy. They didn't look too merciful.

"I was on to them right away," said the saleslady, taking her bow. "Young girls do not buy such expensive dresses without an adult."

"We had money," I protested, tears and coughing muddling my words.

"You may have intended to buy," said Uncle Sam, growing even taller, "but you girls just thought it might be more fun to steal. Wasn't that it?" So he thought I was a naughty rich kid.

"No," I said, but he wasn't listening, just listing the choices open to him: calling the police; suing our families; turning us over to the juvenile authorities.

"Don't do it," I pleaded, and my crying doubled in volume.

"Do you know," he asked, "what happens to girls who steal?" I nodded, and he was pleased.

"First time," I blubbered. "Never before." He left the room. I stopped crying and added up the score. Maybe he wouldn't send us away. But then maybe he would. Would it get in the papers?

He came back with the store detective women. "Actually," said one, "this girl wasn't carrying the stolen goods, and as I understand it, she didn't go into the dressing room either." They looked at me. This was my moment to blame Jane. "Jane made me."

"Did you know what was happening in the dressing room?" demanded Uncle Sam. I dropped my criminal head and nodded. They went out, leaving me to cry this time without audience.

Uncle Sam reentered. "I'm going to call your parents before I decide what to do with you."

"But my mother's not there—she's dead—and my father is in the hospital." Uncle Sam wanted to know if my father was very ill. Then he left me again and came back with a red-eyed Jane and the women detectives.

"I've spoken to Mr. and Mrs. Jones. They asked me not to bother your dad and to trust them to punish both you girls." Was that satisfactory to the detectives? They said it was but made us sign papers admitting our guilt and promising never to enter Saks Fifth Avenue again. It was many a year before I did. And by then I had a credit card.

Dark by the time we arrived at Jane's, we stared into the lit windows of her living room. They all were there: her mom, her dad, her brother, and her cranky grandma, who never liked me to start with. Sitting and waiting. It was a long scene. We eventually admitted almost everything except the complicity of Trudy & Co. Forbidden each other for a month, I was to call Jane's mother every night and report on my behavior.

"Why isn't Jane hanging around anymore?" asked Mel the very afternoon of Hell Night. I'd have thought him too preoccupied to notice.

"She is being punished," I said.

"She must deserve it," said Melvin, and went out to meet punishment more gruesome than Saks Fifth Avenue could conceive.

They brought him home in Richie Levin's car around

three in the morning. He had finally fainted after having
been bound to a stake in someone's cellar for five hours of
blindfolded teasing and torment.

"Don't tell Daddy," he pleaded as he passed out again,
this time in his bed.

A Friend of the Family

Marie had moved in to help care for my father. Teresa was sullen, I suspicious, my brother outraged, and Auntie H. beside herself. She called her "bimbo" when she spoke of her. Only Baby Janice was delighted. Any port in a storm was enough for her. Any mommy, almost mommy, or even temporary imitation mommy was welcome. Teresa was Janice's slave, but it was not enough.

To everyone else, Marie was "Daddy's friend." Auntie H. stopped visiting on Sundays. But she would call me to talk of terrible things. Not just of Marie but of herself as well.

"I know," she would whisper, "my doctors aren't telling me the truth. I have cancer of the rectum. I know it. Save me the plot next to your mother. Just bury me there." If Marie answered the phone, Auntie H. would hang up.

"Is your father's friend staying with you now?" asked Mrs. Donner, our next-door neighbor. Her kitchen window faced our kitchen window.

It gave her a great point of view. From where I stood in

our shared driveway, I shrugged, sauntered off with food I'd smuggled for the stray cat.

"Don't feed strays, Babsie," she said, stretching to see what I was doing. "If you feed them, they never go away." I nodded and continued slipping the cat the remains of my tuna sandwich. Funny how Mrs. Donner called me Babsie, like one of the family. Intimacy born of years of windows and hearing each other's arguments. Years of our cut grass blowing across their lawn and our rainwater flooding their drain. Mr. Donner complained. Eventually Father chipped in to have the shared driveway leveled. Checking out the workmen's measurements, Mr. Donner swept up after them with satisfaction. The first heavy rain ruined his pleasure. Water continued to run down his side. "Rosie," Father had once advised Mother about words between Mr. Donner and herself over Melvin's bike, "Rosie, there are two ways to handle the man. One is to talk to him, and the other is to jump down his throat."

"I jumped down his throat," my mother had snapped.

At five years old I'd taken her literally. "Mommy jumped down Mr. Donner's throat," I informed Melvin, who chased me around the dining-room table.

"Your father's friend seems like a kind woman." Mrs Donner persisted. "Your father needs someone, you know," she went on. "You kids do, too." I stood to my full height, stepped away from the conversation. What did she know about our needs?

Marie had been medical assistant to Dr. Spielberg, a nose-and-throat man who cared for my father's fighters. Us, too. He detonsiled all of us in our season. My season occurred when I hit six.

"There's nothing wrong with my throat," I protested.

"It's to stop problems in the future," my father reasoned. "Nowadays everyone has them out."

"No," I said, "I won't go."

"I'm taking you tomorrow."

The next morning I locked myself in the upstairs bathroom. "You know I can take the door off," my father repeated in exasperation. Staring into the mirror, mouth stretched trying to locate my threatened tonsils, I didn't answer. It was clearly possible that Dr. Spielberg was going to jump down my throat.

"Babsie, I'm warning you," my mother shouted.

Then I heard Melvin's voice saying, "Here's the screwdriver."

I crawled off the sink and into the bathtub, pulling the shower curtain around me.

"Babsie, open the door like a little lady," insisted my father's voice.

The little lady stuffed her fingers in her ears and closed her eyes. That's how I was when he lifted me from the tub.

"Would it help," he said as he carried me down the stairs, "would it make you happier if I had mine taken out, too? Then we could get better together."

"Yes," I said.

So he did.

The ice cream the assistant brought after the ether wore off didn't make up for much. And though my throat healed long before his, my father never complained. That was the first I ever saw of Marie, but she had to remind me of it. Could she have been my father's friend way back then, when my mother was alive? No, it seems not. But she told me she had always liked him. And, it also seems, my mother had noticed it. I heard Auntie H. say so.

Marie was Italian and sexy and hairy. Her bleached mustache shone gold in the sun. The rest of her hair was pitch black. I once saw her naked. She looked as if a huge hairy spider was nesting on her crotch. Her eyebrows were thick and arched to her temples, and her big-toothed smile was surrounded by red, exaggerated lips. The Joan Crawford mouth. Very popular. She had large, swinging breasts, wide hips, terrific legs, and flashing black eyes. I'm sure all the other daddies on our block envied my father his "friend." God knows all the fathers at camp did.

"I'm coming on Saturday," my father had phoned to say. "What do you want me to bring you?"

"Lots of salami and franks and marshmallows. I'm allowed to have a campfire for my birthday." It was our first and only children's camp. Madam Bay's and the other places our fighters trained at didn't count.

"Twelve years old," he said. "It's hard to believe it. Soon you'll be a big lady."

I giggled. That was two summers after he had come out of prison, and somehow he managed to send us there despite the cost. Looking back on it, I realize he wanted space for Marie. At the time Auntie H.'s Sunday visits "to Rosie's kids" were devoted to what a waste of money camp was. So, as she sat and sewed name tags, she spoke of our nice porch, and our big backyard, and our rose garden, and the hose. It wasn't as if we were kids stuck in a slum, the way it had been for her. Auntie H. wouldn't give him a "two cents plain" for his "fancy plans."

"No," he insisted, "it will be good for them." And probably that was part of it. Marie, when she showed up at camp, came as a surprise.

"Remember me, Barbara?" she said after my father stopped hugging long enough to hand me three bags of Lindy's best. I looked up at the woman in her chartreuse dress with its padded shoulders and beaded design, teetering over me on her platformed, ankle-strapped, Betty Grable legs. I didn't remember her at all.

"No," I said, "who are you?"

"I'm Marie."

"She's Dr. Spielberg's nurse, you remember, Babsie," said my father. I thought I did. And that kind of smoothed things. Almost.

"See my salamander," said Janice, pushing the lizard she carried at Marie.

"What a nice pet." Marie smiled. "Does it have a name?"

Janice thought awhile and said, "I'll call it Little Marie." She grinned, exposing in glory the four-tooth gap that had fronted her mouth. She'd wiggled them out before they were ready, despite my warning her against it. It was that way with most things I warned her about. She was to spend a lot of time in braces.

We all went to lunch.

Janice was having a hard time at camp. At least once an afternoon she would come to me crying over something and wanting to go home. But this was her day. She and her salamander were all smiles for everyone. Especially for Marie. It certainly wasn't my day or Melvin's.

Melvin hated Marie on first sight. No, not true. On first sight he had wanted to "do it" to her. At fourteen poor Melvin wanted to "do it" to anything. "She," he said, tucking in his Camp Alamar T-shirt and adjusting his crotch, "is hot stuff." We walked in front of the rest to where the camp band was to serenade us when second sight came upon him. He realized there was something between her and Daddy. So he added, "But she looks like some kind of whore." My friend Jane and I had looked "whore" up in the dictionary. It said "N. Prostitute." "Prostitute" said: "N. Woman who engages in sexual intercourse for pay." I wasn't sure about that. All I knew was, the nicer Marie tried to be, the more uncomfortable I felt. That was never to change. Even when I learned to feel for her.

The worst of the day was the subjunior girls softball exhibition, which I was to play in. Afraid of balls coming at me, I, for reasons best known to counselors, was made catcher. The sun shone hot as I stood sweating out the last half of the last inning. Backed against the mesh behind home plate, I was trying to avoid the swinging bats, which also terrified me. I lived through slow hours of humiliation when it was over. Marie told me how wonderfully I played, how *she* couldn't do anything athletic at all. That was, in Melvin's words, "a crock of shit." She was working hard at saying the right thing. My father said, "You should ask to be shifted to the outfield, where there isn't so much action." He let it go at that. Melvin just said I stunk.

Before they left, my father took me aside to tell me how much he loved me and to give me the special birthday present he'd bought, a heart-shaped locket on a chain. "Open it, Babsie." My mother's face stared up at me.

"I'll never take it off," I said, making a big point of it. "Never. Did you pick it out yourself?" I carefully asked as he closed the clasp at the back of my neck.

"Sure. Why?"

"Nothing."

Then Janice came running to us in tears. "*She* sat on my

salamander" she moaned, pointing at Marie, "and squashed it dead. I hate her," she screamed, as Marie scraped lizard off the seat of her draped chartreuse skirt. I felt much better.

We didn't see much of Marie the following winter except for the two times she came to dinner. On both occasions our Teresa burned the food, I think by accident, but Marie took it personally. I knew the food burning was not uncommon with Teresa, who'd never cooked when our mother was able. We ate alone a lot. But next summer it was more Marie.

"They're doing it," my brother whispered as we pressed our ears against the pasteboard wall that separated the rooms of Hotel Naponach. "Right now they're doing it."

"I don't hear anything."

"Yes, listen, it's the bed squeaking."

I listened hard. Something may have been squeaking.

"Wait," he said, and left me for a moment to return with a toothpaste-stained glass from the bathroom. "Use this."

I pushed my ear into the glass.

"No, not that way, you moron, the open side to the wall. It amplifies sound."

Nothing much was being amplified, but my ear was getting sore from the pressing. Then I heard what might have been a moan and what I made to be the word "Hymie."

My brother grinned with fifteen-year-old wisdom. I listened harder with thirteen-year-old confusion. Did I hear the word "Hymie" again? If so, it didn't prove a thing. Eventually Melvin left the wall. "They're finished," he said. I felt as if I were going deaf. Melvin was hearing things that to my ears were as silent as a silent dog whistle. I didn't like it.

"I told you," he said, "they'd do it as soon as he got up here. Just check out her neck for a hickey." Hickeys were already understood to be serious sex. However, I didn't answer him. It was time to pick up Janice from the kiddie yard.

Hotel Naponach provided a kiddie program. We were

spending August in the Catskills. We kids and Marie. My father on weekends.

"It'll be a real vacation," my father said as he announced the summer's plan. "I need a real vacation." Auntie H. muttered along with something about her "payment after years of sacrifice." Daddy avoided hearing her.

"Why can't Teresa take care of us?" I asked.

"Teresa's taking her boy to her relatives in Connecticut."

"Why can't we stay home?"

"The doctor says Mel can use the country." So we all, including our last prison canary, went to the country. The canary had a wonderful time.

Actually, except for the presence of the "whore," Melvin was having a wonderful time. He was entering masturbation in a big way. And he whispered to me about the who-can-shoot-his-sperm-farthest contests with the busboys. And the intimate details of his flirtations with two princesses from Pelham Parkway. Cousins, blond, big-titted, they were accompanied by adoring mamas. The mamas were blond and big-titted, too. The area of the pool they staked out as their own was always heavy with admirers. "Betty—she's the prettiest—let me suck on her nipple," Melvin bragged. I didn't believe him.

The sleeping arrangements went this way. Melvin and my father, when he was there, shared one room, Janice and I another, and Marie had a small one to herself. All rooms adjoined and took up a floor of one of the little lodges that constituted Naponach. This schedule afforded Melvin midweek privacy with which to fantasize. Melvin's hormones were running wild.

"Daddy's here," I told Janice as I walked her from the kiddie yard to the pool.

"Where?"

"In Marie's room. He said he'd meet us at the pool."

"I want to go to Marie's room and see him." She pouted.

"He said the pool."

"Is Marie coming to the pool, too?"

"I suppose so."

"Oh, good," said Janice.

Melvin was already there, carefully covering the square

brown spot on his chest with zinc oxide, as my father had instructed. He was meticulous about doing it. Each time he came out of the water, he would spread the cream to the exact geometric outline of the mark. "By the end of the summer," my father had assured him, "you'll never know where you got treated." That seemed to be important. When one of the princesses asked about the whitened patch, Melvin talked of a rash.

"Boys who wear patches don't get no snatches." The lifeguard kidded him. The lifeguard was a great kidder.

"Are those your water wings, little girl?" he'd call to Marie as her breasts bobbed past the five-foot level. Marie would laugh, and I would wait till, as always, he'd ask me if I left mine home. The Bronx royalty, as it were, was islands of tits. In spite of myself, I was starting to take pride in Marie's set. It gave our group status.

Marie was having a tough time. Melvin was openly rude, I sometimes surly, and Janice either demanding attention or to be let alone. Only the canary let her change its water and sprinkle its seed without a power struggle.

"Marie is better-looking than those mamas anyway," I commented. Melvin couldn't deny it.

My father didn't look half bad for an old man of forty-one either. His blond hair, when he pushed it to "bunk the thin spots," fell in soft waves around his Duke of Windsor face. His blue eyes twinkled, and his freckled skin grew rosy in the sun. And everyone talked to him. His celebrity preceded him. Damon Runyon and Red Smith and even Danton Walker kept his name current. He still made good copy. And not just with the owners, who were old pals, but with the guests as well. His accomplishments had been cited by Jimmy Grippo, the hypnotist, who was the Saturday entertainment. I'd met Grippo before, at Lindy's, when I was little, the day after one of my father's boys had won a big one. Our table had filled with Runyon, Frank O'Hara, Mike Todd, B. S. Pully, and Jimmy Grippo. My father frequently had Grippo spend time up at the training camps to amuse his lonely, celibate contenders. So now, of course, Grippo introduced my father from the Hotel Naponach stage.

Before my father could stop it, Grippo got Marie up to

be one of his foils. He had Marie and two old men taking imaginary baths, singing love songs, and dancing to finger snaps. Then he commanded her into the audience to sit on the lap of the most attractive man in the crowd. She headed robotlike straight to my father, sat in his lap, and stuck her tongue in his mouth.

The audience roared. Melvin was infuriated, and I devastated yet in awe of the whole phenomena. Janice was asleep in her chair.

"He's turned us into a spectacle," my brother muttered.

"Jimmy Grippo?" I questioned.

"Him," Mel said, "Pop."

I think my father heard him but was busy assuring Marie she hadn't done anything "wrong."

The last Sunday we were there, everyone's hostilities came out of hiding. My father found me necking with a waiter in a parked car and didn't much like it.

"She's only just thirteen," he said, pulling Wally from the convertible by his collar.

"She told me fourteen," protested Wally, the "college man."

"What difference would that make? You're a goddamned veteran. And you, Babsie. What the hell do you think you're doing?" my father demanded.

"Not as much as you do in Marie's room." I felt his palm solid across my cheek. It was the second time he'd ever hit me.

I ran from him.

He stood quietly for a moment, then ran after me.

I pulled at my gold locket and broke the chain. "Maybe you should put Marie's picture in it for me," I cried, throwing it in his direction.

He stooped to pick it up, then turned and walked down another path.

At the lodge my brother was fuming. Janice had gone into his wallet and come upon the solitary Trojan he'd stashed there between a bank calendar and his library card. It had been there at least a year. Janice had presented the crumpled, linty thing to Marie, who took it, saying she ought to show it to my father.

"Marie better give it back," ranted Melvin, slamming stuff into his suitcase, "or I'll say she's been putting out for the lifeguard."

"Has she?" I asked. My neck burned from where I'd pulled the locket chain to break it.

"She probably has, the whore."

Melvin was shouting.

Janice was crying. Me, too. The canary was singing, excited by all the noise. On the drive home we all were quiet.

The next winter my father got pneumonia, and it came back again in early spring. Running himself ragged between New York and Philadelphia, he was trying to promote without a license. The New York Boxing Commission was tough on felons. Too weak to get to the bathroom, he kept a milk bottle by his bed. We hadn't seen Marie since the drive from Naponach, but when he was sick, she called constantly.

"Listen, Marie," I told her on the sixth day of his second attack, "I noticed something funny."

"What?" I shifted the phone to my other hand and plunged.

"Well, there are heavy clots of blood in his urine."

"What!"

"In the milk bottle he pees into. I went to empty it, and it was all bloody."

"Did you ask him about it?"

"No."

"Well, don't." She paused, then said, "Barbara, do you think Melvin would get very upset if I came to visit?"

The question shifted my attitude. Suddenly I was in Marie's place. Melvin would get upset. Poor Melvin, he had more to be upset over than just Marie. The words "blood count" and "lymph nodes" were creeping into his personal lexicon, even if the word "cancer" was still avoided.

"Listen," I said, "Mel's going to the city on Saturday to hear some jazz. Why don't you come over then?" I was crossing over to the enemy lines.

I was glad to see Marie, and I think Teresa was, too. My

father's being sick frightened Teresa, with her own husband ill in Connecticut and a small son to worry over. Marie brought fresh-cut flowers, changed his linen, and gave him a sponge bath with alcohol. So Melvin or no, I invited her to have dinner and then to spend the night. Melvin spent his evening in his room playing Wagner. *Götterdämmerung.* When Auntie H. arrived Sunday morning carrying two avocados (she was educating our palates, we'd just mastered artichokes) and found Marie, she went into shock.

"What's that bimbo doing here?" she asked. "Rose would turn in her grave."

"She came to visit Daddy yesterday, and I asked her to stay over," I said as bravely as I could

"You did what? Who do you think you are, Lady Astor?"

She dropped her avocados into the kitchen sink and backed me against the refrigerator, shaking her finger in my face. Over her shoulder I could see Mrs. Donner at her kitchen window. The sun was blocking her vision. It left us in shadow.

"I'm not staying in the same house with her," shouted Auntie H.

"Ssh," I said. "Daddy's sleeping."

"You are shushing me!" she shrieked, and her hand cracked across my mouth. Did growing up mean getting hit?

Teresa rushed to stop her. "Please, Mrs." she said, reaching out to Auntie H.'s hand.

Auntie H. turned on Teresa. "You stay out of this. You're only the maid around here."

My God, she's jealous of Marie, I thought. But wasn't I? Hadn't I been since the day at camp? And hadn't Auntie H. always had a few biblical hopes about filling her sister's shoes?

"I'm going back to the city," Auntie H. said. "Tell Hymie to call me when he wants me." Her avocados lay among the dirty dishes.

"Traitor." Melvin snarled as we sat around the kitchen table for supper. Marie had taken a tray up to my father. "Traitor," he repeated.

I buttered my bread.

"Who's a traitor?" asked Janice. Nobody answered her.

Three weeks later Teresa threw two black and shriveled avocados into the garbage. She hadn't know what to do with them. Growing up in Carpathia, she'd never seen such produce. In Carpathia she rode bareback and drank sweet water from fresh streams and understood about all the vegetables. Here things were different.

After that Marie visited often. Daddy went to hospitals. She was always there. "Jesus Christ," cursed Melvin, "can't I ever get to see my father alone?" Marie discreetly left the room when we visited. She wandered up and down hospital corridors, smoking and biting at her lips. Her large dark eyes downcast. Her proud bosom fallen. Melvin had always been jealous, mostly of me because I was the "favorite." Favorites aren't fashionable now, but then parental guilt was still two decades in the future.

"Did I ever tell you, Babsie"—my father's voice was raspy—"how we kids used to sneak through the Italian neighborhood and over to Chinatown to kick the gong around?"

"No, Daddy."

"Well, in them days only the Chinks had opium, but we were all curious about it. Songs were written about it. So we'd sneak over to Pell Street and go behind a tea shop and into a room with bunks. Two and three layers high. And there would be this old Chinaman, who was the chef. You see, you gotta cook opium. This old chef, what a face he had, he looked like he'd seen everything and maybe even understood it. It was dreamy stuff. I used to fly to places I'd never been. Or else just see it, like on a television screen, except in color. Very sharp color." He was nodding off as he spoke. Parkway Hospital didn't provide opium, but morphine was close enough. He nodded off whenever the pain would let him.

"There was this old black guy at the gym. A punchy ex-pug who helped around. He used to sing all the time. He sang 'Everybody wants to go to heaven, but nobody wants to die.' I used to laugh at him and slip him a buck." My father's eyes were on the ceiling. "But it's true, you know, it's true."

"I don't want to die too soon," he said, after telling me to blot my lipstick and remember that with makeup, less is more. "I can take the pain, but I can't take the leaving you so unfinished. I don't want to leave you all alone."

"Marie, is he dying?" We were at a coffee machine, something new. It didn't want to work.

She bit at her lips, whacked at the machine, then said, "He's tough, you know. He's got a good chance."

He seemed to get better. He came home and cooked pasta on Sundays. Then he worsened and was back in.

"They're going to do something with the pain," I told Melvin. "They are going to deaden something."

"They are going to put needles in that part of his spine where the nerves are that go to the intestines and try to block the syndrome." Melvin read medical books.

"Do they know what they're doing?"

"I hope so."

They didn't know what they were doing. What they did was kill off the nerves that controlled his colon. So this time, when they sent him home, it was hell.

"I don't want that whore living in our house," snarled Melvin, who was becoming more bitter the sicker he got. *He* might never "know" a woman, and *he* was young.

"It's not up to you," I said.

"Sure, you like that whore because that's how you're turning out. Fucking around with that Belgium bum."

"It has nothing to do with liking her. Daddy needs her."

"You like her. Admit it. You like her more than you liked your own mother."

"Bastard!" I screamed my worst at him. "I wish it were you instead of him." Oh, God, what was I saying? Melvin turned away from me.

"Tell your father," Auntie H. whispered over the phone, "that I have cancer, too." Now that we started saying it out loud, was cancer becoming the way to belong?

"Did you see a doctor?"

"Don't need a doctor to tell me if I have cancer. Didn't I watch your mother? Tell your father what I said."

"I can't tell him that."

"Tell him, but don't tell that bimbo."

Marie was lowering an enema bag that contained a sub-
stance to help him with gas that lay in pockets along his
petrified colon, causing anguish. Her whole day went to
meeting the needs of his daily decay.

"Help me change his sheets, Barbara." God, he'd gotten
skinny. How could anyone that thin be so heavy to move?
When we turned him, his shriveled genitals became exposed, a thing I should not see, loving him as much as I did.
I looked away.

"It's all right, Babsie," he said, smiling to ease my discomfort. "After all, I diapered you when you were little."
When visitors came, he did without the enema. Then Marie
and I would freshen the room with my mother's leftover
colognes and cover the alcohol stains on the parquet side
tables with doilies.

"I bet," said Melvin, when the door to my father's room
was shut and we weren't to go in, "I bet she's giving him a
blow job. Right now."

"Melvin, the man's dying."

"Everybody's dying," said Melvin.

Melvin had given up the Zetas. He went to odd meetings and occasional parties when he had the energy, but
days of college and nights of pain were taxing. He was
back to Bach. And still a virgin. Perhaps something would
change at Queens College. Perhaps some nice intellectual
girl would share her private parts with him. He was
counting on it.

"I like Marie," said my friend Jane. "She's really very
sweet."

"Jane and I are having a party at her house," I tell my
father. "I'm going to make your spaghetti."

"Don't burn the garlic," he says, "and add the tomato
paste slowly, and throw in a few slices of Jewish salami. It
gives it flavor."

"Did Charlie Lucky throw in Jewish salami?" This sauce
was the best thing he'd brought home from Comstock
prison.

"Nah," he says, "that's my own little trick. Charlie uses

pepperoni. Marie, dear, can you help me turn to my side? My tubes are tangled."

"Thanks for the blouse, Barbara. It's beautiful. Where did you get it?"

"Jane gave it to me. It's too big for her." Pilfered presents were easy to part with.

"Barbara gave Marie a real nylon blouse," Janice told Melvin.

Melvin regarded me with disgust. "Just wait," he said, "till she gets the insurance money and we're left with nothing."

"Is your father selling the house?" asked Mrs. Donner from her window. "That's too bad. We'll miss you."

The house went on the market during his final hospital stay. We owed everybody. Sometimes an old friend of my father's would show up, and we'd have grocery money for a month. Sometimes no one showed, and we ate Campbell's soup and bread.

"Teresa's son drinks three whole glasses of milk a day," Melvin complained. Melvin was anxious about his nutrition. Treatments and college depleted him.

"He's only a little kid."

"She's going to have to cut him down, too."

"He can have my milk."

"Share my sandwich, Barbara. You haven't had lunch in three days. I've been watching."

"I'm dieting, Jane."

Then came the day when the huge carton of food was found at the door, between our elegant potted pines. Teresa was on her knees, loading cans into her apron, and gleefully carrying them to the kitchen.

"What is this?" I asked.

She didn't know and didn't care. She kept carting. I pulled off the neat blue envelope taped to the side. It was from the local Hadassah, the same Hadassah that had made my mother so unhappy. The note said: "We heard you could use this."

"Put those cans back," I said. "We don't want their damned charity."

"Barbara, there's no food in the house."

"Put them back."

"No." Teresa understood about food.

I carried the note upstairs, where I put on the Saks Fifth cashmere sweater with white angora collar and cuffs, and my Bergdorf's suede beret, and the plaid skirt that didn't show its spots, all leftover swag, and walked out the door.

"Where are you going?" Teresa called after me. "Eat something first."

"I'm not hungry."

Our front lawn had grown wild, I observed as I marched away. Our bushes were a disgrace. It suited me fine. Tennessee Williams transplants, I decided, and continued on, head high and cheeks burning, to Rabbi Boxer's door.

I'd been there years before, to deliver his copy of my father's prison-written bar mitzvah letter for Melvin. Rabbi Boxer liked me.

"What's wrong with accepting a little help?" said Rabbi Boxer, this time, after reading the note. "It's offered in kindness."

"Listen," I said, "if the Hadassah wants to help, tell them to *kindly* forget canned kindness and send over cash. A few thousand and we'll buy our own groceries."

Boxer stroked his hands and said, "Barbara, one of your relatives asked for this community help."

"Which relative?"

"An uncle called. I don't want to say who."

All those uncles my father helped put in business. Which nervous uncle had felt the need to make that call?

"Listen, Auntie H.," I said, "I think the house is sold."

"Babsie, tell your father I have cancer of the throat."

"What's wrong with your throat?"

"I can't talk about it."

"How's your stomach?"

"Cancer," she croaked.

"We have to find an apartment fast."

"Get a cheap one." Auntie H. was becoming the phantom of the phone.

Now that the house was sold and debts would be paid Uncle Louie started coming around. Louie was childless.

He had failed in many things; that was only one of them. Years before, my father had placed him as a customs man on the docks. Louie was suspicious and small-minded; it was his kind of work. And he found Marie an embarrassment. So Melvin and Louie had things in common: mostly counting up the value of what we still owned.

The small flat Uncle Louie located us in Flushing couldn't hold Chinese vases or Chippendale desks or formal Queen Anne dining rooms. I never saw the stuff again except in bits and pieces on rare visits to relatives' homes.

The day before he died, my father's hand, guided by Melvin's, made three *X*'s on the properly witnessed legal papers brought by Louie. Louie, with Melvin's approval and no one else's knowledge, was to be executor, guardian, and arbiter of our future. The day he died, my father's other relatives showed up. They came and spoke to each other of how sick he was, of his great suffering, of what a blessing it would be when he passed.

He lies beneath the cellophane tent, mouth stretched, gasping at air, eyes rolling beneath blinking lids. Trying like hell to hold back the "blessing." I watch him. Beneath the tent I hold his hand. As long as he breathes, I'm all right. One hand presses mine; the other presses at his heart as if to keep it beating. Nurses come and go. They look from him to the clock. They wait for the tidy ending. They wait to remove the tubes and tie back the tent and cover his eyes. His eyes move. When they pass my face, I feel recognition. I smile at him. They roll away.

From the lounge I hear voices of relatives. Where's Marie? Their words drift into the room: "What about the master bedroom set? The kids won't need it now. . . . Where are the Persian carpets? Did they move those to Flushing? . . . What time is it anyway?"

His hand has stopped pressing. I signal a nurse. She says, "He's dead."

"But he's still breathing. Look."

"No," she says, "that's the machine."

"His eyelid moved."

"That's nerves working. He's dead," she says, and starts with starched white efficiency to strip the tent.

"Stop that," I plead. "His lips are moving; he's saying something."

"You're imagining that."

I fight her. I fight with her hands. Other hands come to stop me. I'm in the lounge with the relatives. It's all over.

We were cramped in the alien living room, sitting on our own furniture, arranged out of order, surrounded by our own friends, who, like the furniture, seemed misplaced. I stared from them to the long carved wood bench pushed against the dinette wall. That bench belongs in the hall. There was no hall. This was not our father's house. This place had nothing to do with us.

My friend Jane was acting hostess. Teresa held Janice tight on her lap while her own son scrambled, to no avail, to find a place there, too. She didn't have room for him. She never had much room for him. We were always there first.

We went to the viewings, which were an agony of trying to please and do right, an agony of being introduced to strangers across my father's coffin. We shook hands with Tammany Hall politicians, who had handshaking down to an art. We shook and looked into faces masked for mourning. We were sobbed upon by old Jewish ladies who remembered us when and whose tears fell so profusely they stopped our own. We were hugged by pugs and kissed by thugs. Then, after we were thoroughly condoled, we went home to sit with our friends.

I tried not to lean too hard on the arm of the couch; it had been damaged when we moved. It was never to be fixed. How Mrs. Donner cried when the van pulled into our driveway to carry off our belongings. She pressed me against her apron-covered chest and made me promise to call her. I knew I wouldn't but said I would. Why, she really liked me! She liked us all. It came as a kind of sweet, sad surprise.

The new people, the Mittmans, stood by their moving van, impatient for us to be gone. "Those trees and bushes," said Mrs. Mittman, "will have to be cut back immediately."

The idea hurt: the idea that these were no longer my trees, that the bay window was no longer my secret reading spot, or my room ever again to be my room. Our belongings piled in the driveway no longer belonged. I wondered if Mrs. Donner even knew where to find us. Of course, she could come to the funeral parlor. Schwartz Brothers of lower Second Avenue was doing the honors. Uncle Louie said we couldn't afford Riverside. Louie was getting a deal.

"Listen," assured Melvin's friend Alfred, "your father wouldn't give a damn about Riverside. Your father liked the streets." Melvin talked some about walking the streets with my father, everyone talking to him, chasing after him. "It used to take twenty damn minutes to go one block." Melvin's grief was unsettling. He was angry with God, my father, and himself. "And the subways," added Jane. "He was a scream on the subway."

"Yeah," admitted Melvin, "he used the subway as a text for us."

"But he did it out loud," said Jane.

Melvin began imitating my father. " 'Look,' the old man would say to us, pointing to his selected specimen, 'look at that mug over there carrying his lunch. Check his shoes, worn but polished. A working stiff, trying to save a penny. He looks like an elevator man, don't he?' " Melvin had him down. "We'd look, and suddenly we *were* looking into the face of an elevator man, most uncomfortable because these kids were staring at him."

"Tell more," said Janice, and everyone started to tell funny stories about Daddy, and soon we were gripped with cramps of laughter.

The AP wire service phoned. I giggled out the information they wanted about services and survivors.

"Jesus Christ," Melvin moaned, "they'll think we're enjoying this. Control yourself."

"Look at that," said Uncle Louie, peering out the window as the funeral cortege rounded the exit leading off the Queensboro Bridge. "See how his procession stretches all the way from Manhattan to here." We looked, and it pleased us. Funny what pleases.

"Where is Marie?" I asked Melvin at the viewings after I

fixed my father's hair to "bunk the thin spots." He didn't answer me. "Where's Marie?" I asked Aunt Birdie at the services. She shrugged. "Where's Marie?" I asked Teresa, who looked at her hands.

"Your brother and I decided it would be best if she didn't attend," Uncle Louie informed me at the graveside, "what with family and all the important people and the press."

"You didn't let her come to say good-bye to him?"

"We thought it best for you kids."

"No one asked *me* about it."

"It's best for everyone."

Then I lost control. Then came tears that would not stop. Then my heart sank wet and weary into the soaked earth that swallowed him up.

They gave her a thousand dollars since she hadn't worked in two years. And they gave her one of my father's watches, not the expensive one. And I never saw her again.

Jane thought she saw her once, years later, in an Italian delicatessen, but couldn't be sure. "I called out, 'Marie,' " Jane said, "the woman turned and looked at me, then walked out the door."

History Lessons

$\mathbf{I}$ lived two lives during those years: one as Hymie's Babsie; the other as Barbara, in adjacent adolescence. These split sides didn't always stay in each other's sight, though sometimes they collided.

"Your father will kill you if he catches you," said my friend Ruth, sneaking a smoke in our downstairs bathroom, my father's bed being well out of sniffing range. She had offered me a puff and eyed me with controlled distaste as I fumbled it. "I don't know why you are making this trip to Peekskill at all," she added, flicking her cigarette into the toilet bowl. "What the hell do you care about the Commie nigger for anyway?"

"I care," I said, smearing my lips with Tangee Tinted. "I care about human rights."

"Bullshit," she said, "you're just going to impress Jane Jones."

Actually I was going to impress myself. It would be something special to be part of Paul Robeson's heroic return to the same concert site he'd been driven from a week before. It was to be "a great thing." "I'll be going up before dawn," Jane had told me, "to join the line of defense. You can come later and bring food."

"How will I get there?" I asked.

"I'll arrange for you to ride with John," decided Jane, whose power in the left-wing youth movement was not to be questioned, not since she'd strolled out of Schirmer's with one of its finest guitars. When she found a radical guitar teacher in Greenwich Village who taught cheap, there was no stopping her. Josh also instructed her in romance. She brought me to meet him one Sunday at his cold-water flat. Complete with crazy neighbors and a kitchen tub, it was very "bohemian."

I stood armed with a hamper of sandwiches, at the appointed place, waiting for John and ready to be part of a "great thing." "He's come all the way from Canada to join us. Watch for a red convertible." The hard part had been sneaking away from the house before anyone noticed.

Why, I wondered, as I slid into his tomato bright car, had no one mentioned that John was a Negro? After a moment's adjustment I decided to be delighted. John, it seemed, was an idealist who planned to be a surgeon to the poor. His family, he said, had come to New York City when it still was a Dutch colony. "They came from the West Indies in bondage," he explained, "but earned their freedom and the right to farm as a reward for years of hard service.

"His name was John, too," he said, speaking of his ancestor. "John Fort Orange. That was in 1644." Imagine, 1644, over a hundred years before Alexander Hamilton left the Indies. John was definitely the most American person I'd ever met.

"He earned eleven acres of swampland in what is now Greenwich Village." Someday, if I liked, he'd show me the very spot. "The British," he told me, "took our property and tried to return us to slavery." John's forefathers weren't having any of that and escaped to French Canada.

We talked as we drove: of brotherhood, of the atom bomb, and whether the Yankees would take this year's pennant. We sang "Joe Hill" and "Union Maid" and Robeson's version of "Ballad for Americans." John knew all the verses.

Then we stopped singing. Misdirected since passing over

the Bear Mountain Bridge, we somehow reached the right road to the glen and were halted. Cars were packed in a single row as far as the eye could see, and farther. Honking and shouting sounded along the narrow road and echoed off the surrounding hills. Surly state troopers issued confusing commands at us and at the cars now wedged behind us. No way in and no way out.

Sitting in our private silence, we pretended to ignore the stares of the stony-faced locals perched like gargoyles on the stone wall that lined the road.

John's hands were tight on the wheel as he inched us forward when possible. We were a provocative twosome, black and white in shiny red. And we got attention. "If she were my daughter," I heard one call from the mix of legionnaires and locals who'd come for the fun, "I'd horsewhip the tramp."

Laughter followed that and someone else shouted, "Why pick on Peekskill? Didn't that Commie learn last time? Just looking for trouble."

"Let's get out of here," I whispered to John.

"We can't," he said. "They're not allowing U-turns."

The summer sun was getting hotter, and so was the crowd. Bottles passed from hand to hand along the stone wall. John and I were fair game. "Hey, nigger," one sports lover shouted, "did you slip it to her along the way? You ought to try us white boys, girlie."

"Don't look so scared," John said. "It will make things worse."

"Can things get worse?"

"I think they're blocking the entrance to the glen."

"Let's get out and walk."

"No," he said, "we can't leave the car. Try and calm yourself." He stared straight ahead and spoke in a monotone. He spoke of freedom and fear and faults in the system. He said not to blame these men who were only victims. Much help he was going to be. These "victims" wanted to kill us.

The cars started to move forward. We rounded a curve and faced a new set of fields. To our right up a gentle slope a beefy-armed man strained as he struggled to move a boulder from between his plantings. His workhorse stood tied beneath a tree, swishing at flies with its tail. What a sweet day this should have been. Could it still be all right? I wanted to be heroic like the Maccabees my father had talked about. "Just like a tree," I sang softly, "that's standing by the wat . . ." John smiled.

"Let's not mistrust the world," my father said. "Being cowardly insults life."

"Being a coward," my father had told us as he lit the Hanukkah lights, "cramps the soul." It was that first winter after he had come home.

"I want you kids," he said, facing the menorah, "to get the right slant on these candles. They are for courage. Jews must have courage. Back in them days," he went on, "when Greek Syria controlled Jerusalem, there was trouble over territory. One Greek mob was trying to push another mob out. A guy named Antiochus won out and took over. But that didn't satisfy the bum. Next he wanted to stamp out Judaism."

"Like Hitler." My kid sister had piped in.

"Exactly," he said, and continued. "The Maccabees saved the day. In this life you gotta stand up and fight. And these Maccabee boys were fighters because their old man, a real guy, had taught them right. Actually," finished my father, "Hanukkah isn't a religious holiday; it's more political."

"My teacher," I told him, when he was done, "says we need a note for staying home the first day. She says it's not legal."

My father lit a cigar. "Do you need a note on Christmas?"

"No."

"Explain to your teacher that if the Maccabees didn't fight, there wouldn't have been no Jews a hundred years before Christ, so there wouldn't have been no Christmas either."

Maccabean courage came more easily as long as the cars kept moving. Another bend, which we drove almost normally, and another. Then the sirens of an ambulance approaching from behind stopped the movement. It passed us on the other side, mostly in the ditch. "A car turned, people hurt" was relayed down the line.

"I'm a med student," called John as we inched by the overturned car. "Can I help?"

"Keep moving," they said. We kept going. Then, stopped again, we waited.

"I should have thought," John said, adjusting his glasses, "before I agreed to drive you up with me. . . ." He didn't continue; he didn't want me more upset than I was. I gave him a bottle of warm cream soda and a salami sandwich.

"What about you?" he asked.

"I feel a little seasick," I said, trying to smile. As if punctuating my words, our car started to heave. Two middle-aged men wearing legion caps had hold of our back bumper and were rocking us.

"You like rhythm?" one yelled. "Black rhythm for a white whore?" John jammed down the gas pedal, shooting us backward into the car behind, where three old ladies sat half dead with fear. The legionnaires saved themselves but were infuriated. Reinforcements ran to their assistance.

"Here it comes," John said. "Get out of this car and run."

Run where?

"I can't move," I said.

"Get out of the car!" he commanded. "They won't hurt a kid."

Men pounded and pulled at the car from John's side. I climbed, clumsily, over my door. A stone grazed my shoulder as I jumped to the road.

"Help," I screamed.

John was sliding along the seat. Somehow he got out just as the car went over. With relief I saw him stagger to his feet and move toward me. He turned his head to see what had happened.

"You black prick!" hung in the air, and a rock, thrown from whose misbegotten hand I'll never know, struck him full in the face, smashing his glasses. Blood spurted. He fell backward the way a bowling pin falls, blood covering his face and turning his white shirt red.

It was all a movie. The state troopers had their backs turned. A man from the ambulance managed to reach us. Then two boys came carrying a stretcher. I heard, "I think he's lost an eye. Get the little girl. Let's move her out of here, too."

It was good to be the "little girl." Good to be pushed into the front seat of the ambulance to sit between "grown-ups."

"We were just bringing food for the kids," I tried to explain. "We didn't do anything wrong. . . ."

The ambulance struggled its way along the other side of the road, which had become a bedlam. The scream of our siren blended into the screaming and shouting all around. We forced a path through and somehow reached the highway.

"Get out here, honey," the man said. "There are cars turning back to the city; someone will take you."

It was all so normal and ordinary on the highway that I stood there a long time before remembering to stick my thumb out, the way hitchhikers do in films. I stood and wondered at how *they* hated us. How ugly *they* were. My politics started to shift. Let *them* starve on their meager farms and slave in their factories without one moment's dignity or grace. It was what *they* deserved.

An old family-filled Dodge pulled off the highway for a rest stop. Their little girl was staring up at me from where she squatted to make her pee, carefully keeping her sandals clear of the flow. Once I'd had sandals just like those. Another car stopped, and a young couple signaled to me. Yes, they were driving to New York City. I got in.

In the Bronx they gave me a dime for the subway and I went home. I never heard what happened to John. But the radio was full of it: the line of defense holding hands around the glen; the overturned buses; the rock throwing; the crying girls; the maimed boys. Righteous voices talked provocation; clever commentators made clever comments.

My brother said it had all been a success. He said it caught the attention of the nation and was "a great thing." I wasn't sure I cared. Teresa, who pulled my bloodied dress from the dirty clothes hamper and didn't understand "great things," said, "I show this to the daddy." I begged her not to. "No," she said, "I show."

He lay thin and pale on the grand parquet bed. Delicate floral designs covered the headboard, making the rubber sheets look even uglier. He'd come home from the hospital this time minus a bladder and one kidney. He'd come with tubes that fed into a rubber hose that spilled into a water-filled gallon jug next to his bed and turned it yellow.

He listened as I told my story. He listened and was very angry at my stupidity and at a world he couldn't protect us from.

"So Jane's running with Communists now?" he asked.

"Not Communists, Daddy. But even Communists have a right to their beliefs." I didn't know why I was defending Communists since I'd definitely decided not to be one. I'd just met the masses and didn't much like them.

"We are not talking rights," my father said. "We are talking reality."

"What about the Maccabees and courage?" I demanded, determined to be on the side of the angels.

"Courage," he said, "comes in many forms. Sometimes courage is knowing when and how to wait for your moment." Taking a hard breath, he continued. "It shows courage to fight with no hope, but that's a kind of desperate courage. As far as the Maccabees go, Communists think religion is dumb compared to Marxism."

"Melvin says Marx was a genius, and he was Jewish!"

"Genius? Maybe. But isms are different from the guys who start them. Listen, Babsie, I know you think your old man is old-fashioned and doesn't understand your friends with their big words and smarty songs. But I tell you survival is your first duty." He pulled himself to his elbows, "And you don't survive going into a street fight blindfolded with one hand tied behind your back. No matter what you're singing."

It was shortly before he made his last trip back to the hospital that I heard about Uncle Jack. His real name may have been Nat, according to Albert Fried in *The Rise and Fall of the Jewish Gangster in America,* but Daddy always called him Jack.

"Who is Aunt Irene?" I asked my father, handing him her postcard announcing her intention to visit him soon. It was a sweet card signed "Lots of love."

"Your uncle Jack's wife."

"What Uncle Jack?" I'd never met any Uncle Jack.

"Jack was my oldest brother," he said. "He was shot down in a gunfight back in 1921 by the little Augie mob." My father closed his eyes; he was having a bad day. Not a day for questions. Shot down in a gunfight, something to think about, like the OK Corral. The morning of Aunt Irene's visit I heard more.

"They called him Dapper Jack," said my father. "He was a real dresser. The girls were wild for him. Irene was always jealous. Girls go crazy for dangerous men, till they learn better. They also called him Kid Dropper." Medication made him drift. "Dapper Jack, Kid Dropper Caplin, a lot of moniker for an East Side boy, but that's how they called him. And it was a name spoken softly. Very carefully." Kid Dropper. That sounded somewhat like Billy the Kid. Perhaps I was close?

> Tough Guy Levi, that's my name
> I'm a Yiddisha cowboy

were the first lines of a song I'd sung when three, at Stillman's gym, to an audience of sweat suits, headguards, and mouth pieces. Perhaps Uncle Jack had been a Jewish cowboy, a gunslinger. Well, why not? Jews were everywhere. The first foot off Columbus's boat onto the New World belonged to a Jew. And then there was Levi Strauss and his jeans! So why not a cowboy?

"Did you live out West?" I asked Aunt Irene as I led her up to my father's room. She was the shadow of a once-beautiful woman who seemed submerged in a dream. No, it seemed it was an eastern gunfight. James Cagney lying across the church steps, bleeding into snow, as the mascara-ruined blond says, "He used to be a big shot."

Aunt Irene started crying. "Oh, my God, Hymie, I didn't know."

"I'm all right," my father said, "only I get to wear my bladder on the outside now. Sh, Irene. It's okay."

She sat close then and held his hand. I didn't hear much of what they said to each other, only something about my mother's not being comfortable with her and that she "never wanted to upset anyone" and my father's saying, "It doesn't matter now," over and over. She stayed about two hours, then left telling me I was going to be a real beauty like my father's mother. I watched the once-beautiful woman walk down the street and back into her dream. When I returned to my father's room, he was dozing, so I curled into the chaise across from his bed to finish *For Whom the Bell Tolls*.

Robert Jordan's death proved more than I could cope with. The final page was drenched with my tears.

"Why are you crying, Babsie?"

"Robert Jordan's dying in Spain, alone, behind a rock."

"Well, that's what he went there for."

"How do *you* know, Daddy?" How could he know? He never read anything but the sports pages.

"Oh," he said, "I read that book upstate." He meant prison.

"Why does he have to die?" I was bitter. "Couldn't Hemingway let him live?"

"It would take from the book if he lived. The whole psychological makeup of this bum says he has to die behind a rock, alone and shooting."

"I hate it."

"Don't."

"I'll never forgive Hemingway," I said at last.

"You won't forget him either. Anyway, Pilar survives, and she's the only one with moxie in the whole mob."

"Pilar," I objected, "the ugly old woman."

"Pilar, all the brave women who ever were. She's the heroine."

"I thought Maria was the heroine."

"No," he said, "she's just injured innocence, something for Jordan to love. Someone to love him after he's gone."

"What good will that do him?"

"Do you think relationships end with death, Babsie?"

"Don't they?"

"No."

"How come I never heard of Uncle Jack? Because he's dead and gone, isn't that why?"

"No, Babsie, because he was hard to translate. But I'll try now."

It was tough, he explained, on the Lower East Side of New York City in the early 1900's. Old rules were warring against new ways. And old men shook their locks and beards at young men with shaved cheeks and bowler hats. They muttered, "Shandah," "shame," on their ways. Shame on those who worked on the Sabbath and told dirty jokes instead of Talmud tales and whose women wore scarves rather than *sheitlech* to the sweatshops. And more than sacrilege seethed in those shops. Unions were being born, and heads were being broken. As far as the police went, well, who could speak their language, much less pay their bribes? So ghetto muscle was called for, and men, sons of scholars even, turned soldier and protected or persecuted as was thought necessary. Dapper Jack Kid Dropper was such a man and a boss of other such men who lived by their own laws. Daddy was trying hard.

Decades later I came across Uncle Jack in two different books about criminals of the Lower East Side. Fried's and one from 1927, published by Knopf, *The Gangs of New York.* My brother found Jack and the Purple Gang given space in Clarence Darrow's biography. But then, when my father was attempting to explain things, I didn't know much about Murder Inc., so when he finished by saying that Louis Lepke was "Jack's lieutenant till he went with Little Augie," I didn't understand all that meant.

"My brother Jack," he said, "lived in a different world. A world apart. I remember one story," he went on, "I was only a kid, but I remember about how another mob was wanting to put Jack away. They brought in two torpedoes from Philly to do the job. Well, your uncle Jack had a habit of starting his day at Mendel the barber's. And he was sitting there one morning, smothered in lather, when two gunsels came in and grabbed Mendel, stuck a gun in his belly, and demanded to know the whereabouts of the Dropper. Poor Mendel was peeing on himself in fear. Before matters could get worse, your uncle Jack spoke up from behind his lather and said he could lead them to Kid Dropper. But he said it had to be done carefully, only one at a time. So he led one away through the alley, a razor of Mendel's slipped up his sleeve, then came back and got the second. One, two, three, and the dead hoods were left behind the garbage pile."

"You mean he killed them?"

"Slit their throats. One, two, three."

"Daddy, Uncle Jack was a murderer!"

My father bridled and struggled to sit up to shake his finger at me. "You still don't understand, Babsie. It was a world apart. And your uncle Jack never harmed an honest businessman."

Artie, a prison pal from Comstock, sat facing my father's hospital bed, telling him how he intended to go straight. When he could. But right now Artie really needed this car. He needed something to feel like a man. "Listen, Hymie, after five years in the slam, a guy needs something."

"What you don't need," my father said gently, "is trouble."

Artie, who I found dashing, winked at me, then smiled down at his fresh manicure.

"Listen Artie," my father went on, shifting to his side, which made his tubes twist and made me nervous, "it's a hot car and you have no business with hot cars. You can't afford it."

"Actually," said Artie, "it's the only kind I can afford. It's a real steal."

"You're laughing now, but you'll cry later. Don't be a wise guy."

"Hymie, I haven't cried since the *mohel* cut too much off! Did I tell you the one," Artie went on, his moustache curving around his words, "about the old lady who wanted her watch fixed and took it into a store with watches in the window, then got annoyed when the guy said he couldn't fix it because he was a *mohel*?

" 'So why hang watches in your window?' she asked.

" 'So what should I hang?' said the *mohel.*"

My father smiled. "All our family used the same *mohel,*" he said, mostly to me, "but your mother wanted Melvin circumcised by a doctor. I convinced her a *mohel* was better, more experienced. In olden times the kid's old man made the cut himself, but nowadays you use a professional. I held Melvin in my arms," he said, "and put a little wine on his tongue and spoke the blessing. What a *tummel* he made. He didn't like being made different from the Gentiles. But an uncircumsised boy can't be bar mitzvahed."

He became quiet, looked at his tubes, and I knew it was because when Melvin had his bar mitzvah, my father had been locked away.

"A Jewish boy must have a bar mitzvah," my mother had snapped back at Auntie H., who'd been complaining about cost. Bar mitzvahs were expensive, starting with years of Hebrew school and special studies and ending with the event itself, which meant a celebration, and celebrations meant money, which was the problem.

"It's ridiculous, all this now-I-am-a-man stuff. A man can go out and earn and help meet expenses. Can Melvin do that?" demanded Auntie H., who hadn't expected this frail and dying sister to fight back.

"Melvin has studied hard and will be a bar mitzvah boy like everyone else. Hymie would die if he wasn't."

"Hymie won't even be there."

"All the more reason."

"Really, Rose."

"Enough," said my mother and began to cough.

Auntie H. gave up, but grudgingly. "Well, all we can afford is sponge cake and punch."

"And wine," said my mother, "and cold cuts and a nice present."

"You better not invite too many people," warned my aunt.

"I'm inviting the whole family," whispered my mother, breathless from the coughing, "and our friends, too."

Auntie H. left muttering about stupidity. On her way

out she took Teresa aside. "You thing she's strong enough to go through such a thing?" Teresa shrugged.

"I'm going to make mistakes." My brother kept worrying the week before the event. "I know it." He made me sit and listen to him chant Hebrew gibberish at me. What else could I make of it?

"How did it sound?" he would ask, his face flushed from effort.

"Like real Hebrew," I would answer, which, of course, didn't satisfy. He would start again.

"Oh, God," Auntie H. repeated to each arriving guest, "oh, God, I hope she doesn't faint." I was worried, too; fainting was close to dying. She was so pale. She held tightly to my arm when we had to stand, then sank gratefully to her chair when she could. Powdered up, in her Persian lamb coat, she sat thin and trembling and proud.

They all had come. Sadie and Harry and the rest. Mouton, nuzzled Nutria, shoved against Sealskin, brushed off on Beaver, and elbowed Mink. They came and settled in for the long service, resigned to waiting for the refreshments. It was winter in the synagogue. The light above the Ark flickered in the airless room. Noses were blown, girdles were stretched, crotches adjusted and asses scratched. Melvin Eugene was about to enter a covenant with his Lord.

When the time came, Mel got up before the lectern, and except for a cracking voice at the very start, he sang his words without hesitation. Murmurs of approval underscored his accomplishing a particularly difficult passage, and one by one male members of his tribe approached the Torah and sang him in. Then, when it should have been over and everyone was ready to rush for food and drink, Rabbi Boxer signaled them to stay in their seats. "I want to read you," he said, "a letter from a father to a son on his bar mitzvah." The letter, written on cheap blue lined paper and marked with a stamp that showed it had passed the prison censor, was from my father to Melvin.

"Dearest Melvin," it began, "my own Pal Mel, my beloved son." Why was he doing this, reading a private letter in front of these strangers, called relatives? I saw my mother's head bend for the first time.

I have been a long time writing this letter. I have been carrying it in my heart since the day I knew I wouldn't be there to stand proud beside you. I wish I could write it so pure and plain that you could never doubt how much I love you and how much having you for a son has meant.

You have gotten many letters from me these past years, and usually I am asking things of you, the kind of things you have a right to ask of me. Usually I am telling you to be steady and strong and to comfort your poor mother and your little sisters. In other words, to be a man much too soon. And now I am doing it again.

Today, son, is a day of change. You may not look different or act different but something deep inside you has been awakened, something in your blood that's been there thousands of years. One thing I want you to remember is that we Jews started as a single family. The family of Abraham. We are still a family, now of millions in spite of the cruelty and hardship we have suffered.

Another thing is that we are called the chosen people. As you grow up and look around, you will notice other people who seem more comfortable and easy. Being a man of the chosen people is not easy. It means being a witness to God's Commandments here on earth and watching men fail to keep them. And sometimes watching yourself fail in the same way. But a Jewish man must struggle against these failures, and that is our salvation, that we know right. It may be hard for you to accept these words from a father in prison, yet I say them. So I must also say that being a Jewish man is often to suffer but more often to be proud. And it is to be glad of life and light in the middle of evil and darkness. It breaks your heart, but it teaches you to love. So have enough patience with yourself to learn and be simple enough to believe.

Please know my sweet son, that you are always in my heart's eye. And distance and walls and even bars cannot alter such a thing.

Your proud father,
HYMAN CAPLIN

It was then she fainted. She seemed to smile, look to the ceiling, and over her shoulder. Then she slipped from her chair to the floor in a crumple.

"I told you," Auntie H. said from her knees, lifting my mother's head off the hardwood floor. "Didn't I warn you? Stand back, Babsie, here, hold her hat and get her purse. No, get coffee, bring coffee, quick."

By the time I rushed the sloshing cup back, she was sitting again and trying to quiet Auntie H. Melvin was still standing on the dais in yarmulke and prayer shawl. His mouth was open. I went to him and knocked on his foot. "She's better," I said, "so come down and start your life as a man."

We moved, he and I, toward the small refreshment room where the wine, food, and presents waited. "What," I asked him, "smells like lox, looks like a box, and flies?"

"What?" he responded by rote.

"A flying lox box," I said. It was an old joke between us, and it was good for Melvin to play his part. "Let's eat," I'd said.

Gathered around the refreshment table, everyone seemed somehow embarrassed. But for different reasons.

I don't believe anyone had ever told my father about the fainting. Certainly I'd never do it now, as he lay on his hospital bed. His eyes were closed.

"Hymie," Artie called softly, touching my father's shoulder to bring him back. "Hymie, I gotta go now. Don't worry about me, I'll be careful." My father smiled.

"Do you think he'll be careful?" I asked after Artie left to drive off in a roar of stolen glory.

"No," he had said. "It's not his makeup."

False Starts

$\mathbf{T}$he thing was how to get the foam-rubber falsies out of my push-up before Buddy's fingers found them first. Before Hidden Treasure and Magic Circle were built in for the "less endowed," if you wanted to look "stacked," which seemed important, you stuffed into your bra nippled pink puffs that could, if not removed carefully, fly halfway across a room at the moment of release. I had to get rid of them before my seduction was any more complete. Later his hands would be everywhere.

"Excuse me, Buddy," I said, "I must tinkle." Then felt like an ass. What a dumb word. Why couldn't I just say "pee" or something honest? Grabbing my evening purse, I made the walk to the door gilded with a female silhouette. Most of the line was in tulle, corsages stuck to shoulders or tied to wrists. I had taken another turn. Draped in crepe so tight, my thighs fought the fabric with every movement. My one perfect camellia was tucked into the upsweep of my hair. After all, I was almost eighteen.

Within the booth I wiggled out of my ankle-length and sat in comfort. I could try flushing the falsies away, but they

83

might not go down. The image of their bobbing in the bowl decided me against it. Forcing the springy things into a half inch of beaded bag, already crammed with makeup, required magic. But I did it. The clasp closed over bunched blobs with bent nipples. Readjusting my own gilded silhouette, I made my way back to our table, chest as high as I could get it.

"Lend me your compact," said a girl at our table. Was she kidding? I wasn't going to reopen that jack-in-the-box bag in the middle of Bill Miller's Riviera if my life depended on it.

"I don't have one," I said, and pulled the purse she was reaching for to my lap.

"Are you having fun," Buddy asked, clinking glasses, "at your first real nightclub?" I touched my camellia.

"Yes," I said, but I'd been in a "real" nightclub before and was remembering it over my brandy and soda. My father had bought me a huge white orchid to celebrate my graduating from grade school, and perhaps to excuse his missing most of the event, he promised me a night on the town.

"Is your father here yet?" Marlene Labinson, whose size had placed her directly before me on the graduating girls' line, had asked.

Twisting my head within the edge of my keyhole neckline, I tried to find him. We girls had made our own graduation dresses in home economics. Mine had been a motherless disaster until my father, tired of watching me rip and resew, sent it to a dressmaker.

"Not yet," I told Marlene. The piano had started, and we marched forward.

My solo, "I'll Take You Home Again, Kathleen," was third on the program. For weeks I'd sung it to the bathroom mirror. Now I was nervous. "I'll take you home again, Kathleen . . ." What had taken Kathleen away? Perhaps the potato famine. There were tears in the principal's eyes. It was her selection. Still no daddy.

"I'm sorry, Babsie, I really am," he'd said, handing me the florist box outside the auditorium. "I missed your song."

I stared at the enormous flower. It was the only orchid

present. "I'll wear it later," I said as we walked home, "to the dance." Later, when Stanley Loeb, who'd tormented me all my childhood, arrived, with slicked-down hair and a red bow tie, to escort me, my father made me put the orchid in the icebox. Stanley'd brought a carnation wreathed in baby's breath. "I'll take you out special tomorrow," my father whispered, "but tonight what he brought you is what you wear."

So the next night we sat at a discreet table on the second tier of the Copacabana, my orchid pinned to the left of my keyhole neck and my father to my right.

"I asked Marie to join us," he said after the strolling lady took our picture. "Is that okay?" It wasn't, but I smiled yes.

Just as Desi Arnaz was finishing "Babalu" and Marie was going to the "little girls' room," a man wearing glasses and a bandage on his neck joined us.

"You remember Damon Runyon, Babsie, from Lindy's?" I remembered, but not quite like that.

"Thanks for the sweet column about my troubles," my father had said. "It might help with my license."

Runyon waved away the remark, then pulled a pad from the pocket of his double-breasted suit and wrote, "What's the occasion?"

"It's my Babsie's graduation."

Runyon nodded and signaled okay at my orchid. Then, reaching to his pad, he wrote, "Did Babsie ever read 'Little Miss Marker'?" My father said, "Not yet."

"When she does," Runyon wrote, "tell her she was the inspiration."

My father had said he'd make sure I read it. After Runyon left, my father added, "You were, you know. He used to watch me tote you at three months old from the Brill Building along to Jacob's Beach, the sporting blocks of Broadway, and over to the Hotel Forrest. And seeing you in the arms of the Shadow or Mugsy while I talked business, he'd say there was a story in it. But of course, he made the kid older."

I asked why Runyon couldn't speak. My father told me about cancer of the throat. "But," he'd said, "Runyon's got plenty of moxie."

Now they both were dead of cancer. And Buddy was

rubbing his elbow across my shrunken chest, whispering, "Let's get out of here." The social part of our evening was coming to an end.

As I sat in Buddy's father's big Caddy and driving east, somewhere between the George Washington and Triborough bridges, chicken a la king, whiskey sour, and that last brandy and soda started rising in my throat. The boning cinching my waist to twenty inches was pushing it all up.

"It's a sticky night," I said.

"Don't you feel well?" Buddy asked.

I moved across the seat to the window to try some air in my face. It was hot, and I was never to be a comfortable drinker. Alcohol might never turn me mean or stupid—at worst I'd want to sing my father's oldies or recite "The Ballad of Reading Gaol"—but drink was always to leave me ill. My first experience had been a year earlier. I'd sneaked off with my friend Ruth and a young Irish cop to a friendly neighborhood bar and downed enough rye and ginger ale to vomit my way home. My last spew was in Mr. Donner's favorite azaleas. Melvin had sneaked me into the bathroom to clean up before putting me to bed. He'd hinted at blackmail—"If I were to tell Pop"—but he never did.

"Do you need me to stop?" Buddy offered.

"No."

"Let's stop anyway."

"I'll have to get out of the whole dress," I said. "It won't pull up." As we scrambled around the front seat of Cleopatra (Buddy's name for the Caddy), my heels were catching in my hemline. It was the second most expensive dress I'd ever owned and had taken all my savings plus a loan from Teresa to buy it at discount at Loehman's. "A sample, a real buy." I'd altered it by hand, and it was getting ruined.

Outside the car crickets chirped in the swampy grass of Flushing Meadows; inside the car we sweated and squirmed.

"You're not wearing panties."

"They make lines."

"I wish I'd known that at the table."

"Why, what would you have done?"

"Who knows?"

Whatever he had in mind wouldn't have worked. The dress didn't allow enough room to kick in a Conga line. It was off, and now only my bra remained, and my earrings, and my pumps, and those markings the boning had left on my body.

"Leave your shoes on," he said, and I did.

"You look sexy," he said. God, I hoped so. What I thought of as sexy was stuffed in my beaded bag beneath the seat. He opened his pants.

A year or so of fumbling attempts of "Let me put it between your legs" or "Just let me rub the head inside" and my trysts with Bobby the Belgian had left whether or not I was a virgin as an interesting question. "Are you still cherry?" my brother had asked.

"Of course," I'd said virtuously.

Actually when Buddy's adventurous finger had first worked its way into the area, it hadn't found one. Was I born incomplete? Was it those bicycle accidents I was always having on Melvin's two-wheeler? Who knew? Tonight all questions were to be answered.

"Spread your legs," Buddy instructed. Hard to do with the steering wheel, the shift, and his bulk blocking my motions. Why we never moved to the back seat I don't know; perhaps that was vulgar. So this was to be *it*. My head crammed beneath the armrest and one leg on the dashboard, the other doing the best it could, I waited for his hardness to push inside. And I waited.

Buddy was a big man. Had he continued in college, he would have gone out for football. The draft had interrupted his education. When he got out of the service, he went to work for the family. Furriers. Buddy's prize pelt was his member, renowned for length and width. One could get the largest sugar-coated cruller at the local T-Bone Diner by ordering a "Buddy Bloom." But since the navy, he later admitted, it didn't always work. And it wasn't working now.

"It's the damn rubber," he said, embarrassed. "Let me get rid of it." He hoisted up and off me and started rolling it down. "I've been hard all night, and now I'm bending."

"I could get pregnant," I cautioned, as girls have cautioned for centuries. And in the manner of centuries of men, he said, "I'll be careful. I'll pull out." (The two most common lies are said to be "The check is in the mail" and "I'll pull out.") So, without a rubber and with some gentle rubbing, he was almost ready. But was I? Would I dare be doing this if Daddy were alive? "Don't believe what boys tell you when they're hot," my father had warned. "They may believe what they say, but hear me well: A stiff penis has no conscience." Well, Buddy wasn't quite stiff, not yet, and he wasn't a boy: He was an ex–navy man. And he loved me. The dashboard turned out to be good for leverage and aside from bumping my brow beneath the armrest, he was, we were, a success. And I was disembarrassed of any doubt as to my sexual status from that moment on. I was fine, I assured my father in heaven, and happily in love and sure to get married.

"Go home and douche," Buddy said, "with cold water."

"What's a douche?"

"That," he said, wise from the war in Europe, "is when you run cold water up your pussy and clean out."

Back home I carried my beaded bag into the bathroom, pulled out the pads, put back my makeup, and sat to consider just how to run water "up my pussy."

After wriggling out of my dress, I stepped into the tub to cope with gravity. Lying on my back, I bent my knees and pushed my bottom forward under the taps. Slowly I worked my legs up the wall on each side of the faucet. Balancing precariously on one elbow, I turned on the cold water, full force, and went into instant shock. But I kept it up till Melvin, whose headboard backed the other side of the bathroom wall, shouted, "What are you doing at this hour? Are you nuts?"

"Taking a cold bath," I shouted back. "It's so hot."

"Suffer," he said, "and shut off the damn water." I did.

Janice was sweet about letting me press iced feet into the backs of her thighs. We shared our parents' floral bed. The airless little apartment Uncle Louis had found meant sacrificing two bedroom sets. Uncle Louie and Aunt Birdie had had their eyes on the master ensemble with marble and parquet. But for once I'd insisted on keeping something, and they took the twins.

"Did you have a nice time?" Janice asked without opening her eyes.

"Uh-huh."

"Your feet feel good," she said. And was once again asleep.

I couldn't sleep. I was thinking about graduating from high school two weeks away and Buddy's father's Caddy back in its garage. I wondered if we'd left stains on its seat. And whatever happened to my camellia.

It's bad enough to feel bad when you know what's wrong but worse when you don't. I kept waking up sweaty and wanting to cry.

"What's the matter with you?" Teresa asked me as I sat in the kitchen and watched her iron my cap and gown.

"I don't know."

"Cheer up," she said. "You a woman now."

I was leaving Forest Hills High forever. And I was scared. This graduation I wouldn't have to look for my father; he wouldn't be there.

But Uncle Louie would, an angry Uncle Louie, recently defeated by my guidance counselor, a scholarship, and his older brother, Dan, who'd stepped in to stop his plans for me.

"Barbara," Uncle Louie said, smiling, "you can't go to college, you have to work."

"At what?"

"Well, you could be a salesgirl or a receptionist."

"I can't be a receptionist."

"Why?"

"I can't work plug boards. I've tried."

"What about selling?"

"I can't add fast."

"You better do something fast," he said. "You aren't any heiress."

"Too bad about your math or you could get into Queens," Melvin said.

I looked at Melvin with suspicion. He'd been so cozy with Uncle Louie that I didn't trust our interests were mutual. He, who measured every mouthful of food consumed at our table, might very well sell me out for the greater good.

"Don't they feed you at home?" Buddy would ask as I shoveled in the lasagna I'd order after the movie. My cheeks would go hot, and a ball of embarrassed hurt would rise in my chest. "You're always starving when we go out. Do you save it for me?" It was just one of those things Buddy was finding fault with since love had calmed. True love had come to Buddy in a flash, worthy of his favorite operas. He'd found in me his own mix of fragile Mimì and fallen Violetta.

How his eyes had lit that first moment he'd seen me on a double date when his pal Howie had walked me to his car. Buddy's date lived in the Bronx. During the ride up we all sat in the front, and Buddy blocked all of Howie's moves toward me. Buddy played chess. We talked chess, philosophy, art, and music. Buddy hogged the conversation. Howie finally retired. He knew when he was checked. I enjoyed the game and moved back and forth from complicated to innocent with the arch of a brow and the hint of a smile. Buddy was totally receptive.

"That was a nice girl," I'd said after we dropped his date home and the three of us, thigh on thigh, drove back to Forest Hills.

"Was that her dismissal?" he asked with a smile. He was really smart, and I loved it.

"Of course," I said, feeling new power. Howie said nothing.

"Are you always so jealous?" Buddy asked.

"Are you always so presumptuous?" I replied.

"Have you ever read Henry Miller?" Buddy asked as the lights of Queens Boulevard sparkled off darkened store windows on this frosty winter night. The conversation had turned literary.

"No," I admitted. It was the third author he'd mentioned that I didn't know.

"Any Colette?"

"When I was a small child," I was happy to tell him.

"Indeed!"

"Indeed."

And indeed, it was true. I'd discovered my mother's cache of unsuitable books hidden in the storage closet in our attic. We read anything and everything, Melvin and I.

"Well, maybe you should read her again," Buddy suggested, "now that you're grown-up."

"Maybe you should read some Damon Runyon," I said when we stopped at my building. "Start with 'Little Miss Marker.'"

On the third date he proposed. I accepted. Several engagement rings already sparkled off fingers in the senior class. I was going to be another lucky one, and I was besotted with love. Buddy, carried away with daring and despite its being after midnight, dragged me home to be blessed by the sleeping Blooms. Mama and Papa Bloom stared at me from under their covers, and Bessy Bloom (his older sister) in her bathrobe from the doorway of her room. Instant hate. Who was this waif their boy had decided to rescue? Wasn't there something wrong with her family? He might as well have brought home a war bride. Actually a case of malaria would have been more welcome.

"I love you," Buddy said as we embraced at my door. "And don't worry, they'll love you, too." Opening my mouth to receive his wet French kiss, I was very grateful. That night in bed I thanked my father for Buddy, who was obviously heaven sent.

"She has a bad reputation," his sister told Buddy. "Just ask the muchachos." The muchachos were Buddy's local pals. Stationed in front of the Optimo Cigar Stand across from Penn Drug, they'd been fixtures for years, stints in the service notwithstanding.

"She puts out," the chief muchacho told Buddy. That drew knowledgeable nods.

"Yeah," echoed another, "she used to do it for that Belgian bum." I was damned.

"He'll never marry you," said Melvin, "just wait and see."

So I waited.

Buddy and I spent time alone. Or with Buddy's other, nonlocal friends, the opera lovers, balletomanes, or that mixed bag that made up the Manhattan Chess Club. But as Buddy frequently found himself more at fault with his family, he found more flaws in me. My future as a middle-class bride was becoming suspect.

Then a small miracle from an unexpected source. Uncle Dan, the college man, the politician, oldest of my father's brothers (except for the long-ago Kid Dropper), worked with the Board of Education and stepped in to decide my immediate future.

Visiting Forest Hills High on business, he inquired about his niece.

"They told me," he said, "that though your grades are irregular, your IQ is very high and you're gifted. College material. And you should go."

"Uncle Louie won't let me."

"She can't afford," said Louie, hotly facing up to his brother, "four more years of school."

"What about two years somewhere that will prepare her for something?"

"For what?"

"Well, she draws."

So I tested for the Fashion Institute of Technology and Design and made it. Uncle Dan may have pulled a small string, though he said he didn't. Louie was livid. I was redeemed. Jane and I did an actual victory dance on the school steps.

The graduation exercise was the prolonged and predictable disaster I'd expected. Afterward Louie and Birdie took us to Howard Johnson's, where we—Melvin, Janice, and I—were allowed one ice cream soda each and no extras.

"Excuse me," I said as soon as it was permissible, "but I'm meeting my friend Jane and going to the movies."

"How does it feel to be an orphan?" Jane asked between bites of her hamburger as we sat staring at each other across the grime of the T-Bone Diner booth. The glare after leaving a darkened movie theater so early in the day made reality unreal. We weren't as close as we'd been, perhaps because we no longer lived within shouting distance, perhaps because I'd given up politics, or perhaps because I didn't want questions like that. An orphan was a poor wretch with a peaked face, a paltry life, and a paucity of memories. I didn't answer her.

"Do you think about it a lot?"

"No."

"Don't you think about your parents?"

"Of course."

"Well?"

"I don't think of myself as an orphan."

"What do you think of yourself as?" I didn't have an answer for that one.

"I didn't," she said, removing the pickle from her burger, "mean to hurt your feelings."

"Let's talk about something else."

"Well, I worry about you. I can't imagine having everyone dead. Pass the ketchup." This treat at T-Bone was Jane's. I'd ordered only a plate of french fries and nothing more. Maybe that's how it felt to be an orphan.

"I have to go to the john," I said, wiggling my way out of the booth.

"That's the third time in an hour," she said. "You missed half the movie."

"I'll be right back."

Inside the small and smelly room I dropped my pants and looked for pink. Nothing. I wrapped the coarse toilet paper around my forefinger and pushed inside. Dry as a bone. I pulled up my pants, washed my hands, and went back to my french fries.

"Are you sick or something?"

"No."

"Then what's the matter?"

I hesitated. "Jane," I said, "do you talk to your mother about things?"

"What things?"

"Sex things."

"Never, why?"

"I just wondered."

Jane paid the bill, and we left. "Where are you going now?" she asked.

"Home, I guess."

"How'd you like *The Spiral Staircase?*" Melvin called to me in the bathroom as I stared down at my stain-free panties.

"Very scary," I called back.

"You always get scared. You always did. Remember *Frankenstein?*"

I remembered.

"I want you to get tongue sandwiches on rolls," my mother would say to Melvin as she handed him the money, "middle cut, and celery tonic. And tell them your mother said lean." That was the way she sent us off those Saturday mornings of our childhood. "And tell the man who takes the tickets your mother said you must go eat between shows and to let you back in." Most kids just stayed on after the kiddie show for the main feature. We went to the deli.

"Why did you bring your little sister to see *Frankenstein* again," the matron demanded, flashing her light in my face, "since it makes her cry?"

"Mommy said to."

"Come with me." Her hard hand around my neck, she escorted me, irritated as hell, to the back of the theater to wait behind the barrier for the bad part to be over. It could happen several times a *Frankenstein.*

"I liked the movie myself," Melvin called in again as I sat straddling the bowl, "especially the opening." Was all this chattiness my graduation present? He reverted. "Aren't you ever coming out?" I did. "I thought," he said, looking at me strangely, "you'd have a ring by now." So did I.

"Mind your own business," I said. Things didn't used to be like this. I'd enjoyed Melvin's minding me. He'd pick seeds out of my rolls because I didn't like them, and he respected my young opinions. "What happens to Tom Joad now?" he'd ask, not satisfied with movie endings, wanting more. "He meets Priscilla Lane," I'd say, "and she marries him so he doesn't have to pick fruit anymore." I was terrific at happy endings. "Mind your own business," I now said again to muffle the little voice whispering "pregnant" at me, "and I'll mind mine."

"You'd better," said Melvin.

"What if I got pregnant?" I asked Buddy as he huffed and puffed over me.

"That won't happen," he said. "I'll be careful from now on."

Buddy had come to where I baby-sat, and we lay loving on the couch. Afterward, I cuddled under his left arm; his right hand held the book while he waited for me to do my memory trick.

"Sonnet One Hundred Twenty-one," he said.

" ' 'Tis better to be vile than vile esteem'd,' " I recited " 'When not to be receives reproach of being, And the just pleasure lost. . . .' " When I finished, he grabbed me tight. "You're amazing," he said. "We read that one only twice. You got some words wrong, but your substitutions were right."

"You lucky devil, you got yourself a genius," I said, proud of my prowess. "Think what brilliant kids we'll have."

"And what looks, if they get your face."

"And my chubby legs."

"Nah, they'll have my legs."

"What if it works the other way?"

"That reminds me of Bernard Shaw and the lady who proposed to him."

"What happened?"

"Well, this lady—"

"Sit up quick, Buddy," I interrupted. "I hear the Bermans."

"Oh, shit," he said.

Three days late. Another count was on. "Nobody," said Buddy, banging his fist onto the roof of the Caddy, "nobody gets pregnant the first time. Shit," he added.

"Should I do something?"

"Just wait awhile. You'll come around. It's only three days."

"What if I don't?"

"I guess we'll have to get it fixed."

One week late and still waiting to "come around." A

full-time job. "Chickadee is dead, turned into a stew, I think," I said, opening the Bermans' door for Buddy.

"Who?"

"Chickadee, the little Easter chick the Bermans gave their kid. It got too big and wasn't cute anymore, shitting everywhere. They got rid of it."

"Probably just as well," said Buddy, plopping on their couch and eating one of their chocolate-covered cherries.

"Are you going to teach me chess tonight?" I asked.

"I forgot the board. What time will they be home?"

"They said eleven. Why," I asked, "do you think it's just as well?"

"What?"

"Chickadee."

"They shouldn't have bought it in the first place. It's dumb in an apartment."

"But they did buy it, and 'it' thought they were 'its' family. 'It' followed that kid everywhere."

"Shitting everywhere."

"So what!"

"So it stinks."

"Sometimes you stink."

"You're in a great mood. Uncle Louie give you a hard time about something?"

"The usual. That's not it."

"What *is* it?"

"The chicken."

Three weeks late. "Maybe you should take a rabbit test," Buddy said.

"What's that?"

"Well, they use frogs or mice or rabbits and inject your urine into them and they check their ovaries and see if you're pregnant."

"Does it kill the rabbit?"

"Don't give me any more of that Chickadee stuff. If you're pregnant, we'll have to kill more than a rabbit."

"What do you mean?"

"I mean, an abortion."

"Oh, my God. Why can't we just get married?"

"Because we can't yet. It'll ruin things with my family. They'll hate you for it. It's no way to start a marriage."

Two dead rabbits later Buddy found a doctor to do it.

"I asked this hooker the boys used to gang-bang. She's got one."

"Did you tell the boys?"

"What am I, a schmuck?"

"Is he a good doctor?"

"Sure."

"How do you know?"

"She's a professional, she knows."

I no longer needed falsies. My cups runneth over. "You're getting fat," said Teresa approvingly and maybe astonishedly as well. On our food budget it was a neat trick. "That Buddy," she said, "he takes care of you."

Saturday was the day, and the late count turned into a countdown. Five days. Four, three, two, one. Buddy picked me up at 9:00 A.M.

"Put on heavy makeup," he'd said, "so you look older." With me wearing the man-tailored suit he'd bought me wholesale for the occasion and loaded with mascara, we were off.

"Do you have your Kotex pad and your belt?"

"I'm wearing them."

"Now I'm not allowed to wait, but I'll pick you up at noon."

"Buddy, what do they do again?"

"I told you, a scraping. It's nothing."

"It's not nothing for the baby. Does the baby feel anything?"

"It's not a baby yet, for Christ sake, Barbara. It's only a blob."

"But does it hurt?"

"Don't worry. He'll give you something."

"Buddy, I can't die or anything."

"Stop being ridiculous."

"Buddy, do you love me?"

"Of course."

*   *   *

With courtly lilt, Buddy handed me out of the car and watched as I climbed the wooden stairs to the house where the doctor waited. I waved good-bye with the four hundred-dollar bills he'd given me.

"Get in here, and let me take the money," said the white-uniformed woman who opened the door for me. She looked like the matron of the Forest Hills Theater, only made up and with an odor of stale lilac. She hadn't been there for our "interview." Just the doctor. We'd told him our predicament. He had told us the price.

"Exactly what do you do?" I had asked.

"If you are going to be a pain in the ass about this, I don't do anything."

"Buddy," I'd said, breaking the silence of our drive home, "I don't want to do it."

"Neither do I, but there's nothing else to do."

Well, this was it.

"Downstairs," said the nurse, "and be quick." I was watching through the window till Buddy was well gone. My heels caught on the cellar stairs. "Clumsy," she said.

That moment was all fear. Dear God, I prayed, knowing God couldn't help. Oh, skip it. I let God off the hook.

"Take off your skirt and pants, and that Kotex, no, leave the belt, and keep your shoes and stockings on. Here wear this." She handed me a kind of apron. It wasn't very clean. "Hurry up," she said, then: "Bend over; this is to relax you." Her needle jabbed my hip.

The table sat in a raw basement room, looking like a butcher block. "Get up there," she said, "and put your feet there. No, not that way, spread your knees."

"I'm still awake," I said as the doctor strapped me to the table. "Is that right?"

"That's right," he said, adjusting the goose-neck lamp to shine between my legs. "I don't give full anesthesia. I want you walking out of here on your own steam. Here, bite on this if it hurts." A cloth-wrapped piece of wood was shoved beneath my teeth. I fought it. The leather straps held me down. "Stop that, you," he said to me. "All the same they are, hysterics. I should charge more. Keep her quiet."

Don't let me die, Daddy, I'll be good.

"Bite down," the nurse snarled as I jumped and moaned. It didn't help. Razors were ripping. Tearing the poor little blob out of me.

"It's almost over," he said. "Hold her still." When it was over, I vomited.

"Clean her up and get her upstairs." There were blood-stains all over my shoes.

Slowly Buddy moved me down the wooden steps to the car. "You look so pale," he said. "Are you all right?"

"Just get me away from here," I said, and nothing more.

"Did you tell them at home you were staying overnight with Ruth in the city?" I nodded. I couldn't talk.

His chess friend lived on the fourth floor of a walk-up on the Upper West Side. I don't know how we made the stairs.

"Barbara, you're bleeding through your skirt. Let me get it off you."

"Use cold water on it," I told him, "so it won't stain." My first words in an hour.

"Get under the covers," he said after he'd undressed me, "and take these, the nurse said they'd help your pain."

Something like laughter started up in me. I couldn't stop it.

"Oh, babe," he said, holding me, rocking me, "I'm so sorry, so sorry." And I guess he was. When I was quiet again, he asked if I was hungry. "I'll run to the deli on the corner."

"Bring me a tongue sandwich and a Dr. Brown's Cel-Ray tonic," I told him from bruised lips. And tell them, I added to myself, your mommy said "lean."

The Sweetheart of
Sigmund Freud

I dressed that morning with the greatest of care, sure that the Lady from Vienna would observe everything I wore. Sure she would make mental notes and perhaps unflattering comments later. I'd never met a psychiatrist before. Despite its popularity in movies, psychiatry was still somewhat akin to witchcraft in Forest Hills, 1950. You had to be crazy to go to one.

I ran the little birthday ring Buddy had bought me under the hot water to make it sparkle. Heart-shaped and covered in tiny diamond chips, it didn't signify what a solitaire might, but I thrilled to it. And I wanted Olga to notice it. Buddy had started seeing Olga (he never called her that except to me) soon after the summer, when sex had stalled. Olga, Dr. Knopf, was a woman of serious reputation, and now she wanted to talk to me.

"The thing about mental illness," Buddy said, "is its contagion. Infected parents pass it to their kids. On it goes. Therapy stops the pattern."

"Buddy, do you think I'm mentally sick?"

"I love you, but I think you are, just a little."

"What a little?"

"Ask Olga, not me."

"Who told her? God?"

"No, Freud."

At home my physical condition was the more obvious concern. "Why are your feet so cold?" Teresa demanded, rubbing them between rough hands and surveying me sideways with her blue, slanting eyes. "You got skinny again."

"I'm fine."

"No, not fine."

"You're sick," Melvin said accusingly as Teresa rubbed and I shivered.

"Leave her alone," Teresa said.

"Shut up," Melvin told Teresa, and pulled two small RX bottles with NO REPEAT stickers out of his pocket and threw them at me on the bed. "Codeine," he said. "I know. I get them for my pain. Well, say something."

"You shouldn't have gone into my bag," I said. Teresa stopped rubbing. "Give them back!"

"No, I'm showing them to Uncle Louie." He left my bedside.

"Drop dead," I called after him, then bit my tongue.

"Don't worry, you'll get yours," he warned. But he was not getting his. Melvin's coughing had ruptured his testicle. Hydrocele, his doctor called it. "What girl will look at me now?" he had moaned after it happened, back when he was still talking to me. Now he only told me what a rotten piece of work I was. Mostly I agreed with him.

I would leave my sister's bed in the middle of the night, to pace off the small hall; it measured two paces wide and four long. When Janice was sleeping over at Uncle Louie's, I'd give Teresa and her son the big bed and sleep in the living room. Sleep is not the word. I'd push myself into the down of the couch and try to contact my father. He had to be somewhere. Nothing leaves the universe. I'd been taught so. The thing was to slip into some other dimension and find him. "No matter what you do in this life," my father had said, "you can always tell me. I may not like it; but I won't stop loving you, and I'll be there to help."

"Daddy," I would whisper, "where are you? If you are

here, rattle the venetian blinds, move the curtain, knock over a vase." The curtain seemed to move. I distrusted it; our windows were drafty. "Do it again," I commanded, "so I know it's you." Nothing. "The dead are God's business," my father once said; "living is yours." "Daddy," I told the curtain, "I killed a baby." The curtain didn't respond. "And I've damaged myself." The curtain rippled. "And nobody loves me."

"Go to sleep," Teresa would say, standing in the hallway. "Go to sleep before you get sick."

In later years I heard that Uncle Louie had been a wife beater. In those days I knew only that he hated women and was obsessed with sin and sex. He stood by my bed, holding the pain pills. "You could go to jail for these. I'm a customs man and know these things. What have you done?"

"Nothing," I said.

"We will see if it's nothing. I'm going to send you for an examination."

"I won't go. I'm eighteen, and you're not my boss," I said.

"Under the law you're an infant—that's the legal word for it—till you're twenty-one. And I *am* your boss."

"If my father was alive . . ."

"But he's not."

"Melvin," I pleaded, "you wouldn't let Uncle Louie force me to get examined, would you? It would be a terrible thing." I grabbed at his hands. "I'm your sister."

The examination never took place. I was saved that humiliation when Melvin, disturbed with discrepancies in our money, was moved to get rid of Uncle Louie. He needed my support at the Legal Aid Society and switched sides.

I never quite forgave Melvin for betraying me to Louie. "That weasel," he'd say of Louie, now that we were allied, "you know, he's charged the estate for every meal Janice and I ever ate there and even for board when Janice slept over. And he doesn't want to pay Teresa; in fact, he wants to get rid of her and . . ." The list was long. "In this life"— my father's voice reminded me—"nothing is for free. It's better to know the price up front and pay it."

"She's no better than a whore," Louie said to Dan and the lawyer, pointing his finger at me, "and he's an ingrate." Whore or no, ingrate or not, Uncle Louie stepped down, and Uncle Dan stepped in. We moved to a better apartment, and I studied at the Fashion Institute and listened to Buddy's new romance with his unconscious, keeping my own personality carefully split.

We were learning a new language, Buddy and I. We spoke of: penis envy and penis failure, vagina dentata and narcissism, denying mothers and rejecting fathers. We spoke of Buddy's uncle who had used Buddy's baby fat to get off on, rubbing his penis against Buddy's baby behind; we spoke of Buddy's childish passivity when it happened. His guilt. His innocence. His shame. We spoke and spoke and spoke. Now Olga was speaking.

"Why do you want to put all your nice eggs in this one broken basket?" Dr. Knopf said, playing with her pencil, thick glasses muting her ancient eyes.

"I don't know what you mean."

"I mean, why does a pretty and intelligent girl pin all her hopes on a man who can't even make love to her properly, who wouldn't marry her when she was in trouble and will need years of analysis before he ever can?"

"Because I love him."

"Do you?" she asked, her Viennese accent rumbling her words with authority.

"Of course."

"Barbara, if I arranged for you to to be tested at the New York Psychoanalytic Clinic and perhaps get some treatment there, would you do it?"

"If it doesn't cost too much." Olga charged Buddy twenty-five dollars a session, which in those days was astronomical. And he went three times a week.

"Well?" said Buddy after I had descended eleven floors to place my carefully pressed skirt next to him on the front seat, where he waited.

"Well, I'm going to get tested."

"Good," he said, then: "What do you think of *her*? Do you like her?"

How was I going to like anyone who told Buddy he was "years away from marriage"? "I guess so," I said.

"She's brilliant," said he. "Brilliant!"

It took months of waiting to get on the Psychoanalytic Clinic waiting list and almost a full year before I was tested. I gathered that a lot of people in New York needed testing.

Meanwhile, I was concentrating on FIT, which took a bit of concentrating. For a girl who'd never seen a home Singer, I learned to operate high-power industrial machines with apprehension. Plenty of pretty fingers found needles through their nails handling those speed stitchers. I learned to drape muslin on dummies, to sketch with a cloquil pen, and to think "on the flat." But there is nothing like fainting a few times in hallways, a legacy of my abortion, to convince your instructors you're a genius. Uncle Dan was proud. Melvin was oblivious. And I? I was amazed. Working late over the kitchen table, correcting my markers, cutting my fabric, and pinning up samples, I'd worry Teresa. It meant dragging heavy loads between home and school. Wedged on rumbling subways, I'd stand with my shoulders pressed against doors for support because my hands were too full to grab poles.

One ride was different and stays with me. I was on the platform, my boxes bruising my arms, and found myself staring into the eyes of a boy about my own age and height, eyes so sad and intimate they startled the way a passing reflection does when it turns out to be yourself. We *knew* each other. When the train came, we both pushed on. Bodies in overcoats were between us. And faces in newspapers. But each knew the other was there.

Through stops and starts we were pressed nearer. I could see his eyes past the bend of an arm. Then I saw more: the soft blond down on his lips and chin; his fine nose between those demanding eyes; his mouth. Then there was nothing between us now but my boxes. Face-to-face we rode, his breath upon my cheek; we rode and rocked and looked. When the lights of the Twenty-third Street station appeared, I turned to move to the door. "Don't go," he whispered.

I hesitated, then went out and watched the train as it moved him away.

"Are you going to faint again?" said a classmate who'd gotten off another car.

"No," I assured her. We walked together to the school.

No green campus surrounded the Fashion Institute of Technology. It didn't even stand on its own ground, and despite its management division, its students were mostly girls. All of them lovingly agreed that Dr. Zucker, ex-curator of the Berlin Museum, was the most exciting man in the world. Zucker, with his eagle's head, was a Teutonic god, and I had a sexual predilection for Teutonic gods. Even as a child watching *The Thief of Baghdad* on the silver screen, while the rest aaahed the heroes, I found it was the villain, Conrad Veidt, looking a lot like Dr. Zucker, who got to me.

Zucker taught the history of culture and art appreciation in a place hungry for charm.

We drank him in. I mimicked his accent, his style, and his wit and bored Buddy constantly retelling Zucker stories. Where I once quoted my father, I now quoted Zucker. Even Buddy couldn't dismiss Zucker's culture.

And I became Zucker's favorite student. It wasn't hard since the first day of his class, when I'd arrived late, wearing full makeup, from a small modeling job.

"Sorry to be late," I'd said, bursting into his room.

"Yes, of course," he'd said, "but late as what? Are you a student, a muse? Who are you?" I was instantly happier than I'd been in a year. "Your student, sir." I half curtsied, the seductive peasant girl before the king.

"Well, sit up here," he said, "where I can enjoy looking at you."

The class was my oasis away from machine techniques and patternmaking. I became brilliant for him. And I loved the person he thought I was. He invited me to take part in his summer tour of the great cathedrals of Europe on a scholarship. It wasn't possible. But the invitation was almost enough.

"Imagine"—I fantasized to Buddy—"two whole months with Dr. Zucker. It could have changed my whole life."

Actually it seemed to me that Buddy's own life hadn't changed, only his vocabulary. "Olga says Freud—"

Dr. Zucker clarified Freud for me: "a brilliant German Jew, and brilliant German Jews are exciting and dangerous."

"I thought he was Viennese."

"It's the same thing."

"About Freud. Is he right?"

"We will all know what was right about Freud in a hundred years," concluded Zucker.

I couldn't wait that long.

Nothing was helping much with Buddy. The only thing I saw that improved was my sexual inventiveness, which would stand me in good stead for years to come. I'd learned tricks to stimulate Buddy's lagging member. And I learned to do these tricks without getting my head between his bulk and the steering wheel. What I might yet accomplish in a king-size bed was a luxury beyond immediate vision.

"Oh, babe," Buddy would sigh, "there's no one like you. There never will be." Once in a while he stiffened on his own, and I would think: Oh, joy. His therapy is working. We will marry.

Even his family's resistance was easing. When I visited his office, his father was sweet. And once Buddy even took me to the home of his sister and her new husband, and I managed to be funny, and she even managed to laugh. Back in school, the girls waited to hear daily reports about Buddy. They lent me dimes to call him at lunch hour. And they sustained me as I talked of my love for him. Zucker had inspired in them a taste for classic tragedy. Good-natured, they hoped for my best.

It was another year of fifty hours a week of classes. I was bent on receiving the gold medal the Designers Guild awarded to the most promising graduate. So to establish my value, I exhausted myself. When Dr. Zucker heard I was top of my class, he was amazed. His "students" usually failed the "industrial" side of the school. But it was my psychological side that was in jeopardy. My testing started, and my life was at stake. I mustn't flunk my Rorschach. It had been a long while since I'd eaten a lasagna with pleasure or enjoyed an opera or anything else. Everything was a test of one kind or another that I had to pass. So I climbed the stairs to the office of the head of the New York Psychoanalytic Clinic on frozen feet.

"Go right in, miss," said the secretary, and I did. The room was empty. Above a huge tooled-leather desk a picture of the great Sigmund Freud himself stared down.

"Hi, Sigmund," I offered. "Olga sent me."

"What's was that?" A voice from nowhere. Then a head and shoulders rose from behind the empty desk. The director, a spindly sort of man, took his chair. "I dropped my pen," he explained. "Please sit." I couldn't wipe the silly grin off my face. He tapped with his recovered pen. He tapped, and I grinned.

"They explained to you how we work here?"

"Yes, sir. They told me if you take me, I get assigned a student analyst who works with me, and then everybody studies my case."

"Not exactly," he said. "But you do have to fit in with our curriculum of study to be of value to us, and I'm afraid you don't."

I wasn't of value to them, and I stopped grinning. "What happens to me now?"

"We'll send a full report to Dr. Knopf, and she'll advise you."

"You've dropped your pen again," I informed him, and exited the door.

"It seems they don't think you're a candidate for Freudian analysis." Olga began pacing around her office as I strained to listen upright and unwrinkled in her chair.

"So," she finished, "there is a man in private practice I respect highly. He's not Freudian, but he's very effective. I'd like you to see him." How much did he charge? I asked.

"I'm not sure, but not as much as me." She waited for me to smile. I didn't.

"Dr. Knopf," I said, "I have no money. I barely have carfare. I don't eat lunch so I can buy pins and pencils."

"Perhaps your family?"

"My brother has cancer. Do you know what that costs?"

"Well, Barbara, if you can't now, you can't. But when things get better, come and see me and I'll send you to see the right man."

"It will be too late."

"It's never too late."

"Olga feels sorry she can't help you." Buddy reported in after his next session.

"Then why doesn't *she* take me and not charge or charge you?"

"Analysis doesn't work like that."

"Nothing works like that."

"Also," Buddy added, staring at the steering wheel of Cleopatra, "she asked me about your ring. She thinks it would be better if you wore it on your right hand. She doesn't think we should think of ourselves as committed."

"What else doesn't she think?" He didn't answer. "Well, doesn't she think you should stop seeing me? Tell me!"

"She thinks it might be better for a while."

"And what do you think?"

"I love you." He heaved a sigh, and all his bulk heaved with him.

"Does she think you're too fat for me?"

I won the gold medal. Were things looking up?

Buddy was pacing up and down in front of the sea lions, his nose sniffing air and looking like a six-foot seal himself.

"Here I am," I called.

He stopped pacing. Then he said, "Your uncle Dan called me this afternoon." I waited. He went on. "He wants to talk to me, about you."

Uncle Dan, taking his guardian role seriously, asked Buddy his intentions. Buddy felt pressured. Uncle Dan reminded Buddy I had just turned twenty and wanted to know how much more of my time he would take up before making up his mind. Buddy resented being told he was damaging the merchandise. Good mink didn't damage with a little handling. Uncle Dan said human flesh was more vulnerable. Buddy left my life. The night he did was swollen with passion and tears. But under it all I could smell his relief. We made love. I did my whole act without mercy. His eyes rolled as sweat slid down both his chins. Two years later Polly Adler told me tales of Silver Tongue Elsie, whose clients left her on their knees in gratitude and sheer exhaustion. I wondered if hate was her hidden weapon. Sigmund would understand.

Night Flights

"Why do all washrooms in cheap Chinese restaurants smell the same?" and "Why am I lying on the floor of one of them?" were questions I might well have asked myself, while struggling to get a brand-new diaphragm in place. It takes a little telling. Starting when Mr. Cohen, my employer, casting a last lingering look at my bottom, had said, "I hate to say it to you, kiddie, but you're fired." He smiled sadly. "I could mention to you your sloppy patterns, but in fact, it's just business. Gone from bed to worse."

After packing up my imitation leather hatbox, I spent the afternoon brazenly using the showroom phone. Cursing myself for not knowing anyone long distance. I wasted time till four when I could meet my friend Ruth. I kept checking my watch: half past three and going on unemployment. Half past Buddy and going on what?

"How's your life?" said Johnny Polletti as I approached the usual table, occupied by our usual group.

"My life," I answered with Mr. Cohen's inflection, "has

gone from 'bed to worse.' " I waited for a laugh, and it
came.

"Sit down, darling," said Polletti sweetly. Usually he
moaned, "Oh, Buddy," in imitation of my torch song. Ruth
must have told him. I sat. Some of the best "sitters" here
looked as if they hadn't changed position in years. Some
hadn't. Some were so familiar you were sure you'd seen
them onstage or screen. Some were not. Some pored over
casting calls in *Variety*. Some did crosswords. Most were
good-looking or once had been. And mostly I sat among
them with a touch of awe, well covered with makeup.

"So," persisted Polletti, a song and dance man featured
in *Hazel Flagg*. "I hear heaven has neglected to protect the
working girl."

"Leave her alone," said Ruth, who frequently spoke for
me here.

Polletti grinned and pushed over to give me more room.
Ours was a good table. A good table at the "actors' drugstore" in Radio City needed at least one "working actor" or
acknowledged "genius" to signify. Today ours had both.
"Oh, Buddy," someone whined, an old joke. They'd all
heard about Buddy, a diversion from their cold coffee and
rehashed tales of failure, or success. My broken heart was
considered fair game, like contacting the ghost of John
Garfield, their own existential hero, dead before his time,
whom they called to as Julie.

"What you need," said Ruth, checking the crowd, "is a
project."

"Why not an acting class?" offered Polletti.

"I'm a designer," I said. No one heard me.

"She needs the right class," said someone.

"Well," someone else said, "the Piccolo Teatro de Milano
is setting up."

"No, she'll hide behind the mime and the mask."

"I don't agree." The debate was on.

"She needs something deep and revealing."

"She'd never get into the Studio."

"Not even the Playhouse."

"Stella would chew her up."

"What about Uta?" suggested Polletti. The possibility

that I was only an excuse for the dialectic never crossed my mind.

"They say good things about Carnovsky." Everyone discussed Carnovsky. Then someone remembered the point of it all. "Mark Gordon from the old Actors' Lab is starting something. He'd be nice to her."

"He's at that booth across the room with Barbara Glenn and Jimmy Dean," said Ruth, putting out her cigarette. "I'll introduce her."

"If I asked you to become a flower," Mark Gordon suddenly demanded of me after ten minutes of listening as they weighed whether action brings forth emotion or comes out of it, "which would you choose?"

"A rose."

"You are now a rose. Tell me about yourself?" Was he kidding? The table turned silent and expectant.

"Well?"

"Well, I'm red and I smell good."

"Go on."

"That's it."

"If you come to my group," said Mark Gordon, "you'll have to be a rose for me. Have you the courage?"

"I always wanted to be an actress but—"

"But what?"

"My thighs are too chubby."

"Thighs! Bernhardt only had one leg."

"She's got a fine stage mask," Ruth pointed out. "Nice visible features, a strong nose."

Mark observed my nose. It decided him. "Come next week," he invited.

Then it felt as though they were wanting us to leave so they could get back to their real talk. I stood up. "If you want to know about roses," said Jimmy Dean, looking up at me over the rims of his glasses, "get a copy of this." He tapped the thin book under his hand. *The Little Prince* by Antoine de Saint-Exupéry. "This guy," he said softly, in that voice that would woo the world, "knows roses."

"Jimmy always carries Exupéry," Ruth informed me as she puffed me back to our table. "Like a rabbit's foot. Usually *Night Flight*." I tried to look as if I understood the significance. James Dean was an already developing legend. Someday his ghost would replace Julie's.

"So," said Mark Gordon the next week, "are you ready to be a rose? Okay, stand near the arch and close your eyes."

I walked across the makeshift platform that was the stage and stood next to the arch. "Feel it," said Mark. "You're a rose. Now what do you like about being a rose?"

My last vision was of Ruth lighting up at the back of the room. She'd come to remind me I had courage. After a long silence I whispered, "Being beautiful."

"Do you think you're beautiful?"

Silence.

"Well, are you a beautiful rose?"

"Yes."

"Speak up. Keep your eyes closed and tell me about yourself. And not that you smell good." I stood silent.

"Where are you?" demanded Mark. "Are you on a bush? In a vase?"

"I'm in a vase."

"Where?"

"In an empty room."

"Are you in sunlight?"

"In shadow."

"What do you see?"

"A dirty window and faded curtains."

"What are you doing there?"

"I don't know."

"Feel your petals," he instructed. "Feel your stem, your leaves." I felt.

"Well?" said Mark.

"I'm afraid I'm dying."

"Why?"

"They've forgotten to give me water."

"Open your eyes," said Mark.

I opened and looked around the loft. Everyone was watching me. "How did I do?" I asked at last.

"That wasn't a test," said Mark, "just an exercise. Sit down now and watch how it works."

So I sat and watched a shaggy-headed boy in tattered corduroy pants turn himself into a dog: hungry, then angry, then beaten. I watched a girl with a clubfoot become a ballerina, without moving her legs, and I believed her. It was wonderful. Yes, I was going to be a serious actress and respect my art, and damn the Garment Center.

"So you liked it?" said my friend Ruth when we achieved the safety of her room. She now lived in a West Side hotel populated with hustlers, hookers, and assorted offbeat types. A perfect place, except for being charged for overnight guests, which meant sneaking me in.

"Yes," I said. "I liked it a lot."

"Why did you choose a rose?"

"It was my mother's name."

In the silence with which we weighted down her Murphy bed, the most exotic contraption I'd ever seen, I thought about acting. There had always been actors around our life. In the thirties the theatrical world had been prizefight mad. Glossies of my father in embrace with Victor McLagelen, Mae West, George Raft, and the rest of the fight gang had adorned our basement bar. Yet my father hadn't thought much of a life in the theater. "Babsie," he'd explain, when I complained, as I always did, about the time he'd turned down a child's role for me in a movie, "it's an unnatural life, especially for a kid. Better to duck it."

"But"—I'd rebelled—"I could have been Shirley Temple."

"Actors"—my father had gone on—"turn into actors. Something real gets lost."

"I think the acting is better than the real," I had insisted.

"If so," he'd said, "you've got something else to be mad at me for."

"Are you still up?" asked Ruth as I shifted position.

"Yes."

"I think," she said, "it's because you like Mark."

Could she be right? "Better get yourself a diaphragm," she mumbled, and went back to sleep. Actually I was worrying about how to break all this to Melvin. He'd become frightened when I told him I'd lost my job.

"Well," said Polletti after I'd been a rose twice more, "is Mark going to put you in his opening production?"

"I'm not ready for that. I've only been a rose."

Polletti pushed away his dead cup of coffee and said, "You're ready for something. You've stopped moaning, 'Oh, Buddy,' and now all we hear about is 'Mark.'"

So, when the last fortune cookie crumbled in Mark's hands, I retired to the washroom, and that's how I came to be on the floor, trying to do the right thing. At first I'd tried it sitting on the toilet seat but after I'd squeezed the dollop of contraceptive jelly into the rubber-ringed dome (and a little extra around the rim), as instructed, and squeezed the slippery thing into the required elliptical shape, it jumped out of my hands and into the bowl. With a grimace I fished it out and dropped it into the sink. After a moment's thought I rinsed it under the faucet from which only cold water ran, then held it under the liquid soap dispenser and rinsed it again. And made another stab at it. Horizontally. Overhead the bare bulb bounced off the peeling ceiling and glared down on bent knees and rolled-down hose. Beneath my back and my best black sheath and my bunched-up girdle, the tile was cold. Using two hands, I got the thing inside me and me back on my feet. Rewashing hands, rearranging clothes, and rerouging cheeks, I decided spontaneity was a wonderful thing.

"It's only one more flight," Mark encouraged as I panted my way up the bent and broken stairwell that led to his place. The December iced metal clanked with every step. "I'm the last one left," he said as we reached the top floor of his condemned tenement on Columbia Street, "and if I can hold out, I'll get relocated into a good cheap project."

Mark's flat had no steam, a sparking electric heater, a leak in the roof, a cat named Mike with five toes, and a wonderful big bed.

Looking like a mountain man in his slightly dingy long johns, reminiscent of the Dr. Dentons of my crib, he joined me on that bed. With his unshaved actor's mug and his active Adam's apple, he certainly wasn't Buddy. Buddy's Adam's apple was buried under layers of costly flesh. Mark's flesh looked as if no one had thought to invest a rich meal in it for years. He helped unbutton me.

Afterward, hungry, he made us dinner on his hot plate,

mixing several Campbell's soup cans and chopped meat. "Beef Stanislavsky" he called it. Passion is more easily shared than sentiment, but we managed both with the help of Paul Muni, George Arliss, and hungry talk of art and beauty. I attempted to do the dishes and shattered the first. Teresa always did the dishes. He said a person, especially an actor, had to develop survival skills. I certainly agreed, so I moved in.

If life in a garret on the Lower East Side wasn't cushy, it was cozy. I still was officially at home, but really that was only where my laundry was done. Here I was enlarging my survival skills. I learned to warm a room quickly, using a mirror as adjunct to the electric heater. "The more reflection," Mark said, "the more heat." I learned to bathe in a sink, rewire a broken plug, and make coffee and love with profound simplicity.

The cozy part was the sleeping in serene privacy with Mark and Mike. Five-toed Mike was the first cat I was to know intimately.

"What's he doing?" I'd asked in alarm when Mike walked his five toes up my thighs and over my belly and, pressing his two front paws into my breast (claws delicately withdrawn), began his dance.

"He's loving you," said Mark.

It was bleak on Fortieth and Broadway, and chill gusts rushed down the Manhattan canyons and up my sleeves and under my skirts. I remembered how my father had folded a newspaper under my coat to protect my chest and my back against such wind. I considered going to the corner and buying one. Instead, I just stood frozen beneath the marquee waiting for Melvin. On decent terms again, we had a date to see Eisenstein's *Alexander Nevsky*. The Stanley Theater was the only movie house that showed these Russian films Melvin was addicted to. "They say," he told me, "that government agents film everyone going in, looking for reds." The Rosenbergs were on my mind as I stood with my face in the shadows and shivered. Melvin took me by surprise. For an instant I didn't recognize him. He looked thinner than only the week before. Much thinner. "You're going to love this," he said. I sat with my coat on, still too frozen to love anything.

"Where's this genius director of yours?"

"Busy, coaching someone for money."

"Ah, the magic word."

"Sh," hissed a serious film student behind us, and we gave ourselves to the film. Back on the street Melvin looked like a specter himself.

"Let's go for a hamburger," I said. "I just cashed my unemployment check."

"Unemployment checks, you've really joined the theater."

There is a glare in restaurants of the sort we sat in that is found only in New York and under which Melvin's face looked even worse. I needed to talk and said, "Melvin, what do you think will happen to the Rosenbergs?"

"They'll kill them."

"Even if they're innocent?"

"It doesn't matter. They're dead already. And speaking of dead already, I have to go back to the hospital soon, so I think you should be at home more."

I was quiet.

"There is Janice, you know." He looked strange as he said it.

"She has Teresa."

"You really are a selfish cunt."

"And you have a filthy mouth."

"It's my only sexual outlet, so allow me."

"What about Nina?"

"Nina, well, I think she'd do it, but I'm ashamed of my swollen ball."

"Tell her about it."

"I can't."

"Then keep the damn light off and do it."

He sipped at the last of his milk shake, wiped ketchup from his fingers. "How do I start?"

"With a kiss, then with your fingers."

"I think Nina's a virgin."

"Then you're even."

"What about protection?"

"Well, don't use that old Trojan, get some of those new wet things. Fishskins, I think." What a woman of the world I was.

"I'll louse it up," he said, brushing crumbs from the table.

"Melvin," I said, the words coming out before I could stop them, "what's it like to have cancer?"

"I don't know what it's like. I only know what it is."

We walked down the subway steps.

"Do it before the hospital," I said.

"Do what?"

"Nina."

He blushed. It was nice to see color on those cheeks. "So, what will you be when you grow up, Babsie?" Old-joke time.

"Shirley Temple, of course."

"Too bad you don't dance."

"Yeah, isn't it?" I rushed away from him for my train. We were going in different directions.

Climbing those five flights to Mark's flat on Columbia Street made me think of my grandma. The tenement smell, like Broome Street, two blocks away. Broome Street was where my mother's mother had lived, since stepping onto free America, and where she died. It had smelled the same. As children we would spot her at her windowsill, leaning on her red brocade pillow, and as soon as we could, we took over that pillow and the view, good enough to hold us till egg cream time.

"Let's go," my father would say at the exact moment we grew restless, and we were off.

"Hymie, don't stuff them up. We're going for Chinese."

"Don't worry, Rosie."

"And don't let them near those Gypsies."

"They won't get stolen, Rosie."

We'd skip the stairs ahead of him, knowing he'd greet at least three old people in their doorways before making it to the street. At the entrance we'd wait, Melvin kicking at a brown stone and me marking time. Then, cigar between his teeth and a hand for each kid, he'd parade us along through the streets.

Not a full block could we go when over the honking cabs of Broadway or the yelling of the fish vendors on Fulton Street or the babble of Chinatown someone didn't call to "Hymie" by name. Of course, the Lower East Side was best. It held our history.

"On that spot there"—Daddy points—"is where I first noticed your mommy. And this here is Irving Berlin's block. And that building there is where Auntie H. and George Burns danced, before they were married."

We nod and note every landmark. He gives us a nickel apiece for the organ grinder's monkey, which tips its hat, then we are on Second Avenue, and sipping soda with pleasure. "This," my father says, "is the home of the egg cream."

"I didn't see him put egg in it."

"There is no egg in egg creams."

The gypsy-eyed men watch us as we approach Grandma's block.

"What do Gypsies do?"

"They survive. They're an old people."

"Why can't we go near them?"

"Well, they have bad reputations. But if you promise not to tell your mommy, we can have your palms read."

Taking the dollar for her pocket, she stares at the pretzeled palms pushed at her. Melvin will grow tall and be smart. I will be lucky, marry a foreign man and travel and have lovers, and I'd better watch my money as people would be jealous and—At that point my father stops her and moves us along.

Then back to Grandma's good-bye cuddle and my struggle against two crumpled dollar bills always forced into my hand.

"No, Grandma."

"Take, take."

"Babsie, give Grandma back that money."

"Rosie, let her keep it. It makes your mother happy." Grandma nods, her hands covering mine, forcing it to hold the bills.

"She can't afford it, Hymie."

120

"Rose, don't make her feel poor."

I, as usual, carry the money away. The money smells like Grandma, like Broome Street and very like Columbia, too.

Mark was there when I reached the fifth floor.

"Shadow of a Gunman," he announced, looking up from where he was wadding the windows to help hold back the wind. Hard for Mark to put his mind to these minor irritations. He'd decided on a little O'Casey to launch his group.

"You like O'Casey, don't you?" he asked.

I'd never heard of O'Casey but nodded yes. Certainly I was willing to learn to love him.

Our dimensions, Mark's and mine, didn't leave much room for the drugstore now. Between rehearsals we prowled Irish pubs listening to old IRA men tall tales of ambushed lorries and Black and Tans. I perfected three different brogues. That was the best part. The worst was getting financed. We used food money for lights and curtains. I, assistant to Mark's genius, scrounged sets while secretly memorizing the part of the girl, just in case. As the production fell together, I started falling apart.

"What did you do in the sink?" shouted Melvin from the bathroom during one of my pit stops. "It's all plugged up with hair."

I looked. Handfuls of my long hair swam in the stopped-up water. Also, I was having to urinate every five minutes. "Probably cystitis," a friendly druggist said, giving me purple pills. "Keep yourself warm." I had a cough that racked, old abortion pains were hurting again, and all that black coffee was making me shaky.

"That old friend of yours Steve Schwartz keeps calling," said Janice, now fifteen and frantic. "He says he's going south somewhere, and for you to call him before he does, if you want to go, too. If you don't want to go with him, maybe he'll take me."

"You're too young."

"Not for long."

"See," said Melvin, "what a nice influence you are on your sister."

"When," I asked him, "are you due at the hospital?"

"Next week."

"I'll try and be home, but next week's our opening."

"You're not even in it."

"How are things with Nina?"

"Don't change the subject."

"Where you going?" demanded Teresa. "Stay here, in bed."

I awoke the next day to find an icicle descending from where Mark's faucet usually dripped. When I turned knobs with blue hands, nothing happened. The pipes were frozen. That was when I called Steve Schwartz.

"What's the matter with you?" Steve said when I joined him for lunch at the sleazy little Syrian restaurant his group had used as a meeting place for years of covert Mideast operations, working towards Israeli statehood. "You look like the last act of *Camille*. What have you been doing?"

My stiff hands burned hot as I forked up spicy kibbe and sipped at rose-scented coffee. My head was spinning, and my chest hurt. Through the window of the Mecca restaurant snow swept down East Thirtieth Street. I could have said my new survival skills were failing me. I said, "I think I'm getting sick."

"I'm taking you," said Steve Schwartz, whom I'd described to Melvin as a nice Jewish armaments dealer, big in Israel. "I'm taking you," Steve said, wiping a manicured hand across his balding brown skull, "to Santo Domingo. It's warm and beautiful, and all you have to do is rest, eat, and you'll be well in a week."

God, it sounded good, but what about Mark? Well, I wasn't even in a play, was I? And I was cold and sick, so I nodded yes to Santo Domingo and Steve.

"The play opens in five days," I said. "Can I go after that?"

"I'm leaving tonight. What will it take to get you on the plane?"

"I don't have a passport."

"I'll fix a visa. We are guests of the number one Dominican bigwig."

"I'd have to go to Mark's and get my things."

"So go."

"He has the key with him at rehearsal, and well, I don't want to tell him I'm leaving."

"Look, that stuff's up to you. If you want to come, meet me at La Guardia main terminal at seven o'clock tonight. Here's cab fare."

I counted the money after he had left me. It was over two hundred dollars. After pulling out a twenty and the singles, I folded the rest into my brassiere. I'd give that to Mark. Something had come up about an actors' bond. But could I get into the flat without the key? If I could, I'd go.

The wind rushed around me as I climbed over the roof and onto the metal ladder that dropped to Mark's fire escape. Don't look down, I cautioned. I'd heard that in movies. Attached by only one rusty bolt, the ladder shimmied in the storm. My stockinged feet froze to the rungs. It was the only way. I'd left my high-heeled shoes at Mark's fifth-floor landing.

Once I made it down the ladder I found the window wouldn't budge. All that tacking and wadding to hold back the weather. I banged at it, my hands turning raw. It finally groaned and gave. Five-toed Mike, startled by my offbeat entrance, purred and paraded around the sink, signaling pleasure.

As I opened him a can of fish, I explained that I wasn't really deserting and how much I loved him, Mark, and the theater. And as soon as I felt well, I'd come back. He knew I was lying, but he licked his whiskers and had the good sense to enjoy what he could. I crammed what I owned, including my just-in-case diaphragm, into my hatbox, wrote Mark a good-bye on the mirror (with lipstick, also learned from the movies), Scotch-taped the two hundred next to it, got my shoes, and ran.

The wheels of the taxi churned helplessly in the snowdrift, making a sound closer to an animal in pain than a machine in motion. Then, catching and holding, they pressed through. The sound returned to normal.

It would be ironic to miss the damn plane now, after managing to push Mark and Mike and Melvin and hospitals out of my way. I'd be left with nothing but shame. C'mon, God, I bargained, let me owe you now. I'll pay for it later.

I made the plane. Flushed and rushed and little realizing it was the first in a series of such choices. Survival skills.

"Have another strawberry," I said, offering the spoon to the smiling moustachioed mouth on my left. Steve on my right wasn't smiling. He's jealous, I thought, and kept up my flirt. I was having the kind of wonderful time only guilt-ridden cowards know how to have. Time that really costs, so you'd better relish it. However, I didn't want to think about that. I was warm, bronzed, and happy, and all the pearl-handled pistol-carrying puppets of Trujillo's island were admiring me. How well the poor can play at the pleasures of the rich.

"Guapa," murmured the number one man's son. *"Muy guapa y muy simpatica."* My high school Spanish assured me I was on top of the situation despite Steve's face signaling otherwise.

Back in our suite I stretched out on the rattan chaise on the balcony and drank in the Caribbean.

"You've got to stop that stuff."

"What stuff?" I asked in innocence.

"Strawberries-from-your-spoon stuff."

"Just being friendly."

"Barbara, you are in a backward banana republic, and you are an unmarried American girl. I told them we were engaged. That was to give you some status. Here women are either family girls or whores. Do you follow me?"

"No."

"Then take my word for it. And behave yourself. This is a tricky deal we're involved in."

The "deal" seemed to center on guns and planes slated for Somoza in Nicaragua, to be used against Arbenz's new left-wing government in Guatemala, bought through Trujillo and surrogates. Melvin could say, "I told you so." My reaction to the white-suited men, accompanied by armed guards, who met us in fanfare at the airport had been: "It's just like the movies."

"It's for real," Steve had said.

But not for me. I was on holiday.

The best brothel on Hispaniola was preempted so our

124

group could enjoy its cuisine. The place was a national treasure, our guide (you traveled nowhere in this republic without one) assured us, and used only for political parties of importance. He thought it too bad we didn't choose to savor its more exotic delights. Gold-toothed darlings, relaxed and expansive, advised us which of the moro crabs in their rocky pen would be most tasty. They taught us to dance the meringue and giggled at our awkwardness, as the blazing sun set and houseboys scurried up palms to bring us back fresh fruit. *Agua de coco,* the pure water from green coconuts, turned out to be the very backup rum was intended for. It was the happy overture to what should have been Steve's and my first night of passion. But the next thing I knew we were hurtling back to Ciudad Trujillo. It seems the guide, who'd gotten drunk and expansive, too, said something in comradeship to Steve that altered all plans.

Steve sat silently behind the chauffeur and signaled me to stay the same. Through the windows of our car the jungle flashed by in threatening shadow. Eventually jungle yielded to shabby civilization, and shacks with corrugated roofs and thatched huts made themselves noticed along the roadside. Modern, brightly lit, yet somehow dismally deserted, the airport came as a shock when it arrived. I smothered all questions till we were well inside and relatively isolated.

"I'll bring your stuff back with me next week," said Steve. "But take my jacket, you'll freeze in New York in that dress." He stuffed a wad of money in my hand.

"What's happening?"

"Not now. You must leave immediately. I'm going to say you got ill."

"I don't understand."

"Just get on the plane and look sick. You're good at that. And don't talk to anyone. They'll report back." His bald brow was wrinkled in anger, and he spoke through tight lips. And under my ten-day tan I felt my color growing pale.

The plane, empty except for six in the crew, took off as the hint of dawn touched this beautiful island, discovered by Columbus on his first voyage and since then steeped in blood and sad stories.

"What are you doing in such clothes? It's cold out," demanded Teresa as I stepped sandal-footed through the door of our apartment. At La Guardia I'd thanked God it wasn't snowing. "Get in a hot bath," she insisted, "and I make strong tea."

"There was some trouble." I stabbed at an explanation I didn't know.

"Always trouble," muttered Teresa.

Melvin in the hospital was too preoccupied to ask me questions about my trip.

"I don't think I'm responding to the new mustard nitrogen," he said through cracked lips. Huge acnelike swellings distorted his handsome face. I hesitated before kissing him. "It's the medication," he said, embarrassed. "They say it will go away."

I nodded.

"The problem is there are nodes starting up under my spinal column, and if they don't start shrinking soon, I won't be able to walk out of here. I have to get back to school. I want to graduate."

"You'll be back in school soon," I said.

"Do you think so?"

"Sure. Dr. Chow says so."

"You have a swell tan," he said.

From the hospital I took the subway down to the drugstore. With each stop I envisioned Melvin younger and healthier in my mind. By the time I reached Radio City I could see him chasing me around our old backyard with a water pistol.

"Well, everyone's talking about Mark's production," said Polletti. "It may even make a star or two."

"I wasn't in it," I said.

"You were part of it," said Ruth.

"Was I?" It all seemed light-years gone.

"Funny," said Ruth. "Mark just walked in. Did you call him?"

"No." Light-years contracted.

"I got your card," said Mark. "It looked very pretty. And warm."

"I felt odd sending it. How's the play doing?"

"Harry Guardino is getting good comment. I guess it's his showcase."

"How long will you run?"

"A few weeks. Long enough to get you your two hundred back."

"Never mind that, how's Five-toed Mike?"

"Not dancing. He misses you."

"Tell him I'm sorry."

"He knows."

Back in our crowded apartment I thought about how no one used Melvin's room while he was gone. Janice rushed by me to get the ringing phone. She turned her back and giggled into the receiver. I moved away to give her privacy. As I reached our bedroom, she called to me.

"Long distance for you."

Steve was speaking softly from Texas. It seemed he'd heard that night from the "guide," who'd heard from an aide of the number one man's son, that I was to be abducted to the Island of Women, a retreat kept for the amusement of Number One and Company.

"It might not have been true," Steve finished, "but there is such a place, and it was better to fly you out immediately. Someone will deliver your hatbox and coat tomorrow."

"Thank you," I said, and put down the phone, suddenly realizing I was still wearing the unfulfilled diaphragm I'd so carefully placed inside me, in Santo Domingo. So much for southern nights.

The Thing About Dying

"Death is both an acquired skill and an inherited art," confided Melvin to Nina and me between the fifth and sixth puffs of the only marijuana he was ever to smoke. "We spend our whole damn lives learning to die." It had become a time for this kind of talk.

"He's so brilliant," said Nina hoarsely, trying to retain her inhale as I'd instructed. Smoking marijuana, or gage, as it was called back when Chicago Green was the most highly prized stuff a reefer could be made of, was still a lesser-known art.

"The point is," Melvin went on, "that death must come sooner or later. So is it worth the effort to fight the inevitable or—" His coughing interrupted his inspiration. After he stopped, his theme varied. "I mean," he said, reaching over to touch a lank strand of Nina's blond hair, "the thing about dying is you're living while you're doing it."

Silent in front of his expertise, I concentrated on rolling another smoke. He wasn't going to die a virgin if I could help it. These were the first I'd ever rolled for myself. "Use two papers, it's easier," I'd been told. "Stick one to the other and fold a ledge and don't put in more than you can handle." So far, so good, if the gum held.

"God says," continued Melvin, "here's how it works. I'm going to put you through shit, then later I'll stop your breath, but first, a little entertainment."

The gum held. I started a third.

"Einstein," said Nina, studying my handiwork, "says all he's interested in is whether God had any choice in creating the universe."

"There's the question." Melvin sighed. "Barbara, who showed you how to roll like that?"

"Big Al from high school."

"Big Al?" questioned Nina.

"A Forest Hills zoot-suiter, would-be musician," Melvin explained. "She collects mysterious friends." On a sad inhale, he added, "It came from hanging around Lindy's with our old man. She likes being one of the boys."

He is right, I thought, carefully twisting the ends of the papers. I loved to hang out with the boys, especially the bad boys. And especially when playing hooky and going to the city.

Manhattan was the "city" to us kids in the suburbs. On that particular spring afternoon Big Al's invitation to go along had been irresistible. Our first stop was at Seventy-ninth and Central Park West, where they had a "meet." The shuffling sunglassed *schmecker* slid Big Al down the street while we waited on the corner. Al returned with a brown paper bag. "Turkish Tobacco," he'd assured me. I suspected differently. But, "Turkish Tobacco, sure is dirty," was all I said, as I helped them separate sticks and seeds.

After they'd smoked, we wandered up to the Palms on 125th Street, where they hoped to jam with a real jazz group. Al handed me the brown bag as they joined the session. The bundle sweetly in my lap, I sat sipping a ginger ale, thinking myself lucky to be included. Then two policemen entered and arrested a junkie, and my guilty bundle became suddenly heavy. "Get rid of that bag," commanded my dead father's voice, and I let it drop and kicked it under an adjoining table, where it lay almost glowing in the dark. One cop noticed me, asked my age, and sniffed at my ginger ale. All smiles and fifteen-year-old innocence, I'd murmured of waiting for my brother, who'd come to sit in with the band. He believed me. When it was safe, I recovered the bag. The boys declared me a hero, entitled to smoke with them. It was a few years before I took up the invitation. But this "reefer party" wasn't for me. It was for Melvin. For therapy. I handed him the fresh-rolled joint.

"Start another," I offered.

"Do you think I'm getting high?" asked Melvin. "It's not like the pain pills."

"Sure you are."

"How can you tell?"

"By your face."

He veered toward the bathroom to peer at his face. "Me Tarzan," he said to the mirror.

"Me Jane," called Nina.

Had he told her about that? About jungle. Jungle was Melvin's childhood invention to satisfy his precocious but thwarted sex life. He played Tarzan and whatever girl he could trap into it played Jane. I was always Cheetah, the monkey. My part was to bear witness and "lay chicky" against adults. Once, while visiting Aunt Ida on Staten Island, he intrigued a cousin's cousin into Masai country, located behind Aunt Ida's green velvet couch, and taught her a few tribal rites. Tired of being lookout, I'd looked on, entranced, as Tarzan and Baby Jane sat facing each other with legs spread, and bottoms bare. Just as Tarzan had started to pee all over Jane's naked triangle, Aunt Ida, worrying about her velvet, discovered us. We were in disgrace. Melvin beat me up for not warning him.

After five minutes of peering at his face, Melvin came back in. "I don't see a thing," he said. Nina and I laughed. It was a good Sunday. Teresa had taken her son to visit relatives, and Janice was staying with a girl friend. Tomorrow Melvin would go back to Francis Delafield Hospital, and we both secretly feared he'd never leave there again. But today we still were able to laugh.

"I think I'd like to lie down and listen to some music," said Melvin.

"Me, too," said Nina.

Tarzan led Jane into his room, and from behind his closed door some Ravel started up. Good choice.

The sun faded over Queens. April wet trees reached up toward our new taller apartment building from whose window I could just about make out the Aquacade. I always looked for it, always worried they would tear it down. Did Melvin look for it, too? It was left over from the 1939 World's Fair. Daddy used to take us there. Billy Rose, a pal of his, had built it to star swimmer Eleanor Holm, and the city had kept it alive as a public pool. We'd gone swimming there once. That was long ago.

Sex, that prepubescent summer, appeared every evening in the shape of Herman Fryberg, a German boy, who came to water the Donners' lawn. It worried me finding Herman so attractive, him being German and it being wartime. But Herman, full of allure, did bad-boy things that impressed me, like smoking Lucky Strikes in the Donners' garage. Mostly I'd been impressed with Herman's designs on me. Did Melvin notice? When Herman suggested we swim with him at the Aquacade, I held my breath. If Melvin didn't want to, I wouldn't be allowed either. Melvin wanted, so we went.

The "ladies' " locker room, to which I was sent, was a madness of sexual preparation. Tough teenagers, looking like the V girls reviled in Sunday supplements, lipsticked their mouths, adjusted their curves, and puffed their pompadours. Frailer types stuffed bosoms with socks or hankies.

Having nothing to stuff with, I considered toilet paper but discounted it. It would disintegrate. So, having used the safety pin Teresa made me carry to attach the cloth-looped key I'd been warned not to lose to my suit, I followed the line of breasty Italians from the Bronx, swing-assed blacks from Jamaica, and freckled Irish out to the pool. The "ladies," I noticed, wore their keys around their ankles, as a kind of invitation. But like Nina, now moaning behind Melvin's door, I had been new to the game.

My chest, as I'd stepped through the disinfectant foot bath the Aquacade insisted on, looked skimpy. But so did the Aquacade. It wasn't the same as when Billy Rose had run the show. Seats were laden with wet towels, and no colored lights sparkled off water nymphs creating designs with their bodies. I searched the crowd for Melvin. Then sin took me at the four-foot level while I clung to the side, trying not to drown. Herman swam up between my legs and pulled the bottom of my suit aside and stuck his finger into my most private part. He kept it there till Melvin pushed him away. Later, on the bus ride home, Melvin had said girls could get pregnant being in water where men did things. If, I thought, he meant peeing, I was done for. Everyone had peed in the Aquacade Pool.

"I'm not a virgin anymore," Melvin proudly grinned, hours later, as he slipped into the bathroom. I shook his hand, more thrilled than he. No, not so. He was beaming. It was as if he had met God and been well received. Maybe he had been.

"And he's going to make Phi Beta," boasted Nina, as we picked the icebox clean to stuff our midnight appetites. "And he's a cinch to get the poetry prize, too. He's so brilliant."

"But is he good in bed?" I couldn't resist asking.

"That," objected Melvin, grabbing at the pickle jar, "is not a sisterly question." We discovered some saved Roman candles, which at two in the morning we shot from our window over the silent streets below. At seven Melvin left for the hospital.

I hated visiting that hospital, a hospital without a maternity ward. A city hospital, big on experimentation and small on comfort. I hated the sound of my shoes on its stone floors, the smells, the faces of the nurses smug in their sinecures and the doctors brittle with betrayal. Francis Delafield Hospital hanging over the quiet of the Hudson facing the lush Palisades was a cancer hospital. Terminal.

"I'm having a terrible time lately," I told my friend Ruth when I met her after my new part-time job modeling at Milgrim. "I am finding it hard to avoid the fetal position."

"What do you mean?"

"I mean I keep wanting to curl up in a ball, my head to my knees."

"Jesus Christ," said Ruth.

I watched her inhale and went on. "Of course, I fight it,

except when I'm in bed. Then I give in and do it. But when I'm in public places, like now, I fight it."

"Good," she said.

"I don't always win. The other day in the movies watching Olivier's *Hamlet,* I did it for half the picture. I feel like doing it now."

"Now?" Ruth looked around the restaurant. "Right here in front of everyone? You are kidding me, aren't you?"

"Yes, I'm kidding."

Picking up some modeling money and feeling flush, I gave a week's salary to Teresa for her and Michael's birthday. Teresa was so grateful it embarrassed me. Teresa, who was keeping us almost intact.

"Why," I asked suddenly, "did you come back after Michael was born? I thought John wanted you to stay home."

"You," she took her time saying, "make me."

"Not me."

"Yes, you and Melvin. But most it was Janice." She paused and remembered. "It was very cold spring when Michael born and very sad time for your family." And out came one of her occasional histories.

It was a damp April day, and she recalled shivering inside Mrs. Caplin's old spring coat as she hurried to the Continental Avenue subway. And she remembered how despite the war, the little neighborhood had grown up since she first saw it. Children and trees stood taller, and the empty lots were filling, and even with the slow spring, dogwoods were threatening to bud. Her baby was quiet in her belly as she rattled toward St. Mark's Place and her little, mostly unused bed with her husband, John. Climbing the four flights to their flat, however, forced Teresa to stop and rest. Unusual.

John was still at work, and she decided to lie down while waiting. Even the dirty dishes in the sink didn't compel her. She dozed, and Forest Hills seemed very far away. Awakening at six in a pool of wetness alarmed her. John wasn't back, and there was no phone. Water ran down her legs, racing her to the sink. One towel. Another. Leaving a note, she went, by bus, to Bellevue Hospital.

It was eight by the time they got her in a wheelchair, and it was eight-thirty when five pounds eleven ounces of screaming son introduced himself.

John arrived too late for the birth. "Your wife is sleeping now," he was told. "Come and see your perfect baby boy." Tears from John's cheeks smudged the window of the nursery. His brothers might have to stand before firing squads on faraway fields. But here, in America, his woman was sleeping in a safe ward and his son was wrapped in clean cloth like fresh holy bread. It was right to come here, Beautiful America.

"I have one son," he telephoned Mrs. Caplin, blocking her troubles from his mind. He was not to think about them now. "Teresa must stay home and care."

Resigning herself to the inevitable, Mrs. Caplin said what was right to say. "Give Teresa my love and kisses. Tell her to be happy. Give her all the children's kisses, too, for her and the baby. And send her Mr. Caplin's blessing. He will be so happy for her." She was out of breath. "What will you name him?"

"Michael, for my father and Teresa's brother."

"A beautiful name. Say happy birthday to Michael." She put down the phone.

And John, who had his cigar ready despite his lungs, lit it with a powerful puff.

When Lily and Pearl carefully approached her, as she pushed Michael's carriage along St. Mark's Place, Teresa was stunned. What were these old Caplin friends doing here? What had happened? She waited for them to speak.

"He's a beautiful boy." They admired Michael, peeking in at him in his hand-crocheted bonnet and sweater. Teresa had matched the blue ribbon ties to his eyes.

"Sixteen pounds," she bragged, despite her confusion. "A good eater." Then, in spite of herself and dreading the very question, she asked, "How's Forest Hills?"

"All split up. Oh, didn't you know? They closed down the house. Locked it up. Sent the children away. Mrs. Caplin's in a nursing home now. No place else after the hospital." Lily kept talking. "She wanted to come home, of course, but what could we do? She couldn't stay alone, could she?"

Teresa's breath had felt as if it were coming from some-body else. "Send away the children." She questioned them. "Where's Janice?"

"Janice is with Hymie's brother Ad, but you remember his wife, Martha, very nervous. She says she can't keep her. I think Ruthie from the candy store may take her, but Jack, you know Jack, her new husband, well, who knows? I guess she'll take her."

Teresa had rocked the carriage. "Janice is so frighten, like little birdie," she mused sadly. Her own little Michael was sleeping too deeply to hear the swing of the pendulum. "Does she eat?" Janice would not eat well for anyone but Teresa.

"Well, I guess so," Lily had said. The women looked at each other. "I don't know. Do you know?"

Pearl didn't know, but sensing a strong card, she threw it down. "Come to think, I heard she's lost weight."

"Maybe Martha no patient."

"Patient! Well, Martha's too nervous. Perhaps when Ruthie takes her." Were they passing Janice around like unwanted garbage? Teresa's fate had closed around her.

"If you could consider coming back," said Lily, "only for a while. So Rose can leave the nursing home. So she can be with them for a little while. Before . . ." She didn't finish. She couldn't. This was no game. Rose's friend Lily was crying for her.

"I will talk to John," Teresa finally said.

So the two old friends, with Teresa's address awkwardly written by Rose still clutched in Lily's hand, had accomplished their mission.

Thanking her, blessing her, and telling her how God would reward her, and meaning it, they left her standing in the thinning February sunlight. Teresa remembered everything.

Nina was helping. And because of her help, I found myself avoiding Francis Delafield Hospital as much as was decent. And perhaps a little more. Frequently, when I went, Melvin would be mean, as he knew how to be, but I'd never learned to handle it. After my visit, mean or kind, I'd find myself truly sick. Sometimes right on the hospital steps. So I needed the comics. The funnymen who ate cheesecake and roared with laughter at the same Lindy's were I'd sat as a child.

"Did I tell you the one—" became my favorite words. Laughter was life.

"Did you hear about the fat little actor," began George De Witt, a Lindy regular, "from the Yiddish Theater on Second Avenue, who shows up for an open audition at the Hollywood Bowl's prestigious Method production of *Richard III*? And with a thick Jewish accent you can cut with a knife asks the director when he should begin.

"The young director is embarrassed for him. 'I don't think the part is right for you,' he demurs, trying to be gentle.

" 'Listen,' singsongs the actor, 'give by me a chance. Is it an open call? Yes or no?'

"The young director gives in. Suddenly the actor straightens up, pulls in his stomach, smooths his brow, raises a regal eyebrow, and elegantly sneers in the best of Oxford English ever to be heard in the hills of L.A. . . . 'Now is the winter of our discontent. . . .' When he was finished, there was awed silence.

" 'What did you do?' begs the earnest Method director.

" 'Do! What you think I do?' The pride of Delancey Street shrugs. 'It's called acting.' "

De Witt was Italian and gorgeous. Later I learned that the thick black hair crowning his head was his only in that he had designed it. However, it looked great and got him much laid. I was next on his list. "Meet me," he'd said, "at the Greek's party." And that's how I came to find myself locked in a bathroom in the Park Sheraton Hotel with a madman beating at the door.

The Greek's suite was full of I-can-get-you-into-pictures men. "Lots of TV people will be there," the comic had promised. "You can do yourself some good. I'll come after my club date."

"What's your name, baby?" asked the host as I arrived at

midnight, looking for my date and still feeling the leer of the elevator man who'd taken me up.

"I'm Barbara," I said, hoping that explained all.

"A pretty girl is always welcome," said the host, Greek expansiveness covering the fact that he hadn't a clue to who I was or even what I was. My comic was loose in his arrangements.

But I stayed. Perhaps I could do myself "good." When the party was down to a final dwindle, the Greek realized I was still there talking earnestly to his head writer, Nat Hiken.

"You mean," he bellowed as Nat left, "that dumb comic stood you up?" I nodded, and he picked up the phone to find my comic passed out at home. "You want me to get the rude wop over here?" he asked.

"Not anymore," I said, and he hung up the phone.

"Good," said the Greek, pouring himself another drink he didn't need. "Let's talk." I should have excused myself and left. But I was all dressed up with no place to go.

So for the first time since I arrived, I stopped secretly looking to the door and looked at my host. Except for an irregularity of nose and a slightly ironic turn of lip, he was classically handsome. Black eyes fringed with long lashes looked at me with real warmth. Aristocratic hands with long, strong fingers patted my own. "Lay odds," he said, "you long to be a serious actress." I smiled and started my best drugstore chat on the "Method" and "inner motivation."

"The only motivation," my host said, "a real actor needs is his job. All this new thumb-sucking is bullshit." He picked at his own thumbs. I noticed flawed cuticles. And he drank too much.

"Does liquor," I asked, sounding a little silly even to myself, "make you feel happy?" Most of my funnymen smoked grass.

"Listen, kid," he answered, "drinkers enjoy the drinking if it doesn't bring happiness." He pointed his fresh cigar toward heaven. "Besides, I'm a dying man. I've got only six months to live." That can't be so, I thought; death hasn't followed me here, too. Slipping his cigar band on my finger, as I used to with my father's, I became quiet. He fumbled his matches. I didn't want to ask him of what he might be dying. It would be too cruel.

Finally I broke my quiet, saying, "I'm sorry," though I wasn't sure of what.

He leaned over and kissed my cheek. "You smell so young," he said.

"And you smell something like my father. I guess it's the cigar. I like cigars." He couldn't be dying.

"Most women say they hate the stink of them," he observed. Succeeding at last in getting a match going, he spoke between puffs. "But you're too young for that yet. Are you really sure you don't want me to get that wop to escort you away?"

"I'm sure."

"It's a lousy life," he said, "chasing after comics and musicians. Yet nice little girls like you do it. Shit, when I played stage shows with big bands, you had to fight little girls off with a big stick. All kinds of dumb broads used to hang around, just begging for it."

"I'm not dumb," I said.

"Are you sure?"

"Very."

"Well," he said, starting the matches again. "Well, I hope you don't disappoint yourself."

"Do you disappoint yourself?" I fought back wondering if I was being unkind to a dying man.

"All the time. Like right now. If I were good, I'd be giving you cab fare home. Instead, I'm figuring how to get into your pants." He laughed like the devil in disguise, and I joined him. I shouldn't like this man, I thought, but I do.

"Here let me," I said, taking his matches and striking one. He studied me from over his cigar, then concentrated on getting it properly lit.

"You're young," he said, waving away smoke, "so don't pay attention to what I'm saying. What the fuck do I know? Jump right in and swim like hell. That's what young is for. Don't be a coward. God hates cowards. My Greek papa used to say that, and he knew a few things."

"My Jewish father said the same thing." I felt almost happy.

He started to speak of that night's telecast of Martha Raye, his estranged wife. Their marriage was dissolving into divorce. "The old Greeks," he said, his face becoming heavy, "say, 'Spare us from the women,' and they are right. She thinks she's in love with a dancer from the chorus line. Ah, what's it all mean anyway?" Certainly I didn't know. But I listened, sympathized, and helped find his cigar when it slipped from his fingers and got lost in the couch. His face was kind of contorting in pain, and I remembered his proclaimed coming death.

"Of what are you sick?" I asked awkwardly.

"Of my life," he snarled, and something happened to the muscles of his cheeks.

"Bitches, all bitches," he suddenly hissed, lunging and grabbing my arm in a lock that was to leave marks. "All you bitches are the same." I pulled from his reach and scrambled across the cocktail table, scattering smoked salmon and olives to the floor.

"Are you crazy?" I screamed.

"Yeah, crazy, you fucking bitch! Crazy to give you what you came for."

I ran to the door, but he was too fast and cornered me into his bedroom.

"No-good bitch," he yelled after me, tripping over his own feet. I had no time to wonder what had happened to the sad soul whose head had rested on my bosom only moments ago. Racing for the bathroom, I barely made it, but not without hearing my best and only black dress go rip from my neckline to my waist. The lock held as the mirror on the door shimmied with each pound. "Bitch," he ranted. Then all was silence. Had he left? Died of natural causes? I was afraid to unlock and look. Perhaps he'd jumped. I'd hear about that. My heart beat painfully against the bones of my corselet. In the morning there would be maids and bellboys. I'd wait it out.

A tub is not a good place to sleep. Despite lining it with all the towels the Park Sheraton provided, I could feel every vibration of the subway that runs beneath the hotel's foundations. "Bitch," it rumbled. "Bitch."

In the morning my repentant host persuaded me to unlock the bathroom door. "I have nothing to wear." He handed me his robe.

Heavy with moral hangover and handsome with sad dark eyes that didn't want to look at me, he apologized awkwardly. "I sometimes go nuts with booze," he said. "It releases my devil, and I'm sorry my devil ruined your dress." We breakfasted while waiting for the replacement he ordered for me from Bergdorf's, which turned out to be the most expensive dress I'd ever owned. Breaking bread with this restored madman was easier than facing the "devil" of my own life—the hospital. I skipped that day's visit.

He sat before me, sniffing at his coffee in a way I decided was decidedly Greek. I watched him mix the rice, onions, and chili sent from Reubens into one steaming heap and shovel some into his mouth. He nodded, face growing brighter and calmer. The line of his brow smoothed, and after he had swallowed, his mouth softened into a smile. He was definitely not a dying man.

Now it seemed easier for him to speak. "What did you say your name was?" he asked.

"Barbara Caplin," I said, smearing marmalade on hot toast. Food did help.

"I'm Nick Condos," he said sweetly, "and happy to meet you. Listen, Barbara, beware of Greeks bearing devils. The one that popped out on you makes me ashamed. He's a dirty bastard. Sometimes I have to drink to forget I own him."

I pursued his mortality. "You said you only had six months to live. That was a lie, wasn't it?"

"Yes, a lie. I just feel that way a lot. But not right now. Gee, you're pretty."

"Am I?"

"Uh-huh." Through the chili I could smell the freshness of after-shave. It smelled like the one my father had used.

I finished my toast.

*   *   *

"What do you mean you're dating Nick Condos?" demanded Ruth across our booth. "He has the reputation of a wild man."

"Not really."

"Well, maybe he can put you on his show." Since my unemployment had run out, I was living on cab fares. Nick turned out to be great with cab fares. Cab fares sustained more "actresses" than free lunch.

"Now that Melvin's back in the hospital, you hardly sleep here anymore," complained Janice, rummaging through my makeup.

"It gives you the bed to yourself, doesn't it?"

"I miss your cold feet," she said.

"You really should come to the hospital more often," Nina whispered to me in the hall outside Melvin's room. "He asks for you when you don't." Nina was looking tired; her pale hair and skin were lusterless.

"It's hard for me, these hospital visits. I've done it too much."

"It's harder for him," she said, turned, and walked off, her arms burdened with Melvin's books and papers. I cut her off to run after Dr. Chow.

Dr. Chow was inscrutable as I caught him in the hall. Racing doctors down halls was something I was getting good at.

"The codeine," I said, "he's been taking it for so long that the amounts you prescribed don't affect his pain."

"We have regulations."

"Yes, but he's in terrible pain."

"You don't want him to become an addict?"

"Who cares? He's dying!"

"We have regulations. You're his sister, aren't you?"

"Who do I talk to about the regulations?"

"Why don't we have some coffee and discuss his case?"

Dr. Chow was lonely. Life wasn't as it had been in the Singapore of his youth. His family was in Brazil. He was here, finishing his residency. Dr. Chow wanted a pretty girl to talk to. I desperately needed codeine for Melvin. "Be nice to him," Melvin had begged from his patient-prisoner's bed. The prescription was increased.

It was the third travelogue documentary Dr. Chow had dragged me to. Columbia University showed travelogues on alternate Tuesdays. Tonight I was to discover the Maori and, I was afraid, other mysteries of the Orient. Tonight after the show, Dr. Chow, lank of hair and heavy of breath, was to cook me a "truly" Chinese meal in his rooms.

"Wasn't that truly educational?" asked Dr. Chow as he opened a cupboard and brought out various cellophane-wrapped bundles.

"Dried shrimp," he said, "and mushrooms and noodles."

"What's that?" I asked of a particularly strange-looking lump.

"A hundred-year-old egg, a real delicacy." For a kid with experience only in wonton soup. "Western people are so provincial," he said, "about cuisine. In China we eat many delicious things you wouldn't dream of. Our ancestors said we could eat anything with four paws to the ground and back to the sun. Dog is a favorite," he went on, "and in Singapore, where I was raised, a special treat is live monkey brain."

"Live?"

"Yes, we take a live monkey and pin him into the center of an open-topped table. Just his crown shows, and then his skull is sliced and then—" He was dead serious.

"Please!" And this was the man in charge of my brother's pain.

"No, Dr. Chow, I really don't want to see a film on snake worship in the Appalachians."

"Are you positive?"

"I'm positive."

Melvin, pale and trembly, asked why I thought Dr. Chow wasn't giving him as much attention lately. "Did you say something wrong?"

"Maybe." He looked terrible.

"Sit down. It makes me nervous, your standing there like that."

"I brought you ices."

"I hope I can taste them—what flavor?"

"Chocolate and coconut." He smiled, his skull seeming to shed the thin skin that covered it.

"Did you get it at the Ice King in Astoria? Good girl." I removed the cartons from the insulating bag. They'd held well for the long trip. "Have some," he said. "It's too much for me. There are spoons over there." I didn't like using his spoons. Hating myself for the feeling, I took one dip.

It was hard when he was cruel and harder when he was nice.

"What have you been doing?" he asked.

"Looking for work."

"But not very earnestly, huh?" he said, and smiled.

"And what's that bruise?" He indicated the green and purple oval on my neck. The scarf I had draped over it had slipped. A testimonial to Nick's violent lovemaking, it was certainly more than the infamous hickey of our youth. Sex with Nick was trick-or-treat. I blushed.

"Don't hurt yourself. Stay healthy," he said with sudden harshness, his bony hand reaching toward my arm. "For God's sake, stay healthy. Don't let this happen to you. And eat more. Let those models be skinny; you put on a little muscle. Exercise." Melvin was not yet totally bedridden. The doctors were planning another experiment: removing part of his spinal column because of the pressure of the malignant nodes pressing on the spinal cord. It might save him some pain but would cripple him.

I smiled. "I'm healthy as a horse," I said. "You need help with your ice?"

"Not for another week at least," he said wryly.

I wanted to run from the room and out to the sunshine of the perfect June day. I didn't. I played at eating my ices and made conversation. "When do you take your exam?"

"Tomorrow," he said, "they'll quiz me orally. They're sending two proctors, and if I pass, which I will, I'll get my diploma and awards. Nina says I'm sure to get the awards."

"That will be wonderful."

"Will you think of me, Barbara, later, when you eat ices?"

"Oh, Melvin."

"I want you to think of me. I want to be remembered. Do you love me a little even though I'm mean to you a lot?"

"Of course I do."

144

"But you hate to come here." I was silent. "I know," he said, "I know."

"They're graduating my brother today," I said to Nick, still mostly asleep. Sleeping with him was so warm. "I have to go to Forest Hills and change my clothes, then get up to the hospital in time." Nick shook himself awake; within a minute he would be clear-eyed and alert. It was amazing how he did it. A quart a night and never a sign of it in the morning. "The Greek's an iron man," his friends would say. "You should have seen him when he danced."

"Don't bother going all the way out to Forest Hills," he said. "It's too damn hot, and you look tired. Go to Sam Chapman's, you met him last night at La Vie, and pick yourself up something nice. Something very nice. I'll give you a check. Get a couple of things, it's wholesale."

Sam Chapman manufactured Ceil Chapman clothing. Once I'd tried for a job there as an assistant designer. They'd liked my book but didn't need anyone.

With sweaty palms I carried the thousand-dollar check down to the Garment Center. Would there be something simple enough for a graduation? A hour later I returned with three dresses and seven hundred in change. I handed it to Nick.

"What's this?"

"What was left over."

He started to laugh. "You're a funny girl," he said.

Was I supposed to keep the money? "I don't understand," I said.

"That's good," said Nick. "Now don't be late."

So I stood in my new gray silk with the gathered skirt and organdy bow tie alongside Melvin's bed and watched as he received his reward for dragging his mustard nitrogen-seared, cobalt-burnt, surgically severed body through Queens College with straight A's.

We watched—Teresa, Janice, Uncle Dan, and Nina and I—as the dean presented him with his Phi Beta Kappa key and poet laureate medal. He was graduating magna cum laude. Dr. Chow across the room was impressed. He even smiled at me.

"I'm so proud of you," I said as I kissed Mel's cheek.

"Are you?" he asked, sunken eyes shining. "I said I'd do it."

"You did."

"Get married," he said as I was leaving. "You're going to need someone soon." Janice and Teresa were crying in the hall. A passing nurse admired my dress.

"Lemme present the next Mrs. Condos," pronounced Nick, kissing the hand of the new Mrs. Berle in drunken gallantry. Milton and Ruth Berle looked at me.

"She seems too smart to make that mistake," said Ruth Berle.

I said, "He's only kidding."

"Have a cigar," continued Nick. "Oops, I'm all out. Sorry."

"Have one of mine," said Milton Berle.

Ruth Berle opened her purse and promptly handed Nick one of the cigars she always carried for Milton. Then they went back to their cheesecake.

"What did she mean by that?" questioned Nick as we sat down with Joey Bishop, Jack Carter, and Red Buttons. They, too, had TV shows. Live television had room for comics. But Berle was king.

"She means you're a bad-boy Greek," piped Sid Gould, a comics' comic. "A real bad boy."

Nick laughed and took a bow. He'd introduced me that way before. Usually it was accepted, as intended, as a joke. It depended on how many Dewar's he'd downed. Nick was mourning Martha, and they'd made book against another marriage for him. Me, too. I was in love. But it was something I'd get over and be wiser for.

The love I was in centered on Nick's scents. His cigars, more expensive than my father's, smelled the same. So did his after-shave lotion and his starched collars. Of course, his good looks, generosity, and weaknesses helped, too. I was sure I could cure those weaknesses as Priscilla Lane had cured John Garfield, if given the chance.

"What are you thinking of?" I asked Melvin as he lay there, no longer able to lift his head. His brow was icy cold.

"Pâté."

"Pâté? You mean that liver stuff? Do you want some?"

"No. I'm thinking how they make it. They peg up these geese so they can't even move. Then take funnels and force-feed them so that their livers swell, and then, when their liver is so heavy the geese couldn't move if they were allowed to, they butcher them and make pâté." It was a long speech for him now, and he smiled at his own effort. "Sometimes I feel like one of those geese, you know, when they come at me with those spoonfuls."

"You have to eat."

"Do I?" We turned silent.

"I'll tell you what," Nick said the night before he and Martha and their group were leaving for their annual summer stint in Vegas, "I'll let you use the apartment while I'm gone. It's closer to the hospital than Forest Hills. I don't like to think of you fighting subways in this heat. Be a good girl."

"Good Babsie" my father had called me. Being good meant staying sad. But Bad Babsie had a two-bedroom, elegantly furnished apartment Nick had just leased to play around in.

"I don't want the morphine," Melvin pleaded when I got there. "Tell them no more morphine. It muddles me so I can't think. Remember when we used to hold hands in the movies during the bad parts. This is a bad part." I grabbed the boniness that was his hand.

"Who do you see when you imagine Lincoln?" one faggot asked as he sprawled across Nick's couch, sipping Nick's Rémy Martin and sniffing one of his cigars.

"I don't think about Lincoln," said a second fag, "but I guess I see Raymond Massey."

"I see Henry Fonda," I said, pushing my way into my favorite kind of conversation, the kind I used to have with Melvin.

"How about Thomas Edison?"

"I see Spencer Tracy."

"Who invented the telephone?"

"Don Ameche."

"And radium?"

"Greer Garson," I said, quickly adding, "I always wanted to be Madame Curie."

"Who didn't?" said the first fag.

For a week I'd become, thanks to Nick's generosity, the Perle Mesta of "gay" Third Avenue. A new pal, Claire, and I would tour their hangouts and bring back a handful to amuse us. It was safe fun in that no one got laid. But it had its dangers. The haphazard herd we'd corral sometimes contained crazies.

"Bang, bang, you're dead," screamed the wild-eyed boy from the hallway as I tried to push him out the door. He was pointing Nick's huge silver table lighter at me like a gun. "Bang, bang." Flames shot toward my bosom. Claire, who outweighed the boy by twenty pounds, came to my rescue.

"He stole Nick's lighter," I said as the door closed him away. We did a quick inventory. Several objets d'art were missing. The parties stopped.

"You look tired," said Melvin. "What have you been doing? You haven't been here in days."

"I know," I said.

"Well, what have you been doing?"

"Wasting time."

"Don't," he said seriously. "It's all the things I'll never know, never feel that torture me. More than the pain."

"Is the pain bad?"

"Bad. But I don't want the morphine. I want to stay conscious while I can. Come tomorrow, Barbara, please."

"Have some wine, little Barbara," said Polletti over the table of the Greenwich Village apartment where we were dining. "It will do you good. This evening is meant to relax you." I smiled, sipped, and sniffed at the good smells coming from the half kitchen. "Louisiana prawn, stuffed with spinach and cheese."

"Are prawn shrimp?" I asked.

"Huge luscious shrimp from the Gulf," said the host.

"You'll love them," assured Polletti. "Clark's a great cook."

What I loved was California actors; they knew how to make a girl feel good. Actually I'd started smiling as Polletti led me up the stairs on Tenth Street to his friend's flat; I'd tasted his cooking before. When Clark saw the surprise guest, he had smiled, too. So far we hadn't shared our secret with Polletti. The dinner was fabulous and funny. The wine flowed, and soon I was relaxed enough to say, "You know we are all related."

"What do you mean?" asked Polletti, with whom I had shared a moment of magic getting over Mark.

"I mean," I said, feeling mischievous, "that we have all known each other in the biblical sense."

"She means," said Clark, "that she and I have had the pleasure."

The idea captured our imaginations; we drank to it. We drank to everything.

"Let's drink to Barbara's tits. There is one for each of us."

"Then let's drink up her tits and forget the wine." So they both started making love to me. Nick was far away in the land of chorus girls, and I,—I started to feel quite lucky.

The three of us squeezed into the cool, scented water of Clark's tub. The Aquacade was never like this. "Jasmine," he said, "for an Arabian night, for a perfect houri."

"I'm no whorey!"

"A houri is a beautiful girl who waits to reward true believers in Allah's paradise."

"Ah," said Polletti. " 'Some for the pleasures of this world and some, for the poet's paradise to come.' "

"Omar Khayyám," I piped in, not wanting to seem ignorant.

" 'Ah, take the Cash, and let the Credit go' is the advice," said Polletti. Outside, the heavy hustle of the Village on a summer's eve could be heard. Inside, it was moan and sigh.

The night went on. So did the next day and the next night. It was a time of rockets. Then, weary with fireworks, I sobered up and remembered Melvin.

"Can you get good ices around here?"

"You can get them at Ferrara's." I took a cab.

His bed was empty. Standing with my lemon ices, I stared at its immaculate sheets. They must have moved him.

"Where's my brother?" I asked the Jamaican attendant.

"Let me get you the doctor, miss."

"He died yesterday," said Dr. Chow.

"Where is he?"

"Downstairs in the morgue."

"No one told me."

"We didn't know it right away. He was gone a few hours before we did."

"A few hours!" Then he had died alone without a hand to hold, without a good-bye.

"I called your home; you weren't there. I didn't think I should break it to your young sister. We were able to reach your uncle today. He's coming over. He didn't know where to find you either. Come down to sign the papers.

"The office wants to know," said Dr. Chow after they slammed the metal doors shut on the frozen drawer where Melvin lay, his hospital wristband still on his withered arm, "if you would consider donating the body to science. It would be very helpful. They're doing such good research in the field."

"No."

"Take a little time before you decide. Perhaps your brother would have wanted it."

"Melvin didn't want to be pâté."

"Excuse me?"

"Don't touch his body anymore." The ices were melting down my dress. I walked to a trash can and threw them away.

"We must bury him before the Sabbath," said Uncle Dan, "but I don't have enough to lay out for the undertakers. They insist on being paid first. Banks are closed for the holiday, and well, I'm short anyway." As Melvin lived, he had died, without even enough money to get decently into the ground. I wired Nick, and he sent the three hundred necessary to get the job done.

It was a meager assemblage. Apart from Uncle Dan and his wife, almost no "family" bothered to show up. Teresa was there, and her little Michael. And our last loyal friends. "He died alone," I told the officiating rabbi, a stranger hired by Schwartz Brothers on Queens Boulevard, "in unrelieved pain. Twenty-two years old, his Phi Beta Kappa key in the hospital drawer."

"Ah, he was a scholar," said the rabbi, grabbing on to something nice to talk about and breaking my heart.

Janice held on to my hand at the graveside. How clumsily we threw some soil on the unadorned pine box as they lowered him down, my high heels sinking with him into earth soggy from a summer rain. The family plot Auntie H. had selected for our mother was half full.

"I want that place," said Janice, "under Mother and next to Melvin."

"All right," I said.

I though for a moment to lie down over what would be my spot and see how it felt. Would they know I was near, those already in their places? Would they feel my heart beating? Would it disturb? I didn't cry as strangers shoveled. And I didn't lie down. Instead, I comforted Nina, who handed me a page typed on Melvin's old machine, titled "Three Out of Five." A last "poem" Melvin had written:

Three out of Five

''Suture, please,'' said the white-masked doctor, and from my stiffened position I knew that the operation was over and a black-bordered page of my life was turned.

Two weeks later my father's grim face told me what he had just discovered in his confidential meeting with the doctor. Later I learned the name of my disease.

The year was 1946, three years since that malodorous name and all it stands for had robbed me of my mother, and only three years to go before cancer robbed me of my father and set me upon a road that would test my very flesh and soul, fiber by fiber.

The medical campaigns proclaim that one out of five people will eventually perish from cancer. Don't let that fact lull you into peaceful oblivion. Cancer is not a mathematical machine which picks one and rejects four in straight and wonderful columns. It can wipe out whole families and it can spare whole families.

I am now twenty-two. I have fought the silent and painful battle with my corrupted body for over six years. Hodgkin's disease

breeds in the lymph glands. It can infect
other body sections. It is cancer of the
lymph system, a system practically as vital
to life as the circulatory system. This
lymph system is a fighter of disease and in
my body it must also fight itself.

It is generally considered a good sign if
a Hodgkin's patient can outlive the first
three years of his illness. I am now a very
good sign. But this sign doesn't presuppose
a good life. I will not confuse or upset you
with my other personal problems. All I wish
to add to that score is that I am the oldest
of three surviving children. I have two sisters. Our financial, legal, and domestic
problems are a public scandal. There is no
clear future for them in sight. But let me
now relate abbreviatedly what the good and
hard fight is with cancer. Let there be no
doubt that every extra year of life is as
sparse of tribulation as exceedingly heavy
drinking is of hangovers.

I will manage to misplace the fragile paper Nina handed
me and think it lost along with so much else. But it will show
up again, surviving the years.

BOOK TWO

Love and Kisses

Marriage, and Other Pleasures of the Flesh

El Borracho was covered with kisses. Lipsticked imprints of the famous and beautiful papered its walls. Even in the ladies' room, where I practiced my own blottings on toilet paper, kisses surrounded me. Back at the table I sipped champagne and hoped to be asked for one. It would be nice to leave my mark.

"When my wife died"—the mogul of a thousand tankers sighed—"I didn't dispose of her wardrobe. It occurs to me you're just her size." Mopping his brow with his monogrammed handkerchief, he continued. "I'd just bought her a full-length sable when she had the accident. It would suit you well."

"Sable is lovely," I said, trying to sniff proposition from suggestion, "especially full-length." Then, pulling my own fur a little closer, I considered how like Nick it had been to give a girl who boasted but two pairs of shoes and owed her dentist thirty dollars a mink stole. And how wonderful. But I was determined not to think about Nick.

"I liked you the moment I saw you," said the mogul, selecting our opening course. Vichyssoise for me and celery remoulade for him. He was avoiding potatoes. "You look so much like her—my wife, that is. I was nervous about calling you." He snapped his fingers for a fresh bottle of champagne, remopped his brow, and went on.

"I thought, What could a beautiful young girl like about me except my money? Then I thought, What's wrong with that? Women love handsome men for their looks, poets for their verses, artists for their paintings, so why not me for my success? My talent is money."

"You're a very nice man, too," I murmured.

"Am I?"

"Yes, very."

"Do you like the champagne? I brought it from my own private cellar."

I nodded.

"Do you like it?" Nick had asked that sweltering August in Atlantic City as he slipped the silver blue stole over my shoulders. "Well," he'd said, smiling his crooked smile and flicking the ashes from his cigar, "move around in it so I can see you."

"It's the best," said Harry the furrier, who chased after show biz folk, carrying his cases of furs. "You couldn't find a mink better at Maximilian. Just blow on it. Real plush."

"If you like it," said Nick, "it's yours."

"I like it."

"Such a price you're getting it for," moaned Harry the furrier through his long nose while stroking and caressing the pelts. "I'll probably kill myself later."

"Good," said Nick, pulling back his wad of bills. "In that case, you won't need the two grand."

Harry looked worried for a moment. Then his glasses bobbling and his jowls jiggling, he grabbed at the money. "Always joking, he'd said, quickly pocketing it. "Let's drink on the deal."

"Drink up," said the mogul. "This is an important evening in your life." He lifted his glass, and I, putting Nick from my mind, lifted mine, carefully so as not to splash his mohair sleeve, for the clink. The mogul liked to clink. And he liked to talk. It was as if he'd waited years for the right audience. He talked of his island off Greece, his fifteen rooms on Park Avenue, and his horse farm in Ireland. "Do you ride?" he asked.

"I'm afraid of horses."

"I can teach you." He smiled, bringing back Nick.

"Let me teach you how to handle furs," Nick had said as I'd stood frozen on the hotel rug, facing the mirror. "Not like that, not stiff. Fling it around. It's yours. No one's going to take it back." I tried flinging and flopped. "Throw it on the floor," Nick commanded. "Throw it, that's right. Now walk on it."

"I can't," I pleaded. "It's mink."

"Walk on it."

I walked, worried that the God of all twenty-one-year-old Jewish girls would punish me for such disrespect. But Nick, his black eyes glowing and his finger pointing, was more immediate.

"You are not to be in awe of mink," he said. "For Christ's sake, it's only a thing. Use it, enjoy it, but don't you dare treasure it."

"Can I stop walking now?" He nodded and picked up the six-foot piece of beauty and dropped it over a chair.

"I guess I'll have to make love to you on it before you relax," he said. And we did.

"Your mind is somewhere else," said my mogul.

"No." I smiled.

"I was so happy when you called me back," he went on. "Who was it I gave the message to?"

"My kid sister."

"Well, if she's as lovely as you, we'll have no trouble finding her a good man, too."

When Janice gave me the message, I'd slipped it into my purse and promptly forgotten about it. I was on my way to meet Nick at his new apartment, where we were to celebrate his lease quietly and alone. Choosing the same gray silk I'd worn for Melvin's graduation and funeral, because it went well with my stole, I ignored the November weather. My only coat, designed and self-tailored back at FIT, had become too shabby for such a romantic occasion. How sweetly he'd said he wanted to spend the first evening in his new home with no one but me. So, with a chicken under my arm and love in my heart, I'd arrived.

"What's in the bag?" asked Nick, opening the door wide to let me in.

He looked so handsome I became shy, "Supper," I said, Teresa's roasting instructions seared in my brain.

"It won't be enough," he said. "Freddie and Long Sam are coming by, and maybe some others. Put it away, and I'll order in from Reubens."

I wanted to pout, like a child and say, "But you promised." Instead, I smiled, wrapped the fresh-killed bird in plastic, and closed the freezer door over my best-laid plans. Freddie was a short show biz fancier, and Long Sam was a seven-foot hooker he was playing with because of her novelty. Sitting in my silk, I listened as Nick called Sherry-Lehmann to stock his liquor cabinet and a dozen boozing buddies to come help him drink it. Nick was the best action for spongers in town. Always wanting a party, he was more than willing to pay for it.

"You like the pad?" he asked as I looked around the apartment with its mirrored walls and velvet sofas.

"Yes, but it's much smaller than the other."

"Well, I'm single now," he'd said pointedly, and gone back to his phone. Another small left jab to the heart.

The mogul was still talking on a wide range of topics. It seemed he knew everything about everything boring. I could, perhaps, bear the weight of his body but never his mind. Stop that, I warned myself. He has horses in Ireland. Definitely a man to marry, if only for the divorce. Nick had several such lady friends, well married and waiting out their divorces. I'd find them, these women Nick seemed to think so clever, their legs crossed over two-hundred-dollar shoes, their hair teased at Bergdorf's, their fingers flashing the tokens of their worth, smiling slyly while Nick poured them drinks.

"That one," he'd say after she'd left, "likes to have a hair pulled out of her ass when she comes."

The thing about being involved with a practicing play-boy was the room it left for your own life. I wasn't bound by any debts of honor. At least that's what I told myself as I drowned in jealousy.

The chef was sizzling steaks Diane before us on a chafing dish, and the mogul was patting my hand. "Your fingers are cold," he said.

"Frequently," I answered, "my feet, too."

"Let me send you to my doctor," said the mogul, "for a checkup." Did he check out his tankers before he bought them? His horses?

"I'm fine. It happens when I'm excited." Were those steaks on fire? No, the chef had everything under control. I admired his expertise. I, too, would learn to play and not get burned.

"Eat up," said the mogul. "Do you want a change of wine?" No more wine. I shook my head and tried to eat up.

When the assortment of platters arrived at Nick's apartment, I had arranged a buffet and watched the mixed group he'd collected go at it. Between mouthfuls of corned beef, Nick answered the ringing phone and said, "Sure, come over. It's a housewarming." As his house warmed, my heart chilled. It was a night like any other night. I'd watched them all summer.

On late summer afternoons, not having the hospital to go to anymore, or to avoid, I'd take Nick's daughter to the zoo or for an amble in the park. Melodye, only nine then, was on leave from the parochial school in Florida, where she was well out of everyone's way. "No, Melodye, don't throw tennis balls to the giraffes. . . . Stop chasing those pigeons." She would grin, her broad mouth reminding one of Martha, her mother, and decide whether or not to obey. She'd had a series of irregular nannies and wasn't sure but that I was another. Yet she touched my heart. Despite her being so obviously parented, there was definitely something of the orphan about her, too. "My brother," I told her, "used to take me here when I was your age."

"Do you have a brother?" she asked.

"I used to," I said.

Returning to Nick's old apartment, where I was in half

residence, we'd find parties in full swing. Musicians, comedians, writers, and weirdos enjoying spontaneous fetes.

One was for Polly Adler, in town on her way to Europe, where she would "crawl on my belly" for culture. Since writing her book, she felt it behooved her. Taking one look at me, with Melodye hanging on to my hand, she decided I was Shirley Temple confronting the Legs Diamond mob. Moving me aside, she asked, "Can you handle this maniac? Even I couldn't live with him. Listen," she'd called to Nick as he approached us, "let me take this gal of yours to Paris with me. One night in the House of All Nations, and she'll be prepared for you."

My father would have known how to handle a Polly Adler. I didn't. Instead, I'd removed Melodye to the kitchen to make her lunch.

"Are these people friends of yours?" Melodye had asked, wiping tuna fish from her mouth.

"I don't think so," I'd told her.

"I want you," said the mogul, "to know I'm a serious man and you won't regret our relationship. When I see a woman that moves me, I appreciate it. I appreciated my wife. It's too soon to think of taking another, but we shouldn't dismiss the possibility."

"Get married," Melvin had implored from his deathbed.

I pushed away the remains of steak Diane and smiled as warmly as I could manage. My face resented the effort.

After three hours of Nick's open house I'd had enough, I'd rescued my mink from the careless cigarette of a chorus girl and called the number Janice had scribbled on the slip of paper. Yes, I'd shouted over the laughter and the noise, I'd be happy to meet him at El Borracho. No need to send his car. I'd take a cab. No one, especially not Nick, noticed my leaving. It was a lonely ride, and I told my troubles to the driver, a habit to follow me all my life.

"My advice," said the driver, married twenty-five years with "two wonderful kids," as he zipped through the November rain (one could really tell a cabdriver anything and remain anonymous), "my advice is forget the bum and find yourself a nice man who'll take care of you. If possible, a rich one."

But I loved Nick, and he *was* nice. His drinking was a thing of ritual, not of addiction. I was sure of it. A little love instead of lust, and he would change. I didn't say any of this to the driver. I just watched the rain.

"Don't worry from the rain," Harry the furrier had assured me in Atlantic City. "I never yet seen a mink with an umbrella." Nevertheless, I skipped hurriedly into the waiting shelter of El Borracho.

"Would you like to stop by my apartment," asked the mogul as the final crepe suzette died on my dish, "and try on the sable?"

"Let's do that tomorrow." I stalled. He'd already invited me to the theater with him the next night and to the country for the weekend. "All this is so exciting, and well, I'm tired. I have a small modeling job in the morning. Early." I was lying, of course. That seemed fair and square. Once he wrapped me in that sable, a deal would be consummated.

"I'll get the check and see you home," he said, signaling to the hovering captain.

"It's too far." I demurred. "Why don't you put me in a cab?"

"No, you use the Rolls and the chauffeur. You'll be more comfortable. You can drop me on the way." I went again to the ladies' room, this time to blot not my lips but my eyes.

As the Rolls-Royce and chauffeur neared the Queensboro Bridge, I tapped at the window separating me, in my solitary splendor, from the chauffeur. He rolled it down.

"Would you mind making a stop first? I forgot something at a friend's apartment. It's not far."

"Call me Roger," said the chauffeur.

"Wait here," I told Roger, and scampered to the brownstone that held Nick's new East Side home. Laughter and shrieking resounded down the stairs. God only knew what was happening there now. Pausing at the landing, I half turned to retrace my way out. What I'd find would hurt and I knew it. Below me waited a Rolls equipped with a Roger.

"What the fuck's the difference?" I heard Nick bellow from behind the door. My hand pushed the bell. No one answered. No one heard its chimes above the chaos. I pushed again and kept pushing. Nick opened, wearing not even a figleaf, a drink in one hand and the perennial cigar in the other.

"It's my Barbara," he yelled to the other naked bacchanals whose romping reflections I could see in the mirrors "I told you she'd come back. She loves me." I moved away and started to back down the stairs. Behind Nick I could see naked bodies and even more naked faces starting to crowd around. It certainly wasn't one of his better productions. "Where are you going now?" he asked, smile broadening and cigared hand fumbling to reach my own. "Come back here, you love me. Never mind that in there; it's background noise. I got bored. You shouldn't have left. "You love me?"

"No, I hate you. You're a monster." I started to cry. Nick stepped out into the hall.

"Give them some privacy," said the girl who had earlier almost singed my stole and half closed the door. I sat on the steps, crying all the tears I'd held back at my brother's grave and a few more. Crying for the cabdriver and his two wonderful kids, crying for the mogul in his loneliness. Crying.

"Sh," said Nick, stepping past me and grabbing my hand, his nakedness looking more ridiculous and vulnerable against the harsh red commercial carpeting. "Sh, don't cry like that."

He dropped to his knees, his bare behind hanging over the floor below. "Barbara Caplin, will you marry me, Nick Condos, and save my life?"

"No," I said, mascara burning into my eyes. "No, never. I'll get over you like I got over the chicken pox, with just one small scar. See," I said, pointing at an almost invisible depression under my left eye, "my mother put socks on my hands so I couldn't scratch." Out tumbled my earliest memory, the high chair. "Hymie, she's scarred herself." One small fingernail had found its way free to attack a scab.

"Let me look," said Nick, and suddenly off his knees he started scanning my cheek, with my father's caring eyes. "I can't find it," he said at last. "Your mom didn't have to worry. Your face is perfect."

"Is it?" I asked.

"Absolutely," he said, and belched. "Excuse me, my love." He attempted a bow. "Reubens pickles," he added. Then softly and soberly: "Save me from Reubens pickles and all the rest. If you save me, you'll save yourself, too, and I can make you happy. I will make you happy. Your father would want that."

Below us I heard the street door open and shut and cold air rushed the stairwell. Winter was coming.

"You'll get arrested if someone sees you out here like this," I finally said.

He smiled. "Say yes," he said, "and we can go inside."

"Yes."

Triumphant, his balls bouncing, he bounded up the steps, dragging me after him. Inside, former partners in orgy fumbled to get dressed as Nick announced in formal tones our marriage. From a corner Long Sam disengaged herself from Freddie and rushed, teary-eyed, naked, and deadly sincere, to embrace me. Everyone wished us well. Flies still open, seams unzipped and bras in hands, they left us to ourselves.

"I'd better call my lawyer," said a businesslike Nick, "and find out where we can do it right away. I don't want to wait." So the worst had happened. I'd said yes. And suddenly I was as intoxicated as Nick and almost as happy.

Three phone calls later, all starting "No, I'm not drunk," he reached his lady lawyer. "What do you mean? Who am I going to marry? My Barbara, of course." We'd go to Augusta, Georgia, and get married in the shade of the magnolias. The hotel was run by Nick's pal from Vegas.

"I'll call for a car," said Nick, now dressed and cramming some things into a bag and a bottle of Dewar's into his coat pocket.

"Don't bother," I said, "I have one."

Nick never asked how I came by this Rolls, and I never volunteered. Instead, as we sped through Queens toward the airport, he said, "Jesus, I don't have enough cash on me!"

"We can stop at my apartment," I said. "I've got four hundred hidden under my rug."

"A Jewish girl"—he sighed—"is a thing of joy."

"What do you mean, you get married?" demanded Teresa as I presented a slightly weaving Nick and rushed for my money.

"I don't have time to talk. We'll miss the plane." A hundred was missing. "Janice, you stole a hundred dollars from me."

"I did not," said Janice, all wide-eyed and innocent.

"You did, too."

"Never mind," slurred Nick. "We can manage on three." He was looking less steady. "It's just till we get to the hotel," he added, taking a long slug from his bottle. Teresa stared at him in silence.

As the door closed behind us I heard Janice call, "Why can't I come, too?"

Augusta, Georgia, had the prettiest airport I'd ever seen. Green with lots of flowering bushes and friendly faces, it was wonderful. Like spring, not November. Everything was wonderful, like a movie with a happy ending. John Garfield had chosen to reform for Priscilla Lane. Barbara Stanwyck saved Gary Cooper from the brink of his John Doe precipice, and Irene Dunne reclaimed Cary Grant. I stared around me. I didn't want to forget a thing.

"Can I get your luggage, ma'am?" offered the porter, his black complexion shining with goodwill.

"I don't have any," I confided. "I'm eloping."

"Well, now," he said, "how 'bout that?" and joined me in laughter.

"If you can wait, you can take my fiancé's bag," I said proudly. "My fiancé has gone to see about transportation."

"My pleasure, ma'am. I hope you like our city."

I was relieved to see how straight Nick walked as he returned. He'd been so shaky, even staggering, when we boarded at La Guardia I was afraid they wouldn't let us on. "I'll take care of you," I crooned, helping him strap himself into his seat. The stewardess eyed him with suspicion, then moved away to tend to her takeoff duties. Ours was a milk plane; it made four stops before Augusta. That's how it was in 1955. At each stop Nick woke to tell me how he loved me and that I'd never be sorry. "I'll make you happy," he said and lapsed into Greek love poems. In between he passed out.

"You're all I have," he said. "I have no home, no country, no place I really belong. Just you. And I'll be your brother and father. I'll dance with you, drink with you, and dream with you."

"Can't we dream without drink?" I asked, but he was sleeping again. Sometimes between the stops he woke, stirred, and tried to unstrap himself. I didn't want that. Unstrapped, he'd slide to the floor, his legs tripping people in the aisles.

"You sure he's all right?" questioned the now-alarmed stewardess.

"Absolutely," I assured her, with newfound authority. I was almost a married lady.

"I gotta pee real bad," mumbled Nick, reaching toward his fly.

"Wait till Augusta," I pleaded. He smiled and happily passed out again.

"Everything's arranged. The Bon Aire's sent a car," said Nick, handing his small case to the porter. "We'll meet you at it. Jesus," he added, "I've really got to pee."

"Me, too," I said, and hand in hand, fingers interlaced, we walked toward the rest rooms. Suddenly I stopped walking.

"What's the matter, baby?" asked Nick. Then, seeing what I was staring at, two drinking fountains, WHITES ONLY and COLORED, he added, "You are in the Deep South, you know." My mind remembered Peekskill, smashed glasses, stones and blood. I stood there rigid and confused.

"I knew they had things like this," I whispered, "but I never saw it before."

"It really upsets you, doesn't it?" he said. "Well, I'll fix that." Then right there Nick, given to gestures and more than ready, opened his fly and peed all over the WHITE ONLY spigot. And no one noticed.

"Thank you," I said

"Consider me your Spartacus," he said, with his crooked smile as he conducted me to the waiting car. "Who do you think you can trust," he said, "if not us madmen, artists, and exiles?"

"Are you sure you know what you're getting into?" Nick's pal, the manager of the Bon Aire Hotel, asked me. "Well, anyway, it's too late to get your license here, but we can drive to Aiken and get it there. Then you can be married in the morning."

The drive was short and sweet, and we gave our vital statistics and birthdays to the clerk. "January twenty-sixth," said Nick.

"That's the same day as my brother," I said, marking the coincidence.

"See," he said, "fated." This new Nick who would stand there and let me love him without risk was amazing to me.

"Will you protect me from the concentration camps if they come?" I asked Nick later, as he downed his fifth scotch, in the cocktail lounge of the hotel. It was a question that in my mind I'd always wanted to ask of my Gentile beaus, but never dared. Nick sweetly and drunkenly proclaimed he would if ever it should come to that, as of course, it wouldn't. I believed him and leaned forward to kiss his strong hand. He smiled, then, seeing himself as my protector wrapped my stole more securely over my shoulders, to defend me from the ceiling fan. And poured me another drink. The bottle boggled as he replaced it slightly off center, but it didn't fall.

Nick, who could hurt me more than almost anyone, knowing instinctively where my pain lived, also knew how to comfort.

"You have a man now," he said, "who loves you." He liked the idea.

"Please, don't drink too much, Nick. We have to be at the justice of the peace by ten."

"I'll be clear by ten," he said, downing his drink in one toss. "Tonight's my bachelor party." We'd agreed that night to wait for sex till it was sanctioned. "It will be sweeter that way," said Nick as I slipped beneath the sheets with him.

In the morning the valet was late pressing my dress. I draped a towel around my underwear and moved impatiently around the suite.

"Take off the towel," said Nick, a finger over where he'd scraped his chin shaving. "Underwear is sexy."

"My underwear has holes in it."

"So do your stockings," he observed. "It's all right, kid. You had three hundred under the rug for emergencies."

"Four hundred," I said, realizing I hadn't called home.

The dress arrived.

Our wedding was as sweet as a Jean Arthur–Jimmy Stewart movie. The justice presided in a vine-covered cottage, through whose windows children's faces peered with excitement. Nick, a white rose tucked in his lapel, smiled as I held my bouquet of orchids in trembling hands. We slipped the solid gold bands on each other's fingers, and "till death do you part" was vowed.

The local paper, picking up the item from the town clerk had run a little story in the morning edition. Several Greeks, who manufactured furniture in the area, showed up, uninvited. Also present was a member of Scotland's Logan clan who having trod the boards with Nick in Glasgow, didn't want to miss a chance to summon up his youth. Nick welcomed everyone.

"Call for hors d'oeuvres and champagne," said Nick, at the hotel, "while I make our guests comfortable."

"How do I pay for it?"

"Just sign. You have the power of the pen now. Add a good tip for the waiter." So the Scotsman did Sir Harry Lauder, and the Greeks linked arms to ancient rhythms and, as befitted the occasion, broke glasses, added, of course, to our bill. Eventually everyone left.

Alone and naked, Nick took me for the first time as his wife. "I want you to know," he said, "drunk or sober, I love you." Slowly kneeling, he slid me to the floor beneath him, where we joined with no extra kisses or caresses. But we had to stop. I was being rubbed raw by the rug.

"We should have used the bed," Nick said. "We're paying enough for it. Take a nice long bath."

I sat in the soapy water, staring at the wide gold band on my finger. Jane Eyre, when she became Mrs. Rochester, would have worn hers through wet or rash, and so would I. I, too, had my fierce, wild man happily hooked.

He would turn faithful and docile, and I was going to have it all, after all.

"Guess who?" said Nick, springing into the bathroom, his reading glasses perched over his penis and surrounded by swollen testes. "Look closely," he said, pointing to pubic hair curling over the rims. "Who does it remind you of?"

I looked. "Why, it's Harry the furrier," I said in sudden recognition.

"Isn't it, though?" said Nick.

"You're not supposed to be in there together," bleated the stewardess for the fifth time. Her whine blended into the noise of the engine, as Nick rezipped and I reattached the remnants of my hose. Nick had been having me with one foot on the toilet, the other unfortunately pressing the red assistance button, bringing the stewardess to the door.

"Is there any trouble?' she called politely.

"No," Nick shouted, shifting my leg so it wouldn't happen again. "We are fine."

"What?"

"Just fine," I called.

"Are there two of you in there?" she demanded, little courtesy left in her voice.

"Yes," stated Nick, irritated by her rudeness.

"That's not allowed."

Her rapping turned into pounding. "You-all have to come out. We have regulations."

"In a minute," shouted Nick.

"Immediately."

"We'll finish in Miami," Nick said in apology as he stepped me out the door, past the hostess and down an aisle of curious faces to our seats. The remaining flight was mostly uneventful.

"She must be crazy," said Nick's lady lawyer, kissing us at the arrival gate, "to marry you, Greek."

"Crazy," the welcoming committee confirmed: Nick's doctor, his lady lawyer with the warm smile, and her pretty roommate. "Don't drive with anyone who has booze on his breath," my father had warned when dates showed up in cars. I didn't seem to have much choice.

"You come with us," said the lady lawyer, wedging me between herself and her roommate into the front seat. Two huge boxers fully occupied the back. "Nick will ride with Doc."

"How romantic," said the roommate, her auburn curls bobbing as she moved to make room. "Running off without any luggage at all."

"I'd love to get out of this dress," I told her. "I've had it on since New York."

"Oh, you sweet thing," she said, taking my hand. "I'll give you something of mine." I felt very welcome.

"I think Doc's jealous," said the lawyer as we sped down the ramp.

"Why should Doc be jealous?" I asked, not sure the remark was meant to be remarked on or just heard. Nick considered Doc his best friend.

"Because deep inside," said the attorney from the side of her mouth, "Doc is a little in love with Nick."

"Doc's not homosexual," I objected. What were they talking about? "He's married." Actually I hadn't liked this separating of Nick and me in different cars, yet I hadn't known how to stop it. Through the windshield I stared into Doc's car immediately ahead and watched Nick's cigar waving to the rhythm of his words. This was just cocktail talk I was hearing. I dismissed it. It didn't dismiss.

"What Maud means," said her roommate, Mignon, "is that in the cellar of his soul Doc would rather be with Nick than with any woman."

"Where are they going?" I asked as Doc's car pulled off the highway.

"Nick's buying booze. He'll meet us at the house. Cheer up," continued Maud as I retired into silence. "It's a party."

Then I met the "girls."

"Let me present Nick's child bride," said Maud in her best courtroom voice to the clique of show biz wives who had gathered, without their husbands, to view and advise.

"Let me freshen her first," offered Mignon, and led me to her dressing room. "Do you want a bath?"

"No, just something cool to put on."

"Here, this should look pretty on you." She gave me a

hostess gown of lavender silk. "Let me tie up your hair in a ribbon." She is trying to be nice, I thought, watching in the mirror as she groomed me. "Now," she said, pleased with her handiwork, "you look like a bride. And don't let the girls upset you," she warned, leading me back. "They seem catty. But it's only a game."

After five minutes of sweet introductions the game was on.

"Any man," proclaimed Maud, the lawyer, winking at me, like family, "who announces his wedding plans by saying he's going to elope with that nice Jew-broad he'd met in New York, and he needs a place where they don't take medical exams, in case he has the clap, is not a good bet." They all laughed, and my face went hot in spite of the wink.

"He was drinking." I defended him.

"My dear child," said one who was obviously the queen bee of this hive, as she sat sparkling in satin and sapphires, "he will always be drinking. Get used to it."

"He says he's going to stop for me."

"Fat chance," the Queen Bee went on, "but if you're smart, you'll take advantage of it. I've pulled over a hundred thousand from my husband's pockets, a little at a time. He'll never notice."

Another concurred. "He'll just blow it or give it to some other broad."

"What other broad? We just got married."

"Oh, there will be other broads," they all agreed.

"Hello, Nicky, darling," called the Queen Bee as he and Doc arrived, carrying bundles. "You look so handsome, you Adonis you. If it weren't for your child bride, I could go for you myself." The game had changed. So did the party. Sipping on my one scotch, I listened as I was turned from "me" to "she." In Augusta I was a full partner. Here I was somehow disenfranchised.

"Has she met Martha yet?"

"Melodye?"

"Just wait till Ollie gets a look at her, she'll think Nick robbed a crib."

"Nick says she's an intellectual."

"I haven't heard her say anything intellectual," said the

Queen Bee. Was she going to ask me to say something intellectual? I could recite them a sonnet. No one was listening to me anyway. Give me a year, I vowed, and I'll show them.

"I brought my maid's gefilte fish balls," said someone.

"My maid makes them better."

"Half the hookers on the beach," said the doctor, "went into mourning when they heard the news, Nick."

"What do they care?" answered the Queen Bee. "What has marriage to do with fun?"

"Try some chopped liver," offered one of the girls, addressing me personally for the first time. "It's the best on the beach."

I wasn't sure who made the offer. I'd lost track of who said what. I couldn't tell Ritzy from Fritzie, Cookie from Candy, or Sunny from Sandy. What names they carried down here. Only Maud, Mignon, and the Queen Bee were distinct.

Nick was talking earnestly to them about talent, a favorite subject. "For every big star who's made it," said Nick, laying a hand on the Queen Bee's satined knee, "I know at least five others with more talent who haven't." Nick, who had worked the Palace Theater at thirteen, spoke with authority.

"That's show biz," said the Queen Bee, who obviously was not outauthorized by anyone.

"That's life," said Nick, who hadn't quite decided if his own was a success or failure. It hadn't turned out as it was supposed to. When twenty, he'd been spotted by Jean Harlow while performing as a dancer at Hollywood's Trocadero. And on her say-so he had been tested by MGM. He'd had his eyebrows tweezed and been offered a fancy contract. So he bought himself a fancy car, took out a fancy lady, and had a fancy accident. His ankles were in casts for months. The girl was unhurt. The contract was torn up. Nick went back to work, dancing in bandages to pay the hospital bills. I'd seen the scars on his Achilles tendons. Nick had lots of scars and lots of stories that went with them. The problem was that he was hostage to his own stories. They obligated his behavior.

The conversations moved inevitably to Miami's "season" and Martha's coming engagement at the club she and Nick had an interest in.

"Nick," I said at long last, "I think I'd like to go to bed."

"Don't damage the child bride," bellowed the Queen Bee as we left.

At midnight the bewildered "child bride" crept out the bedroom door, alongside the house, past the pool, and down to the dock. If this bride wasn't careful, she started to fear, this honeymoon might prove fatal. If, for example, the housemaid, Henry Mae, big and black, with a broom in her hand hadn't prevented him, Nick, with the kitchen knife he was passionately brandishing, might indeed have cut out that piece of her flesh and eaten it, as he kept promising to. Shouting Greek oaths of love and death, he had proclaimed a marital rite involving blood was called for. Was he serious? At this point the tired bride couldn't tell theatrics from threat.

"Stop scaring that little girl, Greek," Henry Mae had ordered. She had seen enough of Nick's shenanigans over the years and attacked him with her broom.

Nick dropped the knife, sat down on the bed, grinned, shrugged, and said, "I'll do it in the morning."

"He don't mean no harm," said Henry Mae as we stood side by side, willing Nick into slumber. "He's just crazy." She giggled. At the first reassuring snore she suggested getting me something solid to eat. "You better keep your strength up."

I had no real appetite. The moment of terror was over, but not forty-eight hours had passed since El Borracho. I needed a place to sit and think or, if not to think, at least to unwind.

Alongside the darkened pool were plump lounges. I chose one. Would the drinking never stop? No, he had promised. And he loved me.

"A drunk is worse than a thief," Auntie H. once said. "At least a thief is predictable." But Nick wasn't a real drunk. Images of the Bowery in winter crossed my mind: bare feet, cracked with cold; stubbly cheeks; idiot grins of broken teeth; and bottles in brown paper bags. No, Nick wasn't like that. He drank out of social frenzy. When he realized the frenzy was finished, he'd stop.

Yet, "Believe me, drunks are drunks," Auntie H. always insisted. "I've seen drunks drink away their children's milk," she said. "Even on the Lower East Side, nothing was lower than a drunk. In Russia drunks made pogroms. In America they made messes." It had been unusual for Auntie H. to bring up Europe in that sort of way. Accents, green-horns, and Hasidic Jews embarrassed her. When Auntie H. talked of "abroad," she didn't mean that sort of stuff. She meant the Palladium in London, where her second hus-band, the "headliner," had wowed them. She meant meet-ing royalty and doing the Charleston in Piccadilly Circus on New Year's Eve.

No, they all were wrong. All I needed was love and patience. And to have Nick to myself.

Maud and Mignon's screened-in pool stretched past the Florida room and the master bedroom, which were lit like stages. From where I lay I could see the evening's cast. Doc had left, but the party was going on. I certainly didn't want to join them, but I didn't mind peeking. And it seemed neither did they.

"I peeked in on the newlyweds before," the Queen Bee boomed. "Nick was riding that poor little thing like a bronco." She's making that up, I thought, recoiling into my lounge. Everyone was laughing, and I should have left; but I stayed, shrouded in darkness, to hear more.

"Well, maybe it will thin her a bit," said Mignon, pop-ping some kind of pill and downing it with scotch. "She's a little chunky, and you should have seen her underwear. I've got to take her shopping."

"Wait a week," said someone else. "She'll be a full size smaller." One of the girls moved toward where the screens separated me from the Florida room, where they sat not ten feet away. She stood there and looked out. She didn't see me and turned back to the group.

"She might be young," said that one, "but she's no in-nocent, not after spending time with Nick."

"Do you think he did it on the rebound because Martha remarried?"

"She has cute tits."

"Nick says it's her ass."

"She's pretty," boomed the Queen Bee, "but she has no style." That seemed to finish that subject, and the conversation returned to themselves. Then I listened as the Queen Bee, bored with her husband, described how he couldn't get it up and how their sex consisted of her getting him off, an act which took longer than she liked, but still only twenty minutes a week. Mignon, a southern belle, who was starting to wrinkle around her velvet neckband, dressed like a garlanded ballerina. I liked her; she'd been sweet to me, giving me her own jade necklace as a wedding present. Actually it had almost felt as if she were flirting; that amused Nick and confused me.

The whole scene was confusing. Nick had pulled me, his slightly soiled Alice, through the looking glass of a fun house.

The action was slowly shifting to the bedroom, where some of the girls were trying on Mignon's new gowns. Bodies were exposed, and all the giggling, pattings, and pinchings started to excite the big boxers, which slept on special pallets at the base of the king-size bed. That bed was becoming a mass of laughing women. I couldn't quite make out what was happening unless I moved closer, as I didn't dare do.

"That damn dog," roared the Queen Bee's big voice, "has got its nose up me."

"Let him." Mignon giggled. "You'll love it."

It was time to go back to Nick.

I found him, sleeping on his back, his hands clasped across his chest, like a child in prayer. The Queen Bee was on the mark about one thing: He was an Adonis, and better than he knew. Certainly better than his critics. I curled in beside him and went to sleep. The first day of my marriage was ending.

The second day broke brilliant of sea and sky. All was quiet. Not a cigarette butt or unwashed glass gave testimony to the night's activity. It was a picture clipped from *Good Housekeeping*. As I approached the garden, I half expected to find someone painting the roses red.

Instead, I found Mignon pulling ticks from the two huge dogs, which lay obedient and all-suffering as she pinched and tweezed.

"Florida is terrible for ticks," she said as I approached her in her Florodora bathing suit.

"Does it hurt the dogs?" I asked as she nabbed another, burned its bloated body with a cigarette, and dumped the remains in a bowl of water.

"Yes, but they trust me, my dogs. The thing is not to leave the heads in. That causes infection."

Huge mouths, with tongues lolling, slobbered on the tiles as she worked. I sat down to watch and ruminate. Last evening's words, the words of the "girls," were like the tick heads. But I decided to push their words away. I had married-lady duties to attend to. "I ought to visit Melodye at the academy," I said to Mignon, letting my feet dangle in her pool.

"Not today," said Mignon, finally releasing the boxers from their torture. "Today you should relax and enjoy your honeymoon."

"Well, at least I ought to call my aunt." I was wanting something to relate to. Real family.

"Hello, Auntie," I said happily when the operator got her on the line. "I'm married."

"Who is this?"

"Barbara."

"Who?"

"Your niece Barbara."

"You gave me a start," she rasped. "I thought it was some stranger. Strangers sometimes call."

"No, it's me. I just got married."

"Married! To who?"

"Nick Condos."

"Is he Jewish?"

"No, Greek."

"You're sure."

"I'm sure. You'll like him, though."

"I doubt it. Nick Condos, isn't he married to Martha Raye? The one from television with the big mouth."

"No, he's married to me."

"I was positive I heard he's married to Martha Raye," she said, sounding annoyed.

"He used to be," I reassured her, and she felt better. She didn't like being wrong.

"So," she said with grim satisfaction, "you went and married an actor. I knew you would come to no good."

"He's not an actor," I said.

"An actor," she ruminated. "One of the Shubert boys once told me, and he should know, that actors weren't worth the shoes they stood in."

"He's not an actor," I insisted. "But he used to be a dancer." She couldn't find fault with dancers, having once been one herself.

"You're sure he's not still married to Martha and lying to you?"

"No," I said, "not legally anyway."

"Well, at least you're married."

"At least," I agreed. "I'll call you in New York."

"Is this long distance?"

"Yes."

"Then hang up. Long distance is expensive." The line went dead, and I was once again unrelated.

The third morning Nick woke me with a kiss. "Get dressed. Mignon is taking you shopping for your trousseau." A trousseau! So I was married after all.

Nick's honeymoon was a success. I spent hours pinned to the mat of his passion, listening to declarations of love and learning new ways to seal our oneness, but we never talked.

The only disappointment Nick had was Martha's sudden decision not to appear at their nightclub. He sat puffing on his cigar in dismay. "It's that damn chorus boy she's married. He'll ruin her career." Once in a while he'd light an extra match behind the boxers' behinds. They were given to flatulence, and he was attempting to burn up their gas.

"I guess we'll have to go back to New York sooner than I thought," he said at last. The idea didn't disturb me at all.

The welcoming committee escorted us to the airport for fond farewells. Nick, as before, rode with Doc, and I sat with Maud and Mignon while the boxers sprawled across

176

my new luggage, looking rather sad. "We want you to know," said Mignon, moistly, "that we now consider you our own. And if that Greek gets to be too much for you, come on down to us. And don't let Martha march all over you either. After all, you are Nick's wife."

"And," added Maud, whom I'd really started to trust and love, "if you get tired of being his wife, don't forget I'm the best divorce lawyer in Miami."

We boarded our plane. "Nick," I remembered as we took seats, "Nick, I called my auntie, but I never called my home."

"I'm your home now," said Nick, and clicked my seat strap close around me.

Wife No. 2

Darwin and my high school biology teacher promoted the idea that animals actually changed body structure to survive. But that took aeons, and I couldn't wait. Of course, I didn't have to go from gills to lungs to adapt. Just tighten, toughen and develop a veneer. Those were my brave new thoughts as I dressed for my first New York night as Nick's wife. I put on lots of mascara.

We started at the Stork Club. Caesar salad, champagne, and Sherman Billingsley saying, "Martha was in last night, and she looks great." I smiled at the compliment as befitted my successful association. Then the Latin Quarter, where the B'way and Lindy's crowd drank to our wedding while ogling the chorus. It established status to greet the chorines by name. Old man Lowey, the owner, clapped as the half-naked ladies lilted through a czardas. Hungarian production numbers, he said, reminded him of his mother. Our future was drunk so often it was in danger of being drowned. In the audience I saw my friend Jane's father.

"Barbara," he called, "I almost didn't recognize you.

You look twenty years older." Mascara worked as well as Darwin.

"How about the Copa?" asked Nick as he gallantly handed me into the limousine he'd hired. "That calypso singer you jumped on is there." A reference to confessions I'd made in the wake of our wedding, which I was learning to regret. "You're lucky," he went on, "I married you, or you'd have wound up a Greenwich Village Commie fucking every freak you could find."

"How about going home," I said, not liking his tone.

"No," he said, imitating Joe E. Lewis, "it's the shank of the evening. Let's sally forth."

We sallied. The brass-buttoned doorman at the Copacabana was happy to see him. "Where've you been, Nicky?"

"On my honeymoon," said Nick. The doorman didn't seem impressed. Nick tipped him handsomely anyway.

"Jeez, Nicky," said the maître de, "it's an opening. He's just going on. I don't have a table in the house."

"Make one," said Nick. And they did.

As the Copa Girls swirled off, they set us up a table virtually onstage. Nick stumbled slightly as we took our seats. Then fell into a coughing spasm. We certainly had everyone's attention.

"Work de banana boat all day long," crooned the star to welcoming applause.

"Day-O," Nick chimed in between coughs.

"Sh," I said.

"Don't sh," snarled Nick. "Day-O, Day-O."

As the spotlight spread for the star to enlarge his number, it included us in its bright beam. Nick started slipping from his seat. I jerked him upright by his sleeve. He smiled. "Day-O," he caroled.

Another song was introduced and cheered. Nick stayed with "Day-O," and slipped right to the floor. I scrambled to reseat him and signaled frantically to the waiter. The check arrived, and as I reached into Nick's pocket to pay it, a hand clamped itself around my wrist.

"What do you think you're doing?" snarled the captain as the crowd looked on.

"Paying the check."

"Nobody rolls our customers here. Get your hands out of his pockets."

"Day-O," sang Nick rather softly.

"I'm his wife," I protested as firmly as I dared, with the whole nightclub and my famous singer all watching. I was losing my brave new grip on wifedom.

"That's a hot one," said the captain, squeezing harder on my wrist. "Now don't make more trouble."

"But I am his wife." Tears were threatening; I stopped them. "Nick, tell him I'm your wife. He told the doorman. He did. Just ask!" It became a nightmare.

"Day-O," sang Nick sweetly. I gave up. We were paraded out. The captain gently keeping Nick almost on his feet. And me trying to regain myself as a gun moll.

"Day-O," Nick thanked him. I lifted my nose.

"Day-O," Nick trilled to the doorman along with a hundred-dollar bill.

"Day-O," he exulted to the limousine driver as he drove us home.

"Day-O." Mascaraed eyes obviously weren't enough, but I'd figure it out. In the morning I told Nick what happened. He didn't remember but said, "It must have been funny," and, "Forget it. There's a couple of things you could do for me today."

"What?" I asked, amazed at how all echoes of "Day-O" had vanished.

"I'd like you to pick up a sample of the fabric in Martha's gown at Katherine Kuhn's, and get pumps dyed to match. They know her size at Delman's. Just charge it."

"Okay."

"And when you drop the pumps off at the studio, get a snip of her hair for her new switch. Ernie's salon is on West Seventy-second Street. See you later." He was gone. I got up and started to straighten the apartment. It was pretty but too small. You couldn't raise a child there.

It took Katherine Kuhn a bit to get the facts straight. No, not a cousin or married to Nick's brother. Yes, I was young. Yes, it was sudden. Yes, Martha knew. No, I was not in show biz, though I'd studied theater. No, I didn't think Melodye would be a problem.

"Why didn't you get yourself some snow shoes?" Nick asked as I walked wet feet into Martha's dressing room. "You were right there."

"I didn't have money."

"You could have charged them, too."

"I didn't know."

"Meet the new Mrs. Condos," Martha said, entering with two fans. Was I supposed to take a bow? I did. The fans studied me with suspicion. I smiled and asked how the rehearsal was going.

"The changes are too fast. They'll have to set up an extra dressing room behind the set," Martha said. And Nick went off to see to it and other problems of live TV. Martha watched herself in the mirror. "You and Nick are coming for Thanksgiving," she stated, meaning up to her house in Westport. The fans sighed in envy. "Well," she asked, "how do you like being married to Nick?"

"I like it."

"Wait," she said. The fans roared.

"I need a piece of your hair," I got in when I could.

She snipped me a wave.

"Why, that's Melodye, isn't it?" said a spectacled lady, peering in the door. "My, how she has grown."

"This isn't Melodye, you dope," corrected Martha. "This is Nick's new wife."

"Oh, sorry." The woman blushed.

"Nice to meet you anyway," I said. My wet shoes left marks on Martha's floor.

"God, you're all damp!" Ernie had said. "Let me get you some tea. I'll be through with my customer in five minutes. Then we can chat." I sipped and watched his handiwork.

"Well, you went and did it," said Ernie, settling in for a bit of gossip. "I would have thought a Jewish girl would have more sense. What did your family say? They must have had a fit."

"They're all dead except for my kid sister. She thinks it's great."

"Never mind me. Nick is really a good guy. I was only teasing. Your hair is hanging like a mop. Let me give you a little trim and a nice French twist. Stop looking in your purse. You're one of the family now."

"Try and remember," Ernie advised as he tacked the final stray hair into place with the last invisible hairpin, "you are dealing with a great actress. And like most actresses, Martha is waiting for her cue. If you cue her, she will respond. Now," he said, holding a mirror to the back of my head, "go change into dry clothing. I'll bring the switch to the dress. See you there."

It was smoky and hot at the dress rehearsal. I sat in a row where I could see the action both live and on the monitor, amazed at the illusions of space. It was an audience of "friends of the show." I sat alone.

"What do you think?" asked Nick after it was over.

And I made a serious mistake. I told him."Well, it seemed to me that the second skit should have—"

He cut me off with a "What do you know about show business anyway?"

"You were right," whispered Ernie, who'd witnessed our exchange, "but they don't want to hear it now. It's too late. Learn to lie a little. It's your job."

As I watched the real show from home, it struck me that no one would have known if the pumps matched or not. Not in black-and-white.

"Barb," Nick said the next morning, "go get yourself some nice winter clothes. Martha said you were dressed like a waif." He handed me a bunch of bills. "I love you, and don't bring back any change."

"When am I going to meet your mother and your sisters?" I asked, counting money.

"Soon, soon. I just hate going up there since my dad died." "Up there" was upper Riverside Drive opposite the Cloisters. It could have been China, so thick was the wall between his worlds. And Nick was a coward about death. In Florida he might dive into a canal to rescue a dog without a thought to the fact that he couldn't swim. But the real residue of death was something he wouldn't deal with. So I met his Greek mother over the phone. Nick translated.

*　　*　　*

The drive to Westport was mostly uneventful. That was good because Nick, piloting the old Cadillac (borrowed from his chum Freddie), was doing it without a license. His had been suspended for drunken driving. The Merritt Parkway was still beautiful with leaves of changing color. The large bunch of yellow mums bounced gaily in my lap, and the champagne bottles rocked gently in the back seat, clinking at every turn. Thanksgiving in Connecticut, how bad could it be?

I was feeling surges of sweet domesticity. Everything domestic seemed attractive. At this moment when I thought of Mr. and Mrs. Condos's plush little apartment with its gleaming silver and polished wood, my heart swelled. I wanted to pull Nick into my mood.

"Nick," I said, studying the brook that ran alongside the highway, "I think we need a blender."

"So get one."

"And I think the table by the doorway could use a pretty bowlful of dried flowers."

"Okay."

"And maybe a down comforter to watch TV under and cuddle into."

"Sure."

Then, coming under the spell of remembered television commercials, I said, "Nick, what kind of toilet tissue do you prefer?"

"Who gives a shit?" said Nick, his cigar clenched in his teeth and both hands tight on the wheel as if he were taking the north turn at Indianapolis. "Put on the radio." The mums continued bouncing, only not so gaily. A sign said WELCOME TO CONNECTICUT—DRIVE CAREFULLY.

Despite that, I plunged again. I said, "Nick, sometimes I don't feel like a wife."

Nick removed one hand from the wheel, fumbled for the press-in lighter, and re-fused his cigar.

"Not that I'm sure what a wife really feels like, but I think I know what a wife is supposed to feel. Of course, I can't be positive, so maybe I'm wrong, but I don't think I feel like I'm supposed to."

"What the fuck are you talking about?" said Nick, taking

a curve at such speed the champagne bottles clanked dangerously in the back seat. "Watch for our exit."

White birch and silver spruce flashed by the car windows as we turned off the parkway. I tried again. "It would be nice," I said, "to live in the country."

"What for?" said Nick, now doing battle with the road signs.

"Well, eventually we'll need a bigger place."

"Why?"

"Well, for our children, when we have them."

"What children? Watch for Martha's road, will you, and remember to be sweet to her. Since her faggot husband ran away from home, she's upset." The car weaved. "God damn, we've got a flat!"

I stood by the side of the road, my backless Spring-O-Lator shoes slipping off the rubble of the shoulder, clutching the mums and thinking about Nick's "What children?" while he changed the tire. "We'll be late. From now on," he swore, "I'll get a limo." I decided I had misheard him, but somehow I let the subject die.

As it was, we were the first to arrive. "Just take a peek at my turkey, Nicky," said the cook, sister to Henry Mae, Mignon's housemaid in Florida. "But no picking now, Greek." She slapped at his fingers with a ladle. I was glad to meet her.

"Well, little beauty," said Martha when she appeared. "So how'd you get him to do the right thing? You never told me. Never mind. If he gives you any trouble, come to me. I can keep Nick in line."

"Thank you," I said, not knowing what else to say to this competitor-in-law, who was obviously trying to be friendly.

"When do we eat?" said Nick. The words brought back the good Thanksgivings of our childhood. "Let's eat," Melvin would chant, marching around the formal dining-room table, counting plates and worrying that there might not be enough for him to have his fill. We used the dining room only on holidays. "I want one whole drumstick just for me."

"You'll get it," my father would say.

"Are you sure? There are only two." Melvin was never trusting.

"Have patience," my father would say, honing his carving knife, while we watched with mystic awe.

"We eat," Martha said, holding a pitcher of martinis (Westporters were big on martinis), "we eat when all my guests come, and when I'm ready."

"Wait till you get a load of these Aryans from Darien," Nick said. I could hardly. Such people were exotic to me.

Westport had taken Martha to its material bosom. Time would sour the milk of the welcome, but not then. Then the Westporters hung expectantly on her every joke and gesture, as they sold her enough Early American to change her name to Martha Washington. They started to arrive.

"Some Jews want to buy the old Hennessey barn and convert it," said one neighborly pal as we sat before the fireplace drinking Thanksgiving toddies. "But I don't think the Hennesseys would do that to us." Oh-oh . . . exotic was proving toxic. I looked to see if Nick was listening. Since I'd become his wife, he was fierce about anti-Semitism. But the lady was on the wrong side of the deaf ear that had kept him out of the army.

However, Martha shot me a fast look and said, "Most of my best friends are Jews. I even married one." Certainly a big surprise to these folks.

"Oh, Maggie O'Reed," gibed the one who'd spoken, "you are a scream," triggering giggles from the rest.

"What's so funny?" asked Nick, who had missed the action but was ready to hate her guests on general principles.

"Nothing," I said, and signaled Martha an it's-all-right sign. The conversation moved to the relative safety of politics. But was it safe? I was suddenly afraid to say what I thought, as we heard how "Joe McCarthy was the bravest man in Washington," and to "Watch out for parlor pinkos, they may be real reds," and "What about that writer of yours, Maggie, the one listed in *Red Channels?*" The question hung in the air and faded.

Now other guests of indeterminate sex arrived. More drinks were served, more hors d'oeuvres passed. And more and more I started wishing I were eating plain chicken with Janice and Teresa. Not so fancy, all this fancy.

"When do we eat?" Nick demanded again, belligerently.

"Later, Nick," said Martha sharply, "can't you control your damn appetites?"

"No," said Nick. "You always serve late because you want everyone drunk and starved so they think it's the best food in the world. "Behind their family bicker I could almost hear my Auntie H. complaining about her own annual complaints about our family manners.

"Your cousin Norman"—she would chastise us—"would never behave that way. Really, Rosie, your kids are the worst I ever saw."

"Behave yourself, Nick," Martha was saying. I ached with memories. A holiday ache. This big Thanksgiving dinner of hers was my first in so long and I hadn't been sure how to "behave." Now I knew it didn't matter. Nobody was much interested in my manners or, in fact, in me. Even Henry Mae's sister's turkey had to wait till midnight to get attention. And both drumsticks were left untouched! What everyone did seem interested in was getting drunk. So I joined them. When in Rome.

Sometime in the wee hours of Martha's upstairs guest room, Nick rolled over onto me and almost unconsciously began to make love. Over his shoulder I saw the bedroom door slide ajar. Someone was standing there watching us. But in the drunken darkness I couldn't be sure who.

Another morning of another show. I opened my eyes to a fully dressed Nick already on the move. "Do me a favor, Barb," he said, going out the door. "Stop by the furrier, and pick out the best mink for Martha's finale number."

Here we go again. I pushed back my messenger-girl resentments and asked, "How do I know what's the best?"

"The one you like most. A dark one. I'll see you at the run-through." He was gone.

"Are you going to the rehearsal today?" my sister asked on the phone.

"Yes, I have to."

"Oh, it must be fun. All those actors and movie stars."

"Not so much."

"I wish I were you," she said. And for the moment I wished she were, too.

"I want you should meet Barbara," said Harry the furrier. "She's married to Nick Condos, who used to be married to Martha Raye." I took my bow.

"Nick says dark?" I ordered, reminding myself to do my
"job" well.

"I got lovely Azurene," offered Harry.

"Nick says dark," I repeated. He spread three long coats
across the floor for me to study. I pushed at the pelts, tested
their puff, and looked to see if they were dyed or had the
proper light underground. "That one," I finally said.

"You're developing an eye, kid," said Harry. "That's the
most expensive. Make sure it gets returned in good condition. You want to take it with you?" I nodded.

I lugged the large pink box into Martha's dressing room,
dropped it, and started to get out of the way.

"Where are you going?" called Nick, stopping me. "Let's
see what you picked." He opened the box and shook out the
mink. "Put it on so I can see the lines."

"I don't want to."

"Put it on." The coat hung full and heavy.

"Was it the best?"

"I thought so."

"Then consider it yours." He grinned. "Merry Christmas, Mrs. Condos. I knew if I had told you it was for you,
you'd have been afraid to take the best. We're all going to
the Copa tonight after the show, and when you wear that,
there won't be any confusion about who you are." So he
hadn't just thought it "funny" after all. Day-O. Things were
looking up.

"Very nice," said Minnie, a crony, as I enjoyed myself in
Martha's mirror. "Nicky just loves to buy furs. You should
have seen the collection he gave to Maggie. But get him to
buy you jewelry. Furs can depreciate." She was right and
was depreciating mine with every word.

"That must be somebody," said the boy with the pimples and autograph book as we pressed through the stage-
door crowd into the waiting limousine. He pushed the book
at me.

"Sign it," said Martha. I did.

"What did you write?" asked Nick as the car rumbled east.

"Margaret O'Brien," I said. Nick, Martha, and Minnie laughed. But at the Copa everyone suddenly knew my name.

"We lose about ten fingertips every Saturday," said the rink attendant, watching me survey the rushing juvenile monsters whose blades flashed as brightly as their grins as they cut you off.

"Ten fingertips?"

"Yeah," said the attendant, leaning on his slush scraper. "Little kids, they fall and their hands get skated over."

"I'd better get my kid out of there." It was the first time I'd referred to, or thought of, Melodye as mine.

"She's all right," said the attendant. "She's a natural."

I sat and watched my "natural" skim the ice. "Don't shift weight in the middle of your stride," I shouted. Melodye ignored me. We were engaged in a "natural" tug-of-war known as "You are not my mother." How will she feel when Nick and I have a child? I mused. Well, she will be a little jealous at first, but eventually she'll enjoy it. It's hard not to enjoy a new baby. I snuggled deeper into my mink on the rink fantasy. A baby, if it were a boy, I'd name it Melvin, after my brother. Two Mels in one family, not good. But Hymie Condos didn't sound quite right either. I was two weeks late with my period and, for reasons I wasn't sure of, keeping it quiet.

"Let's go home," Melodye said, startling me. "I want to bake a cake."

We reached the freshly scrubbed and waxed apartment. "Have you ever baked before?" I asked as she demanded pans, bowls, and flour.

"No," she said, "but I'm going to now."

My clean red linoleum floor with its black border lay between us like a battleground. "Melodye," I said, "I spent a whole day so the place would look nice for the weekend."

"Get a maid," said Melodye.

"I want the kitchen to stay clean."

"And I want to bake a cake. It's my father's place."

"You are not baking anything."

"I am."

"You're not." I was not going to lose this one.

"Yes," she hissed.

"No." My voice went icy.

"All right." She relented after the frozen silence. "Let's go to a movie."

"I'm feeding you lunch and taking you to the museum. Trust me. You'll like it."

We marched up the stone steps through the massive metal doors into the main hall. "That is the Egyptian section with real parts of a pyramid reconstructed so that you can actually walk through it."

"Uh-uh," said Melodye, who on school break was thoroughly bored. So I bypassed the medieval armor. "Come on, Melodye Athenia Condos, I'm going to take you to the halls of your ancestors." That got her attention.

"Greek stuff?"

"In all its glory."

"Who were all those men?" she asked as we roamed through rows of unnamed, undressed Adonises.

"Probably Olympic winners. The Greeks loved sports."

"But why are all their *things* knocked off?"

"Their what?"

"Their men things. They are all knocked off."

"They are very old statues, and parts that stick out get broken, noses, fingers, and—"

"Things," she finished for me. "So they are not in all their glory." Why, she was quite witty for a kid.

"Not quite," I agreed, and she grinned.

"They weren't Catholic, were they?" she asked as an afterthought.

"No. They lived way before Christ was born."

"I thought maybe the nuns knocked them off."

"They may have done, centuries later."

"I bet they did." She grinned again. I grinned back.

And so it went. She was finally interested. And there were thousands of things I would tell her, stuff my father told me. She held my hand. Peace negotiations were under way.

"If you get pregnant," said Martha's buddy Minnie at rehearsal, checking her manicure, the room, and me in one glance, "don't *ever* leave Melodye alone with the baby."

"What?"

"Just that." Melodye sure had a fan club.

"Martha says," lisped the stand-in, "that Melodye is either going to grow up to be a truck driver or a football player. Can you imagine?"

"Melodye loves to dance," I said, "and she's wonderful."

"Martha wouldn't like that," said the stand-in.

"Have you met my father's new wife?" Melodye asked Rocky Graziano, Martha's TV boyfriend.

"Sure, I know Babsie from Stillman's gym. With her pop."

"Was she a boxer?" asked Melodye.

Rocky laughed. "She could jump a good rope."

The challenge came later that day. Nick invited the writers and some of the cast for an Italian dinner. After they had discussed Frank Costello and the Kefauver hearings, the talk turned to comedy.

"The best comedy," Nick said, spooning up Patsy's pasta, "is spontaneous and natural. Give Martha a mike and an audience, and she'll get laughs."

"Comedy is not mindless, you know," said one writer, defending his high-paid position and swallowing his wine.

"But writing life is easier than living it," interjected Norman Lear, Martha's newest writer. "In life you can't change the punch line. You can't say, 'I did that wrong, let's erase and rewrite.' "

"Yeah," agreed Rocky loudly, and the subject changed to the street fights of Rocky's youth, the arm-wrestling contests at the friendly neighborhood bars. And suddenly our table was into it. Writers and producers rolled up sleeves to expose somewhat skimpy forearms, and contests were on.

"Let me try. Let me," demanded Melodye after watching a series of bouts. And one of the writers obliged. He started out in condescension but soon was in dead earnest. Melodye, almost as big and strong as she would grow, and coached by Rocky, downed him. "Who's next?" she demanded, flushed with victory, and turned to me.

"Don't be silly," said Nick as I sat down and allowed my once-shattered-in-three-places arm to be positioned for the press.

Melodye was grinning. "I'll have Barb down in thirty seconds," she announced as her large hand swallowed up mine. Minutes later we were still upright.

"I'm going to break your arm." My stomach knotted under the pressure.

"You'll have to," I whispered, the pain so bad I couldn't speak out loud. Our arms, still vertical, trembled. Then slowly, and I couldn't believe it as it happened, Melodye's arm started to give. Slowly, but inexorably, I pressed it flat to the table.

"She psyched me," Melodye complained, and would for years to come. "I am really stronger, but she psyched me."

"Excuse me," I said, and walked to the ladies' room. The bowl turned red beneath me. I didn't need my old biology teacher to tell me I wouldn't have to think about my baby, not this month.

"When are you going to make a baby?" Nick's sister translated from the Greek as Nick's mother held on to my much-kissed hand and beamed at me. It had taken months to get to that visit.

"Tell her, soon," I said, smiling proudly.

"Tell her, not so damn soon," amended Nick. His sister ignored him. His mother looked pleased.

"She says," his sister translated, "that when Nick was a boy, he was good and loving. That underneath he still is. And to be patient with him." I nodded.

Then Nick's mother started to spatter rapid, harsh Greek. "What's she saying now?" I asked.

Nick's sister laughed. "She's asking Nick, Why do you have cuts on your hands? Why are your nails not long and painted? If he's making you work? She is telling him that with all the money he throws away he should get you a servant. She says she worked all her life, and it's no good. It left her old and weak. She says you are Jewish and your people have suffered for thousands of years, and as a Greek, another ancient people, he should understand this and try to make it up to you. All the suffering.

"She says," his sister went on, "that the next time she speaks to Nick, she wants to hear that he has hired you help." So I fell in love, and once more things looked up.

My period was late.

"You did it on purpose," said Nick, and I ignored the accusation in his tone.

"Nick, we make love so often it's hard to know when or when not to take out my diaphragm. I can't just keep adding jelly."

"We do fuck often," admitted Nick, flattered enough to be distracted.

"You know," said my sister, Janice, when I told her I might be pregnant, "alcohol damages genes and can affect a baby." Janice was becoming a natural hygienist, an eater of raw foods and a propagator of such statements. I usually dismissed them.

"Don't make your sister nervous," said Teresa, who received the news of my expectations with joy. A brace of rabbits confirmed it.

"Congratulations," said Dr. Mead, "you're going to be a fine, healthy mama." Dr. Mead was old and gentle. He'd been Nick's doctor since early hoofing days.

"My sister says a history of venereal disease can produce damaged children." Janice had left an imprint.

"Not with Nick. Look at Melodye."

"But my sister says—"

"Who is this sister, Sister Kenny? Tell her there's no danger. Now be happy and give Nick my congratulations."

Walking along Central Park West to our big new apartment in the sky, I tried out words to congratulate Nick. He washed them down with three-quarters of a bottle of ninety-proof comfort. "Someday," he warned the city thirty stories below, waving his bottle out the window, a scene he'd seen in lots of B movies, "I'll own you."

"Nick, please come away from the window." Nick ignored me and climbed up onto the scanty sill, over

the casement, and out on the ledge. He was tilting and tot-
tering.

"Someday—"

"Nick, for God's sake, come in off there!"

Nick lost his grip on the bottle."Oh, God!" I shrieked.
"You'll kill someone else as well as yourself!" Nick finally
came in, grinning from ear to ear.

"I have perfect balance," he said, and tripped to fall flat
on his face and pass out.

"It's too soon, Barb," said sober Nick the next morning.
I looked at my fingers, which were valiantly trying to sprout
elegant nails, and then at my feet, at the ceiling, but not at
him. "Too soon. We're not married six months." A part of
me had been expecting this conversation, while the rest had
sung "Just Nicky and me and baby makes three."

"It takes nine months," I said at last.

"Too soon."

"Nick is just not ready to be a father, Barbara," said one
of the "boys" from the William Morris Agency, sent to talk
to me at the back of the rehearsal hall. "Do you think it's fair
to push this on him?" It was actually funny, the Morris
office taking such an interest in my belly. Its business was
supposed to be Martha and her show. But a disturbed Nick
didn't produce good Martha, so it seemed I was interfering
with business.

"I am a married woman," I said, "and I have a right."
Did I mean to a child or only to a fornicate?

"You're a woman married to Nick," he corrected. "You
knew what kind of life you were getting into." Did I? I must
have. But I was expecting to change him.

"Ah, Barbara," said this Jewish agent who had dubbed
me Queen Esther and would send me Purim cakes for
years. "You're young enough to wait awhile. Give him time.
Let him want it, too. Have the next one."

"And murder this one?"

"What murder! Medical men don't even consider it a
fetus till it's three months."

"I'm not a medical man."

"Ah, Barbara."

"Have it and I'll leave you," said Nick quietly. "I mean

194

it." Then, when we were home: "Have it and you'll have it alone. You'll have it alone," he repeated as he went through the door. Not to return till morning.

Could I have it alone? Did I want it alone . . . without a father? I was avoiding thinking of my own father. "What's happened to your moxie, Babsie?" he would have asked. Somewhere I'd lost it. My moxie. Whom could I talk to about it? Auntie H. hated babies. Little Janice?

"Do you think he means it?" my sister asked when I called her from the next run-through.

"Yes." She and I held on in silence.

Eventually she broke it. "Maybe they're right, maybe next year, when you're more married. Do you think he would let you have one next year?"

By the dress rehearsal everyone from the executive producer to the stand-in had given me "good advice," which was "next year." That "next year" might *never* be this year lurked in the shadows. Eventually I gave in. So Maud, the lawyer, would reluctantly accompany me on the quick trip to Cuba that Nick didn't have time for."Buy yourself something," he said, "while you are there." I certainly would.

"You'll just love Havana," said Minnie. "Go down a few days early. It's so gay. Make sure Maud takes you around a bit before the clinic. I'll tell her to take you to a circus."

"Errol's there," said a somewhat recovered Nick at the airport. "He can show you around. Flynn knows Havana. He keeps his yacht there, or something. Have a good time, but not too good."

And I was off to the land of good times . . . "Siboney," Hatuey Beer, easy love, and easier abortion. Especially if recommended by Doc from Miami.

I guess everyone thought I'd love it. Didn't most tourists brag of going? Wasn't it the thing to do in gay pre-Castro Havana?

The girls, some very young, stood in a line in the dim-lit room, wiggling their breasts and buttocks and smiling bad-toothed smiles. "Take me," they said in accented English. "I'm the best . . . I'm the youngest . . . I do tricks." We had already selected the two men. Superman, renowned in circuses across the continent, wasn't available, but the men we picked looked like proper stand-ins.

"Five," Errol had advised earlier, "always order five. Five is a good number: it gives everyone something to do." Just Errol's name lent us status.

We selected five, and all the jiggling and giggling stopped in mid-stroke. The rejected filed naked from the room.

"Make yourselves comfortable," said the gold-dentured madam, plumping up the cushions on the sofas we were to sit on. They faced a small semicircular raised dais on which two soft spotlights had started to beam. Earlier she had asked if we wanted animals mixed with the people. She had a girl and a donkey that were "amusing." I had shaken my head no.

"This is your first exhibition, isn't it?" asked the madam. I nodded. "You look nervous; just try to relax."

While I worked at relaxing, our selected group of five huddled at the back of the stage like a naked football team deciding plays. Soon a bongo drum started to beat, and a slow, sexy melody started up. They came out of their huddle and carefully moved into Position A. Then to Positions B, C, and D. E was the big one. For E the whole group heaved and hurled into one another as if they were attached by wires. Like a profane circus act, indeed, and to distract myself, I remembered the joke Nick had told me about the man who forced his way into an agent's office announcing that he and his sisters had the most sensational act in the world. "We open," the man said to the agent, "tapping in to 'Shuffle Off to Buffalo.' Then I screw my one sister while the other does somersaults over us. Then I screw my other sister while the first one sings 'Honeysuckle Rose.' Then . . ."

"What," interrupted the wide-eyed agent, "do you call this act?"

"The Aristocrats," said the performer proudly.

Later some other anxious-to-please Cubans killed two white chickens and a small monkey for us tourists. That was part of the floor show at the Tropicana, an indoor-outdoor nightclub of mammoth proportions, our last stop of the night. It had a huge banyan tree growing right up through the stage. When the giant black man in the neon red pants, his breast bare except for a necklace of bones, jumped onto the stage from the tree, carrying a white chicken in each hand and a little monkey, hanging by its tail from his teeth, I thought they were props. Only when I separated the monkey's terrified chatter from the music and sound effects did I realize this was live entertainment. The man bit off the heads of the chickens and strangled the monkey. The theme of the show was voodoo. Voodoo made for a hell of a production number.

What of my own little production number scheduled for tomorrow? Would I get bongo drums and marimbas for accompaniment? Would the doctors have bare chests and dark gods? Would the nurses wear bone necklaces?

"Sleep well now," said Maud, tucking me in for the night, "and try not to think about tomorrow. It will be over before you know it."

"Will they give me anesthesia?" I asked. It was the first direct question I'd asked out loud.

"Of course," she said. "You won't feel a thing." Poor Maud. She looked so uncomfortable, even as she comforted.

"Count backwards from one hundred," said the doctor in harsh Spanish accents, after he'd succeeded in jabbing the needle of sodium pentothal into a proper vein. He didn't like my veins; they evaded him. But it was a real medical place and reasonably clean, and I didn't have to bring my own Kotex napkin, and the nurse looked like a nurse, and no one was threatening me with jail. Illegal abortion was a totally sanctioned tourist activity in pre-Castro Cuba.

"Ninety-nine," I said, "ninety-eight, ninety-seven." The numbers were getting harder to hold on to. And for some reason I tried like hell. "Ninety-six," I said proudly, "ninety-five." I was terrific. Why didn't the doctor look happy? "Ninety-two," I pronounced carefully, but my lips had gone wrong. When, hours later, I could move them again, I assured the Cuban nurse, who was taking my pulse with dispassion, that "I never felt a thing." I lied. Lies, everyone liked them. Even I.

The night after the night I got back from Cuba was the night we were to see Auntie H. It was her birthday, and it had been arranged months before. I hadn't seen her since my marriage. Nick guilty, with his own relief that everything was over, kept telling me how much he loved me. And how he wasn't going to drink anymore. He didn't, not for one day, the whole night, and all the next day. And because of it, when we picked up Auntie H., he was sober, elegant, and beautiful.

My father had warned me about wishful thinking, but I was becoming addicted to it. Nick really feels bad about Cuba, I told myself; he's going to change his ways. He and Auntie H. will love each other. He's handsome and so well dressed, and she'll like that. She always likes that. They'll talk show biz. She'll admire my dark ranch mink. All male skins, I'll tell her. She'll like that, too. Nick will be sweet and charm her. She will have seen my name mentioned in Leonard Lyons's column and the description of me as "stylish." That will please her. She'll mention it. She'll like seeing me so slender. She hates fat. I'd dropped seven pounds in five days in Cuba. But I wouldn't mention Cuba.

Auntie H. had dressed to the nines; she was in mink, too. It was really too late for the full-length mink season, but you'd never know it from us. She was wearing the one Almost Uncle Eddie bought her just before he died. She'd had it remodeled. Tonight, however, was her birthday, and she was all set to enjoy herself. She even told a funny mink story.

"Some years ago," she told Nick and me as we sat at Marino's, "I was at the Yankee game. A World Series. I was a big Yankee fan always. Anyway, I was walking down the aisle along the good boxes—Eddie always got good box seats—and I heard a voice call 'Hannah.' Nobody had called me Hannah in twenty years. Except Mama, God rest her soul. And so I thought to myself, quick as a flash, It's Nat. You know him as George Burns, of course, but he was Nat Birnbaum way back when we kids were married. Sure enough it was him. 'Hannah,' he said, 'you look wonderful,' and all I could think was, Thank God I'm wearing full-length mink."

Nick laughed, and I thanked God myself. God had other things in mind. Nick ordered a club soda, but as the waiter went for it, he snapped his fingers for a Dewar's to go with it. I pretended not to notice.

"Teresa tells me," said Auntie H., adding for Nick's benefit, "Teresa was my sister's maid, you know. Rose had the first maid on her block. Teresa says you think you might be expecting." I blushed red, and Nick downed his Dewar's in one gulp.

"I was mistaken," I mumbled.

"Better," said Auntie H. "You have plenty of time for that. Enjoy yourself while you can. I was never one for children myself. Her mother," she said to Nick, who was starting to signal the waiter for a repeat, "her mother lost her first boy before Melvin and Barbara were born, some sort of infection picked up at the hospital. After she had Melvin and"—she now faced me—"you, she thought she was finished, but five years later she found herself pregnant again. Rose really didn't want another baby. Who could blame her? You two kids were enough for anyone. Well, she decided to try and stop it. Your daddy went *crazy*. Hymie just loved kids. Anyway, they argued about it." Auntie H. sipped at her sherry as if trying to remember clearly. Nick downed a fresh double. I tried to change the subject. I failed. She went on.

"So your daddy went all the way down to the Lower East Side and brought back our mama to shame Rosie in her home. Well, Mama cried, and your father screamed and yelled. 'A sin,' they pleaded, and both told her she might die, and then what? Seven months later your mother gave birth to Janice." That was it. Auntie H. had finished her story, the sherry, as well as Nick and me.

"Have another," Nick said, and snapped again for the waiter.

By the time the veal piccata arrived Nick was drunk. I ate as fast as I could, but Auntie H. spiced each mouthful with long theatrical memories. She was heavily into her tours of Europe, where her second husband was knocking them dead at London's Palladium, when Nick's transformation completed itself.

"You don't want dessert do you, Auntie? It's so fattening." I was almost imploring, hoping against hope that I could save the evening.

"Actually," said Auntie H., happier than I'd seen her in years, and oblivious of Nick's new glower, the ominous slant of his brow, "I usually don't take sweets, but since this is an occasion . . ."

"Why? Are you afraid of getting fat?" slurred Nick. The gong went off, no saving it now.

"I've always kept my figure," said Auntie H. proudly.

"You can keep it, 'cause who the hell else would want it?" said Nick.

"What?" said Auntie H., totally unprepared.

"Who would touch your figure with a ten-foot pole? You old bag."

"Nick, please," I said, "or I'll leave." Leave to go where? Back to Buddy? The actors' drugstore? Daddy?

"Well, who would?" said Nick. "Who could get past her big, boring mouth?" Auntie H.'s biscuit tortoni lay in its ruffled cup, untouched.

"Just who do you think you're talking to?" Auntie H. fought back loudly. Heads turned.

Nick leaned across the table. "To you, you old bitch!" My heart stopped.

Auntie H. reached for her mink and rose to her five-feet-two inches. She looked very little.

"I'm going," she said, tears starting up in her eyes. "I'm sorry, Barbara." I didn't leave. I sat and watched her walk out the door.

The cab ride home was deadly. The elevator took forever to climb the thirty-one stories to our nest. I feigned drowsiness and leaned my face into its wall. I didn't want to look at him.

"Nick," I said after we walked into the apartment and he turned on the TV full blast, "Nick, I'm very tired. I want to go to sleep."

"Go to sleep. Who's stopping you?"

"Please lower the volume."

"Plug up your ears."

I'd taken to using ear stopples as a buffer to the noise in my life. The stopples weren't working. I could follow his thumping over the new carpeting. I could hear him bang into things, the shattering of a glass, the indistinguishable rantings. I had to sleep. Sleep would save me. In the medicine cabinet was Nick's bottle of three-grain Tuinals.

There were five left. I took one, went back, put the pillow over my head, and wished myself dead. Then he'd be sorry. I pushed off the pillow. The bumping and cursing seemed to have stopped. Perhaps he'd passed out. Had he passed out? Maybe he was hanging off the window again. Had he fallen? I moved, rather unsteadily, to the window and stuck my head out to see. The living-room ledges were vacant. Below me the gray pavement lay empty as well. I carefully got back in bed. The pill was working. Morning would restore me. I floated toward it.

"Shit," I said as Nick stumbled clumsily through the bedroom door, slamming the knob against the wall like a gunshot. "Oh, shit, oh, shit."

"I love you, Barb," Nick said, groping his way onto the bed. "I really love you. We'll have the next one. I promise." His mouth was on mine. "Bullshit." I spat into it. "Leave me alone."

"I want to have you, to love you," he said.

"Let me sleep. I want to sleep."

"Sleep later. We need to love each other now."

"Now! I need to sleep *now!*" Buried emotions started to bubble up. Hate, hot and impotent, burst in my head. Did I scream it? I left the bed in one brutal bound. Reached the bathroom before Nick realized I was gone. Opening the bottle in the dark, I shook the four remaining pills down my throat. I'd sleep, damn him. I slumped onto the john and laid my head on the sink.

"Barb? Where are you? I'm sorry. Hate me, but love me, too." I didn't answer; my brain was shriveling back.

"Barb?" He was off the bed, coming closer, "I'm sorry, Barb." I felt for his razor lying alongside me on the sink. I unscrewed it and removed the blade. "Don't come in, Nick." The blade pricked my fingers. "Leave me alone," I warned. Then I pushed the razor against the soft inner skin of my left wrist. And I pushed again. Hard. The razor sank into my flesh. I could feel the wet of my blood. It took the pain a moment to reach my brain. Had I really done that? Dropping the razor, I turned on the light. Blood splattered the white tiles. It wasn't such a big cut. But it gaped deep and black, and it spurted. Arteries spurt, my biology teacher had taught that. I stared at it.

"Are you crazy?" whispered Nick. "What have you done?"

I held my left arm out to him, the empty bottle still in its bloody grasp. "It's my first suicide," I said happily.

"How many did you take?" He seemed quite sober. I liked that. I could love him sober. I smiled at him, seductively. He wrapped a towel around my wrist and got my mink.

"I'll stain the fur." I worried as he got me into the cab.

The doctor forced the rubber tube down my throat. Not Dr. Mead, a new woman Nick had sent me to. I choked; she eased up, waited a moment, then shoved it hard all the way down.

"Silly child," she said, attaching a hand pump. The tube gouged and gagged me. She kept pumping. "Not enough to do serious harm," she reassured Nick, examining what she'd brought up from my depths. Had I intended serious harm? I didn't know. It was an act devoid of decision.

I don't remember the cab ride home, but I do remember waking up to bowers of flowers and a repentant Nick. "I don't know why I do these things," he said. "That poor old broad! And you." So it was roses for everyone. He sent three dozen long-stemmed American Beauties to flood my aunt's room at the St. Moritz, including with them a sad note of apology. When the flowers died, she saved the note.

Dear Aunt Hermosa,

I hope you will allow me the privilege to call you that, after my rudeness. My only excuse is Dewar's White Label. And I am afraid I use it too often. So for the sake of your niece, who I love and who loves you, I beg your forgiveness. Please give this damn fool another chance. You might even help him by doing it.

Yours,
Nick

Easy Come . . .

The grass was soft and green and moist. So soft it was difficult to remember we were in the desert, where it took gallons of water daily, sprinkled from sundown to sunrise, to keep every blade in Las Vegas green. I bared my feet to its freshness as I walked toward the pool. The grass and I, both displaced, put up flashy fronts. We were doing the best we could.

Smiling to the attendant, who promptly provided "Mrs. Condos" her lounge, mat, and towel, I lay back to take in the quiet. Those gamblers still testing the tables of this counterclockwise city were hidden in air-conditioned casinos. Or at the constant "chuck wagons" for late suppers or early breakfasts, depending. So the sweet long-shadowed morning was mine. Only the chirping of a few fat sparrows, frolicking in what passed for dew, marked the time. These birds of leisure were not out to catch early worms, but rather waiting for breakfast crumbs when hot rolls were buttered and sagas of last night's luck spread like marmalade across the tables that surrounded the Sahara Hotel's bright blue pool. I was beginning to understand these birds too well.

Somewhere several hundred yards away in a gilded room, Nick was snoring across the foot of our bed. His shod feet arched against carpeting, his burned-out cigar hanging from one hand, and an angelic smile on that part of his face not crushed into the covers. He'd half awakened me, crashing into the suite. But it wasn't till he stood weaving over me, shins propped against bed frame, thinking it the toilet, that I came to full attention.

"Nick, you madman, you're peeing!"

"Oh, sorry, so sorry, sweetheart." He half turned, then fell across the bed and seemed instantly out.

I pulled my wet way clear and made for the bathroom. My concern was for his money. Obviously the worst had happened. And I started blaming myself. For weeks I'd stayed up, my eyeballs dry in their sockets, keeping him company. Keeping him from drinking, from gambling. Keeping him amused under scrutiny. Trying to do my "job."

We'd achieved a kind of truce, Nick and I, since my bout with the razor. In a strange and terrible way it established me as a "character," and one of the family. Martha could ask me, "How are you fixed for blades?" and get a laugh. Trying to "be good," Nick would get up each morning, all charm, and make his own kind of effort. Which was not easy for him. And I knew it.

"How are you this morning, my beautiful wife?" he'd say, and soon we'd be making love. Usually on the couch, where he'd spent the last part of the night, returning from his "one drink with the boys." Nick was letting me "get some sleep."

So this summer I'd sworn to hang in and listen to as many comics' comics, late-night gags, Lord Buckley wit, and Joe Frisco lore as necessary. This summer I was going to earn my keep as wife, warden, and Wonder Woman. Warden was the role the rest of the group relied on. But lulled at last into false security and lapsing into fatigue, I'd wanted one night off.

"Sure, Barb," Nick said, "stay in bed. I'm fine. I'll hang

out with Jay. And stop looking scared. I promise I won't drink, maybe a beer or two, but that's all. And I won't go near the crap tables. And when they ask me, 'Where's Barbara?' I'll just say, 'They're not making child brides like they used to.' " He would. He liked the line. So much for good intentions.

I could have said, "Nick, you've broken your word and my heart again." But I'd stopped saying such things. They didn't help.

Everyone would enjoy horrifying me with details of drunken Nick screaming at pit bosses, demanding markers despite his self-imposed limits. I'd hear how they tried to protect him, till he turned so ugly they let him destroy himself. Getting an alcohol-possessed Nick away from a gambling table was like trying to wrest a bone from a starved dog. Polly Adler, who loved Nick, once watched me attempt it. After ten minutes' abuse, tough enough to stun even her, she'd removed me to the bar to talk to me "like a mother." Ordering me a Ramos gin fizz, she gravely advised me in her gravel voice, "Let the cocksucker blow it all. Nothing is worth losing your position as a lady."

There was no doubt about that either. I was to be the "lady" of our crowd. Whenever they needed one. So I'd hear about Nick's great run of luck, till it turned, the hundred-dollar chips to cocktail girls, and the hotel sheriff escorting him, shouting, from the casino, when the money was gone. I'd respond, reading my lines like a "lady." Later, laughing at himself, Nick would buy me some extravagance he could no longer afford, and I'd let him. I'd show it off to our group, and they'd say, "That crazy Greek." That was the script: "Easy come, easy go."

Should I swim across the pool to where the attendant was vacuuming up yesterday's tarnish? No, it would be too cold yet. I would wait and watch the silver plane slide across the sky. It was a morning sky so perfect that despite whatever else had happened, it washed me with a wave of promise, the kind of wave that can engulf you, at twenty-two, for no reason other than sheer beauty. I stopped thinking about Nick's money and thought just about Nick himself. About being on his arm. The pride I could take in his company, when he was sober. The same pride I had walking along the streets of my childhood, watching my father charm all comers. But even sober, Nick preserved his status as a drinker like a trophy of itself. I fingered my own little trophy. New to my neck, it was a gold talisman that Martha bought me from the casino gift counter. Martha bought lots of jewelry there. Sentimental stuff to keep her group feeling special. Lots of St. Christopher medals for Nick; for me, mezuzahs or Stars of David.

"She won't be satisfied," I'd murmured to Ernie, "till I'm wearing yellow stars stitched on all my clothes." Ernie had laughed and shown me Hebrew cuff links she'd given him. Allowing me to be bitchy, Ernie was my Vegas safety valve. We were pals of convenience; in entourage politics there's a need for allies and accomplices.

But I was glad to be alone with the sky. Later it would shimmer in the hundred-plus-degrees of July in Nevada, but now it was silent and very, very blue. Even the silver airplane slipping across my vision was silent. Suddenly it was gone. A half flash, then a dark line of descending smoke where it had just been. A line of smoke and black flecks. I had to be imagining this. There'd been no sound. One second it was there; next, black smoke straight down. I sat up and called to the pool man. "Did you see that plane?"

"What plane?"

"It was there"—I pointed—"a moment ago."

"Where?"

"Where that line of smoke starts. It's disappeared."

He smiled uncomfortably. "I didn't notice," he said politely.

"Haven't you a radio at your post?"

"Yes."

"Put it on. Something just happened."

"It's too early to put it on."

"Put it on softly."

"I'm not allowed, Mrs. Condos."

"Then call and tell someone. I think I just saw a plane blow up."

"I wouldn't know who to call. Will you excuse me, ma'am? I have to set the lounges." He left me staring at the smudge, widening and fading. It was erasing itself out. A room service waiter carrying a tray was passing.

"Did you notice a plane a moment ago?"

"Pardon?"

"Never mind," I said. The sky was once again a perfect unmarked blue.

It got hotter.

Spreading my arms, I watched the ripples they made as they moved through the water. I stroked the length of the pool, trying to time the thrust of my arms to the push of my legs. I was performing my one aquatic perfection, the breast-stroke, learned at camp, the summer of Marie. I liked it because I didn't have to put my face underwater. And my father, whose splashy strokes were self-taught in the East River, had admired it. Would he admire these luxurious laps while my husband lay in his drunken sleep? What would he have said to this husband altogether? Nick was so sure my father would have loved him. "Your pop and I would've been pals. He was a regular guy." I allowed Nick his visions, and he indulged mine.

"Hey, Barb," he would call out to me at a nightclub restaurant, "here's an old friend of your dad's." Depositing the man at my side, Nick would stand back, beaming with bounty, and watch as I listened to wonderful stories about my father. It pleased Nick to bring me such gifts. Usually, as soon as Nick was out of earshot, the "old friend" would ask sotto voce if I was "all right." And "Quite a playboy you got," followed by "If there's anything I can do for you . . ." The card he'd slip me would announce him as a liquor distributor or the representative of a produce company or a waste removal executive. In Vegas they sometimes owned points in the hotel. I held on to the stories and lost the cards.

The lounges were filling. I had some extras set up and reserved for our group.

"Have you heard anything yet?"

"About what?"

"The plane."

The attendant shook his head at my persistence and wandered off.

"Hi, babe." It was our drummer. He flipped the mat next to me and flopped onto it. Behind dark glasses I could see red-rimmed eyes fighting off the daylight. The faint aroma of illegal pot said he'd already prepared himself for the heat. He smiled lazily. "Oh, is the wild man locked up?"

"Sleeping it off."

"Martha's not talking to him."

"What happened?" The last throbs of possibility, all those secret maybe-it-wasn't-so-bad hopes started to fade.

"He was still cool after the second show. Then the next thing I knew he was at the craps. Rolling and roaring. Where were you?"

"Sleeping."

"Expensive nap. Martha tried to stop him. She really did. She tried her jokes, but they didn't work. But they had a fight. You know, I love the Greek and gave it a shot, too, but when he's bad . . ."

"How bad?"

"Probably the limit," the drummer said, tip-tapping his fingers on the mat. "He was still going strong at five when I split for the desert to catch this week's blast." This was the time the government regularly tested atom bombs in the Nevada deserts. And no one thought to complain.

I retired into cosmic acceptance, smiled elegantly, and asked, "Tell me about this week's blast."

The thing, it seemed, about watching an atom bomb blow on schedule was somehow not believing in it. That precise mushroom, celebrated in so much newsreel footage, was so familiar it became just another show. I would never go.

Earlier that year I'd sat with Nick watching one of the new big-money quiz shows that were so popular in the late fifties till someone yelled fraud. A ten-year-old blonde, with pigtails in her hair and spectacles on her nose, was, for a huge sum of money, describing the effects of strontium 90.

"It gathers in the clouds," she lisped, "then falls as rain and is absorbed by the grass. And when the cows graze on it, they store it in their milk in high dangerous density." She then went on to list its deadly effects. Everyone, even Nick, applauded her answer and her prize. No one heard her.

There was some thought among the patriots who pooh-poohed my alarm that I was subversive. It was more than that. I was terrified of cancer.

Melodye hit the water like a flying wedge, creating such a splash that growls greeted her from poolside. Surfacing, she churned happily, oblivious of local disapproval. Spotting me, she dived again, smooth as a seal, and came up from beneath, almost but not quite breaking my stroke. She flexed her broad shoulders, and a strap on her suit tore loose.

"I'll get a safety pin for it," she said, and in one bound was out of the pool, racing toward the room she shared with the maid next to her mother's suite.

"Bring a needle and thread," I called after her. "I'll sew it."

"Too much trouble," she shouted back, and I liked that. I trust a little sloppiness. Even after so much time in the hands of the sisters, she was still pagan. Quite like her father, and I loved her for it. In fact, we loved each other, which was good. We both needed it. I slipped into my private game. What I Love and Hate About Nick. Every day the list shifted. Today it went:

> I love Nick because he's untamed
> I hate Nick because he's out of control
> I love him because he's generous
> I hate him because he wastes his money
> Love that he's unconventional
> Hate that he's without convention
> Love him sober
> Hate him drunk
> Hate that he can't control it
> Hate that I can't stop him

The game started turning like a roulette wheel, becoming:

> I hate that I don't accomplish
> I love that I don't have to
> I hate being a lazy charmer
> I love learning to do it well
> I love making it pay off
> I hate that I love it

Enough of this empty stomach game. I was hungry. What about Mel? Had she eaten?

"Had any breakfast?" I asked when she bounded back. Her hair shrouded about her face at an awkward angle. I'd get Ernie to help it.

"I want pancakes and sausages and fried potatoes," Melodye said as we moved to a table, "and chocolate milk and pie. And I'll treat. I've got silver dollars." Yes, she had her father's ways.

"No," I said, always establishing position. "No, I'll sign."

"Did you," she asked as I spooned up a fresh strawberry floating in cream, "hear about the plane crash?"

"What did you hear?"

"A big liner went down in the desert right near here. The guy on TV said everyone's dead. Blown to pieces." Blown to pieces! As I sat here, waiting to deepen my tan. After a moment I said, "I saw it!" And wondered if I was bragging.

Melodye stared at me. Perhaps she wondered, too. "I wish I'd seen it," she said. "I never get to see anything." Was "I" becoming "them"?

I listened as poolside started buzzing with the crash. Its horror was paraded and marveled over. Body counts made up conversation. Between sips of screwdrivers or soda pop, speculation soared. The attendant was apologetic. He acted as if I deserved a medal. "She witnessed the whole thing," he kept telling people as he reported in new statistics for my approval. The only description he missed was the smell of it.

"Martha's pissed with me," said Ernie, piling onto a lounge and pulling me away from the crash to what was really important. Show biz. He said, "I need a little help with a problem. I want to do something sensational with Martha's hair tonight. Since Judy, she thinks I'm neglecting her. I may need an extra switch. Can I borrow yours?" I nodded. I was happy to contribute something.

Since Judy Garland arrived, all other entertainers became second-page news. Even Sinatra. *Everyone* loved Judy. It was the law. Actually Judy put the noses in our group a little out of joint. We murmured among ourselves how our

Maggie was a bigger talent, who didn't need eight chorus boys to make *her* look good. Ernie, the best in his business, had been drafted to do Judy as well. It meant exercising all his tact. By the time of Judy's opening night half of Hollywood had flown in.

"Shall I wear my black chiffon?" I'd asked Ernie the morning of the night of . . .

"Judy will be in black, you know, tails and tights, and there will be all those black tuxedos around. I'd go brighter. How about the pink satin and carry the little parasol bag?" And we were into our constant conversation: how to look.

"Too wide for the crowd."

"Perhaps that embossed beige knit with all the rhinestones and that great push-up bra. Might as well give 'em a little tit."

"Even if they're not all mine."

"And get long beige gloves, up to the armpit." Ernie had done the hair for *My Fair Lady*.

"Not with the knit, Ernie. For the knit, it's naked Marilyn Monroe time."

"Then wear the white georgette with the pearl beading and your little pearl tiara. Let's outqueen them. The place will be swamped with tit anyway. Long doeskins, and you'll be divine." It was definitely my role to be "divine."

The afternoon of the "night of" Ernie was frantic.

"Judy's made me promise to bring her something to get her *up* for the show. She's very nervous, and she made me swear."

"I've got diet Spansules," the drummer's wife offered.

"The point is," said Ernie, "she is not supposed to take anything. It's bad for her."

"So," reasoned Maud, the lawyer, whose job it was to hold the line, "what she needs is psychological first aid. Let's empty out the Spansules, fill them with sugar, and give her those." And that's what we did.

Judy went on, with sugar, and was sensational.

This afternoon in lotus land was wearing down. I sent Melodye to fetch me a sun hat. I was still unwilling to enter our suite.

"How's your dad?" I asked, tying it on.

"Well," said Melodye, "he's under the covers now, but I'm not sure he's undressed."

"Is he sleeping?"

"I guess so."

"It's up to eighty-five dead," the pool man rushed over to say, "and that's not counting the private plane." He seemed to be losing his audience.

Melodye was getting cranky. "I thought," she complained, "Daddy was going to take us water-skiing on Lake Mead."

"Maybe tomorrow."

"It's always tomorrow for me."

"That's not true." I defended Nick, but usually it was.

"Boy, she's going to be a headache when she grows up," said someone as Melodye shrugged off. Melodye scowled and kept walking.

Twenty minutes later she returned looking secret and pleased. Plopping down on the grass at my side, the pocket of her terry-cloth clinking, she wanted to tell me something.

"I just," she said with hushed excitement, "won thirty-six silver dollars." She jammed her hand into her heavy pocket and jingled the coins.

"What were you doing in the casino?" I whispered back from under my hat. "You're not allowed."

"I wasn't *in* the casino, Barbara, *dear*. Only almost. I asked a man to play me a number, and it came in. So there!"

"Stop that"—I stayed her arm—"and keep it to yourself. It's against the law for minors to gamble."

What might her nuns make of her now? Melodye had been the pet of Miami's Sacred Heart Academy. Really wanting to belong somewhere, she'd converted from Greek Orthodox to Roman Catholic, winning parochial hearts and a lot of attention. At ten the nuns had seemed the best bet she'd found.

"You must meet the mother superior," Melodye had said to me, on my honeymoon, when I visited her at school. Solemnly she'd taken my hand and led me through the garden, the chapel, and into the inner sanctum behind the altar. Melodye's determination was only equaled by the mother superior's surprise at finding us in so unlikely a spot. She ushered us out to less sanctified ground.

"This is Barbara, my father's new wife," Melodye said formally, adding, "She's nice. You can't even tell she's a Jew."

The mother superior shot me a glance and took a bit of time studying her hands. Finally, looking at Melodye, she'd said, "Christ, our Lord, was a Jew."

"Is that so?" said Melodye, in amazement after two years of religious training. "I never knew that."

In the recess of my memory my father had lifted a knowing eyebrow.

"You better get out of the sun," Ernie advised. "Why don't you get shampooed? I'll be so busy with Martha I won't have time to do you." A small surge of jealousy rose up from the rich catalog of my hidden jealousies, but I squashed it. It was too dangerous a feeling.

One of our "kids" was sitting under layers of salon foam, turning her from dross to gold. "I needed a new look," she said as the beautician tilted me back against the sink. "Why not?" The rush of water drowned my words. Slumped beneath my dryer, I watched the new blond toss her curls in pleasure. Then I closed my eyes. "Don't be a mope," my father used to warn. "Stay away, alive." But I kept my eyes closed. Suddenly the drummer's wife was shaking me.

"Something terrible has happened," she shouted.

"You mean, the plane?" I asked.

"What plane? I mean Melodye. Melodye just poured a bottle of beer over that chorus kid's head. You know, the flirty one she didn't like. The girl was showing off her new hair, and Melodye picked up a bottle of beer and poured it over her head."

"Oh, my God."

"The girl started to cry something awful."

"What did Melodye do?"

"She asked her not to tell Martha and handed her a bunch of silver dollars."

"Then what?"

"The girl took the money, that's what. Maggie's going to kill her." I dropped the dryer lower on my head.

Later, back in our suite, I found Nick in the bathroom, showered and sober, dots of toilet paper decorating his newly shaved chin.

"I'm sorry, Barb," he said, bleary-eyed and sad. "I really am."

"I know, Nick, so am I. I should have stayed with you."

"No, you've been a goddamned trouper. It's not you, I keep telling you, it's me."

"Oh, Nick." I felt the salt of failure wash the back of my throat. "Oh, Nick." We'd lived through this scene before, and I was out of words.

"Fuck it," said Nick. "It's only money. We'll make it up in Miami this fall."

"That," I said, "is the difference between Greeks and Jews. You say 'fuck it,' and I say Kaddish for the dead."

"We are both wrong, aren't we?" He changed to a smile. "C'mon," he said, "let's get some chili. I'm starved."

Nick turned off the TV just as the announcer was tally-ing the score of the crash. His fact-filled voice enhanced the foreboding I'd been avoiding facing all day. My period was late. Again. And I was frightened of facts to come.

... Easy Go

Five months later I lay listening to a bird outside a hospital window. My hospital window. A Florida bird, surprising me with its strange, insistent sound. I was surprised that I noticed it, much less cared what kind it was. But it seemed I did. Maybe my nurse would know. Miss Wilmott knew about things like that, the difference between night-blooming jasmines, the life of poinciana trees, when the tides changed. But a man, a lawman, wouldn't let me hear the bird. He was demanding my *sane* attention. To seem sane was all-important, Maud had warned. The Payoff to cover my "little mistake" would have brought me a Jaguar sports car. It didn't much matter. I couldn't drive.

The "law" was drowning out my bird, politely demanding my attention. "Little lady," the sheriff said, slumping further into the blue Naugahyde armchair to stare at my tubes, "little lady, you ought to be more careful." I lowered my eyes and nodded. He removed his ten-gallon hat and rubbed at the dent it left across his brow. "Doc says he don't know how you-all got hold of those pills." I waited. "Doc

215

thinks," he went on, playing with the sweatband, "that you took them from his bag. Now, you didn't do that, did you? Suicide, little lady, is a criminal act, and that's a fact."

"I don't remember about the pills," I lied. But of course, I did. Playboy Doc had put that bottle of fifty three-grain Tuinal right in my hand, saying, "Here's some sleep shit, Barb." Then he'd taken Nick out for a "few drinks." Nick needed relief. Having to accompany me to Cuba himself this time, since Maud refused, had been a strain on him. So Doc plunged some Demerol in my hip to hold me for the night. And "Wouldn't it be silly," he'd said, "for Nicky just to hang around and watch you sleep?" They talked me into it. They'd talked me into a second trip to Cuba. Why not this?

The sheriff was still talking. "You won't do this no more?" he asked. "Will you, little lady?"

"No," I promised, smiled him out of the room.

"Has Barb done it again?" I could imagine people asking. "Pills or razor?"

"Both!"

"She should give up razors, too messy."

"You must have answered properly," said Miss Wilmott. "The sheriff removed the guard from your door."

"I didn't know there was a guard."

"That's because you haven't been out of your room. If your pressure is good, we can consider a wheelchair ride into the sun. It's pretty by the pier, lots of flowers. And why don't we get ourselves pretty, too?" she said, bringing me my first mirror. I discovered I'd finally achieved *Harper's Bazaar* cheekbones. Should I consider that a silver lining? I pinked them up carefully. Too much rouge on thin cheeks bespoke half-crazy ladies who walked streets talking to themselves. And as Maud cautioned, craziness was touchy in my position.

Everyone smiled as we wheeled by. They were proud to have saved me. Suicide was a mortal sin.

"We are all so relieved to see you better," said Father Laughlin as we passed him on the ramp. I, my wheelchair, nurse, and rolling IV stand.

"Thank you," I said, and certainly meant it.

"All the sisters prayed for you."

"Thank them." I meant that, too.

"How's Nick?"

"All right."

"Tell him to be a good boy for me and to behave himself."

"Uh-huh."

"Do you know what time it is? Be careful. You'll upset her intravenous." It was Miss Morgan, my night nurse, struggling to get Nick upright and off me and my bed. It was dark. I'd been asleep, and sleep was such a luxury.

"Leave me alone, you old bag." Nick was making a lot of noise. "She's my fucking wife."

"Sh, Nick, " I said, "it's late."

"I'm going for Sister Francine," declared Miss Morgan, and I heard her feet clip down the hall.

"Hiya, Barb," said Nick, crooked smile, eyes glazed. "I wanted to kiss you good-night."

"You better go, Nick."

"Fuck 'em, let 'em throw me out. I'm not such a villain, you know. You know that. Admit it." I admitted it, and he grabbed to embrace me.

"Nick, you're hurting my arm."

"Oh, sorry, my darling, I'm sorry." Straightening up, he dropped his cigar, and bending again to get it, he slipped to the floor. Fumes of Dewar's White Label floated up from the left of my bed.

"Nick, get up."

Miss Morgan and a lot of starched white women bustled in and almost tripped over him. "I think he's passed out," I said.

"I'll get an orderly to get him to his car," said the sister.

"Have the orderly drive him or let him sleep in the car." What an effort to be effective. And really did I care, or was it habit? "He's had a few drinks," I continued to explain.

"Oh, I know all about Nick," said Sister Harmonia, redeeming his cigar and depositing it in the toilet. "I've dealt with him before." She patted Nick's hand. She liked him.

A large man came to drag Nick off, like so much used

laundry. I could hear his voice echoing back from silent halls, insisting he was all right and telling the world to go fuck itself.

"Do You Know Who I Used to Be?" he shouted, and I realized I was smiling. Poor funny Nick. I liked him, too! When had I gone from being upset over him to be upset with him? It occurred to me that Nick drank to forget he was a drunk, but I never could forget. I had failed to restore him as I was supposed to do. And now he had disturbed my needle, and it hurt. Maybe it would be all right. It wouldn't. Miss Morgan fetched the resident.

Blond and big and capable, the yawning young doctor removed the intravenous.

"The needle, it slipped through the vein," he said in brisk German accents. "I will find a better place. Relax, open your hand. You have such beautiful hands," he said. "Like a Van Dyke. You know Van Dyke?"

"Of course."

"Ah," he said, "an American with culture. I see you in the morning. *Schlummen Sie gut.*"

The *Schlummen* wasn't so *gut*. It wasn't even *Schlummen*. But I lay very still, the sky outside my window black, and listened to the click of Miss Morgan's needles. She sat and knitted in the dark, till softly she snored off. So God had saved me to lie in darkness. Could that be? Had he done it through the German resident? Eventually and reassuringly the sky turned violet, then pink, into morning. Godlike magic.

"Was it the German doctor who saved me?" I asked Miss Wilmott as I pushed away breakfast.

"No," she said, pushing it back. "It was a young Texas intern. He's left. But he was very dedicated to you, slept right here on a cot till you were safe. No, the German doctor wasn't on this floor then. You must try to eat."

"Does the German doctor know I'm Jewish?" I can't eat.

"What a funny question. I didn't know you were Jewish myself."

"I dreamed last night about my friend Anna Berger," I told her, pushing at the tray of ham and grits again. "I haven't seen her since grammar school. Her family were refugees from Germany." Miss Wilmott wasn't listening. Giving up on breakfast, she was getting a brush for my hair.

"Not too tight?" she asked as she braided me.

"No," I said, "fine." Teresa used to pull my braids too tight. Teresa! My God, I hadn't spoken to them since I left New York. They'd think I was dead.

"They brought you in DOA," Maud had said. "Dead on arrival. How much do you remember? You know, they found you both in bed. Nick snoring peacefully at your side, stained in your blood."

"I remember nothing," I had said. It wasn't quite so. The last thing I recalled were the stairs, falling, crawling, bleeding up the duplex stairs, a note pinned to my nightie. Too bad no one saved the note. What had I written? I could have framed it. "That's my last suicide hanging on the wall," I could have said.

I asked Miss Wilmott to help me call my sister in New York.

"You've been in the newspapers here," Janice said. Her voice sounded tight.

I tried to warm her up. "Another item for my memory box."

"You don't have a memory box anymore," Janice snapped. "I burned it."

"You did what?"

"I burned all your stuff. Your dumb box. Everything. In the incinerator."

"What's everything?" I was shouting, Miss Wilmott looked perturbed. I tried to lower my voice.

"Daddy's letters," she said flatly.

"Just the ones to me or everyone's?"

"Everyone's."

"My diaries?"

"Yes."

"My poetry?"

"Yes."

"The picture albums?"

"Just yours."

"Melvin's stuff?"

"Some."

"Oh, my God. How could you?" I was yelling again.

"Don't yell at me. If the stuff was so damn important to you, why'd you leave it here?"

"Couldn't you have called to say you were going to do it?"

"Call who? I just did it; the papers said you were going to die. So I just dumped it all in the incinerator."

"Dump it in the toilet," Doc had ordered that final phone call, "and flush it away."

"Nick," I'd said on the first call. The hotel operator had located him and Doc at Ollie's bar. "Nick, I'm in a lot of pain. Something's wrong." Doc had taken the phone. "Relax," he'd said. "You're just passing a little clot and overreacting because of the Demerol."

"I hope so," I whispered, and lay on my side, waiting for the clot to pass. The pain grew worse.

Worse became insanity. I was falling off the bed. Then, crawling across the floor, I got to the bathroom. Doc's clot was stuck. I tugged at it with my hand, and it came out, head first. My clot was green and purple against the white tile floor, an almost man-thing in a shiny sac. I could see its sex.

"That damn clinic never finished the job." Doc said accusingly over the phone. "Get it into the toilet and flush it good," he'd said.

"It's transfusion time," interrupted Miss Wilmott, full of cheer.

The German doctor arranged my bags and bottles. "I was born in Bonn," he said, trying to make it a social occasion, "but I was raised in Berlin. Things were bad then; money wasn't worth anything. You had to carry a suitcaseful to buy groceries." He worked as he talked. "I was only a child, but they told me. Shall I call you Barbara, and you call me Siegfried? That is better, yes?" Pausing, Siegfried sat on the edge of my bed. "Do you play chess?" he asked.

"Not seriously," I said, thinking of Buddy.

"Ah, chess is either serious or nothing. I learned in the Russian prison camp. I was captured on the eastern front."

All Germans who weren't Swiss seemed to have fought in the East, I thought.

"We had nothing to do all day," said Siegfried. "It was so boring you can't imagine, so we made a chess set. No, you cannot imagine such boredom. Do you know, for six months we ate nothing but cabbage, borscht, and potatoes?"

"That doesn't sound so bad," I said.

"Just try it." Siegfried laughed. "Actually the food here isn't much better. I was on duty twenty-four hours, and all I could get was ham and cheese and milk."

"You should be working at Mount Sinai Hospital," I said. "I hear the food is good there."

"No, thank you. They work foreign interns to death at Mount Sinai." He smiled. I smiled back.

"I wonder whose blood I'm getting?" I said, trying to be social, too. Why was I working so hard to get someone I didn't like to like me?

"Don't worry. It isn't Jewish or anything. Would you mind the needle in the back of your beautiful hand? It hurts a little going in but will be more comfortable for you as the transfusion goes on."

He readied the needle. Why didn't I say something? Tell him I'm Jewish. Was I afraid? Had I been "saved" to be a coward? He was still talking about Russia. "If you silly Americans had any sense," Siegfried said, "you would have rearmed us and let us finish the Russians off for you. Cold war, pah! You would be thanking God for us."

"I thank God," I said suddenly and joyfully, "for Stalingrad. And for Russian peasants who threw themselves under German tanks."

"You're crazy!"

"No, Jewish. Hymie Caplin's daughter and Jewish for five thousand years." The needle was tearing my hand. "Jewish like the blood at Mount Sinai. Jewish and still alive in spite of you. Even in spite of myself. And I'm glad."

He slapped adhesive over the needle, did something with a valve, and walked out of my room.

Had I really wanted to die? Yes. Finally and forever and without heaven or hell. I'd mistrusted this world. God seemed a god of terrors. Years away, when mystics will assure me death ends nothing, I will cringe at the idea. Blankness was what I wanted. Not to punish Nick, as before, or as the "cry of help" people reassure themselves suicide is. No, only to end the pain.

However, the God of the Jews and everyone else had decided otherwise. And I was glad, glad to be alive to curse at Siegfried. Glad to smile at Nick's idiocy. As for Nick, I'd find a way. Or if not, well . . . I grew dizzy with gladness. But something was happening. Miss Wilmott and Siegfried were pulling my needle and unhooking me from the blood in a kind of rush.

"It's all right dear," Miss Wilmott was reassuring, "just a little reaction. It happens. Sometimes the body doesn't like the new blood." Siegfried said nothing but carried the rejected, non-Jewish transfusion from my room.

Suddenly it was important to me to speak to Janice again, to tell her I might not have a memory box, but I had life. And so did she. And we needn't be so scared.

"Hello, Janice, it's me. I want to tell you—"
"I'm glad you called." She cuts me off. "Teresa is angry I didn't put her on. She saw those headlines, and she's been all upset. Here, talk to her."
"Barbrula? It's you."
"It's me." I'd tell Janice later. Now I take pleasure in the voice of Teresa, caring.
"You okay?"
"Yes, I'm okay. I'm fine."
"But they say you die."
"They were wrong. I'm still here." A little silence. A little sigh. A little question.
"And you baby?"
"No more."
"Again, no more?"
"Again. I'm sorry." So, for the fourth time in my life, I hear Teresa cry. She was so sure, as I turned pear-shaped, she'd have a new "Caplin baby, for us happiness." At last I stop her, saying, "Teresa, darling, it's long distance," which as with Auntie H., works.

"Okay," she acknowledges, and Janice is back on. A little softened.

"Listen, Barbara, when you come back, I'm going to change your diet. You can get strong and healthy again with fruits and vegetables." Vegetables sound better than ham, which is meat, which is flesh.

"Sure," I promise, and Miss Wilmott helps me hang up the receiver and gets me to the commode.

I find a copy of the *Miami News* dated December 11, 1956, lying neatly folded on the tank of the toilet, weighted down by a jar of Vaseline. Two weeks old, but still news to me, so I pick it up and read:

NICK CONDOS' WIFE
FIGHTS PILL DEATH

by Milt Sosin

Barbara Condos, 23-year-old wife of Nick Condos, actor's agent and former . . . critical condition at St. . . . "40 to 50 barbiturate capsules," says her . . . Barbara, a daughter of Hymie Caplin, New York fight promoter, has been unconscious since . . .

I put down the paper. It must have belonged to the night nurse. "Never mind, Babsie," I almost hear my father's voice saying, "yesterday's news belongs to yesterday."

Siegfried, his head cautiously peeking around my door, tried a nervous smile. I smiled back, easily. Armistice.

"*Ja ja*," Siegfried said, "you are feeling better."

"I'm making a comeback. *Grüss Gott.*"

"So you own some German words."

"Why not?" I called after him.

Miss Wilmott watched me finish my whole fruit salad. And then there it was, with its strange little song, my bird.

"Miss Wilmott," I said, "let's take a peek at that bird." She wheeled me to the window.

"Why, it's a spotted-breasted oriole." She pointed. "Some blew in on a hurricane a few years ago. They're kind of rare. We are lucky to see him."

"We certainly are."

Then, singing its odd sound, the beautiful yellow bird with black dots spread its wings and flew. And so eventually would I. In the end it would seem easier to leave Nick than to kill him. So I will leave. And we all will grieve. Especially Teresa. After five years she had managed to accept Nick as family. Teresa loved the family.

Teresa

Standing in the space allowed to steerage for their breath of air, Teresa can see nothing of Halifax Harbor. But excitement ripples the decks of the ship, and she can certainly feel that. It's over. She has passed through all the small horrors and humiliations passengers of her class are heir to and has survived.

Of course, that one loss, the loss of her mother's recordings, which were pressed the important year her church choir toured, was brutal. That clear lead voice sent along to comfort Teresa in foreign places all broken during the theft of her father's brandy. She keeps the pieces anyway. Never mind, perhaps she can replace them when she goes home. At least in a few years she'll be able to return her father's flat leather purse bulging with Canadian gold. Till then she'll try not to mourn.

Now, what are they saying? Something about a train to Winnipeg. No, she must get to Toronto. Her brother is waiting for her there. She doesn't want to board. "Get on," the man in uniform tells her in bad Russian, while pushing her toward the line. "You have to." He insists harshly: "You signed to work the farms. The farms are in Winnipeg." A whistle blows.

"What?" She knows some Russian, but not enough to be sure of what he is saying. He repeats himself in angry tones. It still means nothing to her. She signed so many things. Her chest cramps with fright. Her shoulder wants to jerk away from this hand poking it. But where to run? The crew is already hosing down the area she used for her small person and belongings. She is prodded into line, turned into cattle, just like the rest. The rest are not talking or arguing. Their faces say it all. Not hers. She will wait for her moment.

Feeling for the part of her blouse where her brother's address is sewn, she swears she will get to him. Her grip on her linen satchels stiffens. The year is 1928, the month is May, the wind is moist, and Teresa has just turned twenty-two.

The train slows down to a tentative stop. On the rickety wooden wall that signifies a station, a sign says CORCORAN. And next to it a simplified map shows the word "Toronto," a dot away. Teresa hesitates, then grabs the moment, her sack, and slips to the open door. It's only a few steps from her seat. It means a small jump to the ground. She does it quickly and deftly. She has jumped from the bare backs of her father's horses too many times to consider this a hazard. However, the little couple who had been crowded into the seat with her and who followed her move have more trouble. He wrenches his shoulder and she lands on her knees.

Once down, they hide behind the wall with pounding hearts and wait for the train to move on. Finally they hear it go. And when all noise and smell of it disappears, they run like crazed rabbits down the country road. Small wild flowers cluster here and there. Teresa would like to pick one to tuck in her braid but doesn't. She is leading a band of three.

When the tall blond man catches up with them, they huddle against each other. Teresa realizes they are still wearing their Winnipeg tags on their bosoms. She puts her hand over hers. Could he be the police? Was an alarm sent from the train? Removing his hat and rubbing the heel of his hand across his forehead, damp from rushing, he speaks politely.

"Please don't be afraid," he says in proper Polish, and smiles anxiously at them. Especially at her. His eyes are very blue. "My name is Valchek Sadowski, and I am a friend."

Later, when she comes to tell of this, she will call him an angel. Now she holds on to her breath.

"Don't be frightened, please," he repeats softly. "I am from Krakow, and I will help you." First, he tells them, they must come to where he lives, and he will give them supper and listen to their stories. But now it's starting to rain, and they have to hurry. It's not far.

He rents a small cottage in a little cluster, all exactly the same. Perhaps "cottage" is too fancy a word. He has no family in Canada, where he has been for five years, working in a factory and sending his money home. He treats them like cousins. Which helps. Teresa asks where to relieve herself. Different from the stinking cubbyholes of the ship or the closet on the train none of them dared use, this is a real room, clean and cool. A shaped wooden seat crowns a porcelain pedestal. But after soiling the clear water, how to make it clean again? Nervously she pokes at the chrome workings, and then one experimental push suddenly releases a torrent. My God, she's broken it! What should she do? Miraculously it quiets down and regains crystal calmness. Washed away are all the droppings. So this is how the pee places work in this new world.

Then, full of Valchek's soup and bread, they sleep on his floor, and in the morning he escorts them back to the rambling station. Like a "good angel."

Teresa hands him all twenty-five of her hoarded Canadian dollars. Taking what he needs to buy her a ticket to Toronto, Valchek carefully folds and gives her back the rest. She must be very careful, he warns. "Be slow to unfold it." She nods. He copies her brother's address on two pieces of paper, one for her and one for him so he can write her, and waits with her for the train. He is missing a morning's work for this, but he doesn't mind. He is really happy to help. Teresa kisses his hands before climbing on board and waves from the window till he is out of sight.

As the train rumbles along, this window of hers frames nothing spectacular, which is fine with her. Waiting to see Toronto is enough. A man in a plaid suit is trying to flirt with her. He likes her, she can tell; he's been working so hard to catch her eye ever since she sat down. It must be English he's speaking. How will she ever learn to sound like that? She smiles back, moving her hands helplessly to signal her lack of language. He keeps trying, talking louder as fields turn to lots and a city creates itself before her eyes. She now wants this man to shut up. She needs all her attention to hear if the conductor says "Toronto." "Sh," she says loudly. The plaid man is startled but obeys.

"Tor-on-to," singsongs the conductor. Smiling her apologies, Teresa pushes by to get to the doorway. It takes forever for the train to stop. But this time she doesn't have to jump. This time little metal stairs are placed beneath her feet, and Teresa steps into Toronto in style.

Those cars with words painted on them must be the taxis Valchek explained about. She approaches one carefully. The driver spits out his toothpick, studies her piece of paper, and signals her in. Later she will find out that he charged her two important dollars for a fifty-cent trip. But now all that's important is that he knows where to take her and is willing to do it.

Stopping before the wooden house with the stairs in front, he points her to its gray door. Stepping onto the curb, she finds herself staring into a shiny black face. She has never seen or heard of such a thing. Wheeling in terror, she wants to get back into the taxi. It's already moving down the street. Crossing herself, she circles widely and sneaks by this apparition and up the steep stairs to the gray door where a fat woman in a housedress is fanning herself with the morning mail.

"Kowalski," she says timorously. The woman seems to understand. She then goes for her first English word. "Sister" she pronounces, hoping it's as Valchek taught her. Pointing to her heart, she repeats, "Sister." The landlady takes her to his room.

Sitting on her brother's bed in the cramped darkness, she waits. When she is back in Carpathia, she and her mother will laugh at all her fears. She will make the stories funny. She stares at the bundles at her feet and clasps her hands tightly as if in prayer. She is not praying; she is just holding on to herself. "Pins and needles," she will someday describe, "every bit." When the door opens to his familiar silhouette, Teresa leaps forward to embrace him. Startled, he pushes her away. Hard. Something she will always recall. "It's me, Tereska," she calls from where she tripped. The Carpathian sound of her Polish goes straight to his heart. He lifts her to her feet. Yes. Yes. And he can get her a room; someone just moved out. And yes, find her a job; someone he knows has a wife in housework. And he's happy. He dries his eyes with a worn sleeve. No, the black man was not a fiend, just an African; they are all black from there. He'll show her on the new atlas he saved for. Yes, she's safe. Teresa is surprised by his shabby appearance in this land of plenty. But she doesn't say so. And she isn't quite safe. The narrow, recently vacated room is not empty after all. Its last tenant left behind his bedbugs. The bugs nip at her from the mattress, sheets, and pillow. They sting her to her feet, where she spends the night whisking them off. In the morning her brother returns from his night shift to find her still standing. Speckled and spent.

The next two days they use her brother's bed in turns. Just when the landlady is ready to object, Teresa moves to Borden Street, where she has been hired as a family maid.

"She accepted me right away," Teresa brags to her brother as they walk back to get her things. Teresa's braids are pulled so tight across her crown they are giving her a headache, but her polished apple cheeks are bunched in pleasure. Now she will be a person again.

She gave her name as Mary, it seemed easier to her than Tereshka and somehow offered a better protection. Important if you are going to share a roof with Jews. "In Canada," her brother explains, "Jews have a good place." She is not to worry. And, despite what she may believe, they are generous. She listens, but in Carpathia such a thing could never be. In her town only two Jewish families live and work. They've been there for generations. One butchers, under kosher laws, the red meat hardly eaten by villagers and sells it to the city. The other owns a saloon where Teresa's father and his farm friends take their after-work vodka and listen to the news. The Jew owns the only radio in the district. In Teresa's town one might tilt a glass with a Jew or buy his goods. Certainly no one would ever harm one, but no one would willingly touch one either.

The Dwarkin family nickname her Marinka. And Marinka she remains for the next three years. Mrs. Dwarkin is deaf and devoted to quiet Marinka. They give her a lovely little room with ruffled curtains right next to the room of their daughters. She has her own radio and a mirror and a window that faces south over the back garden. Waking to the craw of a crow reminds her of home. And the small Dwarkin girls cling to her skirts and kiss her good-night. Their parents talk to her lovingly in Russian, and all in all, she feels she has done "okay," as her brother likes to say, using the Americanism with verve.

"I understand them good," Teresa explains to him on their Sunday excursions to church. She is free every Sunday from after her breakfast till 10:00 P.M. They attend Roman Catholic though they are Eastern Orthodox. God will forgive. "I just can't speak back."

Actually the only persons she can speak with are her brother and an occasional churchgoing Pole. And if her Russian is muddled, she has no English at all. A serious problem the day she gets lost.

As well as her Sundays, when her brother collects her in the morning and returns her at night, she has Thursday afternoons for herself. On her first Thursday she sat in her room, looked out the window, and listened to her radio. Understanding little but proud to do so. On her second Thursday she set out for a brave walk.

Borden Street is in a pleasant treelined part of Toronto, and Teresa, high with adventure, rounds its corner and keeps going. June rosebuds on their trellises scent the warm afternoon air. And boxes of geraniums garland windows. Her eyes absorb one exotic pleasure after another. Imagine a boulevard so ample that horse carts and motorcars and a train, without an engine, that spits electric sparks from an overhead wire all move compatibly down its cobblestones.

She admires the wide, clean pavement under her feet and all at once realizes she has no idea where she is.

I haven't walked for long, she reassures herself, turning back. My house must be near. She can't find it. She turns corners, looks up and down streets, and recognizes nothing.

When the mounted policeman, with his broad-brimmed hat, climbs down from the grandest horse she has ever seen to ask her why she is crying, she can't tell him. Finally a bearded ragman rattles by, his horse more ancient than his clothes, and is enlisted for help.

After much chin scratching and nodding he gets the message, which he translates brokenly to the mountie. The mountie turns out to be a gallant. He parades Teresa, perched on the wobbly cart alongside the ragman, through turns till Borden Street suddenly appears and her house is in front of her.

Teresa's brother is bothered by this story. "You must always have your address in your hand when you walk." So through twelve changes of season Teresa walks away her Thursday afternoons with a cardboard in her left hand, announcing to all interested, her name, language, and domicile. That is, until she takes to walking out with John.

"Don't just stand there," her brother admonishes her under the crepe paper rosette "dance." He knows John to be a churchgoing Pole who holds a steady job at the Royal York Hotel, and he brought her to this social hoping they might like each other. Teresa hasn't mentioned going home in a while. And Valchek, from Corcoran, just wrote to say he got engaged.

John is holding out his hand and waiting for Teresa to step forward. She likes his face; his black hair, blue eyes, and pink cheeks remind her of the boy she left behind in Carpathia. Encouraged by the smile, the enthusiasm of the band, and the giggles and cries of the dancers whirling by, she takes the inviting hand and is swung onto the floor. It's a heady harvest celebration, and ancient peasant rhythms pulse. Elbows fly and skirts kick high and the floorboards burn the leather from her shoes. She sings to the songs; some are well known to her. John's hands are square and hard and hold her fast. His short, sturdy body matches her own. For the first time since boarding the boat at Dansk, she is not afraid.

They rush to each other at social after social, let the accordion gush hot or cool. And they dance. They dance till their thighs ache and their breaths burst. At Christmas he proposes. And they are married in May.

"Are you sure, Marinka?" Mrs. Dwarkin shouts at her, cupping her ear for the reply. She pours Teresa steaming tea from a gleaming silver samovar salvaged from Russia. This kind of tea Teresa understands: the bags, no. She passes her the cube of sugar to be held by the front teeth. Teresa has polished that samovar many times but was never before so honored as to taste from it. They drink out of five inches' worth of red lacquer cups with no handles, also prized possessions. Teresa's fingers embrace the warmth of these wood "glasses" without burning. She nods that yes, she is sure. Mrs. Dwarkin sighs, sips in the news with her sugar, and enough has been said. Occasionally the image of the boy with the sad eyes who promised to wait for her return pulls at her heart. But not too often.

Then she manages a bit of foolishness she will regret all her life. In the house next to the Dwarkins works a Ukrainian girl. Eventually she and Teresa exchange shattered Russian greetings. Then small talk. One fine April afternoon, under a surprisingly warm sky, they pause in the hanging of their separate washes and walk to the fence between.

"So you marry, Marinka!" Olga says, perhaps wondering how this old-fashioned greenhorn has managed such a trick while she, who chews gum and talks Canadian, can't.

"Yes."

"You should fix up."

"I bought one pretty dress."

"I mean your hair. Those silly braids. And look your shoes."

Teresa looks down at the lace-ups she bought for two dollars. "They are strong."

"Ugly. Black high heels; patent you should get."

"What about the hair?"

"Cut short. Real American."

A half hour later a teetering Teresa regains the Dwarkin kitchen, two long braids, still tied, lying next to the brogues in the bottom of her empty basket. Ninety cents' worth of Olga's cast-off high patent-leather heels squeezed onto her feet. Her ankles buckle, and her toes won't go right.

"Marinka," calls out Mrs. Dwarkin, her hand to her breast, "what have you done?"

"What have you done?" repeat the little girls, looking at the crudely sliced hanks, hanging below her earlobes. Between sighs, Mrs. Dwarkin does what she can to even it off. By the time her brother sees her, Teresa can stand straight in her shoes and almost wave a few tendrils toward her cheeks.

"I don't blame John if he refuses you."

John doesn't refuse. "It will grow," John says, and marries her right on time.

She packs her braids with her mother's broken recordings, to be kept and wept over in private.

The Dwarkins attend her wedding with pleasure and relinquish her service reluctantly. But Mrs. Dwarkin must have a sleep-in to act as her ears. So for a while, with their references, she goes to work for a rabbi. Then for a while she doesn't get work at all. Then she and John set south for New York, where her language handicap will again become her burden. For the next fifty years it will make her wisdom sound too simple and her advice adorable but not to be heeded. At least not by us Caplins, who inherit her in 1937.

"I lucky," she will say while shoveling the hated Wheatena into my five-year-old mouth. "In Winnipeg they give five dollars in one month. In Toronto they give thirty. In Manhasset, forty, and Mrs. Caplin give me forty-five."

I think forty-five dollars quite fabulous myself. Especially since I was reduced to five cents a week after abusing my candy-store privileges. Teresa is a wellspring of optimism. Except when superstition comes to sit on her tail. Then luck becomes the all-powerful goddess to be spoken of most politely.

In Manhasset, where she had the forty dollars, Teresa worked for a family of Scots. John had an aunt in Bayside they'd gone to, seeking shelter from the hard times of 1932.

For that job she tells her first Depression lie. John is reduced from husband to boyfriend. The Scottish family, it seems, prefer its help single. On her day out she and John barricade themselves behind the doors of the bedroom John shares with a cousin and sneak an hour of semibliss. John's aunt is almost as rigid as Teresa's employer.

"Very strictly," Teresa recalls of the Scotswoman with resignation. "Very nice but strictly." Every two weeks on Friday at 4:00 P.M. Teresa must wash her hands, neaten her hair, and stand, in clean apron, outside the study door. After a moment or two the lady of the house will tell her to enter and approach the desk. Then Teresa must ask for (or it will not be given) her salary.

"My wages, thank you," Teresa has been taught to pronounce. John decides Canada may be the better deal after all.

Before returning, they take a weekend for modest sightseeing in Manhattan. They've been there only twice in three years. Leaving their trunk in the cheap hotel room near St. Marks Place, they promenade the nearby streets. It's an Eastern European neighborhood, and they are comfortable. Teresa is wearing the print dress and felt hat with feathers handed down from her Manhasset lady, and John has on his best and only black. They watch other weekend strollers, some wheeling baby carriages. They talk of the children they hope to make when there is money and time. Lost in such daydreams, they almost don't hear the man calling to John by name.

"Benyo," he calls back, and rushes Teresa along to embrace his chum from the kitchens of the Royal York Hotel.

"I live right upstairs," Benyo invites. "Please come to meet my wife." So they walk up the four flights of the neat brownstone and into a roomy flat. Mrs. Benyo serves sweet Czechoslovakian charm along with tea, hot bread, and ham. A friendship forms.

"Don't go back to Toronto. Try the city. It's good here," Benyo implores. "Share with us. We have room." Then the cardboard trunk is settled at the foot of the double bed in the back room and Teresa is helping clean the chicken they chipped in for. Her next few years are decided. In this area Teresa can even shop for herself. They spend six months sharing with the Benyos, then take a one-room flat for themselves—their first and last.

It is still hard times, and there are hard moments to face. John's jobs are on and off. Walking every night, except the very coldest, from St. Marks to Wall Street, where Teresa cleans offices for twelve dollars a week, isn't easy. When she does take the bus, she worries herself over the fare and thinks of the farmers of her village who walk, rain or shine, every day to their far-flung fields. John decides again to take a look at Canada—they liked him at the Royal York—but it is too expensive for Teresa to go along with him—"Not just to look."

Lying in bed, he reassures Teresa's turned back that he will stay only a month or two. Unless something good comes up and "In that case," he whispers, "you will come to me." Teresa is silent.

"What's wrong?"

"I feel funny to stay here like a widow," she says at last, "to sleep alone in this room."

"It's too much money for both," he reasons.

"Then I would rather be at a job in a house, near children. I hate the offices, dark and empty." He kisses her solid shoulder and agrees.

The next day he walks her to a household agency on Eighth Street, where declaring himself her brother, he registers her as available.

At 11:00 A.M. she sits nervously next to John and across from five serious women, who eye her, weighing her job potential against their own. They cross legs over mended hose and touch for their earrings.

At noon the first possible employer, a matron from Brooklyn, inspects them. English is a factor. And Teresa doesn't even know where Brooklyn is. She never heard of it in her two Slavic years near St. Marks Place.

At 1:00 P.M. enters Hymie Caplin, fight manager. His Rosie needs help. Three kids, one only nine months, and a new house with ten rooms, including attic and basement, are too much for her. Teresa thinks he's quite a gentleman, stylish with his big cigar and bigger smile. So does John, who talks for her.

"I got three at home, the youngest a little doll," Caplin brags after the "brother" asks if there are children. "And the older girl, why, you'll go crazy for her. Cuter than Shirley Temple and smarter. Three great kids." He puffs in pleasure. "And wait'll you see my son of seven, a real boy." He describes her big room, which used to be an attic but is so transformed she'll think she's in the cabin of a luxury yacht, complete with hatchway and steering wheel and three porthole windows. "Yes, there's a radio, of course."

"Should we tell him I'm only temporary?" Teresa asks John. She doesn't want to deceive this warm, smiling man. But Depression ethics evoke a severe negative warning from John. And the deal is made. She must get her things and be back at the agency at three. Then they will be off to Forest Hills. Money is passed, and hands are shaken.

"I think he's Jewish, too," Teresa tells John as they walk back. He agrees that it is all to the good.

At 3:00 P.M. a resigned Teresa and a relieved John watch the blue Dodge sedan pull up in front of the agency. John's relief is short-lived. Something is wrong. He doesn't see the natty Mr. Caplin sitting inside. Instead, from behind the driver's seat lumbers a burly man with a pug's face.

"I came for Teresa," the brute announces, studying the paper in his paw.

The agency woman reassures John. "This man works for Mr. Caplin. It will be fine."

John demands and gets the family phone number, then reluctantly hands Teresa into the back seat.

At 4:30 P.M. the silence of the car ride across a bridge and through little citified communities attached by a road and separated by barren fields and even a farm or two ends. The thick neck in the front seat twists, and the pug-faced man says, "This is it."

It is a nice suburban house set in a well-groomed lawn on a street of such houses. At the door stands a pretty dark-haired woman with a curly-haired blond child peeking around her hip. Another lady, less pretty, stands protectively nearby. A friend came to look me over, Teresa guesses correctly. Down the block a boy, in knickers, detaches himself from a bunch of other boys, all of whom seem much the

236

same, and starts ambling toward them. That must be the son. Taking her bag from the driver, she follows Mrs. Caplin into the front hall along the corridor to the kitchen. There Mrs. Caplin tells her to sit at the dinette table and asks if she would like coffee.

"No, thank you too much," says Teresa, trying her best to sound correct.

The two women glance at each other. It's a mark against her, but not a big one, she judges from their expressions.

"Well," asks Mrs. Caplin, "do you have a uniform?" Mrs. Caplin is also trying to sound correct.

"No," mumbles Teresa, starting to wish herself back on St. Marks Place.

No one seems quite sure where to go from here. Then a baby gurgles from a wicker bassinet near the warm stove.

"Don't be upset if she starts yelling," Mrs. Caplin quickly advises Teresa. "She always screams at the sight of strangers." They approach the bassinet, and the fragile little baby girl, with the face of a fair china doll, throws her arms open wide and gives Teresa the prettiest one-toothed smile her mother has ever seen. So uniforms be hanged. Mrs. Caplin never had help who wore them anyway. She hands my sister into Teresa's arms, where the baby cuddles in to hold on for the rest of her life. And Teresa, well, Teresa is hooked.

"She was glad to be free of the German," Teresa will tell me years later as we watch the flickering of the Yahrzeit candle my brother had lit, for our mother's memory, before he recited Kaddish.

"What German?" Janice will ask. "German" is the dirty word of her four-year-old world.

"The German who wash your diapers before I came. Your mommy"—she unconsciously crosses herself—"she was afraid from her."

Janice sticks the thumb in her mouth—that will mean braces—and burrows into Teresa's constant softness. "No German," she insists.

"Yes, a German maid. Mrs. Donner from next door tell me. She say the German don't sleep in." Mrs. Donner, from next door, could slow down her elegant Odessan Russian and communicate with Teresa. It was she who translated how to use the washing machine. A miracle which astonished Teresa's eye. Even the lady of Manhasset did not own such a thing. A big round tub with propellerlike blades to gyrate the wash and attached to that a steel drum with a basket that spun and pushed the water right out of the clothes and readied them for the line. Teresa mastered it quickly. Then she would talk to three things. Mrs. Donner, her friend the wash machine, and Baby Janice, who required only cooing and kissing.

Mostly she kissed Janice in secret, afraid Mrs. Caplin might not like it. Janice certainly did.

"Get Teresa," my mother would call when Janice's crankiness was out of control. No sooner would Teresa lift her than all sobbing ceased.

"Get Teresa" were the watchwords of the next two years. Actually they were good years.

"Your daddy make plenty money," Teresa will remember with pleasure. "Mommy she go beauty parlor and buy things."

Even before Mr. Caplin's car pulls into the driveway, Teresa can smell his cigar and hear his "Anybody home?" Even from the basement with the machine going. Teresa is happy.

John had remained in Canada only three weeks. They gave him a job at the Royal York, but he hated it. His friends of old were gone, and the garbage cans he was meant to tote were too heavy and hurt his chest. He left almost as anxiously as when he'd run from Polish conscription to Czechoslovakia. Back in New York, Benyo gets him a job as handyman, jack-of-all-trades, where he is working. It's a small chain of restaurants Teresa refers to as Charleys. John wants her in Manhattan. She stalls him. Where else could she get such nice wages and do such pleasant, easy work? Even if Mrs. Caplin gives her only every other Sunday to go with her Thursday afternoons. She wants to stay. After all, poor Mrs. Caplin thinks she's unattached, and poor John doesn't know she's become attached, but to another man's children. Teresa is definitely in love.

Every morning by seven-thirty she is in the kitchen helping Mrs. Caplin feed breakfast to the brood of "bad eaters." Then it's time to brush out Babsie's ringlets and make sure Melvin is all buttoned, especially his fly, which he insists on neglecting. Or does he? Then, singing the songs of her mother, she washes dishes, mops floors, and does whatever else is asked of her, with pleasure. Twelve o'clock is lunch by the radio. *Stella Dallas* and *One Man's Family*. At first Mrs. Caplin, who does the cooking, has her eat on the little white utility table under the salami that hangs by the kitchen door. Hymie Caplin likes his kosher salamis a little withered and hard. But soon she is at the dinette table with the rest. Mrs. Caplin can't quite get the right tone to these things, and such distinctions are hard to explain to willing, smiling Teresa, who can't speak back. So we take our family meals together. She is one of us.

When he is home, Hymie will throw as many choice chunks from whatever he is enjoying into her plate as into his kids'. This means she must smile through such experiences as her first hot Italian sausage. Dr. Brown's Cel-Ray is another surprise (she never sipped soda before) and bubbles out her nose, to delight us kids. Even Baby Janice giggles as my brother and I nudge happily at each other to Teresa's coughs and gasps. Mr. Caplin, on the other hand, is talking politics while waving his knife and fork in accompaniment and doesn't notice. He does notice her shoes.

"Rosie, get the girl some good crepe soles with arch supports. She's on her feet all day. She can save those pointy things for her Sundays. And what do you mean *our* rainwater is upsetting Mr. Donner? For a nice guy, he sure is picky." Teresa understands little of this as she eyes the purple skin and strange texture of the eggplant before her. It's a vegetable she even today views with suspicion. Breads, cereals, eggs, and potatoes are what she is comfortable with, and what she eats on the sneak to allay appetite before sitting down to share our somewhat exotic fare. We know her secrets. No, not all. We don't know that her brother is her husband. It will take a series of emergencies and one more year before that pops.

On the Sundays she isn't off she sometimes goes with the family for its walks. She is allowed her "pointies" if she wants. I wear my Mary Janes, and Janice sits in her stroller in spotless high laced whites. Melvin's oxfords are also polished, but scuff marks still show through. My mother puts on perfume and even a flower in her hair, tucked into one roll of her pompadour. Daddy, with his hat tilted back, exposing all the pride and pleasure on his face, leads us forth. For a Broadway wheeler he has a true Victorian streak.

Teresa loves it when she goes. Her coloring is the same as my father's, inherited from Jenny, his long-gone Swedish mother, and indeed is the same as us kids. Mother's aquiline darkness will come forth later, just in time for Nick. Right now we all are bouncing blondes, and Teresa could be a stocky cousin from the country. She sometimes fantasizes that she is.

But when Teresa watches Mr. Caplin lift the baby from the stroller to sit on his shoulders and bounce along, fantasies cease, and she wants to rush to support the slight spine and even pull from his hand the cigar that's a touch too near a well-pressed eyelet ruffle. She, of course, restrains herself. Eventually Janice will tire of this and be handed back to Teresa for the necessary cooing before her return to the stroller, where Teresa feels she properly belongs. Then Teresa can push her out front and enjoy the sights. She will ever be fascinated by people on parade. She will ever by astonished by their variety. Shorts, talls, pretties, uglies, rich, or poor. And she will always be in awe of the big brick houses and stained glass stuck in Tudor windows and stone balustrades, framing front balconies and doors. Forest Hills Gardens has lots of stuff like that for her to marvel over.

For me, at my age and inches, it all takes on a different angle. For one thing, these walks turn to be highly competitive. Discounting the sibling rivalry of who gets to hold whose hand or who walks in front or pushes the baby or picks the streets, we also watch the adult eyes check each other out. How pretty does the wife look? How well is the husband doing? Then they check us.

"She's bigger than mine at her age."

"He's going to need braces."

"Don't the Steinberg kids look sweet?" asks our mother as we approach Stafford Avenue. Even Teresa knows the answer to that one.

"You must be kidding, Rosie. Steinberg's kids don't come close. Look at the flat nose on his middle boy. They didn't turn him enough. And the girl's got knock-knees. No beauties there. We got the beauts all right." I tuck my knees as straight as ligaments allow and smile sympathy to the Steinberg girl as we pass by. I can afford to be generous. Teresa pinches me; she senses something in my attitude she's not sure about.

"Why is Babsie walking like that? All stiff. Stop that, Babsie, and throw your shoulders back, and everybody, breathe." Daddy's cigar stains the summer air. Teresa tries breathing in another direction. "In Carpatska Rus," she tells me, "air more sweet." Her English is growing but in its own very personal way. We take on another group of contenders.

Pausing by a fire hydrant, we find the Gold family. They own a spaniel. "Rosie, how would you like a pup? We could call him Champ." Rosie shudders for her expensive carpets and her prized drapes and doesn't respond. We kids hope against hope anyway. "Yeah, your little guy is nice-looking all right." My father pats a small, frizzy head about belt buckle high. "But take a gander at our pal Mel here? Look at the head on him. Lots of room for all those brains he's got." The Golds fight back.

"Well, well." Mrs. Gold smiles narrowly. "So little Janice is looking healthier, isn't she? It's a shame she was such a fragile baby. She may even grow to be prettier than Babs here. But she'll never be as fat."

"Babsie's not fat." My mother's eyes are taking on a red glint. "She's solid and perfectly formed. She doesn't need ankle highs to control her feet." This is a real below-the-belt shot.

My father rushes to soften the blow. The Gold kid walks a little funny. "Well," he says, "Baby Janice may need them for a time. Her ankles are real weak." We move on.

"Hymie, how could you say that about Janice's ankles? Her ankles are just fine."

"I had to say something, Rosie. You hurt the kid. He heard you."

"Are you saying I was cruel?"

"No, just careless."

She's silent. Then: "Listen, Hymie, I never get into that stuff. You always start it." She wants fairness.

"Let it drop, Rose. Walk home, and I'll go bring some Chinks." Teresa dreads "Chinks." Who knows what's under those strange-smelling sauces? And lobster Cantonese, a household favorite, scares her to death.

Once Teresa even got to Stillman's gym. "I never see so much dirt," she recalls, "and so sweating."

Walking the high, creaky steps to Stillman's, our shoes scuffing against the iron edges and our fingers clutching at the worn handrail, Teresa sniffs in strange smells. Sandbag odors, leather and liniment, fight rosin, wood, and canvas for a place in your nose. To say nothing of old cigars and ground-out cigarettes. That men would exercise in such smells is unthinkable. But Teresa sees that they do. As our father's voice rings, "Melvin, stop moping and, Babsie, lift your feet or you'll trip," we arrive.

"This is our Teresa." He introduces her. "She helps Rose." Teresa, pretty and strong, is getting a bit of attention from the local citizens, who are used to regulars like Melvin and me. "Listen"—my father jollies her, half on the square—"there're some likely single Polish boys sparring up here, so be friendly." Teresa flushes; she gets his drift and knows that John won't like this. Should she tell Mr. Caplin now? She doesn't know how. Astonished by these men whose heads and hands are bound in padded leather, while they pound each other or dance around in roped-off spaces, she shakes her head. How they poke those big leather mittens in the air, even at no one. Snorting just like her father's bull. She must write him about this.

"Cut Allie's hair even closer, will ya, Willie? Every punch he takes looks like a wallop." Allie Stolz, handsome and muscled, stops sparring and prances over. He knows Teresa from the house. "Hi, Polska." He teases her, then turns to acknowledge me, his true love. He lifts me up and passes me through the ropes, where I do, by request, "Animal

Crackers." I feel I am getting too old for this song I've been singing since I was three and cut it off to do "Down by the Old Mill Stream," with gestures! I get my usual big hand.

"Send the boy in for two rounds, Hymie," shouts someone, and Melvin moves closer to Teresa, in case they are serious. Everyone laughs at him. He blushes red.

"I'll go two rounds," I say. I don't like them to laugh at my brother. Now they start laughing at me.

Allie's bandaged hands lift me up for a kiss. His face is wet. "Put her down, Allie boy, you'll get her all dirty."

"Am I going to marry Allie when I grow up?" "We'll see, Babsie. How did you get that blood on your blouse? Teresa, get that washed off. Rosie will kill me." Then the gym medic looks up Teresa's nose. She's been having sinus trouble, and that's why she's here. "He knows more than a specialist," my father insists.

"Pollops" pronounces the grizzled little man. "Need to be cut." Teresa gets that word "cut" and panics.

"Don't worry." My father reassures her. "What does he know? He's just a fight guy. I'll take you to see Spielberg."

Spielberg is the doctor who will pull my tonsils. I met him and his fancy nurse, Marie. "He won't hurt you," I tell Teresa. "That's what they promised me, anyway."

More blood; now it's my hand. I'd picked up a razor from the tape box.

Teresa shows my gashed palm to my father. "How'd she do that? Benny, get over here! Teresa, keep her hand off her skirt. Benny'll fix it, he's a great stickman." Gauzed and taped Babsie, the Stillman's gym "regular," sits mournfully in Teresa's lap all the way home.

"I don't really want to be a Brownie," I tell my mother as she checks my barrettes and pulls them even tighter.

"Why not?" she demands. "It's good for you." Everything I don't want is good for me, from oatmeal and kasha to the long tan stockings that hook to my undershirt with their own special snaps. If I am late getting to the toilet because I dallied, the whole block knows. Deep brown stains appear down my legs as I run home in obvious humiliation.

"Because I just don't want to." My mother's patience is notoriously short, and over her shoulder I see Teresa trying to warn me off. I am not to be warned. My jaw tightens. "I won't go."

"You'll go if I have to drag you."

"Drag me." She does. Teresa watches as we go, eyes red from the tears that won out over my will to hold them back. I am welcomed into the troops. This little pack of Brownies meets at the "other school" in the Gardens, the one with no Jews at all. (Why she insisted on this trial by fire among such aliens I can't figure.)

So, I am still sullen, and she is silent, as we walk the pretty streets with their English names back home. The streets run the ABC's starting with Austin but end somewhere before the problem of Zed. I know them and would sing them out for her; but that would be making up, and we are definitely on the "outs." Actually, running away would express my feelings best, but I always fail at that.

"Someday I'll figure out how to run away right, and nobody will ever see me again," I mutter at Teresa as she pulls the flower-printed cotton nightgown over my mouth.

"Be shut," she says.

"Why don't you speak English?" I taunt back when my mouth is unhampered. She is not perturbed.

"So, little Babsie became a Brownie." My father's voice is phoned in from Philly, a place he goes with the fighters. "How was it?"

"Silly."

"Such an actress. I bet you really like it. Tell me you liked it." His expectant pause is too much for me.

"I liked it." Very low. Sometimes even he fails me. "What are you going to bring me?" I want a different conversation. He obliges, promising kisses and goodies, and I promise to stay his "best girl."

"Nobody understands me," I complain to the bathroom mirror, dragging my mother's nightgown as a train, while I clump the tiles in her new open-toe spectators and make cigarette faces in the mirror.

"Me, too," says Teresa, rescuing the gown and shoes. Teresa is worrying over Hitler. Hitler and his Germans are menacing her family. And, Mr. Caplin is not helping her by pointing his fork at heaven each meal, saying what a monster he is. "Mussolini is a monster, too," she explains to John every other Sunday, "but Mr. Caplin, he says Hitler is worse. A devil, who will march on Poland, then the world." What Teresa can't fathom is if everybody knows this, why isn't the household god, President Roosevelt, taking care of Hitler like Mr. Caplin keeps saying he will? What's going to happen to her family if Hitler marches? She was a child during World War I. But she remembers how Germans took her town. Soldiers were everywhere, perhaps a thousand, perhaps more. They slept where they could. Some lived in tents, and some in the deep trenches they'd dug throughout the surrounding fields. The rest were assigned, in groups, to the local houses. Teresa's father's house was large, so twelve German infantrymen were billeted there. All the houses clustered in the valley of her village were of the same design; only details and size differed.

You walked from the courtyard into a huge room which was kitchen, parlor, and family bedroom all in one. Next to that was a hall, which led on one side to a larder, a linen room, and a storage room for serious clothing and heirlooms. On the other side was a long, window-less room for keeping grain. The wheat and oats lay dry in its bins, and behind its far wall was the barn, where, depending on the season, lived three horses, two bulls, and eight to ten cows. In winter they gave welcome heat. Then came the small husking rooms and mill, where wheat and chaff were separated to become fodder or flour. Then the sheep pen, where about thirty lived, across from the pigs. "Our pigs live clean on sweet hay," Teresa says. "Pigs got brains, too. We children love and kiss and pet, and cry when the town pig killer comes to do fast to die. But after it over, we eat them anyway." She sighs with resignation. "That's the life."

The dread of Hitler brings back the first time she knew fear. She was only a child when the Polish army conscripted her father's horses for the war. They were sad but not scared, not yet. Not even when the cannons miles away had started their booming, and everyone ran to root cellars to wait it out. German patrols caused some consternation, but it was livable.

"When you young," resolves Teresa, "soon as you don't

feel any more pain, you forget. Even to laugh, when a Germans steals your ducks."

But when the Germans took the town, the laughing stopped.

Teresa's father housed a lot of women. Her mother, her grandmother, the great-grand-*molta*, her father's sister, and an older girl cousin, who was staying for the war. And they all were nice to look at, these women, even her father's sister, whose arm had been crippled in early adolescence and who afterward avoided men's eyes. The robust German infantry stationed with them would have been attracted to much less. But the official Russian commandant was having no molesting of civilians. So a tense truce existed, as the men watched after the rounded hips and swishing skirts. The boredom of delayed battle pushed hard, and eventually the boys would indeed be boys, despite orders. They wanted a party and would have one.

So the twelve soldiers of her house ganged up on Teresa's father; hog-tied him, and removed him to a campfire in his fields to be left there till morning. Then Teresa and the small brothers still at home shook with cold and fright as the Germans pulled the blankets off their beds to block the windows from passing eyes.

"They want use the womens," tells Teresa of it. "And us children hide in dark and see."

One German was musical and played his harmonica as his compatriots drank and chased the women. "Dance," they demanded. Even the great-grandmother must dance without a blouse so they can laugh at her shriveled tits. By firelight Teresa watched the ancient face go gray as with death, never to be the same. "Smile," and as the women danced, they smiled from stiff lips and behind terror-filled eyes. Recalling the Octoberfests and carnivals of their past, the soldiers beat on pots and pans and grabbed at tits and asses. The women evaded drunken hands and mouths as best they could. They were delaying, watching for signs that beer and schnapps were drowning the madness. Her father's young sister was not so lucky. She didn't dance well and couldn't achieve the thinnest of smiles. Petrified, Teresa and the children watched in silence as the frustrated soldier seized her heels and dragged her, head banging across the floor, to the far side of the fireplace, where they struggled in the shadows of her parents' bed. Teresa remembered the pleas from the darkness and, to this day, tries to deny the horrible things she saw happening.

In the morning her father rubbed his raw wrists, surveyed the wreckage of his home, and went to the commandant.

Then the apple trees and cherry trees of their courtyard sported odd attachments. Twelve soldiers, hands pulled behind and up, were strung from their branches. Twelve heads drooped forward, and a dozen pair of boots dragged in the dust. Another group of Germans guarded them and threw water in their faces when they fainted. A day and a night passed this way. Then they were cut down. The guilty soldiers were sent to the trenches, and no new ones came to take their place.

For years after children herding cows around Ustrzyki would beware of these trenches where bullets and live grenades lay in the covering grass to be stumbled over. When the Germans retreated, they took every cow, sheep, and pig they could find with them.

The only people among the Carpatska Rus who didn't rush out on their rag-covered feet to cheer the Cossacks, who came to chase the Germans, were the town Jews.

"Jews must worry from pogrom," explains Teresa. "Cossacks are Cossacks. You know." She will add, "But sometimes I feel scare like a Jew, too."

Feeling like a Jew was not so comfortable, not in 1939. On March 15 of that year Prague fell without a fight, and even earlier than that Benyo and his wife whispered to Teresa of bad things happening to Jews, nasty stories sneaked out by those Czechs lucky enough to get out to tell them. Teresa worries over these stories all the way to Florida. She also worries about admitting to her married state. John complains he hasn't slept with her one night through in two years. When they get back, she promises him, she will tell. Maybe Mrs. Caplin will fire her. John hopes so. Teresa's not so sure.

Serious Considerations

Spring marched with Teresa from the Houston Street subway stop to St. Marks Place and up four flights of steps to her little flat. Sun spread through the dusty windows and over Teresa and John as they lay together on their brass-trimmed bed. That bed was the most expensive purchase of their lives, and today, she hoped, or perhaps it would be tonight or maybe again in the early-morning hours before she hurried her way back to Forest Hills, they would make life on it. But it was to take them two years. And long before that the troubles started.

They began with phone calls from unfamiliar voices and lots of whispering into mouthpieces. It started with Mr. Caplin's frowning, saying, "Teresa, don't answer the phone," or, "If that guy calls again, Rose, say I'm not here." Ruthie, the Caplins' good friend from the candy store, spent summer afternoons in shady conversation with Rose. Under the bing cherry tree that was the pride of the yard, they talked beneath their breaths. And Mrs. Caplin started holding her mouth in a hard way she never did before. It looked to Teresa as though she might be trying not to cry.

Slowly Teresa began to notice that the "big shots" were not coming home with Mr. Caplin anymore. At least not so often anyway. No more George Raft to go bang-bang at Melvin or beautiful Barbara Stanwyck with her even more beautiful husband for Babsie to sing to. Less and less laughing mouths around the bar in the basement, drinking up all the Caplin liquor. But when the Roman Catholic priest from Our Lady of Grace, where Mr. Caplin put on the exhibition fights for charity, stopped dropping by, and the new Rabbi Boxer, too, Teresa felt something wrong was in the air. Though less company meant less work for her, like Mr. Caplin, Teresa always loved a party. Now there were none.

Still, there were a few guests. Auntie H., Mrs. Caplin's sister, brought her man friend, the Almost Uncle Eddie, a lot. And Lou Salica came with his family, bringing strong cheeses and rich pastries. Also Allie and his brothers, Abe Feldman, and Lew Jenkins—all the fighters were still there to feed and fuss over. Teresa couldn't make out one Texas word said by Jenkins or his wife, which made her suspicious, but they seemed cheerful. So perhaps she was wrong. She brushed the shadows away into the corners of her consciousness and put a smile on her face.

The shadows wouldn't stay put. They came creeping out to breathe the autumn air, to chill her heart and chatter her teeth. For one thing, war had come to Ustrzyki, her hometown in Carpathia. And the movie newsreels showed her German Stukas breaking the crisp dawn of Polish skies, bringing new words to understand like "blitzkrieg." Teresa worried and waited for news of her family while the Caplins worried and waited for the next big bout. This bout was the one the Caplins were counting on to cover new expenses, like the lawyers recently come into their lives.

The morning of that fight two rather nice-looking men in suits and ties arrived at the side door. They didn't ring the bell. Instead, they signaled to Teresa, watching them from the window over the sink. It was very early. What could they want? She couldn't just ignore them, so she opened the door a crack. Then they pushed through the door, knocking her to the side, and started for the stairs.

Racing ahead of them, the word "pogrom" pushing at her mouth, she stood before the bedroom door, blocking the men while knocking at it with the back of her knuckles. "Mr. Caplin . . . men."

Their voices rode right over hers. "Stay where you are in there, we're coming in. Don't move a muscle." They went in.

Teresa waited a moment. No bad sounds, no screams, no pogrom. Back downstairs in the kitchen she wondered at her panic. It must have something to do with the fight, she told herself. Tough fight business people were sometimes rude. Breathing more easily and putting up coffee, she set breakfast for four. Yet she was glad the kids had left for school and missed these men. Only Baby Janice still sat bemused in her high chair. "Cookie," called Janice, "cookie." Handing her a zwieback to chew, Teresa got the bacon stretched and ready for the pan.

"Your mommy come down all dressed up and white like a wall," she told me years later. And she described my mother sitting in frozen silence, not answering whether she wanted her eggs. "You daddy drink coffee standing by sink. The two men wait till he's done and take them both away." So it was some kind of pogrom after all. Teresa put the bacon and eggs back in the new Frigidaire and started to watch the clock. At noon, home for lunch, Melvin raced Barbara to the radio, won, and got his pick of programs, and they munch away, unknowing.

"Where's Mommy?"

"She go someplace." Teresa didn't want to say more. After lunch they went back to school. Barbara returned for a moment. She had forgotten her pencil case, and that was all.

Around 2:00 P.M. the phone started to ring. First the trainer from Hymie's fight suite at the Astor Hotel. "Has Mr. Caplin left yet?"

Teresa answered yes. She didn't know what else to say.

Then it was the man from the weigh-in.

Then the corner handler from the gym.

Then Mike Jacobs's office.

Then Mike Jacobs himself. "Where's Hymie? . . . Well, then, is Rose there? . . . When did he leave? With who?" Hymie Caplin, it seemed, had disappeared.

The reporter came to the door sometime before three. Teresa watched anxiously for the children and said as little as possible. No, she didn't know about any arrest. Please to leave, she had work. At last confounded by her lack of English and blank looks, he did leave. She sighed in relief and started supper.

"Do homework first," she ordered Barbara and Melvin, who ignored her to throw down their books, drink their milk, and run to their friends.

Cutting Janice's lamb chop off its bone and into little pickable pieces, and warning Melvin about too much ketchup, and getting Barbara to pay attention and not drop her potatoes everywhere took up the evening meal. The clock ticked; the children tired; she tucked them away. No, they couldn't stay up and listen to the fight. "No, Mommy say no." They'll hear about it all in the morning. Melvin must give Barbara back the movie magazine. It's hers, and yes, it's okay if she reads it in bed. Yes, she can sleep with it if she wants. "Mommy say yes." And they must be quiet and not wake Janice. "Stop flush toilet, Babsie. No toy!" Then all was calm except for her heart.

A worn Mrs. Caplin came at last. She didn't want to eat anything. She sat by the big Atwater Kent in the darkened living room, her head in her hands, and heard the familiar voice of the sports announcer wonder why "Hymie isn't in the corner with his boy." She listened as they joked and debated if a Caplin boxer could even lift a mitt without the colorful Hymie Caplin shouting his blow-by-blow directions from ringside. Rose Caplin smiled a weary smile in spite of herself and started rooting "Hymie's boy" home.

The next morning she answered the kids' questions with as much normality and cheer as she could muster. Then she sat by the phone, for the long hours that would pass till he came in the door.

It was after four before he was home, hugging his babies, being tender with his wife, and preparing to wait out the hard months till his trial.

"All those phony bums stop to calling him," Teresa recalled. "All those no-goods who eat food and beg for their pocket. Only reporter people call all daytime and nighttime,

too ... You think nothing else happen in whole world."
Teresa started hanging up on them. She stopped passing
the time with the neighborhood maids. Even when John
asked about things, she would cut him off. Things were bad.
And words didn't help. She gave up going to church. She
was getting too angry with God. She would never quite
forgive him for Hitler. And for Mr. Caplin, too. Especially
as she watched how the children from school made Babsie
cry or heard Melvin, without a friend, alone in his room
spending long hours rattling tin soldiers across the floor.
She wondered if God feels pain.

The day they convicted Mr. Caplin was a slow news day,
so that the popular fight figure Hymie, hero of John
O'Hara's "Flannistan & Flannistan," originator of the fine
art of double-talk, a genuine Damon Runyon prototype,
and the subject of countless newspaper columns, was a
crook, made good copy. He left the court handcuffed and
went straight to jail. The picture in the newspaper looked so
unlike him that Barbara and Teresa almost convinced themselves it was someone else.

"Don't look at that, Babsie," called candy-store Ruthie a
second too late. It was hard to avoid looking, splashed all
over her newsstand as it was. Barbara and Teresa brought
Melvin to verify it. Baby Janice in her stroller was oblivious.

Inside the paper were pictures of the family as well.
Follow-up stuff. Me at two, feeding the heavyweight Abe
Feldman, while my mother smiles. Another showed a happy
champ bouncing a baby Melvin on his knee. This stuff
wiped the war right off the front page. How could Winston
Churchill's warnings compete with that?

"Auntie H. and Uncle Dan," Teresa remembered, "go to
beg big shots to help. Poor Daddy, he is frame." The big
shots, it seems, feel some waiting is in order. It's a bad time
to unfix the fix. Wait till they get their boy in as mayor.
Their boy doesn't get in. Not this election anyway, and
Teresa gave up on big shots. "You Mommy brave, but the
big shots break her heart."

At first it was just the littlest of lumps, noticed by accident when some tensions were being massaged away. She

had Teresa feel it. It couldn't be seen, not even when she angled her neck. "It feels like baby pea," Teresa said.

"Have it checked," commanded Auntie H.

"Only if it doesn't go," fended my mother, too busy fighting for appeals and trying to hold the stable together to deal with a lump. It didn't go. It even got a little bigger. At least she thought it did. Teresa thought it felt the same.

When Babsie got a D in conduct, her mother must visit the principal at P.S. 144. Every other teacher seemed to be standing in the hall, just to watch her as she walked to the office. "We like Barbara very much, you know. And she has such a sweet singing voice. But she's always late, you know, and she is starting to disrupt the class. She's not a real problem, you know, not yet. Perhaps you can talk to her."

Teresa watched Mrs. Caplin slap Babsie hard. The fingers left their print on Babsie's cheek. "Don't make them send for me again," Mrs. Caplin screamed at her. Janice hid behind the door, sucked at her thumb, and whimpered. "I warn you." Mrs. Caplin was now talking low, "I have too much now. Don't add to it."

Later Teresa patted two curly heads buried in her bosom. "Mommy upset." Teresa comforted. They were not comforted.

"She wouldn't dare do that," protested Babsie at last, "if Daddy could see her." Teresa wanted to explain that that was exactly why it happened. Because Daddy was away and Mommy was hurt and scared. But she hadn't the right words. Babsie wouldn't listen anyway.

The Germans had already reached the gates of Leningrad when Teresa's Michael was conceived. But so much was going on in Forest Hills, Teresa hardly noticed either event. She did know that Mrs. Caplin's lump had gotten bigger and very visible. Several doctors had shaken their heads over it, as their fingers probed at her lymphs. Tired of fingers pricked for blood counts and veins invaded for extra analyses, exhausted with shrugs and smiles the lawyer offered instead of hope, Mrs. Caplin hid in the bed she had shared with Hymie and tried to ignore that something was happening with Teresa that she hadn't the energy to deal with.

Sitting in terror behind the steering wheel of the blue
Dodge, trying to get straight what her instructor had taught
her, trying not to shift into the wrong gear, and to remember the scheme of it, she had somehow passed her driver's
test. That she had actually tricked them into giving her a
license amazed her. Deserved or not, it didn't matter, she
must drive. She had treatments to get to, some in Brooklyn,
some in Manhattan. Praying her way past traffic. Nobody
seemed to notice that she was a fraud. "Don't tell Hymie,"
she instructed those people writing and visiting him, as
Hymie knew her too well. Hymie would understand she
could never be a real driver, and he would panic. Him,
locked away up there, knowing she was out on the road.
Still, he might be proud if he knew. Most of all, it was kids
she had to watch out for. Little children were everywhere
on her street. Playing and trusting her to take care. She was
a mommy. What if she hit a strange child? What if she hit
her own?

"But you can't leave your car in the driveway all day,
Mrs. Caplin." Mr. Donner of the shared driveway was ad-
amant. She was over the boundary, breaking the diplomatic
quid pro quo.

"It's hard for me, for my neck where they cut, to keep
backing it in and out of the garage." If only Hymie were . . .
"I always have it out of your way before you get home."

Even so, he pointed out the inconvenience at the side
door. "I'll move it," she said. And did.

"Really, Rose," Auntie H. marveled, "I wouldn't have
the guts to drive a car. And here you are, sick and everything. . . ." It was a big compliment because her sister
had outtoughed Rose all her life. "If he were my
husband," she would chide, "I wouldn't let him hang
around Lindy's so much. Too many bimbos there," and
"If they were my kids, they'd have some manners," and
"Really Rose, you shouldn't be so familiar with help. Teresa is just a nice ignoramus. She can't even speak English. Just give her her orders; stop saying 'please,' and
explaining everything."

"Really, Hannah," said Rose, pulling out the long-aban-
doned given name with a rare smile, "driving isn't that

difficult." Solemnly she added, "The day we get Hymie out, I'm going to drive right up there and pick him up."

"He'll get a big kick out of that, Rose," said her sister, "but it looks like it'll be awhile. Five-to-tens don't even come up for parole for a few years."

Rose touched her neck. "I'll wait," she promised.

"Teresa, you are getting fat!" said Ruthie from the candy store accusingly. Teresa smiled slyly. "Not fat," she said, "one baby boy, right here." She pointed at six months' worth of Michael.

"Stop kidding," said Ruthie, appalled. "That's all Rose needs is you pregnant."

Teresa didn't press it. She was avoiding the problem part herself. The part about leaving. After the biopsy Mrs. Caplin got worse. And there were new lumps. "Since they moved Mr. Caplin even farther up north, Mrs. Caplin came home from her visits like a drown cat," Teresa told John. He didn't wish to hear.

"Let me make you hot food," she was always offering. "Eat some." Mrs. Caplin said she had no appetite. Out the garage and into the streets and across the parkways, Mrs. Caplin ferried the kids to the painter she'd hired, who did them in oils. He had been commissioned before the real trouble started and sympathetically took photographs for her to send to the prison because she couldn't take the kids up too often. They wore her out.

That very few people were visiting at the house was a "good thing," Teresa decided. Mrs. Caplin was so tired and there was not so much food to share and what good were they anyway? But underneath it hurt her. Where was friendship? Friendship sprang from unexpected sources. Harry Magid, the mouse of a cabdriver who had survived the same Lower East Side streets as his pal Hymie, but hadn't become a somebody, had stayed a little shot, and sometimes called to say hello, came riding his Checkered cab to the rescue. If not exactly to the rescue, at least to the comfort. "How can I help you Rose? How can I help Hymie?"

"Could you drive the kids up to visit him sometime?" Rose asked of this little man she hardly remembered. "He's dying to see them, and I haven't the strength anymore."

"Sure, Rose," became his bywords. After a while Harry Magid, known as Chulky, was allowed visiting privileges. Prisons, it seems, are cautious of corrupting influences, but eventually he was on Hymie's mailing list.

"I'm only allowed so many outgoing letters a week," his childhood friend told Chulky from behind the iron mesh barrier, "so don't think I don't want to answer more, but I'm saving them for Rosie." Teresa was touched when she got a handmade birthday card from Auburn prison signed "With thanks, Hymie." She saved it for years. Then, like the broken records of her mother and the long braids of her innocence, it somehow disappeared.

The boxers were still boxing. Loyal to Rose and the kids, "I'm doing it for Hymie," Allie Stolz told Red Smith for his column, before a big bout. But soon the trainers were demanding more money. So less and less was coming in.

"They are taking advantage of you, Rose," declared Auntie H.

"What can I do?" asked my mother. She counted bills and worried. Teresa heated up lots of canned spaghetti instead of meat. Melvin hated canned spaghetti. Barbara did, too, but not so loudly. Luckily the baby loved it. When our mother decided to sell her best mink for ready cash, Teresa mourned more than she. Almost Uncle Eddie was embarrassed into buying it for Auntie H., who was to wear it till it was worn and frayed. She then passed it back to a maturing Janice, who resented it, resigned herself to using it till embarrassed by its shabbiness, she gave it over to Teresa, who shared its split seams in regretful respect till it died.

Still, the bills were mounting. Doctors for Janice, for herself. Barbara was outgrowing her clothing, and she couldn't manage to beg hand-me-downs from friends. She couldn't manage to beg at all. Not even for Melvin's lessons at synagogue.

"It's expensive to be a Jew in America," Teresa told John. John grunted; he was saving up for a big christening himself. Jews didn't get baptized, but his son would.

December 7, the day that will live in infamy, didn't even

dent Teresa's memory. "I know it happen," she will tell me, "but not exactly." By the time Michael bulged beyond all secrecy, the new War Production Board was limiting the length of skirts and forbidding trousers to have cuffs. It didn't matter. Teresa couldn't afford new clothes for herself anyway. She had taken a five-dollar-a-month cut.

"Teresa," Mrs. Caplin begged when she came home from her third trip to the hospital, "Teresa, don't leave us. Since they cut me again, I can't even lift Janice." She held out her arms. The bandage on her neck seeped. "Have your baby here in my bed. Please take my room. It's more comfortable for you. I'll take the attic. I don't care. But don't go."

John would not be moved. "After you have the child, you stay home with him." With money a little better and his weak lungs warding off the draft board, John wanted a bit of what he had never had: his own wife at home.

Babsie studied Teresa's stomach. "Are you really going away when it's born?" Teresa didn't answer her.

"Are you going away from me?" cried Janice, grabbing at her. Little hands hitting against her belly, Teresa shifted away from the frantic fists. "Don't go," sobbed Janice. "Promise me, promise me. Cross your heart."

Teresa would promise her all and everything. Janice was the child of her heart. Teresa would take the little hands and kiss them to fight down the waves of fear. Usually she didn't want anyone to see her kiss the child. Usually was not now. She was preoccupied with how to answer the questions in those bright blue adored eyes. Instead, she kept kissing.

"Promise me. Say 'always,' " begged her tormentor.

"Always," lied Teresa at last. Later she will think that God didn't let her lie after all. She will remember how the ladies from Brooklyn found her and bound her to her word.

Daily Bread

Teresa was annoyed with our finicky food habits and finally said so. She knew about hunger, she told us, she had learned during World War I, as she prepared baked eggs for the third evening that week.

These eggs, a wartime luxury, came from Aunt Ruth. Ruth was Mother's younger sister, living her long, hard hours somewhere in the country, holding together a family deprived by Depression and ineptitude. When times were good for us, they had come seeking relief. Aunt Ruth liked to remember how "Little Babsie went right up and brought me the nickel she had in her savings bank" when I'd overheard her plea. Now a touch of it was being returned. Teresa told us Mother's sister understood how life could sometimes be and was grateful for the gift. I wasn't. I hated eggs for dinner and decided to reject these baked blobs and would stay hungry instead. "Could be," Teresa suggested to me, "you eat tonight at Jane Jones."

"Can I come, too?" Little Janice always asked now that she was able, and she liked listening when Jane and I talked boys.

"No," I always answered automatically.

Eating at the Joneses meant doing dishes, too, something I was not altogether handy with, having had Teresa to
deal with such things. I was also unable to make a bed, hang
up my clothes, or even set a table. And was for years to
come. "Your fault," I accused Teresa years later as I burned
my fingers in Nick's kitchen and she smiled indulgently and
told me how good I was at other things: how well I could, as
a child, entertain and answer phones and keep myself busy
and not ever bother the grown-ups and draw pretty and fix
flowers.

"You never brat." I'm not so sure. However, life was
different with Jane. Her family assigned chores. Her
brother must sweep the steps, rake leaves, and help mow.
And Jane must dust, do dishes, and keep her pretty flowered room perfect. Not sure whether to admire such accomplishments or hold myself aloof of them, I was
nevertheless always glad to sit at their table. At home things
kept getting worse.

"Shouldn't Mrs. Caplin be in a hospital?" Mrs. Shulman,
our other neighbor, had asked Teresa. Her bedroom and
my mother's faced each other over the shrubbery. "She
coughs so hard we can hardly sleep." Mrs. Shulman may
have spoken with concern, but Teresa heard only selfish-
ness. She mourned with me over our mother's beauty now
blackened by X rays, her body ravaged by such sores and
sensitivities that even fine cotton could not be tolerated
without effort. She bravely hung on. Worried for her husband, us children, she tried to do for herself so as not to
burden. Speaking with fear to Chulky, the cabdriver, she
designated what he should do, if he could do, after she'd
gone. Mrs. Hymie Caplin, as polite to the angel of death as
he would allow her to be, turned in her grave many times
before she got there. "Barbara is a strong one, but my poor
little Janice, she will be lost." She whispered these things
when she could. Chulky waited. "She will need—" Mrs.
Caplin wasn't able to continue.

"I'll help her, Rosie, don't worry."

Hearing him, she smiled. "Melvin," she said when she
was able, "is angry. Try to get him to forgive us."

"Forgive?" questioned Chulky.

"Forgive. We promised him such a good life and pulled it all away."

"He has nothing to forgive. What are you talking about?"

Smiling at the sweetness of this little man willing to give his Sundays to her children and his money, too, after all the Roxy Theater costs, and candy, and sodas and piña coladas at the Seventh Avenue stand, she smiled and stopped trying to explain herself. Instead, she drifted into thoughts of David, her long-dead firstborn. He'd have been the handsomest. It was the hospital that killed him. A hospital infection gone to her teat. Sucked in with her milk. Spread to his little brain. Oh, God! Better to remember her father praying his Saturdays away at shul. And the day she was married in the most beautiful gown ever hand-beaded on the Lower East Side. Beaded and bought by her sister Hannah with real show business cash. Hannah, who gave her the prettiest hand-me-downs to dance down Delancey Street. Hannah, the dancer who has no knack for kids. Hannah will have to keep helping, too. Helping Hymie and the children. She will make her promise. It will be a deathbed promise. Hannah will keep it

"Take good care," she instructed Teresa as she left again for Memorial Hospital. "I'll just be a couple of weeks. Something called mustard nitrogen that they're trying." Teresa supported her back to steady her. "And don't let Melvin bully." Gasping in air under her words, she squeezed Teresa's arm and went on. "You're the boss." Teresa nodded. What a little squeeze that was on her arm. No pressure. Her baby, Michael, could squeeze, not Mrs. Caplin.

"And forgive my sister if she's sharp. It's just her way—" Coughing stopped her completely. The malignant mass of cells whose panzer divisions had swept her lungs were blocking her supply lines, cutting off her oxygen, shooting down her red corpuscles, and stealing her reserves. *Götterdämmerung* on rampage.

I watched Teresa help dip my mother's head into the taxi. She could only hold it tilted. Her neck was no longer able to support it straight. Chulky, whom Teresa called Hooky, was driving her on company time.

"Can't I go, too?" begged Janice.

Chulky looked confused. He had to pull his wages. "You stay with Teresa this time," Mother whispered.

"You stay Teresa," Teresa echoed as they drove away.

"Did you know Joe Louis is in the army now?" Melvin asked Teresa. Teresa was shocked; the army gave only twenty-one dollars a month. Mike Jacobs once brought Joe Louis to the house, and she heard Mike Jacobs tell how much he earned for a single fight. It would be better if he fought at the Garden and gave his money for guns, she argued.

"No," Melvin explained. "It's for our morale. Our morale needs all the help it can get." Posters were pasted everywhere, Teresa studied the menacing slanty eyes behind glasses and bloody bodies squashed under giant iron swastikas that shouted to her to buy bonds and shut up because the enemy was listening. She heard Tin Pan Alley join Gasoline Alley to encourage her to razzberry or Bronx cheer right in "Der Fuehrer's Face." And at the movies Charlie Chaplin's Adenoid Hynkel, the Great Dictator, danced for her in a classic which also featured Paulette Goddard. When Babsie, playing in Mrs. Caplin's mirror, pushed her hair into a puffy pompadour and greased up her lips, she looked quite like Paulette Goddard. Teresa, as she pulled the borrowed silks off Babsie's shoulders to hand them back away, agreed to that.

"Paula Jewish, too," she informed Barbara. Teresa was getting more worldly. John, who now spent his Sundays with us, could testify to that. She handled a ration book with the best.

But John was not feeling good, not since a bad bout with pneumonia, though proudly bouncing young Michael around the house, he hid it.

When Teresa had bought the twenty-five-cent tablecloth on Houston Street and climbed four flights to bundle little Michael's diapers and assorted clothes in it instead of a suitcase, John had thought she got a bargain. It was to be for only a while after all. How could they not help these

Caplins of hers? Teresa had begged. The poor sick woman wanting to be with her children. John didn't have the heart to refuse. That their nest on St. Marks was permanently broken never entered his mind. Or hers either. Mrs. Caplin stayed home with them only three months. Then it was Memorial Hospital. She never came back.

That Teresa was not the boss, as Mrs. Caplin had said she would be, became self-evident. First, it was not her nature, and second, no one there would let her be boss anyway. Not the kids and certainly not Auntie H., who came once a week to check money and ration books and to repudiate such an idea. Not that Teresa could have managed without Auntie H.'s visits, but she could have managed well without her tongue. There was something in the way Auntie H. told her she was the "maid" that ached her the rest of her life. Even much later, when a sick Auntie H. begged her for a visit, a small reminisce, or even an unbelievable kiss on the cheek, she remembered. Strangely enough, Teresa loved Auntie H. because somewhere along the line Auntie H. became one of her own.

The day of Mrs. Caplin's funeral was the first time Teresa had seen Mr. Caplin since the last morning he left for court. It had been two and a half years. He looked very changed to her.

Teresa's day started early. Auntie H. had called at the crack of dawn. "Make sure they look nice. Check Melvin's knickers for stains. And if Barbara wears that white blouse she wore last week when we took her to see Hymie at Rose's hospital, for God's sake, sew up the rip under the arm. It looked terrible."

"She will wear different one." Teresa started to describe it.

Auntie H., who was fatigued and frantic, rode right over her. "And clean socks, please, and check their nails, for God's sake. Their nails are always a disgrace. Now what can we do about serving something after the cemetery? Oh, never mind, if anyone comes, they'll understand or the hell with them. What time is Chulky picking them up? Well, get them out quick. They can't be late."

"Janice, she want to go."

"She can't, she's too young. This is horrible enough. Tell her I said no and no tantrums."

"She want say good-bye Mommy."

"Tell her Mommy is in heaven already and can't hear her. Oh, no, don't say that. I don't know. For God's sake, tell her something."

"For God's sake," Teresa repeated to herself after she hung up the receiver. Michael, usually quiet, was screaming.

"I want to sit in front with Chulky," Melvin informed me. "Me, too," I said, surprising myself. I normally preferred to be alone in the back.

"There is no room," Melvin said.

"Yes, there is."

"It'll be too crowded."

"I don't care."

"How about you both sit in back and I'll be your chauffeur?" Chulky suggested. And that's the way it went as the car started west to Riverside Chapel in the city. Auntie H. was trying to do it in proper style. Hard with no money. Almost Uncle Eddie had to lay out his own cash for the new family plot in Beth David all the way from Chicago.

"Hymie will pay you back, don't worry," Auntie H. shouted to him long distance.

No one had thought to ask the "maid" if she might want to see Mrs. Caplin. Or would think to take the kids again either. Every time the phone in the hall near the kitchen rang, the whole household jumped. Finally: "It's all over, Teresa. She's gone, the poor little girl, Rosie's gone. It's over for her." Auntie H. had never sounded so soft and wouldn't again, not for years. "Tell them it's over, Teresa, dear. I haven't the heart for it."

Now Teresa was standing at the kitchen window, watching as Chulky backed the old blue Dodge out of the garage and down the driveway. She looked at Melvin and Barbara sitting in the far corners in the back seat. They were not talking to each other. The September sun was twinkling through the stained-glass candle that filled one windowpane so prettily and lighted up the sailboat that filled another. She remembered when Mrs. Caplin and the glass man figured which panes to put where. Mrs. Caplin spent hours making sure they had decided right. "What do you think, Teresa? Should we do tulips in the downstairs toilet or some iris?" The sun started to fade, and the glass boat lost its brilliance. That seemed better to Teresa, more fitting. From her own window Mrs. Donner across the alley smiled sadly and waved to her. Teresa started noticing that her eyes were wet and grabbed for the dish towel. She didn't care about germs.

"I come," she answered Janice, who was calling for help from the bathroom. "I come."

When the afternoon sun shone on the caravan of cars pulling up around the house, Teresa was stunned. She expected only Hermosa and Chulky and maybe Ruthie from the candy store or Mrs. Caplin's ladies from Brooklyn. She didn't even have coffee in the house. And there was no liquor either or cake or anything. It'd been so long since the house was crowded. And she couldn't do the nice Caplin things. Set a nice Caplin table. Seeing Mr. Caplin, his hands in irons, get out of the second car, she hardly knew what to feel. "I was so glad to look his face and so sad look his hands and so sorry for family, I don't remember what I do," she told me later. "I only remember his hat on wrong. When they free hands, and he fix hat, I feel more better."

The first thing he did was come into her kitchen and embrace her. "Thank you," he said, "from my heart. You are the best champ I ever had." Then he examined Michael. "Good strong back," he said, "and what legs! A fine boy." He grabbed Michael up to kiss him and held him for quite a while. When he finally put him down, he turned his face to Teresa and tried to smile, but the smile slid into such sadness that it was Teresa who turned away. When she turned back, he had been swallowed up by living-room people. The detectives took his place in the kitchen. For two hours she listened to detective talk in there. In the living room there was mostly hushed tones. Once Teresa heard Mr. Caplin say to one of his brothers, "Okay, I'll see what I can do. I'll write him a letter for you." Were they still asking him favors? Teresa hoped she'd misheard. The detectives became busy following the war on the radio.

"They're rounding up all those damn Japs out west and locking them up," they told her. Since Midway, America was feeling a little better, but not much. A terrible day.

Old and so seriously ill she could hardly walk, Rose's mother came to mourn with her. "Nobody will come to sit the traditional shiva for the dead," she said sadly to Teresa in the kitchen. It was wartime, and Auntie H. didn't believe in such things; but old Grandma wanted it. Needed it. She cried about it in Polish. Her remaining daughters came to pull her away.

Then everyone was leaving. Teresa didn't get a chance to say good-bye to Mr. Caplin, and Janice, dislodged from his lap, where she had sat rather too shyly, was sobbing in her skirt. Auntie H. stayed. "I think I'll sleep in the living room," she told Teresa. "Make up the couch for me. Rose's bedroom still smells of the medicine." Mrs. Caplin's bedroom smelled just fine. It was dusted and fresh and pretty. Teresa had seen to it. But of course, she knew that was not the reason. She smoothed clean sheets over the down of the sofa and got the guest pillows from the closet. And that's how it went once a week for a year. Auntie H. did her duty.

They let Hymie out. But his Rosie was not there to pick him up. He came home by train. It was three years and eight months since they took him. Teresa had kept a close count. Now grayer and thinner, he was back. But still the best-looking man on the block. A mixed blessing, his good looks, Teresa decided, because all too soon there was Marie. She would like to have discussed this development with John, but he wasn't feeling good. Then they admitted John to Bellevue. His lungs were infected. The old pneumonia had come back to plague him. He had to quit his job at Charleys. It was too hard on him.

"As soon as I'm better," he called in from the phone near his ward, "you will tell Caplin you have to quit. As soon as I'm better." Right now he couldn't argue against her forty-five dollars a month. Mr. Caplin had restored the five-dollar cut. John didn't get better. At first he seemed to, and Teresa was hopeful.

"I tell him," she informed Mr. Caplin, "to stay with his sister in Connecticut when hospital finish. Fresh air and eggs do good. And she can take care him."

"Don't worry"—Mr. Caplin comforted her—"I got a great lung man for him to see. He'll straighten him right out." Later Mr. Caplin kept what the great lung man said to himself, and John went to Connecticut. His family in Terry-ville was nice. Often Teresa took Janice up with her for a visit. Loving the farm, Janice never wanted to leave. Neither did Michael; only John wanted to go.

"I feel too far away," he told Teresa. "I can stay with the Benyos again."

"You stay there," she insisted. "It's better." Later she worried about that. Feeling a nagging at her conscience that she tried to dismiss, "I have too much to take care," she said of it. But then she was not sure. John visited a herbalist his sister went to and told Teresa everything would be fine. He swallowed bitter powders with his fresh milk. He tried to walk but tired quickly. By Christmas he was determined to come home. "I want to see you," he hissed over the phone. "I want to hold my son." Mr. Caplin said he could stay with her in the attic if she would watch out for his sputum and keep the kids at a distance. Arrangements were made too late.

When John's sister called and told her to hurry, it was too late. Some part of her knew it.

First, she ran to St. Marks Place and collected Mary, the Benyos' daughter, to stay at the house with Michael. By subway they reached Forest Hills. Teresa told her what she must do and rushed back. She knew she was losing the race but stayed over at Benyo's to rush with him to the earliest train. Teresa was never able to manage traveling on her own. She and Benyo missed the train. Distracted, she called Forest Hills from the station.

"Everything here is just fine," Mr. Caplin told her. "Don't worry about things here. Get to your John." Mary Benyo, it seemed, had decided not to stay, but Teresa mustn't give it a thought. Mr. Caplin will stay home and take care of little Michael. "I'm watching the home front," he said, and did. As she feared, they reached the Hartford

Hospital too late. The doctor was cold with her, and Benyo must hold her up when they go to the "freezer," as Teresa will call it, and pull out a drawer to show her John.

She couldn't look. She apologized to me about it as I will apologize to others a few years to come. She just couldn't look. So Benyo did it for her. "John needs a shave," he said, and led her away as the attendant slid the slab shut. Her sister-in-law helped with the funeral arrangements. He was dead on January 4, 1944, and was buried on the sixth. Teresa now owned land in America. She, too, now had a family plot.

The war rolled on. Women were making real money while making real guns. America's Veronica Lakes rolled up their peekaboo bangs to run machines.

"You can leave Michael with us and make a fortune in a factory," the Benyos advised when they visited in Forest Hills. "Mr. Caplin will make out." Teresa agreed with them but stayed where she was. Love had its own economics. And something had gone wrong with Melvin. Melvin, sulking in his room, refusing to socialize with the hated Marie, had actually gone sick with jealousy. At least that's what Teresa suspected. "Every time he want to to be close with your daddy," she recalled, "Marie in his way. You, you make friends and hug and kiss. Janice, she hang on me. But Melvin lose everything." So Melvin had gone sick over Marie, who exaggerated her mouth and painted stockings on her legs when she couldn't come by black-market rayon. Then Mr. Caplin, who couldn't quite put it in words, signified that the trouble with Melvin could be more than Teresa imagined. She watched Melvin, who went for tests.

When the doctor called in the results, Mr. Caplin was away in Philly, trying to do "fight business." Teresa worried all night over the urgent-sounding voice that repeated, "Please make sure Mr. Caplin calls as soon as possible. We must speak to him immediately." Immediately, which turned out to be the next afternoon, had a pale Mr. Caplin listening and saying, "Uh-huh, uh-huh, I see. . . . So there is no doubt, uh-huh. . . ." Teresa watched him hang up the receiver and stand facing the wall for a long time. Then she saw him bang his head violently against it. When he stopped, he walked to the backyard to stare at the cherry tree little Melvin had helped him plant. And she knew why she had said no to the Benyos' factory. She finished fixing dinner.

The dressing room at St. Vincent's clinic was decorated with pinups proclaiming feminine measurements. Melvin studied each with a student's serious application. Men had gone mad for measurements. Watching carefully as the metal plates were taped across his genitals, he hoped his adolescent half hard-on wouldn't get in the way.

"We have to do this," said the X-ray technician, "or you never get to enjoy a perfect thirty-six–twenty-four–twenty-six." Then they pasted poisonous packets under his arms, evaluating reactions.

"I feel like a guinea pig," he told Teresa, who didn't know what he meant, only that Melvin stayed on her mind.

Then Michael pushed Melvin right off her mind and got deadly ill to do it. The world's healthiest child suddenly wasn't. Home for lunch from kindergarten, where he was the youngest in the class, he smiled, sat at the table, and slumped over into his sandwich.

"Something's the matter with Mikey," called Janice. Teresa shut the Frigidaire and came to look. Oblivious of the fact that for once in his young life he had the total attention of the table, Michael seemed asleep and yet oddly awake. His head lolled like a broken marionette. Janice was right: Something was the matter.

"Put him to bed," ordered Melvin, his own skin stinging under medical patches. Teresa carried the drooped child up to the attic. Melvin ran to the corner for Dr. Kalkin. Janice cried for her daddy in Philadelphia. And I just sat. By now Michael's eyes were rolling up and his head was burning in Teresa's hand.

Kalkin took one long hard look and asked for the phone. "Send an ambulance immediately," we heard him command, adding, just like the movies, "It's a matter of life or death."

Teresa knelt next to the inert child strapped into the stretcher all the way to Queens General. God was punishing her for not giving him enough of her attention. But he was always so undemanding compared with the Caplin kids. Undemanding and strong. Where were the rosy cheeks? He was so pale in spite of the fever. Pale and blotchy. She whispered, then shouted his name to no response. At the hospital she heard the word "coma," then "meningitis," then "critical." They took him away from her into mysterious interior halls of medicine. She waited where they left her for two hours. Then a nurse came, carrying Michael's clothes.

"Disinfect these and come back tomorrow. You can't see him till them." Crying all the way from Kew Gardens to Forest Hills on the F train, she carried the clothing home. People saw her clutching the child's clothing and knew something bad had happened. People looked with sympathy, but no one spoke to her. The next day Mr. Caplin was home and went to the hospital. She had been there for hours in the little room separated by glass from the isolation chamber containing her son. She pointed out Michael's doctor.

"I made friends with him," Hymie Caplin told her, pleased that he could still do something. "I gave him some tickets to the Garden and told him all about you. It's all fixed up. They won't charge you a penny." Michael came out of the coma.

Teresa smiled at her son, and he smiled back. She vowed she would pay him more attention in the future. And she did. For a while. She watched as his doctor, Mr. Caplin's new friend, carried him around the children's ward on his shoulders. Michael fell madly in love with the doctor. His little translucent face lit with pleasure every time the doctor came into sight. Teresa still wondered where the rosy cheeks had gone to.

"He'll be good as new," the doctor had promised. That was not quite the case. But after three weeks Michael was good enough to come home, where he continued to grow up a little more slowly than he started out.

Teresa was forced to cope with a new vocabulary. She could almost pronounce "MacArthur," "Pacific," and "Tojo" as well as "Eisenhower," "Sicily," and "Montgomery." Then sadly, "Auschwitz," "Dachau," and "Treblinka." "Buchenwald" and "Bergen-Belsen" followed soon after.

*   *   *

On June 30, 1945, our Teresa, an ocean away, became a war casualty. A hole was torn in her heart.

At first we heard her shout with joy at the sound of her brother's voice. All the way from Toronto. Person-to-person. Then she stopped shouting and just listened. She heard the fate of her father. It was the first news of her family since Poland had fallen. This was what she told me a long time later. Then she didn't talk, just asked me to watch Michael and went for a solitary walk.

Clemente Kowalchek, her father, the headman of his village, was tortured to death in reprisal for a guerrilla attack on a German soldier.

Her town, she will tell me, was very small, and the people were close. When the Germans made its Jewish families dig their own graves and shoot them, naked, to death, no one would believe it. Then they did the same to the Gypsies. One father and mother and six curly-haired children screamed as the machine guns spattered. They had taken the gold from their ears and fingers and left them under so little earth that pieces of them scattered with the next storm. Then they lined up the strong Carpathian boys and marched them away. Teresa's mother had followed for as long as she could, then gone home to wait for word that would never come. When the partisans organized, her father, pretending to be ignorant of their activities, did what he could to protect them.

The German soldier killed was the head of the firing squad. The SS men marched her father from his home to headquarters for questioning. They kept him two days. He returned home with not a tooth left in his mouth. He refused to say what happened to him. He went to his bed, blessed his wife, and died. That was it, all she knew. That's what her brother told her.

V-J day followed six weeks later, and I can remember Teresa celebrating along with the rest of us. Only a little more quietly. And years later, under a dark Mexican sky, I will think of her quietness and understand.

BOOK THREE

Transitions in a Spaced Age

Changes of Heart

If I ended the year of our
Lord 1969 trembling in the psychedelic maze of a Mexican
garden, attempting to be "one" with God or whoever else
was handy, but mostly revisiting my life in Technicolor
flashes and thinking about Teresa, I also realized Teresa
couldn't conceive of where the years had taken me: from
sex to abortion to suicide, none of which she understood at
all, to trying to save my soul, none of which she needed.
Years of struggling against nature for sainted celibacy.
Then setting life free and giving in to nature, adventure,
and my heart. Years of men. Of loving dangerously. Starting with the end of Nick. In truth Teresa would have been
aware only of the theatrical trappings that glossed the last
stages of my staggering marriage, the glamour, the traveling, the clothing, all the stuff Janice didn't have, and
wanted.

Indeed, it was like starring in a Ziegfield production to
descend the wonderful wide staircase to the lobby of the
Hôtel de Paris, vintage '59, to where Nick was waiting,
conspicuous in handsome anticipation. He watched with

possessive pride as I glided step by step, slowly, to allow admiration from the fabled Greeks, elegant French, and eager Americans who began their evenings of sport and pleasure there. I adored that part. It was so charming to have Rubirosa kiss my hand and better than amazing to have Darryl Zanuck have his chauffeur chasing about the potted palms and the casino tables to slip me a series of "meet me" notes. So desperate was I for some sense of triumph that I drank up all the compliments and accepted flattery as fact. Foolish tricks I'd learned from Nick, who had foolishly fallen in love with me again. And wanted to indulge me.

"When you go on to Venice," he'd said, leaving me to tour Italy with Melodye as chaperone, "and if there's moonlight and a man who looks like Rossano Brazzi, forget you're married and enjoy. Just don't tell me about it." I took him at his word. Before that, his only complaints had been my new vegetarian eating habits.

"It's like traveling with a giant rabbit," he protested as I opted for vegetables over gigot and ignored champagne for Vichy water. "You're denuding the French countryside."

These last years Nick's "rabbit" had learned to step over his inert body, go to the kitchen, and cook up greens. And when he stood on the window ledge, raving at New York City, I could continue to read my journals on natural hygiene or do my breathing exercises or simply touch up my nails, barely tuned in for the threatened crash. So it finally ended not when I was wanting to die but when I almost let him finish himself.

Angry over something to do with Martha and frustrated with me, Nick had burst into our Florida bedroom, oozing with booze and 3:00 A.M. violence. I watched him pace, mutter, slam and break. Was I due for another moonlight escape? Could I get to the phone and call a taxi without precipitating more danger? "Where," he had hissed, "are those sleepers Doc left?" Starting toward me, he lurched into the nightstand. "Where did you hide them?"

"In the top drawer." I didn't even put up the usual resistance. I just watched as he clumsily opened the bottle and downed his first three. Good, he'd be quiet. Then, half out of it, his eyes still sly and wild, he swallowed three more. I stayed very still and kept watching. Then more.

When, in and out of consciousness, he started to turn gray and bubble at the mouth, I shook free of my morbid fascination and rushed to get help. Oh, there was plenty of time to rescue Nick, but what was happening to me? I was frightened for my soul. I needed to save my soul. "If a mug turns himself cold," my father once said of a man in the news, "he's turning himself dead."

So I saw a judge, got a writ, and ran to California, where Janice, newly married to her young and beautiful actor, had just, in her own Santa Monica bed, given birth to a baby. She had phoned it in as it was happening, giving me a groan-by-groan of the event. "It's a boy," announced the midwife just like the movies. Then Nick came to Los Angeles, so I ran to New York. When Nick returned East, I went back West to vegetate and restore myself. These crossings kept me in motion for a year. I also visited a fasting retreat. "What," demanded Auntie H., "do you mean, you are starving in a desert?" She had never heard of such a thing.

"What's aura?" I asked my friend Helene Buttons, who'd called my California hideout wanting to do me some good. That was something I'd never heard of.

"The light that emanates from our radiant souls," she explained. "Take my advice and see this man." Back in 1960 vegetarians were a close-knit group who passed along information on the best in organic produce, the best practitioners of the various natural healings, and the very best prices to get them for. And even twenty-five years too early for the New Age, Los Angeles mystics could be found. But not over every brass star on Hollywood Boulevard. And none of them were trying to sell you their crystals.

In this case, Helene knew a fellow who knew a psychic, who read aura, which might give "you some direction for your life." Since Buddy and Olga, I was suspicious of people with inside information on how other people should live their lives, yet I found myself possessing a mystic bent. At first it had taken me by surprise. Originally, more worried about the wobble of my thighs than my thoughts, I'd buffered my last years of Nick with yoga. Twisting into ancient postures, I had breathed prana and harbored a pure and unspoken crush on Majumdar, my teacher.

"Why not drop your leotard one day?" suggested another student, amused by my mute adoration.

"Not with a holy man!" I protested.

"I didn't realize you were so religious," she said, and neither had I until then. But was aura reading kosher? I wasn't so sure. Certainly Majumdar wasn't dabbling in such things. Once Helene had sent me to a witch doctor occupying a dank basement on West Fifty-seventh Street who offered, for a handsome fee, to clean me up with a ritual "limpia." I managed to escape it.

"My friend Eduardo Tirella," pressed Helene, spending an expensive chunk of long-distance time on it, "will drive you to this psychic. He doesn't even charge. He does it for God. And you'll enjoy Eduardo. He's a great vegetarian cook and a fabulous designer. Right now he's redoing Doris Duke's gardens." With those kinds of references how could I but agree to go?

"Call me Eddy," said Eduardo as we spun out toward Tarzana, the Santa Ana wind blowing my beehive hairdo apart. "You are going to love Jacques Honduras." Jacques Honduras, indeed, I thought. What a phony name. Lots of nuts among these California berries. Eddy kept chatting.

"You must be a good vegetarian." He complimented me. "Your skin is transparent in the sun." So we talked God, mangoes, and papayas the rest of the drive.

Jacques Honduras turned out to be a pale retired postal clerk who raised parakeets and lived in a simple house in the middle of nowhere. After seating me against a white wall and taking out a pad, he read me rapidly, scribbling notes as words rushed out of him.

"Big change. Big change. Don't go leave the country. . . . Stay away from Mexico. . . . Mushrooms . . ." How did he know about that? I'd told no one of my plans to join Polly Adler in Tecate, Mexico, for an Aldous Huxley seminar on peyote. It would be good "to climb a few mountains for immortality," thought Polly. "Florida," pronounced Honduras, "important spiritual transformation

... Florida will save you.... Go to your house there and wait.... Something wonderful..." Another shock. I did have a rent-paid house to use in Miami Beach, and "something wonderful" sounded wonderful! So Florida it was to be.

On the ride back from Tarzana, comparing readings and listening to Eddy describe the "marvelous meat-free dinner" he was going to prepare, I saw him suddenly begin to tremble. He pulled the car off the road. What was the matter?

"I don't know," he said, "but something is rattling my spine." Then he reached into the back of his Aston-Martin and handed me a heavy green book. Had I read *The Path of the Masters?* No.

"You must," he stammered. "You must."

Years later, hearing about the accident when Doris Duke hit the gas pedal instead of the brake and crushed Eduardo into the wrought-iron garden gates, I remembered his sweetness.

Waiting for me at the Miami airport was the chiropractor son of a natural hygienist lady from New York, courtesy of the vegetarian underground. In those days of no-direct flights I was glad to see him. It was 2:00 A.M., and most of the drive to my house was spent with me mourning Nick and my prevailing sense of loss and how I needed something, someone.

Noticing something green lying on his back seat, I reached for it. It was the book Eduardo had shown me.

"*The Path of the Masters.* Please, Bernie, let me read it."

"No," he said sharply. "That's not for you with your jazzy life."

I closed my door on him in angry silence. The next morning, full of apology, he knocked on it.

"I want to take you somewhere," he said, "and introduce you to someone very special. I could sleep all night," he continued, "and it came to me I was supposed to help you." I went with him.

"Oh, I know that face," I happily told the bright-eyed Astra as I studied the turbaned portrait on her wall. I'd felt

279

a joy at recognizing it that I hadn't felt since my father's last smile. "I've seen that face," I said, "in dreams."

"Sit down," she'd invited. "Bernie says you are already a vegetarian. That's to the good. Time is so short before the visit." So she talked and I listened; then I talked, cried, and she typed. By the time night fell, we were attaching a strip of instant snapshots to a long letter and mailing it off to India. India wired back. I was to be initiated at the visit.

The "visit" was that of the American representative of Master Kirpal Singh, a yogi saint from Delhi. Turbaned, bangled, and bearded, Mr. Khanna had come to initiate six local seekers into the mysteries of this spiritual science called Surat Shaha Yoga, the yoga of attention and sound. And me, too.

Suddenly in love with God, I worried if it was all too quick. My heart and soul longed for some real truth to cling to. Could this be it? Lying in my bed at night, practicing what little I'd learned about meditation, I prayed for a sign. Something to seal my faith. Something to convince me that God, even though He made a lot of mistakes from the weather to war, actually might know my name.

The night before initiation a whole video screen opened inside my head. A sepia-tinted vision. It was obviously India. A bride, beautifully adorned and veiled with fresh flowers, was paraded on a white horse to her waiting groom. The ceremony was being conducted by the most magnificent old man in a high-crowned turban and flowing white beard. After a while the vision faded, and I fell asleep.

I was glad I had described it to Bernie. For lo and behold, just before initiation, Mr. Khanna set up a vintage projector and, on reels no longer current, screened for us the only film ever made of his and Master Kirpal Singh's master, Baba Sawan Singh. There it was, in sepia, exactly as I'd witnessed it: the wedding. My heart opened.

"No," I would explain happily to old lovers and new admirers. "No, there is no point in our dating. I'm a celibate now.

"No," I would insist as they objected. "The point of celibacy is not moral. It's a matter of attention and energy. If you spend it on sex, you're not giving it to God." I kept a required spiritual diary, which I sent to India, once a month, chronicling my endeavors and my failures. For more than a year my chastity was the untarnished object of my own devotion. Then came Oscar from Venezuela, a leftover infidelity from the days of marriage.

Oscar sat, looking at me, coughing gently and smiling secretly. He knew me as a wandering wife, not, he said, as a "would-be saint, saving it for God." Smug with my sanctified new self, I just repeated my mantra and smiled back. Certainly I could handle taunts as well as temptation. I wanted him to know that the real me was now breathing a more rarefied air. Indeed, if he, who had always claimed to be a mystic himself, would stop mocking and listen, he could breathe it, too. But as his own sly smile continued to grow, mine started to shrink. What was he finding so damned funny?

"They used to," he said, waiting for my reaction. "They used to watch, you know. Back then when you were staying at my coconut plantation."

"What do you mean?"

"They used to sit with their machetes still and most quietly watch you as you removed your top and crossed your legs at the water's edge to do your yoga breathing exercises. Our production fell off almost completely during that hour. Of course, you were only a hatha-yogi then. One could still imagine touching you." He was referring to the time I had run from Nick to visit him.

"I never noticed anyone."

"You wouldn't. They were up in the palm trees hypnotized, like monkeys confronting a cobra."

"I don't believe you," I said.

"Why would I lie? How would I know about your exposing your breasts?"

"I must have told you."

"No, the head machete man told me. As explanation for the poor count of coconuts."

"Well, no one there ever bothered me."

"They are polite, our Venezuelan campesinos. And most probably they were afraid you might stop." Oscar looked very superior. "It was a wonderful thing for them, you see.

You, slender and sweet, sitting there worshiping sun and sea in bare breasts."

"The bra top bothered my breathing, but why are you mentioning all this now? Why didn't you say something then? If it affected you, your production, I mean."

"Perhaps more than my production. But you were my guest."

"Did I embarrass you?" I asked, hoping he'd say yes, which might have excused his embarrassing me.

"I wasn't," he said, "responsible for the behavior of a crazy lady from the States."

"The point is," I flared, with a definite loss of yogi composure, "that one of your María Isabels would never have done it. Right?" My tone was betraying me, and he picked at the weak spot.

"Our women would be more aware," he said thinly.

"Aware of what? Damn you!"

He had me at last and laughed. "Aware of being watched." His laughter caused the thin white scars that seamed his handsome face to fold. Had I really been responsible for those scars? Insofar as the race that had been run because of me. Or so Young Oscar had said.

Young Oscar, his nephew, who'd known me first, liked telling me all about it. He'd come to New York probably just for the pleasure. He'd told me how he had challenged his uncle to race down the Autopista, which goes from Caracas to the sea. And how his uncle had agreed.

He hadn't been sure just what went wrong. But the crash came, glass slashing his uncle's face to pieces. In the Miami moonlight Oscar's scars looked romantic, and when he suddenly touched my breasts, the moment was his.

"No, my Barbara," he said, "these are not the breasts of a saint."

And so I'd fallen. But only for that one night. The next morning Oscar was gone, and I, whose threshold of pain and pleasure had been breached, was trying to hold to the words of Kirpal Singh, who'd instructed that if you fall on the "path," at least fall in the right direction.

I repeated my mantra like crazy and went back to saying, "No, there is no point in our going out, you see. I am a celibate." I did not want to fail again. So I carried the same cry to New York, where I had landed a "real job": fashion coordinator for the Peter Pan bras, girdles, and swimwear. Indeed, I had the staff baffled at Peter Pan. In those days a sexy young woman who didn't eat meat and who eschewed men was unheard of. I was unique, for a while anyway.

Then Michael dropped into my life. He didn't seem to portend a pitfall on the "path," sent, as he was, by some meditating vegetarians, who thought I could use a nice friend.

"He is so sweet," they explained. "We met him at the gym. He knows you're working at being celibate and will respect that."

He showed up at my studio apartment in Murray Hill with a single long-stemmed rose, ice skates, and the rosiest cheeks to be found in February in New York City.

"Do you skate?" he asked after appraising me.

"I used to. A little."

"Well, it will tighten those legs right up and help your chest development, too." Who had told him about my legs, and what was wrong with my chest? "C'mon," he insisted, "let me buy you a pair of skates."

The man at the skate shop was almost irritated with Michael's expertise. We must get the boots right. Then the blades. "Shave down her first point just a hair," Michael instructed. "We are not going for figures. I don't want her tripping and messing up that madonna face." The skate shop man studied my face. I dropped my eyes.

After the skate shop he suggested La Scala restaurant. Michael, it seemed, loved opera. And like Mimi and her lover, we were applauded to our table. Michael was a favorite customer. I became busy explaining vegetarian fare to the owners surrounding us.

"Bella?" Michael prompted them.

"Bella," they chorused, and my "spiritual" romance was off and running.

"Ten more solid pounds," Michael considered, "and you will be magnificent." Somewhere around this time I lost my job. After a year of skidding away from my boss, a man of many mistresses, I found myself on thin ice. And then on unemployment.

So every afternoon I'd scrub Art Students League's paint from my hands, not to offend him, who was neurotic about "dirt," and rush to La Scala, where he fed me.

"Listen, love," he said, "one little piece of meat. Some fegato venezia or veal piccata couldn't hurt you. We really are animals, you know. It'll be good for your blood." Michael frequently spoke of people as animals.

"My blood is fine, Michael. What are you doing after karate?" I was getting curious about the income of this buyer of piccata, bicycles, Japanese woodcuts, and the best box at the opera.

"Checking out a liquor store and looking into a beauty school. Larry Mathews has a proposition for me, about a salon he wants me to open with your friend Monti. I'm thinking of taking it and changing my life." What could that mean? Because I was trained not to ask questions, and since he didn't sleep over, Michael's comings and goings remained mysterious.

"Michael," I asked at last, worn down with oblique references to worlds too dirty for my saintly feet. "Michael, tell me about your old life. The one you want to change."

"It's not for your ears, my life's breath. Not for you to think about. Besides, it's all past. But will you mind standing room at the opera for a while?"

"No, we can hear it on the radio, but—"

He cut short my question. "Sh, my saint. Think of the beautiful babies we will make after we are married. I'll be a sweeter father than your old man was, I swear it. I'll teach them to swim and skate and be strong. I'll beg your magical master to bless our union and he will. Wait and see. By the time you come home from touring with your beautiful master, I'll be ready for you."

In 1962 Sant Kirpal Singh Ji, Majarah, was coming from India on a world tour. And I was to be part of his American "caravan." My breath caught every time I thought how lucky I was to be included. Only the recent slip in my celibacy had me concerned. Not that Kirpal Singh insisted on celibacy, but chastity, he said, was wanted on his seven-fold path. "Man is a social being," he advised, "and needs a companion." Was Michael to be my life's companion? The tour pushed all else to the back of my brain. My master was coming. And seeing him step from his plane at Idlewild Airport (not yet named JFK) would be the best moment of my life.

Crisscrossing America, I slept in cheap hotels, or in garages converted for the occasion into dorms, or on floors, couches, and cars. Rising at 5:00 A.M. to pray, I gave free breakfast to all who came to meditate with truth. And also to those who just came for curiosity or the breakfast. All were blessed by coming, and no one left hungry. So for almost a year I cleaned, cooked, and stayed intoxicated with God and encased in crystal.

Then, on November 22, 1963, in Dallas my crystal, along with most of America's, was shattered. It happened in an open car on a day of drums. So vivid and ever present.

I had been sitting two hours to the west at a fast-food counter in Vancouver. Anticipating the long, religious ride to California. Then the morning Muzak, turned to static, irritating the breakfast faces around me. Then, a disbelieving voice, cracking with anguish, had said, "Something has happened . . . Terrible."

Later we saw it on TV. We would see Frank Mankiewicz step out the doors of Parkland Hospital in Dallas and signal for quiet and soberly tell us John Fitzgerald Kennedy had left us.

Heartbroken, I asked permission of my master to leave the tour for a while. I didn't want to go to California. I wanted Christmas in New York, with Michael. I wanted to skate at Rockefeller Plaza and feel good.

After landing in a blizzard at Newark Airport, I rushed to phone Michael at his karate club. After some whispering, I was told he wasn't around. They would take a message. "Tell him I'm at the airport and on my way home." It took hours to reach Manhattan. I opened my door to a candlelit apartment.

"Hello," I remember calling, thinking Michael, who had my keys, was obviously creating something beautiful for me. The air was scented with fresh-brewed coffee.

"Hello" again. I didn't own a coffeemaker, or coffee. Candles flickered over what seemed like Michael's entire wardrobe, plus some ladies' clothing as well. In harsher electric glare, I saw I was right. And lots of cigarettes. One still smoldering. Michael didn't smoke. What was going on? Michael never showed up. Days later I heard some of the story.

"Oh, St. Barbara." Friend and gossip columnist Alex Friedman phoned to tell me the facts of life. "Just read the newspapers. It's all over the place. Your prince Michael, and I could have told you before, but you were having so much fun, lives with New York's hottest madam. Has for years, and they are in big trouble."

He was right. A trunk containing the corpse of a bookie had floated to the top of the Harlem River. The papers made much of a mystery woman and her accomplice, who had dumped the trunk off the Triboro Bridge.

Days later Michael finally came for his things. Hoping not to find me there, he wasn't up on his luck. With his head between his hands, he said, "Listen, my life, I have to marry her. I can't desert her. I have to be able to refuse to testify. What can I do? She always gave me everything when I was with her. She knew about you. I told her I was leaving the life."

"Why did you lie to me?"

"I never lied, I just never told you. My love, I was changing for you."

I reached for my keys. He kissed the palm of my hand, then gave them over. "She's in trouble. What can I do?" I didn't know. "I'm taking her to Canada to avoid the police. It was a favor, you see, for our best client. . . ." I watched him pack his clothes. And hers.

"Don't forget the coffeemaker," I remember telling him. (In 1987 Michael made a small headline again. In an argument he shot the young brother of his lady friend, then put a bullet through his own tortured temple and his awful quietus made.)

That was how the sixties took shape. Did the violence give birth to the love children? Certainly seeking after truth and love was not truly exclusive to me and my particular group of disciples. But then that notion would hardly enter my mind, spiritual snobbery being as common and as ancient as religion itself. It lent zeal to my pronouncement.

"You are all just jerking yourselves off spiritually," I had insisted to Tim Leary as we dangled our feet in the perfect pool below the Bungalow (a simple stone palace nestled in pines, adorning a hill on a three-thousand-acre estate) belonging to Billy Hitchcock and his twin brother, Tommy, in Millbrook, New York. Andrew Mellon heirs, the Hitchcocks were given to open entertaining and I was one among many houseguests.

In 1963, while organizing the IFIF (International Federation for Internal Freedom, with LSD as sacrament), Tim had announced in the *Harvard Crimson:* "We welcome anyone interested. Participants need only bring their own brain." By '64 Tim was late of Harvard and dangling his feet in Billy's pool.

My father, who delighted in Irish con men, would have declared Tim a "real beauty," and, wisely, "a little Jewish." My father was always insisting everyone he liked was "a little Jewish" or, if not that, then "surrounded by smart Jews."

This, of course, included Franklin Delano Roosevelt, his personal messiah, as well as an early pope he admired, George Bernard Shaw, Cary Grant, Wallace Beery, and Charlie McCarthy, who "must have had a *mohel* for a woodcarver." Sigmund Freud unquestionably had "a big Jewish brain." "Psychology," my father had said, "may be a Greek word, but it's certainly a Jewish idea. Trust me. I read Freud pretty good when I was away." A sports columnist had once quoted my father talking about Lew Jenkins, a troublesome lightweight champ of his. "People don't understand Lew," he quoted. "Lew's a maladjusted neurotic, born with a chronic inability to control his kisser."

Anyway, it seemed, Tim was Jewish enough to get Billy to give him, for a nominal fee, the Victorian mansion tucked away in one corner of the Millbrook estate.

"Drugs are not the way to God," I kept insisting, as Tim's partner, Dick Alpert, now called Baba Ram Das, smiled. I then became more vehement. "For God's sake,

Sandoz Chemical didn't create spiritual experiences. There are older and better ways to get there."

"But slower," said Tim.

"In India . . ." I'd start again.

"The sly man," interrupted Van Wolf, a friend who had brought me, "the sly man, according to Gurdjieff, doesn't have to take the way of the fakir. The sly man can use one of God's own shortcuts." I'd never heard of Gurdjieff, but Van, whom I had known since he worked for Mike Todd and hung around Lindy's, had a knack for shortcuts, and certainly a shortcut had sounded in order, as my celibacy kept threatening to slip away for good.

"My master says not to use drugs. He says we are the living temples of God. He says we are to keep our bodies pure with a strict vegetarian diet and to avoid all intoxicants."

"I am going to christen you St. Barbara," said Tim, who picked up private passions. "Every revolution needs at least one saint. You can be ours."

It was flattery again. And I welcomed it, though at the time I thought it set me more firmly on my pedestal. All things considered, the problem with pedestals is the getting off. And was I getting dizzy up there, perusing all these worlds I had access to? Certainly my gold lamé turban was tilting.

"Better to eat meat, drink wine, and burn the Koran, than condemn he who does," Mhulani Rhumi, a Persian sage, had said. The idea seemed so civilized that I repeated it a lot that summer, especially on the sands of Brooklyn, among a group of health-nut vegetarians, friends of my sister's, where I went when I wasn't at Millbrook or free-lance fashion coordinating. And I liked spreading the good news of what the privileged and chic were up to. Here, in return for such gossip, they shared the best mangoes to be found north of the Mason-Dixon with me. They particularly loved my Barbra Streisand story, my biggest free-lance success.

A minute red-bearded merchant from Egypt had contacted me to help launch what he insisted was to be the starship of a fleet of fancy stores called Les Parisiennes. And "never to mind" its Forty-second Street location. His *maga-sin* was to have the *première grande avec un spectacle fabuleux* and *les stars importants* and *beaucoup de monde* should be there. And please "arrange" by next week. Well, why not? So, taking a wad of his money, I leaped in and hired the best of Eileen Ford's runway models, had them fitted, then coiffed by Monti at Saks for the best of heads. I found a loud little band that would use my sister, Janice, as its singer (singing was her heart's desire). I had her coiffed by Monti as well and flooded the area with flyers announcing our gala opening.

The French Line lent me a covered gangplank complete with a real live sailor in a beret as well as supplied banners, champagne, and giveaways. The boys at the Morris office would fill the place with every sort of celebrity they could push into it. But how to get press? So on the spot I created the first annual Woman of the World Award just for Barbra Streisand, the sensation of *Funny Girl* and the brightest thing to happen to Broadway since electric lights. Sending her the most impressive of imploring telegrams, I announced her good fortune and our pleasure in presenting her this prestigious award. And what time would she find the limousine convenient? I waited on those famous tenterhooks till she said yes. And then did I get press!

The street was so jammed the police had to handle the traffic and people hung off the library lions to get a peek.

I think my red beard had a *classique* Egyptian climax just watching Barbra cross that gangplank into his rather undistinguished establishment while champagne popped and cameras flashed, and I'd done it! Receiving enough of a bonus to keep lazy for a year, if I lived cheap.

"It was a happening," said Van Wolf, who'd introduced me to the Hitchcocks. Now instead of *Around the World in Eighty Days*, starring half of Hollywood, Van was promoting "Around the Cosmos in Sixty Minutes," featuring Tim, God, and the Gang. At Brighton Beach, Brooklyn, I was considered a definite "entrepreneur."

"Have you read Hermann Hesse?" I asked Teddy, one of the Brighton Beach regulars, who was his own oasis of constant amusement. I liked teasing Teddy, who always lifted his long nose in long sneers when he answered.

"He's one of those great German thinkers, ain't he?" Teddy said. Then went back to picking sand from between his toes. He had just done his daily eight-bay run. In those preyuppie days the only visible New York runners jogged the Coney Island shores.

"No," I corrected. "Hesse was Swiss."

"Those are the worst kind of Germans," stated Teddy. "Next to the Austrians, that is." Teddy had never forgiven the Germans. Which was fine with me. Sprawling his lean body alongside my blanket, Teddy organized himself better to observe female breasts bobble on their way to the sea.

And I turned my thoughts to a gentle, serious neighbor of mine who leaned romantically toward me and to whom I was very drawn. Tall and dark, serious and spectacled, he'd finally spoken to me at the corner delicatessen we both frequented, asking if I was a yogi. Totally charmed with being recognized that way, I kind of forced our friendship to live in that spiritual area, taking him to meditation meetings and such stuff, still hard to find then.

He was someone, I decided as the sun started to toast me, my father wouldn't label a "Boy Scout wise guy." But could I move away from my vestal altar toward him after cramming my celibacy down his throat every time he gestured in an opposite direction? No, with him I had pinned myself to my position by my high of choice: "Holier than thou."

"Where's Janice?" Teddy suddenly demanded. "Where is the other Caplin beauty?" He was always secretly in love with my sister.

"Janice is visiting Auntie H. with little Paulie."

"I can't decide," Teddy said, wiping off a slice of mango he'd nicked from an adjacent blanket, "if Paulie looks more like Janice or his father, Bobby, God rest his soul." Mango juice marked his words, and he reached a long arm to the next blanket to garner another. "Anyway, he's a gorgeous kid."

"A gorgeous kid," chorused some of the neighboring towels, reed mats, and aluminum folding chairs.

"Too bad he don't talk so good," added one.

"He spoke at six months." I defended my nephew fiercely. "But after the shock of Bobby's death and Janice's breakdown, he just retreated a little. That's all. So what else's new?" I challenged. At Brighton I fell into a talmudic rhythm of speech. It was my mimic's ear. My singsong went unnoticed by Teddy, who thought everyone talked that way.

Yet how judgmental these vegos were behind their slices of mango. Their life, encompassed by Bay 2, was one of removed and comfortable comment. What did they know of little Paulie's first brightness blighted not only by his father's sudden death but by his mother gone mad with guilt? Bobby had seen Janice on Fifth Avenue and followed her, like the romantic young actor he was, into a record store and even into the booth. They flirted, later fondled, and finally wed. And went west. Where he was to make their fortune. So said the William Morris agents, who always "know star material when they see it."

But how actors' strike of 1960 got in the way. The little cottage in Santa Monica Canyon required rent, and the baby required everything. So à la Steinbeck, Bobby took a temporary job doing roadwork, which was in keeping with the *Route 66* television hero's role he was up for and which would help with his "character." Under a boiling July sky with a pick in his hand he had a seizure, something to do with an old football injury. Janice, in a vegetarian terror of medical procedures, rushed him to a healer three hot hours away in the desert, where, before help was available, he choked to death on his own vomit. She never forgave herself. Neither did his family.

"We don't argue with Big Babs here," Teddy announced after the little silence my words produced, "with her millionaire pals so crazy for her they throw their rubles at her rosy feet." I ignored him and applied some Bain de Soleil to my skin.

"Just look what she creams herself with," Teddy continued to the crowd. "Baby oil ain't good enough for those shoulders. Boy, if Ilsa Koch coulda gotten her hands on skin like that, she coulda showed us a hellofa lampshade.

291

Just notice the way that poor man's Beatle over there is glomming her. Her charms are manifold."

I smiled then at the cute skinny kid with the new Chelsea haircut, just getting popular. He smiled back.

"I think that 'that one' deals in marijuana," said Teddy, "he and his little group of mods over there."

The idea of something soothing on this quarrelsome beach was suddenly appealing. I'd had a drag on my last trip to Millbrook. So I smiled again. And the kid ambled over. "Wanna stroll a bay or two?" he asked.

"Clever as John Daly, ain't he?" commented Teddy. "Such a way with words. I could die." As I stepped across three towels, two mats, and one baby building a sand pile and walked away with him.

"What's your name?" he asked.

"Barbara, and yours?"

"Roger. I'm from California, but I was born here." Twenty yards later he added, "I noticed you doing yoga on the beach last week. You were with your sister and her kid. I asked about you, checked you out. You didn't look like those other vegos over there. You got class."

Between Brighton and Manhattan Beach lay about 150 yards of rock cliff. Not unpassable at low tide, a little tricky at other times. We got about halfway and climbed up to a small ledge and lit up. "I'm a quick high," I warned. "I don't really smoke. So you may have to support me back past the rocks."

"Don't worry," he said. "I can take care of you." A favorite phrase.

"You musta," he added between inhales, "been a sensational sixteener."

"What's the matter with me now?"

"You're dynamite now. I just was thinking of what I missed. You live in the city, huh?"

"Yeah."

"Want me to walk you to the subway?"

"Walk me," New York kids used to demand of one another. I found it sweet. To his credit, through shifting tides, Roger got me back.

"I want to hold your hand," Roger sang, bobbing up and

down the elevated subway platform, from which I could see the parachute jump and roller coasters I had once ridden on with my father. "You like that sound?" Roger asked, testing the water. He was coming along for the ride.

"The Beatles, you mean? Yes, very much."

Tip-tapping his fingernails against the cover of a trash can, he demanded I "dig it."

"Are you a musician?" I asked, knowing he'd enjoy the question.

"I play around with the flute." He leaped up onto the bench and did a little Gene Kelly turn and leaped off. "I'll bring it around sometime and do a tune for you."

"That will be nice."

"Nice! I'll put you away, I play so good. I'll play the pants right off you."

"Did they tell you, those people you checked me with on the beach, did they mention I was a celibate?"

"What's that?"

"That's someone who doesn't have sex. Ever."

"You've got to be kidding."

"No, I'm not. I took vows."

I surprised myself by telling Roger a little of how I'd come to my master. I'd told none of it at Millbrook. Actually no one had asked. They accepted me as St. Barbara on my own recognizance and sweetly catered to my vegetarian tastes.

At my apartment I watched Roger study the photograph of my master with a seriousness that I found appealing. "He got some face," Roger said at last. "It looks like the map of India and Moses wrapped up in one. Does he always wear that white turban?"

"Yes, he's a Sikh. The long, turbaned hair and bands on the wrist set them apart. They are very austere."

"Long hair is really where it is," said Roger, checking his bangs in my mirror. "Maybe I'll grow mine even longer. Nah, it would make me too visible. By the way," he added, getting back to earth, "do you know anybody who wants some good smoke at a good price? Hard to come by this season."

"I may."

"I hope they're rich. I like dealing in high society." So I mentioned the Millbrook crowd, and his eyes lit up. "Tim Leary is gonna shake up the whole world, babe," he proclaimed. "Have you ever done any spiritual acid?"

"No, it's not my way. I told you I'm a yogi, and I don't do those things." I was, and I knew it, protesting too much.

"Well, if you want to get a glimmer of God quick, do it."

I had once written to India to ask about acid. He'd said it was too dangerous. But it was like all apples and all Eves. I was curious. Could Roger be a quiet way to satisfy this curiosity without Millbrook or Miami the wiser? Could he act as a guide? I casually inquired. It seemed he'd done a lot of "trips," as he called them. The idea of trying it with Roger seemed rather comfortable. I could slip off my saint's pedestal with no one to see. Except God, of course. But that was too big a notion.

So Roger brought his flute. I bought some fruit. He brought 350 mics injected into innocent-looking sugar cubes. (Honey balls would have been more to my taste.) I bought flowers and put on fresh sheets. We lit candles, put out my master's picture. And reassuring each other of religious sincerity, we swallowed a little loaded sugar.

One second after swallowing, I was sorry. What an act of madness. Too late, too late.

"What happens now?" I asked Roger in total fear as he lifted his flute.

"Now," he said, "we wait. Listen to this." Looking like Pan, he sat cross-legged on the arm of my yellow velvet couch and piped. I was starting to feel unpinned. There was a quivering in my stomach. "A funny thing happened to me on my way to enlightenment," I joked. Roger had smiled into his flute.

"I think I married a skinny, flute-playing, impoverished, dope-dealing Beatlesque baby last night," I had said to my sister, Janice, the following morning.

"What are you talking about?" she screamed into the phone.

"Roger, that beach boy from Brighton. I took acid with

him last night, and I think—oh, God, I can't bear it—I think we are joined for life."

"You took what? Oh, Barbara, that's so unhealthy."

"Too late, and in the middle of it we were joined in celestial bliss."

"What do you mean? Do you mean you balled each other?" The phone quivered in my hand.

"Ball, hell! We're sun, moon, and galaxy to each other. He was Christ to my Mary Magdalene. Shiva to my Parvati. He was Caligula, and I was his sister. Our worlds collided. Oh, I don't know. Anyway, I don't think we can separate."

"Are you going crazy?" Janice demanded. "Where is he now?"

"Selling some hash to some hotshot record guy."

"Well, then you've separated," she said. "So forget it."

"You know what I mean."

"No, I don't, and neither do you."

"Well, I may love him."

"You're making me very nervous," she said. "Listen, all this crap is because you got laid for the first time in years."

"I did have one glaring exception before," I admit.

"Did you?" said Janice. "You never told me. But never mind, once doesn't count, and neither does this. Not that I'm against true love, but you sound nuts. You'd better fast today and drink juices tomorrow and clean out your system. Then you'll know if worlds collided. But if you were going to collide, why not with one of your socialites?"

"I don't know."

"Do you think your master will approve this collision?"

"He was there."

"Who was there?"

"My master manifested. Roger saw him, too. LSD starts so hard and scary. And I thought I was dying, so I started to pray to the master for help. And he appeared."

My sister sighed and said, "Drink juices at least, and we'll talk later."

I put down the phone and remembered Roger's luminous face last night, lights dancing around his head. "Barbara," he'd whispered, "someone is standing behind you. I think he's the man in your photograph except he's huge and wearing white." I'd turned as best I could, being disconnected from my muscles. And there he was, or almost was, effulgent in white light. "Forgive me," I had prayed. "And please, don't let me go now."

Kirpal Singh, or his image, passed a hand over my head. Then he faded. But Roger definitely had known he was there.

A later conversation that day with Peggy Hitchcock (Billy and Tommy's sweet sister) convinced me I still had choices. "Loving love is usually at the core of such experiences, and actually, Barbara, I'd say, vegetables and meditations notwithstanding, that you were overdue. Don't you think?"

I wasn't sure what to think or even what I'd learned, but there was no doubt I had flunked celibacy again. I took Janice's advice and made myself a carrot juice, as best I could with fingers that still had a tendency to disappear, and I lay down to try to figure it out. It was impossible. I centered on Peggy's talking about "loving love." That was possible, though perhaps more practical for her than me, who was living cheap and running out of the despised unemployment insurance. All this hanging out with the rich was infectious. And there was Peggy the living incarnation of my earliest ambition (except for being Shirley Temple). Peggy was an in-the-flesh madcap heiress. All my favorite movie stars, from Hepburn to Davis to Lombard, had played madcaps. And all those movies boasted happy endings.

"What do you want to be when you grow up?" Almost Uncle Eddie had asked me at eight years of age, over a soon-to-be-rationed steak dinner (one of the rewards of visiting Auntie H. in the city). It was a question I was prepared for.

"A movie star or a madcap heiress," I'd answered snappily, making him laugh. It even made Auntie H. laugh, who wondered "where little Babsie ever heard that."

Usually Uncle Eddie was on the road when I visited the St. Moritz, and I got to sleep in his king-size mattress in the elegant suite he kept for himself twelve floors above the room he kept for her. "Don't worry," she'd always confuse me by saying, "you are sleeping in a virgin bed." Actually, as

I recalled it while sipping my carrot juice, weekending with Auntie H. was an event we both approached with trepidation.

"I'll take Babsie," she'd tell my mother, "but not the two of them. Two is too much." I think one had been too much, but she'd endured. First would come the warnings: "Don't play with Eddie's radio, you may get a shock. . . . Don't touch Eddie's seltzer maker, it may explode. . . . And don't lean over his balcony, you may fall off." She didn't have to worry about that one; I had to be forced onto the balcony at all.

Her "meal ticket," as she frequently referred to Almost Uncle Eddie, had a balcony that faced south. "No park view, but all the better for tanning," she'd say as she basked in black rayon bra and briefs before the windows of the courtyard that faced us. "Midriffs are in, but don't tell Eddie. He worries about my being loose. You know what I mean?" I didn't, but certainly wouldn't say a word.

I sat there anxiously. Heights made me dizzy, and my underwear was white and worn.

"When my legs are tan," she commented, checking their progress, "I don't need hose." That was a World War II plus. Save stockings. Auntie H. sunned and stitched her snags.

"That Hitler," she shouted over Manhattan, "that Hitler will be sorry when all our silk drops on Berlin." Auntie H. truly hated Hitler. She told Hitler jokes. She liked telling about the poor Jewish girl bringing the boss's son home to dinner.

"Mama," the girl begs, looking around the shabby apartment, "clean everything good. And wash off all the dirty words in the hall."

"I'll wash all the 'shits' and 'bastards' off the walls," the mother agrees, "but 'Fuck Hitler,' that stays!"

The only people Auntie H. hated worse were the future mayor William O'Dwyer, for whose career my father had been sacrificed, and the "lousy no good fixed judge, who sold your daddy up the river." Auntie H. had contempt for all justice. Both man's and God's. But she did care a lot about time.

"Who made up time?" I asked as she gave her watch a

third look. We were running late for Uncle Eddie, a very punctual person.

"Who cares?" she answered, pacing in front of the bank of elevators. Wartime meant all the elevators were not operating and we must wait. I cared, yet I shut up. I didn't want to work up her irritation. But I couldn't stay shut, another character flaw. "Do you believe in God?"

"I believe"—she had glared down at me—"that God takes a pint of your blood every time you ask him a favor." She twisted her Lucky Strike into the metal ashtray that hung beside the elevator and continued pacing. "God is not to be relied on," she ranted. "God can make you crazy. God is not fair."

"God let Joe Louis beat Max Schmeling, the German." Family legend.

"It wasn't God. It was either Mike Jacobs or Joe Jacobs." Then she had stopped pacing and started staring down the corridor at a slow-moving figure approaching us. After a moment and almost under her breath she added, "But sometimes, just sometimes, God surprises you and comes through."

Silent as a panther Auntie H. watched the man come closer. Averting her head, she began making strange sounds at the back of her throat. When he was finally standing behind her, she turned and spit full in his face.

"That," she hissed, "is for sending an innocent man to jail." She spit again. "And that is for the lousy Judas money you made doing it." The elevator doors parted, and she marched me in. "Right down, Joey," she had commanded, pointing her finger at the phlegm-spewn face standing outside. "We don't ride with shitheels." The doors closed. My father's judge was judged.

I wondered, as the LSD subsided enough to allow me to start falling asleep, if Auntie H. ever worried about saving her soul. One thing was becoming certain: If my salvation depended on celibacy, I was doomed.

Giving up on heavenly credit, I looked to earthly comfort. Yes, I continued vegetarian. I still meditated and carried reverence for Master Kirpal. However, having flunked Perfection I, II, and III, I changed my major, and it was a relief no longer to be so much "humbler than thou." When Tim Leary left off saying "St. Barbara" and started referring to me as a "love goddess in the tantric tradition" and Peggy named me "Barbara Beautiful," I took it as a tribute to my talents and the ten pounds I'd dropped during my acid transformation and figured it would all work out.

So I gathered my rosebuds, some fine new furs, a few fast friends, and a fashionable address. But somewhere, while gathering, I misplaced a thing or two, like the gentle, serious man who lived down the street and whom I would think about from time to time with some sense of loss. But I didn't judge myself too harshly, or I thought I didn't. Because it was so human to be human.

Then, a few years later, I heard a surgeon advise that he thinks "a little look-see procedure is in order." The night before I was scheduled for the surgery I went on a first date that I'd been looking forward to. It was with a friend from Millbrook, who had all the signs of becoming a real beau. He was a young theatrical producer of extraordinary taste, sweetness and sensitivity. And I, scared to death of the morning, decked myself in my most swan-song beautiful to glitter at the opening he was escorting me to. All smiles, I gleamed for him, till I folded at intermission.

"Let me get you out of here," David said. "You'd do better with a drink and a quiet dinner." So we went to Casey's, a place our friends frequented, and despite my promises to myself not to, I told him of the hospital and more. In fact, everything. Including my current California banker, who, from a safe distance, was more than happy to pay all the hospital bills.

"So," David said, "your mother, father, and brother all died of—"

"Yes."

"What time must you be there?"

"Early."

"I'll take you."

He came by limousine, loaded with magic talismans, Buddhas, incense, and flowers. And, I think, love. He waited with me through the testing, was there at my bedside after the small surgery. And he asked me to marry. I said that if God let me off the hook and I was whole enough for babies, I would. God did. And I intended to. So I gave up my role as playgirl of the Western world and my life of somewhat overcrowded acquaintance to become the producer's perfect lady. I liked it. And I liked David's family. His English horseman of a father, in charge of certain selected racing stables given to finishing in the money. His mother, an American of breeding, warmth, and goodwill. His smart and pretty sisters. David said it would be the melding of two sporting families, and I hoped it would. It seemed so fitting and more than I'd come to expect. But life, full of mystery and mischief, somehow changed directions.

Some of it had to do with the pep-up "vitamin" shots David's dentist popped into him every day, to speed all those wheels he had in motion. He wanted to be a Todd or Merrick for me, which seemed to decree speed for him. And the wheels included his play currently running at his East Side theater and about to be his first Hollywood film. (The film got lost in the shuffle.) Plus a chancy thing on Cuba and Castro that he was determined to go down in flames for (despite opposing political pickets from both sides, Cuba, sí and no). A rock musical in the experimental stage (about Victoria and Albert attempting to tour America). And the ace up his sleeve, a play he was importing from London. Written by one famous actor as a tour de force for another famous actor, it was to be directed by an even more famous playwright. Heady stuff, and despite himself, David was a little in awe of all three. He wasn't alone. His American writers, directors, and actors all were awed by them, too. I, in ignorance or arrogance, wasn't. They were just "important men," a subject I had my doctorate in. So some of what happened had to do with me, too. With ego and what the mystics call my karmic predisposition toward loving dangerously.

"You have to come," David urged over the phone. "*He* is here, and I can't handle him and Bruce alone. I need your touch. Besides, there's Mailer's party in Brooklyn Heights, so you have to." It was after 10:00 P.M., and I was watching the news in lazy legitimacy, wondering what were the benefits of being officially engaged if they were not being spared sudden moves.

"All right," I said. "I'll be there. However, don't expect glamour."

"You are always glamorous." David wooed from his office atop the theater. "Just get here by eleven."

I was there at ten-fifty and decided not to climb all the way up to the third-floor office and sat down instead on the stairs to pass my time chatting up a songwriter who was attending the ingenue.

Below us, the theater anteroom started to fill with the exiting theatergoers. All happy. It had been a fun night; they'd had their money's worth. I found my eyes met by and held by one particular man who, standing alone, looked different. I blushed. He kept staring as he lit a cigarette. The others emptied themselves into the street. He was still in his corner, smoking and staring at me.

"What are you looking at?" asked the songwriter.

"At that face." I nodded in the direction of the smoker. "That's a face one could look at and never tire of."

The man with the face was moving from his corner toward the stairs. Careful! I warned myself. You are spoken for, agreed to. Then the songwriter disappeared down the back, the quicker to adore his starlet, and I stood there, except for the smoker, alone. Now what?

"Ah, there you are, darling." David's voice accompanied the thump of his feet down the steps. "Good girl. Right on time." Reaching for my shoulder, he became aware of the smoke below. "Welcome," he called past me, "I want you to meet Barbara."

"It's nice to meet at last," I said. So this was *"Him."*

Our hands touched in introduction. "And to see you," the playwright answered, and I could feel his fingers tremble.

Sitting in the cab as we three rushed toward the Oak Room, I remember wondering if David on my other side could feel the electricity every time the playwright's leg touched mine. No, my producer chatted amiably, oblivious. Was the great man from London tired by the trip? The time change and all that? Did he enjoy the play? And did he know how much the American playwright we were meeting ad-

mired him? And how thrilled he was that his British idol had
come to see the performance. And how everyone was looking
forward to meeting him. The playwright said that David
should have given him some warning of Barbara's beauty. "A
fellow should be prepared for such an encounter."

"Yes, she's something," agreed my fiancé, proudly patting the knee next to him. The other was otherwise engaged. I was in trouble blocks before we reached the Plaza.

"*He*" spoke of the harsh, electric excitement of New
York City and how he might need a guide. Then and there
David volunteered me.

"Yes, certainly," I said.

"Have you ever been married?" the playwright asked as
he helped me all too gallantly from his side of the cab.

"Yes," I answered, "I remember the wedding."

The playwright smiled, and I would hear that line,
among many others, come at me from the characters he
created. And flattered again, I will feel necessary and think
of myself as a muse. Muses are some kind of love goddess,
too, aren't they? So we—the two playwrights, David, and
I—dined together, and the talk turned to stories of mysterious, sudden violence.

The American playwright was anxious to serve up some
noteworthy morsel for his British idol's approval. Then the
Britisher topped him. And so it went. I didn't say much.
Mostly I smiled and shared self-conscious moments, when
"*He*" and I reached for the same ashtray, or opened our
napkins at the same moment, and I understood when he
echoed my exact supper order of cold salmon and salad. A
signal. Then, noticing a vein in his temple throb, I remembered he had a bad back. I'd even used his back doctor in
London when David had taken me with him to set this deal.
But I'd been in too much discomfort to meet anyone.

"Is it your neck?" I asked.

"Yes, the damn plane."

"Let me help you." I applied pressure at the back of his
neck. He removed his glasses and let his head drop, remaining quiet and grateful as I touched and massaged.

"I know exactly where it hurts," I said as I worked.

"I know you do," he answered.

"He was like a little boy with you," David commented later. "Where did you get the nerve?" I didn't answer, preferring to keep the last secrets of my art to myself.

"It's getting tricky," I said a week after to my girl friend, "all these dinners à *trois,* all these secret touches."

"Be careful," my confidant advised.

"I'm being careful, but it's almost irresistible."

"Resist" was my friend's last word. But I didn't.

Not that I didn't try. But the war eventually went to "*Him.*" Because I fell "in love." And love excuses everything. Or most things. Well, some of it anyway. Also, I was set up. David, taking advantage of the obvious attentions paid to me, sent me in to ease production tension. And since I still loved David and intended to marry, despite this irresistible passion which was supposed to pass, I went.

Of course, David didn't mind if the playwright took Barbara to a concert. And "sure," he would be glad to lend "*Him*" Barbara for an opening he must attend or for "*His*" birthday dinner. And certainly Barbara should sit in at "*His*" rehearsals to hold the fort.

"Has Mrs. Condos arrived?" the playwright called from his eagle's nest in the dark balcony. "Well, send her on up then. And some scotch. And another glass, please, and make sure she has a pad and a pen."

Good producer that David was, he even managed to leave town, for another week of tryouts on his Cuban obsession, at the crucial moment. "Don't you want me with you this time?" I asked, even begged.

No, I was to handle the Royale. "I," he said, "don't need charm at Stockbridge."

And so the fort fell. Up until then it was all still on hold, in waiting beneath linen napkins or in the backs of cabs. If David had not been so speeded up with drugs and drive that he couldn't listen when I tried to cry "danger," it might have never happened. Or perhaps it was, as my playwright insisted, fated.

*　　*　　*

"Here, read this part," the playwright had said, happily handing me a newspaper with an article on him. We were in his suite quite, quite alone.

"Yes," I said, reading. "Very nice."

"Do you like what she says about my arms?" It was dusk. Behind him a gentle late-September sky hung pink and pretty over the park. There was champagne and some barely picked-at salmon on a silver salver. The salmon was even pinker than the sky, even pinker than my cheeks, which I felt to be all flushed and warm.

"You mean the part where she says, 'was wearing a black turtleneck . . . rolled up to reveal burly forearms,' that part?" I asked, and crossed my own legs higher to reveal a touch of thigh.

"Yes."

"May I feel them?" I flirted. The flirting was wonderful.

"Later," he promised. "You'll feel my muscles later."

"Will I?"

"Yes, dearest girl, but now I must rush to the first act. We're using concealed microphones, so I must listen for tinny sounds. It's a bit dangerous."

"What shall I do?"

"Read the scenario of my new play. I'll hurry back. Oh, yes, please make a note of anything in it that disturbs you, so we can discuss it."

Instead, I ran a bath. I was too tired to be brilliant about his work. All the awful lying to David. All the furtive fingers on the backs of theater seats. All the under-the-table titillations. The guilt was catching up. David assumed I was with relatives for the Jewish New Year if he thought about it at all. Instead, here I was, in a tub at the Hampshire House, madly in love and hating myself and my lover for it. This, I swore to unseen witnesses, would be the end of it. It will be over, after this. . . . I took my damp and scented body to wait in his bedroom.

I woke to find him, sitting on the edge of the bed, looking at me. "What time is it?" I asked.

"After twelve," he said softly.

"So late? You stayed for the second act then?"

"No, I've been here since ten."

"Doing what?"

"Looking at you."

"You should have awakened me."

"You were sleeping so quietly, so gently. I kissed you on the eyes. You did not stir."

"I am very tired."

"I know," he said. "I know."

"I ordered supper."

"I saw it. It's waiting."

"Are you hungry?" I asked him.

"I would like to lie beside you now," he answered.

"Come, my love."

"Oh, my darling, my beautiful girl, who wears lace for me and smiles."

So it wasn't the end with this playwright of another life and a wife in London. But it will start the end of David and me. David, more and more isolated, within a madness of speed and pressure. I, isolated in deceit with only my secret lover to distract from self-dislike. Perhaps if I were British, too, I'd have been better at it. Perhaps I could have overcome somehow. But in the end an American girl, raised with MGM morals, can't marry one man while loving another. At least this girl couldn't. So the plays will open and close, and David and Barbara will close as well, eventually to end up as slightly self-conscious friends.

"He" will continue. Arriving at my apartment, checking to see if his picture is in its place, next to my bed, he will warn that the antique mirrors over my bed "are turning dark with shame," to chide me on escapades I took to buffer the terrifying lonely pain of loving him in such a way. I'll answer, trying for charm, that the mirror's darkness is but camouflage. Self-defense. Inside I will feel, rightly or wrongly, that it's all his fault. *"He"* will call, or not if he can't, from oceans away, and I will have moments that go: Please, dear God of the Jews, let this call be *"Him,"* and I won't annoy you about anything anymore. Oh, sweet compassionate Lord, let it be him. I need it to be him. To hear his voice. Please, just this one small thing. I ask—"Hello . . . yes, overseas . . . Yes, thank you, operator, thank you, thank

you . . . and thank you, God. . . . Oh, my darling, it's you. I was desperate for your voice. . . ."

Was I wanting him too much? But he knew that. I listened as he told me his trip would be delayed and after that he would be spending the holidays where phones were difficult. But I must know, must feel, must understand. . . . So had God given me the call, but as a punishment? Hadn't I thanked Him enough? Or was it because I was bad, in a world of so many bad? And I wasn't so very bad after all. I was hurting no one but myself. Does God punish when you hurt yourself?

"Yes, darling, my darling. I do understand. I hate it, but I understand. . . . Perhaps I'll go south. . . . Yes, some friends have taken a villa in Cuernavaca. . . . Exactly, right under the volcano. . . . Yes, of course, there will be men, darling. . . . But just for dancing. . . ."

So there I was in this moonless Mexican garden, searching again for the "pure white light," while tripping across hibiscus and rock with enough of my brain so scattered I couldn't even form the word "help!" which is exactly what I'd come for. Though, if you'd asked me only a week before, I'd have said I'd come to hang out with Van Wolf and company at this season's villa or to swim in ancient aqueducts or climb temple steps and hear the plumed serpent's scream. All of which had charmed but hadn't helped anything. Help, I was realizing, was harder to come by.

"My God, Harry," I finally managed to call out into the darkness to my companion on this hallucinogenic trip I was tripping over. "Where are you?"

Harry didn't answer. But I knew he wouldn't abandon me. Harry was part of this chemically extended family I'd joined, in innocent indecency, to stay stoned for the holidays. And within Van's cloistered garden walls, as within that magic circle at Millbrook, someone who wanted to could still explore his or her inner soul in safety and style. By then most psychedelic experience had turned into loud rock concerts and disco freak-outs.

But not at this villa I was visiting, fitted with its heavy wood beams and conscientious consciousness seekers left over from when trips were still called "sessions" and full of hope and awe. And anything could happen. So rituals of supportiveness as prescribed in Sutra 19 from the Tao Te Ching cyclostyled by Dr. Timothy Leary conditioned correct behavior. One should have:

1. Handwoven cloth
2. Uncarved wood
3. Flowers—growing things
4. Ancient music
5. Burning fire
6. A touch of earth
7. A splash of water
8. Fruit
9. Stone ground bread
10. Cheese
11. Fermenting wine
12. Candlelight
13. Temple incense
14. A warm hand
15. A fish swimming (a toughie)
16. Anything over five hundred years old

Most experimenters settled for clean, beautiful places, candles, and a copy of Tim's version of the *Tibetan Book of the Dead*. I had never actually read that book, but everyone told me it was important to have around.

Sometimes a "sober" guide would sit in with a novice. It was "family" courtesy. This group was very courteous about living in one another's psyches.

"Harry," I managed to cry again, "I think I've lost the path."

Yet what exactly had I taken? I didn't feel the way I remembered it with Roger. That was quite a time ago, and I couldn't be sure. Was I having what I'd heard termed "a bad trip?" What had Harry called it, not white lightning or orange sunshine, or anything? I don't think it was color-coded, just a set of laboratory initials to be washed away on. Only in the future, when entering a home of mine ravaged by Gypsies, will I relive a bit of this feeling of total chaos. On this chancy Mexican night, however, all I could hope for was to get through it. Tim Leary said that there was a moment in any session when the most reassuring thing to cling to was knowing it would eventually end. About that, I figured, he was right.

But why, hours after everyone else who was going to had already downed the damned stuff somewhere between the soup and fish and I had refused it, had I done a reverse and swallowed it down? Was it midnight, madness, or what? In fact, there were two holiday parties going on in that villa that night, the one barely intruding on the other. The two groups mixed and mingled as one. The nonacid group dined and danced to three blind mariachis on a lantern-lit terrace, completely unaware of the black holes in consciousness exploding in the heads of the other.

"Don't take it, Barbara," Harry had warned as I flirted with the idea in front of a huge adobe fireplace in the far corner of a small patio. "The stuff is fast and mean." But I, switching parties, didn't really hear him. I remember him standing in the firelight and redosing as well, so I'd have a companion in psychedelic vigil. And when I complained thirty minutes later that nothing was happening, he smiled.

"Patience, child," he said, starting or organize blankets, juice, and music. "You'll soon wish nothing would." The fire Harry was feeding started to dance. "I'll put on some music."

"Fine," I had said, always glad to be taken care of. "And lots of Beatles, please."

And I wanted to talk about synchronicity. The Jungian kind. The kind so profound it was as if God had given you a peek at his punch line before he pulled it. My father was always insisting that God had a sense of humor. All at once it seemed an important thing to tell Harry.

"My father . . ." I began.

"If your father is hanging around," Harry interrupted, "it means that love doesn't die, Barbara. So stop frowning like that."

"My father." I tried again. Then ability to frame words vanished. It was enough to manage to breathe, like coming up from an ocean bottom. It was as if a breaker, the kind that batters the bulkwark of the Presidente in Acapulco,

308

had crashed my skull and splattered my brain. No, this was not what had happened with Roger, and my master was nowhere around.

I moaned, and Harry, whose face had just turned into my brother's, gave me an ancient nod. The nod one Cro-Magnon gave another when the mammoth charged the mouth of the cave. The nod of the nomad who watched the Red Sea close over the pharaoh's army and walked on. The nod given me so long ago by my father when the Lower East Side cop had grabbed the junkie with the eye-dropper up his vein and slammed him into the gutter. Harry's nod then shimmered itself into a chimpanzee grin, and as he hunched over my bamboo chair, his monkey's paw covered mine.

Watch your wishes, I warned myself as both our sets of monkey teeth started to chatter.

"Watch out for these middle-class magicians called chemists, too," Harry managed to say, referring to the nice family boy who had invented whatever it was we swallowed. And we joined in the laughter of loons and lunatics. "And doctors," he added.

"And playwrights," I had said, "especially English ones."

We had danced ourselves to a drunken bed, my beautiful man of letters and I. We had flirted and fought and fenced our way through the early spring evening into night. He'd bent my arm behind me, causing me to wince, to make his point. I'd snarled seductively, cat to mouse, and made mine.

He gnawed at my whiskers and smoothed my tail. My eyes slanted, and I nudged his head downward, spreading my fur.

"You're my girl," he whispered into me. "Mine," he screamed. And it became later.

Somewhere deep in me a single egg welcomed a single sperm, perhaps the fastest, perhaps the cutest, then closed itself off from the million others swarming past to enjoy a little poetic togetherness.

He rolled at last onto his side, still chewing strands of my curls caught in his teeth. His breathing came in bursts. I began to breathe more slowly and more easily, while still sucking on the knuckle of the finger he'd left in my mouth. Tasting blood, I smiled. I'd bitten him right on his writing finger. A small scar to remember me by. As he moved his hand between my thighs, I watched him smile and close his eyes. Were we finished? Should we start again? I was happy either way. It was good to be with him, alone in bed. The two of us.

But it was not just the two of us, not just he and I in that Plaza hotel room. For there were three now in the bed. And the third was dividing and expanding as joyfully as nature intended it.

The next day he was gone, leaving us to love each other across the sea. We'd spoken hot words into phones, and six weeks, most of them rainy, had rambled by. "I think I may be pregnant," I'd postulated to girl friends one by one. Adding to each: "Anyway, I'm late." A score of mice, two rabbits, and syringefuls of blood disagreed.

"But I feel pregnant," I insisted to the Fifth Avenue doctor who headed his own obstetrics pavilion at this very imposing hospital. "I know how pregnant feels."

"No." He discredited my feelings. "It's something hormonal. A shot or two will fix you up."

Three weeks and three shots later. Floodgates of blood opened to pour between my legs, over my sheets, across carpets, into the taxi, and onto the marble hospital floor.

"What do you mean, 'insulted the embryo'? " The room was still hazy. They had been considering a transfusion before sending me back from postop.

"Well." The elegant patriarch of better breeding through chemistry ahemmed. "Well, it seems despite all those tests, you were pregnant."

"Were?"

"Well, I think it's dead. Or dying, since we went in to look around."

"Dead or dying? Where is it?"

"Still inside. You know abortion is highly illegal and you are unmarried and I don't want the stain of inducing one to answer for. If we just wait, you'll start to miscarry and I can remove it."

"Remove?" The anaesthetic still echoed in my nose. And benumbed my brain.

"Yes, we will D and C when indicated." So I was still able to make babies but not allowed to have them.

He'd left my little room, leaving me mostly alone. Mostly or all. I wasn't sure. We had been insulted.

The insult continued. My body seemed inclined to hold on to this dead or dying baby. (So did my heart.) I did not start to bleed again, but I did start running high fevers. No contractions, just constrictions of the breath and a head that ached from corner to corner.

"Are you crazy? Lying in a hospital with a dead baby inside you?" shouted my ex-husband, Nick, from Bel Air right into my eardrum. "I'll be in New York tomorrow. We'll see about that." A sporadically sober Nick would ride to my rescue. This was his kind of stuff. He always wanted to make it up, to do me some good. We were still sort of family, weren't we?

"Are you kidding, Barbara? Is that doctor a damn donkey? What's his number? I'm going to call him," offered a pal, and sometimes lover, of political position and power. "This is madness."

"You've been there eight days," one of my girl friends complained. "What's the bastard gonna do, let you die there?"

"But, darling." My man of letters was trying long distance to understand what was happening. "You must come here," he said at last. "I can arrange things here."

Nick arrived and signed me out of the hospital on his own volition. Buttoning me back into clothing, he was trying hard to do it right. His cigar unlit, in courtesy, hung from his hand. He got me home and later to the airport. I was surprisingly fragile.

I don't remember that plane ride to London. Except that it was first-class. The stewardess, buckling my seat belt, awakened me. "We are landing," she said. "Are you all right?"

"Just fine."

It was late day in London before I passed through customs and into the arms of my lover's emissary, an eminent actor of the British stage and his lady love, for whom he was about to leave his wife. They were pals, and I was happy to see them there. Of course, *"He"* couldn't chance coming. Back to their illicit apartment we drove, I to a quick borrowed bed; they, to a romantic dinner and evening on the town. It was a long night.

The next morning, delivered by way of the Fleet Street specialist, I arrived at one of England's better abortion clinics. Since I was not on national insurance, but indeed paying ready cash, I was treated better than the long queue of little sad-faced girls and even sadder-faced older women standing with their sanitary napkins in their hands, waiting to be next. I was treated better, but not much.

At the other end of the hall I was hurried into a small, somewhat dim operating room, where a clumsy anaesthetist started fumbling for a vein.

"That arm is used up," I told him, ever ready to be helpful and all too experienced in these areas. I smiled. I wanted to make friends. But he didn't. He was too rushed and harried from squirting sodium pentothal into so many frightened veins an hour to make friends.

"I know my business," he said.

He didn't.

At last it was over. Lying in a hard little bed in an airless little room, I heard that a nurses' strike had just begun.

I lay in that room for three days and three nights of slow-footed service. My arms were so crippled I couldn't comb my hair. It matted in sweat beneath my head, as I prayed for someone to turn my pillow or change my sheet. But I did have the paid privilege of a private telephone, over which I gave and got mixed reviews. Finally, hearing from a friend in New York, I learned how our other friend Patricia's husband had shot her through her head and belly, killing her. And then he shot himself. He was Latin, and she had a lover. She was leaving him. Now they both had gone. I told this to my man of the theater when he phoned from a pay phone in a pub. "Who?"—he sighed—"can measure the depth of human love or pain?" He was right. I held the rest of my calls for a while.

"Didn't I once tell you," pontificated my friend Jakov

Lind, the serious Jewish writer and my only visitor in two days, "didn't I once tell you Jewish girls should hang around only with boys from the neighborhood?" Jakov fingered his moustache. "You, too, it will happen to, with your Mexicans, Greeks, and your Arabs."

I worried if he might be right. I was certainly playing around in some rarefied circles. Hadn't I watched as a young Latin aristocrat terrified his hired musicians, firing drunken shots at their feet with his pearl-handled pistol, later the same evening overdosing his Cuban pal, planning on leaving him for dead on the highway? If worse came to worst that was. He didn't have to do that. I revived his friend and helped the musicians make a getaway.

And hadn't I flirted with Eastern monarchs and ministers and flaunted such strong pro-Zion opinions that would have tempted tongue-cutting-off, if in Arabia?

And hadn't I engendered serious violence between two matadors in Tijuana, both of whom felt, with justification, that they had a claim on my attentions. Jakov was right. While trying not to focus on my feelings, I played fast-and-loose with the tempers of others.

"That hurt," I complained as Jakov's large fingers tried clumsily to help unmesh my hair.

"Where's your big genius?" he asked, continuing to unmesh me. As my London confidant he knew all.

"Avoiding being recognized," I said, my nose in the flowers he brought.

Jakov gave up on my curls. "I think," he said, "you'll have to get it cut."

More phone calls. The acting emissary. His little lady love would bring a list of things I needed, including something to eat. They were being sweet, and I was getting much too fashionably skinny, even for me, who lately held skinniness higher than saintliness.

"My darling girl, I wish I could be with you," had whispered my lover again from yet another outside booth somewhere near Regent's Park. "But it would be impossible . . . impossible. . . . I'm too well known. . . . You see . . . How would I explain such a visit?" My playwright, it seemed, not only wrote in dots and dashes but lived that way, too. And so then did I.

I would have explained all this to Harry as he led me like a crippled child past the dancers and the mariachis, into the quiet of the garden, where we would wait for the sunrise. I way dying to explain everything I'd ever known, except I'd lost all audible sound. Now Harry had left me alone in rustlings of the night to go back to the terrace for a lantern. Mexican nights were not civilized, with their iguanas and scorpions and sudden screams from unseen birds.

But my Englishman was civilized. A gentleman of words and games. Good at everything from cricket (to sneaky fingers beneath the table while taking tea with me at the Savoy). And the muse in me was so enamored of him, his talent, and his touch, and so, eager to serve, I spread my perfume across his pillow, pretending not to notice that he lived between two beds. So if I loved them, I also hated those hidden London meetings. He had looked silly scurrying all bent as he moved between the parked cars that were lined along the Serpentine. With me hurrying behind him.

"Must you rush so?" I had to beg of him. "I can't keep up."

"Oh, my sweet girl, my love." He apologized. "I am sorry. I just want to leave this area. I saw a familiar face. I'll take you," he offered, "to a lovely field where the queen's household guards rehearse parades. We will watch them. Quick, let's get that taxi."

Even from a distance the horses looked hot in that late July sun. So did the horsemen on their fur-draped saddles, under even furrier shakos.

"Must they work out in those getups?" I argued while arranging my white ruffles as attractively as I could. I never stopped seducing him, not for an instant. Not even when wanting to find fault with him, as then, on that shadeless, treeless field that was hell on my hangover. I had spent the night before drinking in my birthday. Hadn't I outlived my mother by two and my brother by fourteen? And wasn't I still well and vital, in spite of myself or this playwright who settled next to me on crackling grass?

"It's good form," he informed me, "to practice horse parade in full dress." Touching my face, he added, "You look so beautiful in that white." Then he asked, "Are you naked underneath?"

"Except for garters and hose," I answered, just to watch desire creep up his cheeks and hide behind his glasses. He flexed his forearms, and my own desire rushed to meet his. Dear God, he was worth anything, everything.

"It will be a long, dry August," he said later, taking my hand, "with you back in New York. I'll miss you till September. I'll miss your face, your mouth. Oh, how I'll miss your mouth."

That mouth was starting to taste dry and sour. Dizzy with heat and him, I was glad to be sitting. Don't, I warned myself, faint again. There had been mirrors in that doorway where I had fainted that first time in New York. My black silk gown had slumped me to the sidewalk under its weight. And my love had stepped from his limousine, engrossed in arty conversation, and walked by me on the sidewalk where I lay fallen and never even seen me. He actually hadn't seen me. That had been a bad night, full of deception and the debacle that was the opening of David's Cuban thing.

Did concentrating on my playwright's failures make leaving easier? Tomorrow I'd cross the ocean, to wait again. There would be more phone calls. And my body would cry out for his. I'd divert myself. Suddenly the summer-dry grass of London was choking off my breath. And I said I'd better go back to the flat. He couldn't come.

"I love you, my own sweet girl," he said, handing me into a cab. "Have a good flight, and I'll call you Monday in New York."

"Say 'Happy Birthday,' " I'd managed to shout out as the door closed and the flag dropped.

He moved forward. "What? Oh, my dear, happy birthday. Happy birthday."

As I remembered how we'd held hands through the window till the light changed, I seemed to be getting the "why" of being stoned in Cuernavaca, in good company rather than being alone for holidays in New York. Harry returned to the garden to light me with his lantern and study me. We both appeared to have stopped shaking. That was a good sign, we agreed.

"But why are you crying?" he asked as we left the garden. "Are you in pain? Stop. That kind of pain is your own invention. Consider this, that you, Barbara, are not really Barbara. That these thoughts and memories were programmed into your brain only last week at the Pavlov Institute in Moscow, You never lived in Forest Hills or ever lost a baby or even were in love."

Could Harry be telling the truth? Was I a Russian experiment? Harry smiled his very best New Yorker kind of smile. My father would have liked him.

"So don't sweat it, Babsie," he said. "And as far as being a muse goes, why, you revel in it and you gotta be one of the best. You enrich things, kid, and you got style."

Had I been speaking aloud, then all that time when I thought I hadn't gotten a word out? I kissed Harry, who kissed me back, then staggered off to stoke up the fire.

On the far side of Van's elegant garden, and much to his annoyance, was a beer factory. I sniffed at its aroma as dawn broke over the separating wall and a couple of Mexican cocks decided to crow. It had turned 1970 and I could use a beer, I thought, and a breakfast.

"Harry," I pronounced carefully (it would be days before my tongue would totally untie), "Harry, when I can walk and use a telephone and face an airport, I'm flying back to New York to write a good story about being a mistress. Maybe I can even sell it. To *Cosmo* or somewhere."

"When did you start to write?" Harry asked, looking a little like my brother again.

"Just now," I said. "Just now."

BOOK FOUR

Mixed Tense

Tale of Three Cities

If there was one thing Teresa was sure of, it was that never again would she witness the devastation of cancer in someone she loved. God, when allotting, would surely balance what was to come against that already suffered. Which meant, of course, that those lumps in Janice's neck were just swollen glands that would correct themselves naturally.

She might mention them to Barbara, but the households were out of touch. Janice was mad at her sister, again. She had changed her telephone number, again. And had forbidden Teresa contact, as usual.

What this particular anger was over wasn't quite clear. Teresa considered it might have to do with Barbara's not introducing Janice to men. Or could it still be about sending Paulie to Peru. It was hard for Teresa to remind herself of that. Struck down with a fever, she had watched helplessly as Janice prepared to pack him off.

"Are you completely crazy?" Barbara had screamed over the phone. "The boy is only eleven years old!" Teresa, holding her breath on the extension, kept hoping Barbara was having an effect. Barbara wasn't. "Janice, you must not do this."

Janice rolled right over her. "Arturo's family are wonderful, beautiful people. I know, I spent a week with them." Janice was using her perfect-mother tone. "They," she assured Barbara, "will take good care of him." Teresa released her breath into the mouthpiece but said nothing. Long conditioned to that, she felt as if a big spider had come to spin a web around her heart.

"Janice"—Barbara fired from the hip—"just for once, think what you are doing. You are pulling the child out of school and shipping him to a world where he can't even talk the damn language!"

"Listen, Barbara"—Janice blasted back a cannon—"he's my kid. You should have had one of your own." Teresa held through the bad silence that followed.

Then, at last, Barbara sighed her defeat. "When does he go?"

"This week."

"Will you visit him?"

"I'm not one of your millionaires, you know. He'll manage. He'll learn."

Teresa had put down the phone and taken to her bed. Her fever hit 102 for three days running. Paulie clung to her hand. "Don't let Mommy send me away," he begged. "I don't want to leave you." Janice sent him.

Janice sent him as deposit on her Peruvian paradise to come. She sent him to seal her deal with Arturo, the soccer player she met on the subway and decided to fall in love with, even as he pounded a reluctant candy machine for its treasure. She sent Paul to a dirt-floored hut in an open-sewered slum in Lima. To live where no one would have time to talk to him, even if anyone could. To a compound of scufflers hanging off the hard edge of a hopeless society. Paulie, smuggling in a wad of Janice's suspect savings, would be welcome. Never able to describe much of his flight from New York to Lima, Paulie will only remember marshaling his strength the way he was taught at karate class. And being determined to help his mother, who had dragged him through a maze of men and melodrama, into her wonderful new life.

Passing Peruvian customs, Paul found himself embraced by a frail European-looking man and a fat Indian lady. Arturo's parents, waving the photograph Janice had thoughtfully provided. And they treated him like a celebrity. He later admitted that he enjoyed that part. He wasn't quite able, however, to pin down the compound they brought him to as poverty. Some people actually seemed to be living in holes. Not like Harlem or the Lower East Side or any other slum, it was more like another planet. Or the worst scenes from *Planet of the Apes*.

Relatively Arturo's family were well fixed. Their place, though floorless, boasted two rooms and a small kitchen with an almost indoor toilet. They even owned a constantly blaring radio as well as an occasionally functioning TV. One of Arturo's two sisters gave Paul her bed and slept on a pallet next to the icebox. The other stared wordlessly at him from across cultures. And sometimes she smiled.

"I was the first blond," Paulie told Teresa, "she ever really saw," adding proudly, "she called me Rubio." Blonds were the stuff their Inca dreams were made of.

So Rubio became the star of the slumyard. And all too soon he was running amok in the street. Hitching rides, smoking grass, and sniffing the cocaine older, sharper boys procured, he danced the "monkey" for their amusement. And he had dollars to toss around as well. Later he was to terrify Teresa, bragging of his adventures.

"One night," he told her, "I was with these guys from the candy store across the road, and they took me to the beach. It was after our neighborhood curfew, but we used to sneak out anyway. We had to go down a big cliff with no light, and I almost fell off; but one guy, a friend of Arturo's, grabbed me just in time. When we got down there, we got really high. And this cop came and said he was going to put us in jail, unless we gave him our grass. He got about a thousand *soles'* worth, too, 'cause I just bought it. Then I was alone and got scared. Climbing back up the cliff was very hard, and my hands got cut. Then a cop car stopped, and one grabbed me by my hair and said something about

the loco American and laughed and pushed me flat into
the gutter. Then they drove away. I didn't even mind Arturo's father shaking me around. I was so glad to get back
there!"

"Arturo's father"—Teresa watched Janice waving the
blue envelope from Peru at her—"writes that Paulie is being
a really bad boy." Teresa purses her lips and waits. Janice
isn't through. "That kid will ruin everything. Arturo will
give him hell when he gets back to Lima."

As it happened, Arturo, who'd left with his team for
South America soon after his romantic but bigamous elope-
ment with Janice, never did get back to Lima. At least not in
time. Arturo and a teammate were sitting shave-headed in
a Bolivian jail. A small street fight. The team had replaced
them and traveled on.

Teresa sighed when Janice sold the blue Cadillac they
were both so proud of. She pined as Paulie's piano was
packed and shipped away. And she actually cried to see the
last of Mrs. Caplin's silver, reverently polished for so many
years, cashed in for what she later told me were "peanuts."
Three big black brassbound trunks stood in the middle of
the living room, waiting for Teresa to pack them up with
Janice's future. Teresa's future remained foggy. When they
fought, as was daily, Janice would tell her to "go live" with
her now-divorced son, Michael. When they made up, as was
nightly, she begged her, "Come to Peru. I can't make it
without you!" Teresa feared it was true.

"It must be the mails down there," Janice explained of
Arturo's silence. And "He's such a dope I bet he's writing to
the wrong address."

Then Janice became desperate and, with great difficulty,
placed a call. Teresa was on the extension as Janice at long
last got connected with the neighborhood bodega, which
sent for Arturo's father. The father spoke some unsatisfy-
ing version of English to Janice, who hurled back what
Spanish she'd managed to learn. Teresa was not able to
follow any of it. But at least she was rewarded by Paul's
oddly husky voice shouting, "Mommy, it's me. When are
you coming?"

"You be good or else," Janice threatened, followed by "I

love you, I love you, you're my baby. I'm coming soon."
They were cut off before Teresa could even say hello.

"I'm in love," Janice, bounding into the apartment the
day after she met Renaldo on Sixty-third Drive, announced
to Teresa. "Fuck Arturo, I've found a real man, a real
father for Paulie. We are going to get Paulie out of Peru
and moved to Chile."

"Please," Teresa begged, bending shaky knees to sit.
"Please call Barbara."

"Which one do you love?" I asked my sister gently,
trying not to embarrass her. There was, however, an edge
to my voice I couldn't quite cover. It told her I disapproved,
not only of her plans but possibly of her, too. We spent a bit
of time disapproving of each other, Janice and I.

"Teresa understands." Janice was openly belligerent.

"Does she?" I commented, considering a cigarette I'd
vowed never to light again. Lighting it at last, I watched the
smoke drift up to meet itself in the mirror over my bed. I
was missing my playwright.

"Teresa," she commanded, "tell Barbara you agree with
me."

"Never mind Teresa," I countermanded. "Just run me
through it one more time. Who is this guy? How did you
meet?"

"I told you already," she whined. "What are you, drunk
or something?" She was definitely hating me. "Listen," she
snapped, "I have to pee. Teresa will tell you." She dropped
the phone with a crash.

"He works in a little restaurant on Sixty-third Drive,"
Teresa told me, "and he smiles to Janice through the window, and Janice smiles back, so he comes out. Well, you
know how Janice is." I nodded into the phone, puffed
deeply, and waited. She continued. "He is interesting to
Janice, so she invites him to the house, and he listens to her
whole story and says why she does stupid things like that. So
now he is all the time here. And Janice—"

"Janice," I interrupted here in spite of myself, "is as
crazy as bad acid."

"I don't understand."

"Nothing, go on."

"Well, now Janice wants to send this Renaldo to Peru to pick up Paulie and take him to Chile."

"What!" I smashed the cigarette and started shouting. "Why Chile, for God's sweet sake?"

"Sh." Teresa quieted me. "Please, no good to yell. It's because this one is from Chile. And him and Janice decided to go there together and live."

I sat speechless. Janice was back on the line. "Oh, Barbara, he is wonderful, beautiful, a real man, so intelligent. I never realized how stupid Arturo was till now."

"Slow down, Janice."

"No, I don't care what you say. You don't want me to be happy. You're jealous because the men you love don't want to marry you." She hung up.

Lying back on the silk sheets one of the men in my life brought me to match the wallpaper of the bedroom in the apartment he loved to love me in, I pondered over my playwright-poet away in his life in London, and I worried whether my mirrors were turning dark with sin. My sister certainly had a way with words.

"Talk to her," Teresa begged me the next day in a secret call. "She is upset. She don't mean to say such nasty things."

I waited another day and called. My sister's phone had been changed to a new unlisted number.

Despite Teresa's head shaking, the new one, Renaldo, went off with almost all Janice's cash to prepare a home in Santiago for Janice, Paul, and some illegitimate daughter left over from a previous alliance. They are loose in their arrangements, Janice's Latins. So, giving up his valuable green card, Renaldo flew away on Janice's magic green carpet.

Teresa bade Janice a frightened good-bye. She hung on to the little money Janice left and all the words. "Don't worry, Teresa. When I'm settled, I'll come and get you. Or maybe Michael will bring you, or maybe he will even move down there with us. Renaldo says Santiago is gorgeous. And with a little money there are opportunities. Maybe we'll even get Auntie H. to come down. With her money, we could do a lot. Maybe even Barbara. If she won't move, she can visit. I'll call you, and I'll send you tapes. Have Barbara play them for you. But don't call her till I tell you." Teresa disobeyed and called.

A week later she and I sat on the steps elevating my bed and huddled close to my Sony. We were trying to understand the tape Janice had sent about the fun filled days of her adventure. It went like this:

"HI, TERESA. AND BARBARA. I HOPE TERESA IS PLAYING THIS FOR YOU, TOO. WELL, I'M HERE IN SANTIAGO, CHILE, AND I MISS YOU ALL AND I LOVE YOU. I LOVE YOU, I LOVE YOU! YOU KNOW, BARBARA, YOU DON'T KNOW HOW MUCH YOU LOVE EVERYTHING UNTIL YOU LEAVE. OF COURSE, THIS IS ONLY MY SECOND DAY HERE. I AM STILL VERY TIRED FROM MY TRIP, BUT NOW I'M CLEANING UP MY LITTLE BOY. I DON'T THINK THIS LITTLE BOY HAD A REAL BATH IN THE SIX MONTHS HE WAS IN PERU, HAVE YOU, PAULIE?"

"NO, THEY ONLY HAD COLD WATER IN LIMA, AND WATER COSTS MONEY, TOO."

"WELL, ANYWAY WE ARE ALONE. RENALDO HAD SOME ER-RANDS, AND WE THOUGHT THAT THIS IS A GOOD TIME TO MAKE THE TAPE. TERESA, DEAR, IF YOU SAW THIS LITTLE BOY, YOU'D PROBABLY CRY, BUT DON'T BE UPSET. RENALDO, WHO LOVES PAULIE WITH ALL HIS HEART, AND I ARE GOING TO STRAIGHTEN HIM OUT. AREN'T WE, PAUL? YOU LOVE RE-NALDO, DON'T YOU, PAULIE?"

"YES, A WHOLE LOT."

"YOU SEE, BARBARA, HE LOVES HIM. AND HIS LITTLE GIRL?"

"OH, YEAH, SHE'S VERY CUTE."

"TELL BARBARA HOW CUTE SHE IS."

"OH, VERY, I LOVE HER."

"YOU SEE. NOW, TERESA, DEAR, PAY ATTENTION BECAUSE YOU HAVE TO DO THINGS FOR ME. FIRST I'M SENDING YOU SOME EXTRA MONEY. I WANT YOU TO GET ME SOME MORE OF THOSE DUNGAREES I GOT. THEY FIT ME, AND THEY FIT RE-NALDO, SO I WANT YOU TO GO TO HARLEY'S SPORTSWEAR. I'LL SEND YOU A DRAWING AND THE SIZE. ORDER FOUR MORE—"

Had she sent the drawing? I asked. Teresa, listening, nodded.

"ALSO, I WANT MICHAEL TO LISTEN TO THIS TAPE. MIKEY, I WANT YOU TO DO ME A FAVOR. GO TO A RECORD STORE AND

GET ME THE CASSETTE OF *WOODSTOCK*. IT'S VERY IMPORTANT.
PAULIE NEEDS IT. AND REALLY, MIKEY, WHEN YOU ARE VERY,
VERY FAR FROM HOME YOU REALLY DO NEED LITTLE THINGS
LIKE THAT."

Her voice dropped.

"YOU SEE A LOT OF THINGS HAPPENED TO PAULIE IN PERU
THAT NO ONE WANTED TO TELL ME AND WELL, I'M TRYING TO
GET HIM BACK ON THE TRACK. AND I WILL, I PROMISE. NOW
I'M GOING TO TELL YOU ABOUT THEM, BUT EVERYBODY,
DON'T GET UPSET."

Teresa moved closer to the Sony. This was it.

"PAULIE HERE IS RECUPERATING FROM HIS TIME IN PERU.
HE HAS BEEN THROUGH SOME ORDEAL, LET ME TELL YOU.
BUT BEFORE I START, TERESA, THERE IS ONE MORE IMPOR-
TANT THING, PLEASE!"

Teresa's eyes stared from the Sony to the ceiling to God.

"I AM SENDING YOU A LETTER WRITTEN IN SPANISH, AND
I WANT YOU TO SEND IT RIGHT BACK DOWN TO LIMA TO
ARTURO'S PARENTS. DO YOU HEAR! RIGHT AWAY! IT'S SO THEY
SHIP ME THAT PIANO I SENT FOR PAULIE. AND THEY JUST
BETTER DO IT FAST. WE NEED THAT PIANO HERE IN CHILE
NOW."

Her voice changed; her mood swung.

"WELL, I GUESS THEY HAD A HARD TIME WITH PAUL, FROM
WHAT HE SAYS, BUT THEY BETTER SEND IT FAST. BY THE WAY,
THE FLIGHT DOWN WAS JUST WONDERFUL. THE STEWARDESS
WAS VERY NICE TO ME WHEN I WAS CRYING. AND I CAN'T TELL
YOU HOW FIFTEEN HOURS JUST PASSED AND I HARDLY EVEN
NOTICED. FOR A WHILE I SAT NEXT TO A VERY SMART MAN
FROM ARGENTINA, JEWISH. AND WE TALKED POLITICS AND I
LEARNED A LOT. YOU'LL BE INTERESTED, BARBARA, BECAUSE
YOU UNDERSTAND THIS STUFF AND . . ."

Teresa dropped her eyes from God and back to me. I
was helpless.

"YOU KNOW, BARBARA, THE PEOPLE FLYING DOWN HERE
TO CHILE ARE A MUCH BETTER TYPE THAN THOSE GOING TO
PERU."

My sister, the geophilosopher, was giving birth to a the-
sis. Eventually she started to wind down.

"AREN'T THEY, PAULIE?"

"YES."

Teresa almost jumped just hearing his little voice again. But Janice was back to praising everything Chilean and condeming Peru to perdition. She hovered and winged off into more packing instructions. Exactly what Teresa should include in the trunks. Here in Chile there seemed to be no Alexander's or Sears where she could go buy such stuff.

"NOW COME HERE, PAULIE, AND SAY HELLO TO TERESA AND AUNT BARBARA."

"HELLO, BABA."

"ISN'T IT CUTE HOW HE CALLS TERESA BABA? AND HE'S LOOKING BEAUTIFUL, TERESA. HE'S ALL CLEANED UP, AND HIS SORES ARE GETTING BETTER. RENALDO SAYS TWO WEEKS AGO HE LOOKED LIKE A WOLF BOY. TELL BABA AND AUNT BARBARA HOW NICE IT IS HERE AND HOW CUTE RENALDO'S DAUGHTER, PAMELA, IS."

"SHE'S SO CUTE."

"AND TELL HOW YOU LOVE PAMELA."

"WELL, YOU HAVE TO GET TO KNOW HER, BUT I LOVE HER. I REALLY DO."

Teresa was starting to cry, so I shut off the tape. After a moment I repushed play. Janice was still interrogating Paul in the manner with which Barbara Walters would someday rend revelations from Betty Ford. Obviously Janice had missed her calling.

"TALK, PAUL. TELL TERESA HOW YOU LIKE IT HERE AND RENALDO."

"I LOVE IT AND I LOVE RENALDO."

"YOU DON'T THINK I SHOULD EVER GO BACK TO ARTURO, SHOULD I, PAUL?"

"NAH. ARTURO'S A BABY."

"AND . . ."

"AND HE RUNS AWAY FROM HIS PROBLEMS."

"THAT'S RIGHT, PAUL. PAULIE IS RIGHT. NOW, PAULIE, TELL US ABOUT ALL THE TROUBLE YOU GOT INTO. HE GOT IN LOTS OF TROUBLE, DIDN'T YOU, PAUL."

"YES."

"HE GOT IN WITH BAD GUYS, BARBARA, YOU KNOW, HANGING AROUND. BY THE WAY, BARBARA, PAULIE REALLY LOVES

YOU AND MISSES YOU, AND SO DO I. PAULIE, TELL AUNT BARBARA HOW YOU GOT MIXED UP."

"I DON'T KNOW. I JUST STARTED HANGING AROUND THE WRONG GUYS."

"PAULIE, WOULD YOU SAY YOU WERE GETTING HIGH AT LEAST THREE TIMES EVERY DAY?"

"YEAH."

"DO YOU HEAR THAT? NOW TELL AUNT BARBARA WHAT WAS HAPPENING TO YOUR HEALTH."

"I ITCHED AND MY EYES GOT RED AND I COUGHED AND MY NOSE RAN AND MY MOUTH HAD SORES."

"WELL, BARBARA, TERESA, OUR PAULIE'S REALLY BROKEN DOWN, BUT STILL, HE LOOKS PRETTY. IN FACT, YOU LOOK DAMN GOOD, DON'T YOU, PAUL? HOW'D YOU LOOK WHEN RENALDO GOT YOU?"

"BAD, I HAD SHADOWS AND EVERYTHING."

"YOU REMEMBER THE MOVIE *LORD OF THE FLIES*, BARBARA? THAT'S THE IMPRESSION I GET FROM RENALDO. ISN'T THAT FUNNY?"

At this point Teresa was in mourning, and I was starting to realize how far from all workable reality this tape was pulling us.

Now it was the next morning, and Janice was telling us she was alone, that Renaldo was walking Pierre. I hadn't realized Janice had dragged her old poodle down there, too. I looked at Teresa, who was shaking her head. Poor Pierre. Janice told us he was unhappy, disoriented, not eating and hiding. She thought he might be depressed. Actually, she confessed, she might be depressed. Not that Renaldo was not wonderful, but she was sad about Peru, and while no one was listening, she admitted that she missed Arturo.

"AH, BARBARA, THERE MUST BE SOMEONE SOMEWHERE FOR ME."

Then she complained that Teresa was remiss. She hadn't packed Janice's nail brush and lots of things that cost money. "MONEY, MONEY, MONEY," she repeated wearily. And she was freezing. There was no heat in the aristocratic old house Renaldo rented. Suddenly remembering this was a tape of triumph, she veered back to how wonderful it all would be.

328

She called for Paulie and pushed him, much to her own shock, to admit trying cocaine. But he won't do it anymore. Now he must tell the truth. If he had his choice would he live in the States or Chile? The States. She was crestfallen. Didn't he like his new minimotorscooter? He loved it. She felt better. Enter Renaldo. Had Pierre done everything? Renaldo thought so. What did he mean, "think"? Oh, never mind, he must say hello to Teresa and sister Barbara, whom he'd never met. He didn't want to. He did.

"HELLO, MAMA, I MISS SO MUCH YOUR COOKING AND FOOD. HELLO, BARBARA. THAT'S ALL."

And that was all. Janice screamed good-bye. She loved us all. The tape whirred and clicked off, and the silence became oppressive.

"Can you believe?" said Teresa at last. She was nervous about sounding disloyal to Janice. Barbara was always a touch the "other," the healthier, the luckier. Barbara was never all hers, not the way Janice was. Teresa readied herself to reject any bad thing Barbara might say. Strangely Barbara said nothing.

It was years before the full horror of that tape was realized. An older, angrier Paul was to tell us, almost tauntingly, that he really started doping there in Chile. He learned to take his comfort in cocaine, pills, and acid as well as marijuana.

Within his first hour on his miniscooter, Paul will find Santiago 1971 convenient to his needs, especially after his last weeks in Lima, when his mother, long distance, had managed to let him in on the plans. He heard that Peru was no longer the promised land. Someone was coming to lead him out of there. But he must not let on. So he'd become Secret Agent Boy.

"Fucking no-good Arturo," that's what his mother had said on the phone. He danced to the words. He sang them over the cliff and out to the sea. He'd show Arturo. But what about his piano? It'd only just arrived. "What about my piano?" he asked Renaldo when he appeared.

"Later," said Renaldo. "Listen and be quiet. I'm here to get you. That's what your mama wants."

In deep conspiracy, Paulie wondered if this slender dark

guy with the light skin and tight mouth was really going to
be his new father. Secretly he preferred Arturo.

"Are you going to marry us?" He asked on the way to
the airport. Renaldo, counting soles and figuring exchange
rates, did not answer.

Now he was flying to Santiago to meet his mother. Maybe
Teresa, too. He started humming, then singing one of his
favorite Beatles songs. He sang out loud, checking to see if
he was irritating Renaldo. Renaldo ignored him. But the
slender Latin stewardess looked at him and giggled. He
giggled back and sang even louder, with gestures. That did
it. Renaldo pinched him hard on his thigh. Tears came to
his eyes. He turned his head to the window and the clouds.

It was greener here, Paul noticed. The neighborhood
looked more familiar. It had real sidewalks. They were to
stay at Renaldo's mother's till they got a house of their own.
His mother, holding the thin arm of a little girl, greeted
them at the door.

Then Renaldo's mother led him to his own closetlike
room; he was glad to have a door to close.

Later he wandered the area. Viña del Mar on the sea.
The next day atop his new miniscooter he set out again.
Some older kids with hippy hair and American jeans were
clustered around a magazine kiosk and attracted him like a
magnet. Pedaling a little closer, he smelled the aroma of
"high" in their atmosphere and grinned at them. Pressing
his thumb to his forefinger as if holding an invisible joint,
he inhaled with a rapid and audible hiss. They clicked in.
He made a small purchase.

Renaldo found a house. A little the worse for wear, in
what used to be an elegant section, it still was quite attractive. It would need some help, this house, but Renaldo
assured Paul that a few dollars here and there would do
wonders. While packing for the move, Renaldo surprised
him and found Paul's grass. Grabbing Paulie's throat, he
shook him and shouted. Scared, Paul feared Renaldo could
really hurt him. He thought Renaldo drank when he went
on his errands. But he thought as little as possible. Mostly
Paul got high. "I will tell Jana about marijuana," Renaldo

warned him. And he did, almost before they were out of the airport.

Standing at the Avianca barricade, Paul was in such a state he thought his head would burst. "Are they in yet?" he kept demanding of Renaldo.

"*Si, si.*"

"Then where is she?" Renaldo signaled at the customs area. There she was, she was coming! No, she was going in another direction. What was she doing? He started to shout. She was bending, watching as an airport guy opened a metal box. She reached inside and pulled out a tangle of gray curly animal. It was Pierre. Paulie couldn't believe it. She was pulling Pierre toward them. Pierre lifted his leg against some baggage. She kept pulling, and they left a trail to the barricade. Paul jumped and yelled and wrapped himself around her. Pierre was underfoot, getting stepped on. Renaldo stood aside and watched.

"I think we better get Pierre some water," she said. "He's been locked up forever." She giggled. Poor Pierre hadn't known he was going to wind up in South America.

"Give water at home. It's more better," instructed Renaldo.

"Poor Pierre," his mother was still saying as they headed for the taxi. "He used to be beautiful. Now look at him."

It was a time of firsts. Janice took her first look at the house her money rented and wasn't sure. "It was very classy," she later told me, "but it didn't have anything. Heat, stove, refrigerator, nothing. And the beds, with your back, Barbara, you wouldn't have lasted a night."

Janice also took her first look at Renaldo's daughter. Somewhat better. But she was glad the child was to stay with Renaldo's mother, who had greeted her with open arms.

It was about two days after they recorded the tape for New York that Janice and Renaldo had their first fight. Paulie retraced his path to the kiosk and made another buy.

News of her retreat from Chile came to New York in stages.

Stage I: I accepted a collect call from Janice. "Barbara, you must help me. He's got my money, and he won't give it back. He's kicking Pierre, he hit Paul, and he's threatening me, I'm scared. I have to get away. What can I do?"

"Go to the consul."

"Please, Barbara, you speak Spanish, speak to him. Call his mother, help me."

It took me four calls to Renaldo's mother, full of repeated threats from my pals Richard Nixon and Henry Kissinger, to get Janice most of her money back and her option to leave the leased house, the bought bike, the new furniture, and old dreams. But she dragged Paul and Pierre through half a day in Lima before setting safe feet in Miami. She had fantasized finding a repentant Arturo, whose love, along with Paul's piano, remained intact. Arturo, they had hazy word, was coming. "Don't," she warned us in New York, "tell Arturo about Renaldo." Then she confessed that in a moment of panic on the way to the Santiago airport she'd given Renaldo back half the cash I'd fought so hard for. "I was afraid," she said, "he was going to kill us."

Stage II: Janice, taking Teresa as "muscle," returned to Santiago to claim back her money. Much to my surprise, the new threats I was phoning in, which included Allende and the U.S. Marines, worked.

Her money in hand, Janice stopped in Lima again. She wanted to introduce Teresa to Arturo's family and see if he had come home. In Peru they found the piano still taking up most of the kitchen and Arturo expected any moment. Janice told them whatever lie came to mind to explain her comings and goings and raced Teresa back to the plane to Chile.

Teresa remembered her six days of South America as one long nightmare. "Barbara, once I see the place they stick Paulie in, I am so angry I can't talk one word. It's worse than anything I dream. People live like pigs in mud. No, in my town in Europe, pigs live more nice." After describing the sewer, she went on. "In Chile, there is Renaldo. She lie to him. She say she needs money to get divorce from Arturo. She lie to everyone all over the place. She even lie to Pat, who buy us tickets to go."

"Pat?" I asked, "Who is Pat?"

"Pat, the nice man she meet when she bring Paul home

from Chile. The nice man who don't know anything and wants to divorce his wife to marry her. The one whose wife shoot him to death next year."

"Oh, that Pat." I remembered. I never knew him. But what energy my sister spent on her madnesses.

"We have hard time get the money," Teresa recalled. "Renaldo he change he dollars on black market. Some just gone. At the airport Renaldo tells Janice he needs dollars. I am holding the dollars. I hear and try to get quick through the gate where he can't go. Janice keep me back. She don't let go of my arm all the time we are in Chile. She say to give him three hundred, but I only give him one hundred and run like heck sake through gate. . . ."

Teresa, till this day, doesn't have any concept of the amounts of money Janice scattered. Teresa worried over hundreds, and Janice spewed thousands.

She's got the cash, she informed me collect, and she's stopping over in Lima. In Lima they found Arturo snoring happily on his sister's bed. He was very glad to see her. He loved her. He will come back to New York with his team. And why didn't they all get in the bus Janice's money had bought them and go someplace *fantastico* for dinner. Teresa bounced along with the rest.

"You should see this restaurant," Teresa told of it later. "It almost as bad as where they live except it has real glass in the windows. Thanks God, because as soon as we sit down next to one, a man comes outside by bushes and opens his pants and pees right against it. Right in front of our face"—Teresa remembered it all in vivid images—"and then Arturo's mother she order something she love. And on a plate comes a small animal like a rat. Boil right in its skin with teeth sticking out and a tail. And she eats it, tail and all. I eat nothing. Janice she see nothing except Arturo. He listen to her lies and she listen to his lies and everything is beautiful make-believe."

The next afternoon they went to the airport. Worn out with odd emotions, she and Janice passed through immigration. "Listen, Teresa," Janice decided, her head cradled in Teresa's lap, "it cost a lot. I made many mistakes, but now it will be all right. Arturo loves me. We will try to make it in the States. I'll keep my friend Pat on the side. After all, he's married, too! And I need the money. Paulie is safe, and he will go back to school in the fall. I hope he's having a good time in Pennsylvania." Actually Paul was having the time of his life hearing from his father's family how his mother had killed their beloved Bob. And how, despite their protests, she'd cremated the body, too. Perhaps to cover up something.

Before Arturo returned, Janice installed a secret phone in the back of her private closet. She would unplug this phone when Arturo was at home and answer only when he was out of the house. She needed money.

"Sell the bus in Peru," suggested Teresa.

"I can't. It's supporting Arturo's family and his other wife and two kids. Besides, if we ever do get down there, we will need it." It was the first Teresa heard of this other wife, much less kids. But nothing surprised her.

That fall Janice took to wearing turtlenecks constantly. They looked good on her, and neither Auntie H., nor I, her sartorial sister, thought anything of it. "She looks well," Auntie H. mentioned to me. "Of course, she watches what she eats. She isn't eating at the Automat like me. She has Teresa to cook for her." Then Auntie H. showed me how loose her own dress was. "I don't eat, I don't sleep, I'm a nervous wreck, and still, Janice takes money from me and tells me her troubles. As if I didn't have troubles. Well, anyway, she's stopped dragging that kid with her when she comes." Auntie H., who never forgot a rotten thing anyone ever did to her, twisted her diamond ring and gave me a list of Paul's latest failings. "That kid is no good. He is driving her crazy."

Teresa later told me that it was Pat who noticed the swelling along Janice's throat and wanted her to go to his doctor. But Janice put it off. Finally she agreed, but the Sunday before the Tuesday of her appointment was the day Pat's wife shot Pat in the head, chest, and belly. Janice, deep in depression, dropped the doctor idea altogether. I'd never met Pat, which was a help to me.

Now Arturo, back in New York, was playing soccer on

occasional weekends, was working in some sweatshop factory, and seemed to be trying. They were as she'd wanted, finally together, but she complained a lot.

"I should have married Pat," she moaned to me.

"Pat's wife might have shot you, too." The idea didn't take.

"Maybe not," she argued, adding, "think how much money he would have left me. What Arturo earns at the factory is so little it's embarrassing. Since his soccer team fired him for fighting, he only picks up a couple of games a month. He gives me almost nothing. If I didn't have extra help, we'd never make it."

"Doesn't he notice what you really spend?"

"Are you kidding! He's so glad he doesn't have to be pretending to attend that beauty school that I enrolled him in he wouldn't notice anything. Oh, Barbara, if only I had some of those thousands I threw away. I'd disconnect that fucking phone locked in my closet and go to work as a damn secretary. Like you always wanted."

"I never wanted you to be a damn secretary."

"Well, you know what I mean."

She meant the job I pulled strings to get her when I was married to Nick, the job of assistant to the producer of a variety TV show. She'd turned it down. She'd wanted to sing, not assist anybody, no matter the career that could have started for her. She wanted to sing. But she didn't have much of a voice.

"Do you want to visit Auntie H. this week?" I switched subjects. "It's almost her birthday."

"Maybe. But only if you go. When I'm alone with her, she picks on me. My hair, my makeup, Paulie, something. Even if I bring her cookies, they're from the wrong bakery."

"That's the price of being on her payroll."

"What a mean thing to say." Janice's voice was hurt, and I wished I could cancel my words. Ah, those festering resentments about Auntie H.'s favoring her over me. Janice was, I was always reminded, her heiress. But Auntie H. never let the heiress forget it either. "Babsie," Auntie H. liked to tell us, "can take care of herself. Babsie, Janice needs me."

"You know," Janice mused, "she used to lock Paul in her hotel bathroom to keep him out of the way." I know, and I knew Janice sat there and allowed it.

"Hermosa's a funny woman," I acknowledged, "an original."

But Hermosa used to be different. She used to be a real sport. One of the boys. Of course, she never wanted anything to do with kids. Even us, her favorite sister's children. She wanted us quiet and out of sight. Auntie H. would have locked all kids in bathrooms if she could. Plaguing our mother about this or that, she overwhelmed us. "It isn't that my sister Hannah hates the kids," my mother explained, "but they *are* noisy." My father would mutter about selfish broads with no maternal feelings, and sometimes I'd start connecting the dazzling Hermosa, our Auntie H., with this constantly complaining sister Hannah. Then decide they couldn't be the same person at all.

Hannah Siegel, it seemed, was born to dance. The whole Lower East Side knew that. "She danced at the drop of a hat." Those who knew her, old-timers, sitting around the Friars Club, still reminisce about her. Usually it was the drop of a monkey's hat she danced to as the organ grinder groaned out "The Sidewalks of New York" or "Little Annie Rooney." She danced and shared in the pennies and nickels they collected, too. That is, if her mother or father didn't catch her. Hannah danced to street whistles, boys with harmonicas, bells on wagons, and quartets singing in front of bars or barbershops. She danced as if her life depended on it. And perhaps it did.

"The Gypsies will steal her if she doesn't stop." Her mother worried in Yiddish. But Hannah thought that Gypsies might be her great opportunity. She tried to get their attention. She auditioned for them on the sly, laughing, dancing. "The Gypsies," she remembered with a funny smile, "never stole me, just wanted to tell my future." Actually she knew her future: Someday someone would dance her away from Broome Street.

Just when she first noticed Nat, she wasn't sure, but she said she noticed him before he noticed her. He had New

York style. Finally, at a dance, a small Sunday afternoon affair, he found himself waltzing her around the floor and fell in love. At least that was the way she told it. "I even," she admitted, "sneaked change from my father's cashbox to buy him a cigar." Soon they were a team. They practiced tangos and one-steps that won them prizes, and Nat talked to her about the stage. The beautiful vaudeville palaces lit and waiting. He talked of the money, the applause, and, most important, the music and dance.

"Why can't I?" Hannah had clenched her fists and stared into her mother's old greenhorn eyes. "This is America, Mama. I can do what I want. It's a free country!"

"I'll give you free! Talking to Mama like that!" Her older sister, Ida, slapped her hard across the mouth. Ida was bigger and stronger and would have hit her again, but their mama stopped her. Only little Rosie, wearing Hannah's hand-me-downs, took her part. Rosie always idolized Hannah when Hannah allowed it.

At last, worn down with fighting and convinced by the young Nat Birnbaum of the good care he'd give their Hannah, her parents had officially blessed them as a team. And they married. That's how it was then.

So they worked on their wardrobes and sexy smiles and strutted into show business, hitting all the circuits. As a Latin dance act they turned themselves into "Hermosa and Jose." Or was it "Jose and Burns," as imprinted all over the steamer trunk they had invested in to carry their costumes? Auntie H. defended that trunk almost all her life. Memories as well as stockings stuffed its faded flowered drawers. And pictures of her naked behind her huge ostrich fan. Her eyes rolled upward toward heaven. Jose and Burns. Nat had dropped the *baum* from his name. All the East Side boys were doing that in "free America."

"There is a broken name for every light on Broadway," my father quipped. Hannah, now Hermosa, wasn't sure that this Hymie Caplin was funny. He came from a notorious tough-guy family, not talmudic like her own people. However, he was handsome enough with that blond hair and those green eyes. Surprisingly her papa seemed to warm toward this wise guy. He even translated Hebrew history for Hymie's enlightenment. They sipped strong tea through sugar cubes and shared ideas. Actually Hermosa was a sucker for a winning wink herself.

Jose and Burns usually got work as the opener on the bill or as a breaker between funnymen. When they didn't get work, Hermosa would "pony" in a chorus for one of the "Shubert boys," as she called them, and Nat would pick up a payday judging dance contests at the "Rackets." But the "big time" somehow eluded them. So when Al Klien, of the Klien Brothers, a headline comedy act that toured Europe and played the Palladium, proposed she divorce Nat and marry him, as she told it, she thought it a sensible move. Nat wrote sad letters to this hardhearted Hannah until their divorce was final. Then he found himself a new partner, a pretty Irish girl named Grace who had a way with her. And Jose and Burns disappeared and Burns and Allen began.

Vaudeville died and took Hermosa's second marriage with it. Eventually she met Almost Uncle Eddie and moved into the St. Moritz. "It was supposed to be temporary," she said fifty years later.

"I don't think I'm going, in all this rain," Janice had coughed into the phone earlier. "Auntie H. doesn't expect me anyway. What about you?"

"I guess I will," I said, eyeing the pink-wrapped bottle of Chanel No. 5 cologne I'd bought for Hermosa. Not too expensive, to avoid an Auntie H. harangue over my frivolous ways. "I'll get over there in an hour. We don't have to stay long."

"All right, I'll meet you in the lobby."

I found Janice, her pretty head hunched into a turtleneck, pacing in Auntie H.'s wet hand-me-down mink in front of the hotel entrance.

"Where were you?" she demanded. "Something's wrong."

"Sorry, I got hung up talking backgammon. I'm entering a tournament. What's the matter?"

"Well, I called her room, and there's no answer." Putting her freezing hand on my arm, she looked about fourteen, a kid in mommy's clothes. "Then," she went on, "I went up and knocked, but still nothing, and the doorman doesn't think she left and—" By this time I was calling Hermosa's room.

The operator, an old hand at the St. Moritz, recognized my voice. "Is this Babsie?"

"Yes. Have you spoken to Mrs. Klien today?"

"No, I haven't, but some days I don't. Let's keep ringing." The Art deco clock in the lobby jerked another minute by.

"Let me speak to the manager."

It took a moment to get the passkey to do its trick. Hermosa's room was dark. The shades were drawn. Janice and I moved like thieves past the bathroom and around the wall to where her bed huddled. She was in it.

"Is she breathing?" asked Janice, backing away.

"Just barely." I was at the phone. "Get the police," I ordered. "Get an ambulance."

The police arrived first. They were sophisticated about sleeping pills. "We better not wait," they said. "Let's get her to Roosevelt."

As innocent of peril as a babe in its bunting, Hermosa dreamed on as we carried her, bound to her desk chair with her blanket, down to the rainy street. Her head lolled; her expression was soft, gentle. Should we have backed out, Janice and I, and locked her door and gone to have a highball? Auntie H. liked an occasional highball. She would spritz herself one in Uncle Eddie's room while waiting for me to get ready for bed. What would have been kindest? I know what happens at hospitals with this stuff. Will she thank us? Does she want to be saved? Will she be saved?

"Hurry, hurry!" I snarled at the cop at the wheel. We all were crowded in the squad car together. The windshield wipers beat time as Auntie H.'s head bounced over to Janice's shoulder and back to mine. She was propped between us. The siren shrieked.

The Roosevelt Hospital emergency room was its own kind of madhouse. Based-up winos, mothers with screaming children, someone with an eye knocked out or almost out, or something awful. Jangled junkies harassed head nurses; scurrying interns shouted at addled attendants.

But with the cops as leaders, we were pushed through to wait and watch as they started saving Auntie H.'s reluctant life.

"Here are all her medications." I emptied the plastic bag I'd thrown her bottles helter-skelter into as we left the room. I'd ransacked her medicine chest and top drawer.

"Janice, have you got any of her pills in there?"

Janice looked through Auntie H.'s handbag. She'd searched for everything she thought important and thrown it in there. "No, but I got her will."

"It looks mostly like it's the Seconal," said the bearded boy, obviously pretending to be a doctor just to fool me.

"Are you a resident here?" I demanded.

He nodded. "Start emptying her stomach and get that intravenous going." Giving orders as he went through her bottles. "Some collection," he commented.

Auntie H. lay naked, her one breast flapping against her bony rib cage as they moved her around. "Her privates," as she called them, were exposed and looked pathetic and bald. "Good God"—Janice grimaced—"is this what they did to you, Barbara?"

"I guess so."

"She may not make it," the doctor warned, wheeling her away behind further swinging doors. "Be prepared for a long wait." I thought about Hermosa teaching me to rumba. And how to place a hairpiece and to "wear your earrings close to your face, Babsie, it's prettier."

We were sitting on a bench in the hall. People with important missions hurried by. "I guess I should call Arturo and Teresa and tell them what's happened," Janice decided, still hanging tightly on to Auntie H.'s big brown handbag, stuffed with all her bankbooks, jewelry, eyeglasses, wallets, and, of course, the will. I was angry with myself for resenting that will. I was angry with Janice for pushing it into my mind. I felt sick.

"Maybe we ought to call Uncle Al," I said, "and Aunt Ruth."

"I'll call them all." Janice was more in control than I'd ever heard her. "I've got her address book."

Spending a lot of time, and all my change, she returned

to tell me she was going home. She'd drive back with Arturo later.

"I'll wait here," I said.

My best buddy, Big Steve Herzfeld, gave up the backgammon tournament to sit with me. Uncle Al's son showed up and was delighted to remember meeting Steve once at El Morocco or someplace important. Not surprising, since Steve cut his teeth on such silver spoons. My cousin was full of compliments on my adult beauty; we'd had childhood crushes on each other. But Auntie H.'s madness preoccupied him. He began recounting eccentric anecdotes of her time selling his father's high-priced apparel. "Once," he said, "she had this rich Italian woman in the dressing room who was ready to buy everything we had." Hermosa, he told us, suggested the woman wipe under her arms because she was very sweaty. Then, it seems, Hermosa went on to ask why she didn't shave. The woman, indignant, said that in Italy no one shaved under there. So Hermosa said, "Listen, when I'm in your country, I'll wear a toupee under my arms, but over here, shave!" Big Steve loved the story. "We lost the sale," Norman remembered with regret and summed up. "It was worse," he said, "when she liked you than when she hated you." He spoke of her in the past tense with an almost affectionate relief.

"Do you think the old broad has a fighting chance?" Steve asked after Norman left and he had listened to Janice and Arturo figuring out their half of the coming legacy.

"I hope so." She was my Auntie H., a piece of my life, my *living* legacy. But as Janice reminded me, I had no financial stake here; everything for me was simple. Would I have felt differently if I thought my freedom and future were having this dance with death? Who knew? But I didn't think so.

Aunt Ruth showed up. Overweight and overworked. Good Aunt Ruth was having a bit of time with her stakes, too. It's hard to be the mother of two hungry and warring daughters who jealously fight each other's every crumb of life. Auntie H. spent some vacations with them in Browns Mills. She treated them with snobbish disdain. They were backwoods and not too pretty either. Then, when the elder got her nose fixed, she ranked better with Hermosa. But nothing about the younger pleased her. "She's sly and greedy," Auntie H. said of her. "I don't know why. Ruthie is so good. She's working herself to death for those two girls!" Aunt Ruth "worked herself to death" in the kitchen of a tuberculosis sanitarium. Eventually she ran it. "The only thing that young one inherited from Ruth is her fat." Hermosa hated fat. She hadn't allowed her sister Ruth to one of her weddings because she deemed her too fat, a hurt that poor Ruth would always carry in her heart. What a pretty face she has, I thought. It had been twenty years since I'd seen it. Janice rushed over to her, dragging Arturo.

"I want you to meet my husband." She sounded somewhat superior.

Aunt Ruth looked expectantly toward Big Steve. "Only a pal." I apologized. Leaving Janice and Ruth to consult, I went with Steve for a late supper.

On the way we found the bearded doctor. Auntie H. was still hanging on, but he wasn't what you might call comforting. "We'll know better by morning," he said. "She does have a remarkably strong heart."

The Sixth Avenue Delicatessen was harsh with glare after the gloom of Roosevelt Hospital. I found myself ravenous. So was Big Steve.

"Two whole turkey legs for me if you've got them," he ordered (Big Steve was really big) "and a Dr. Brown's Cel-Ray for me. What do you want, Babs?"

"One turkey leg and tomato juice."

The waiter nodded. He had it down and rushed away.

"I like calling you Babs."

"Babsie," I corrected. "They called me Babsie."

"Rockabye, Babsie," crooned Steve.

"I never liked that," I said. "All the bough breaks and baby falls stuff. Some lullaby!"

"Some family you got, kid," Steve said at last.

"You'd have liked my father. You'd have liked Hymie."

"You'da loved her father." A rough voice intruded over my shoulder. "Hymie was the salt of the earth," it pronounced. I turned to face watery blue eyes and broken nose beneath a newsboy cap. "It is you, isn't it? You ain't changed since you sang 'East Side West Side' in front of the Turf restaurant for me. Except, what happened to the blond curls? What curls this girl had. You shoulda seen 'em. Her old man taught her all these songs, see, and when us bums would line up to grab a finif or more after he had a win, this kid would sing to us. Them was sweet days."

The waiter was back with the drumsticks. "Is that old windbag bothering you?" he asked.

The windbag was retreating out into the rain. He blew me a kiss. I blew one back. I felt silly.

"Wouldn't he be great in a Fruit of the Loom commercial?" I tried for a laugh.

"Do you really remember that guy?" Steve asked over my humor in favor of turkey.

"No," I said.

"She's going to make it," I shouted into the phone to Big Steve, who cheered madly at the other end. "They've got her in intensive care; but her vital signs are good, and she even opened her eyes." When they moved her to a regular room, Janice brought Auntie H. her handbag.

"Just leave me my checkbook and a few dollars for tipping," she croaked, her throat raw from tubes. "Hold on to everything else; they steal in these places."

The yogis say we bring our worst fears upon us. Alone in an almost pleasant semiprivate room, Auntie H. anguished because I didn't want to take the diamond wedding band, embedded for so long, from her left hand.

"No," I protested, "please leave it on. It makes your hand even prettier." She jerked the intravenous she was locked into, trying to dislodge the ring. She hurt herself and lay still. "This ring was from Al Klien," she said. "I don't remember what I did with Nat's. I think I pawned it. At least take the other one, Babsie, Mama's, with the two big diamonds. Where is that?" She was suddenly alarmed.

"That one is in the hospital vault."

"Take it out, and keep it. I want you to have it, Babsie. Please, enjoy it for me. Where do I ever go anymore? The

Automat." I didn't want her ring. But I thrilled to see her smile; even her complaints charmed me. They had life. And she seemed to feel my caring, perhaps for the first time.

"Take it," she insisted.

"Some other year. It's your mother's ring, and you love it. Enjoy it for yourself. I'll take it some other year."

"Now that's a promise." The oxygen tube up her nose created an eerie embryonic aura, the kind astronauts have. And I remembered St. Francis Hospital in Florida. The smell of jasmine and the confusion of time and sense. The fear. I cradled her and sang her a few oldies.

" 'She's nobody's sweetheart now.'

" 'That's me,' " she crooned along. "Hey"—she brightened—"did I ever tell you the one about the man whose wife charges him every time they diddle?"

She waits for me to say, "No, tell me."

"Well, after twenty years of marriage she shows him a small tenement on the West Side and tells him she bought it for them with all the money she saved. Well, the man starts to moan and beat his breast." Auntie H. was out of breath. She had insisted on giving me something even if it was only a laugh. "So he beats his breast and his wife asks what's the matter, and the guy says, 'If only I gave you all my business, we'd own the Waldorf.' "

"Barbara"—the phone hissed in my hand—"Barbara, do you know what that no-good kid of Janice's has done?" Auntie H. never waited for my "what?"

"That damn kid, that Paulie, stole seventy dollars out of my wallet." She was actually calling from her room, not the cheaper pay phone in the lobby. "Janice feels terrible. She was ashamed to tell me. It's not her fault. That kid is just no good." Why had Janice told her?

"Why didn't you just replace the money?" I called and questioned. "You know Hermosa; she'll never forget it, much less forgive."

"Why shouldn't I tell her?" Janice shrieked, then started to cough. "Why shouldn't she know?" Choking held up the argument till she regained herself.

"Your cough is getting worse," I noticed.

"Never mind my fucking cough. Damn you, Barbara. Why do you criticize everything I do? I can't afford to replace the lousy money. And it's none of your business!" She hung up and rechanged her number.

"Why can't you girls get along?" Auntie H. asked as I walked her to the shoemaker. She hadn't regained her strength; only her tongue was still sharp. "You two haven't talked all spring and summer. Shame on you, Barbara. Her having such a hard time with that animal she married and that damn kid."

"I don't have her number," I explained, supporting Hermosa across a curb. "Give me her number and I'll call."

"No," said Hermosa. "I promised her not to give it to you."

"Then how can I call?"

She misstepped, and I clutched her elbow. She regained herself. "Stop jerking me," she chided, "I can still move gracefully, you know. After all, I am a dancer."

Eventually Janice's voice was once more heard, shrill but comfortable, as if we'd spoken only minutes before. "Turn on Channel Two. It's coming live from Chile. I think they're knocking off Allende, I'm not sure. But they are showing some great shots of Viña del Mar. That's where we had the house. Turn on the set, quick."

I dialed onto danger in the streets. Armored police cars on patrol. Sudden gunfire. Babies screaming in mothers' arms. Doorway-to-doorway scuffling. Army tanks rolling down roads and with them the realization that police have disappeared. I saw soberly dressed businesspeople with newspapers under arms, standing quietly in line for a bus, watching the action. Their manner seemed as remote from the madness as mine. All this Telstar stuff. All this war as you watch it. Not even a thirty-second delay. It took on a slick surface.

"Look, that is our street." Janice coughed. Choking on her excitement. "I'm sure it is our street, right there where that body is. This is worse than an earthquake. I'm glad we got out." More coughing. "I hope poor Renaldo and his mother are okay. Jesus, look at that! That tank rolled over that dog."

"Janice, whatever happened with those chest X rays you took?"

"Oh, nothing. A touch of asthma." That she was inventing and had never even called to find out about the X rays I didn't know till winter. It was still September, and the days were long and warm.

"Do you want to come for Thanksgiving this year?" she asked. It was as near as she could get to "Let's make up."

"Sure, if I'm in town."

"Why? Where are you going now?"

"Just to London again. But it's not definite." My poet was finishing something. A screenplay, I thought. And was somewhere sort of isolated.

"Is that still going on?"

"Mostly."

"Do you think his wife knows?"

"No."

"Do you think your David ever realized?"

"Yes."

"I liked David."

"You liked all my men," I reminded her. She coughed quietly.

I went for Thanksgiving. My man of letters had written in a postponement. "I'll be there, my sweet love, in December."

Auntie H. pecked at the capon that Teresa preferred cooking to turkey. She also pecked at Arturo, Paul, Janice, and me. She was having a wonderful time. So was I. It was good to see them all again. Arturo's teasing broadly set Janice giggling into her turtleneck. Teresa, apologizing for her perfect holiday fare as humbly as a serf, packed Auntie H. a care package.

"I can keep it on the windowsill," Auntie H. said as we bounced our way back along Queens Boulevard toward Manhattan. "Teresa is a good cook. Too bad she still can't speak English."

"We never helped her."

"Never mind. She should have picked it up anyway. My

sister Rose," she added, "never expected too much of her. After all, Teresa is only a peasant girl." Silence.

"Janice never wears the mink I gave her," she mentioned. I don't tell her that Janice passed it on to the "peasant girl." She would never forgive such a thing.

"Janice doesn't make the most of herself," Auntie H. pointed out again. "She's not like you. You know how to be a glamour girl. Even though she's the prettier. Everyone always agreed on that. You just don't want to help her," Hermosa continued. "You never introduced her to anyone worthwhile. She told me. My goodness, look what she wound up with. He's still in the banana tree. A beauty like her. Why, in my day the men would have stood in line just for a 'how do you do.'" She flicked her tongue. "And that no-good kid of hers, did you see how much he ate? Both drumsticks. He never even asked if anyone else wanted one."

"You always like breast meat," I said. She didn't respond.

A Matter of Blood

In December my playwright cabled:"Darling, New York production definitely postponed. Stop. It will have to be London. Stop. Hope you are taking it. Stop. My heart as always." Signed "H," as always.

In December Janice had taken Teresa along on her visit to the union doctor Arturo's weekday job at the factory allowed. The doctor studied the big black pictures of inside Janice's chest. Teresa watched him and tried to follow what was indicated as he said, "Well, the entire left lung is covered with the mass." He turned and in a brusque business-like manner concluded, "I can't tell without futher tests. But I would say it's either lung cancer or Hodgkin's."

Teresa will tell me that was the moment she felt God was dead.

Janice will call me as soon as they get home. No, first she will talk to a health food person. By the time she calls me, she has the name of a cancer specialist, one her nutrition people feel is not too limited. Asking me to meet her at his office, Thursday at four, she will add, "And please, don't tell Hermosa. Not yet."

It's cold, and a skicap is pulled down over her ears.
It has such a gay pompon on top. I can't bear it. We sit in
the old-fashioned and rather elegant waiting room. Her
rounded, narrow shoulders are hunched; she seems crippled. A wounded bird. And her eyes are terrible. My flesh
constricts. I am surprised when she accepts the grimace on
my face as a smile. Trying for a smile to comfort, I know
that whatever my face is doing, it's not that. Yet she grasps
at it as a smile. She needs it as a smile. She smiles back.

"You're looking so pretty," she says, "so rosy. No wonder
men adore you. You're really adorable, Barbara. So sweet."

Oh, my God. She must stop saying things like that or I'll
fall apart. Where is all that "mad at" stuff when I need it? I
take her arm as we pace his waiting room.

"He's studying the other X rays. I brought them," she
tells me. "So he has to take only one more. Too many X rays
aren't healthy, you know. *Prevention* magazine just did a big
article on that." She is pleased to pass this information.

God, I beg, please, Master Kirpal Singh. I'm sorry I eat
meat. I'll stop. I won't have sex anymore. I'll be good.
Please, somebody help her.

This doctor is kinder, but a knell tolls under his tone.

"Well, I think it's Hodgkin's, which is lucky. We've made
some advances with Hodgkin's. But surely you must have
noticed something earlier. Those glands are very pronounced. Why didn't you come sooner?" Janice shrugs.

"I was afraid," she whispers to me as he studies the new
X ray he'd insisted on.

"Do you want me to proceed with the hospital arrangements?" he asks. He operates out of New York Hospital and
can get her right in. Janice looks to me for the decision.

"Thank you. I think we had better talk it over." I'm polite
as hell. So is my sister. Two heroines right out of Louisa May
Alcott. We bow and scrape our way from his office.

"He made me feel Jewish and alien," I say, trying my
smile again. She looks so scared.

"Do you think I should go to a Jewish doctor?" She
drops her head, the ridiculous pompon bouncing.

"So why not talk with one?" I say in synagogue singsong.
"What could hurt?"

"Find me one." She lifts her face. "Find me a good one."
I keep waving to her as the cab carries her away.

"No, I can't come for Christmas," I answered my play-wright across the ocean. "My sister"—I enunciated very properly—"well, I think she has cancer. I'm not quite able to plan anything. It's really rather necessary for me to stay here." "Rather necessary," "not quite able"—why was I us-ing phrases like that, imitating him again?

"Oh, my dear." His voice echoed his distance. "My very dear. I understand. Call Terry if you need me. I'll get right back to you. Take good care, my sweet girl. Take very good care."

I was trying to take good care. Running to friends, to a shrink. Which was the best way to go? Which concept? Which doctor? Which hospital? Predictably it came down to the team at Mount Sinai. At least they would let you moan "oy vey" and understand.

Soon we were checking in at the Klingenstein Medical Center. Not to be confused with the Klingenstein Pavilion, a much fancier part of the Mount Sinai establishment—not for the likes of us. That's for rich heart attacks, rich babies, and cosmetic surgery. This would be expensive enough, though. And we both were thinking of money as we filled out the forms.

"Do you suppose"—Janice fretted—"Arturo's employ-ment insurance will cover some of this?"

"Don't worry," I reassured. "I'll make up the difference." Even as I said it, I was worried. Had I enough to last her? To last her till what? We both were thinking of death. She started to wonder if the other new check-in had cancer. I wondered when it might be me and who would pay for that? God, spare us public hospitals like those Melvin had, where once in their power, you wait in pain to be humiliated.

"We are not dead yet," my sister said, and I thought how dear it was of her to say "we."

High style at Mount Sinai seemed to be a stethoscope sticking out of a side pocket. Perhaps I should get one. Then nobody would question my comings and goings.

"There are"—Janice was reading my thoughts—"medical supply stores where you can buy that stuff. I got a scalpel once and a dentist's pick to scrape my teeth. Do you like to pick under your gums? Sometimes it feels great." Eventually we were admitted. Semiprivate.

"Barbara. Barbara. Oh, Barbara, don't let them! Stop them! I feel it, I feel it. Oh, God, I can't take it." Wanting to run into the hall, I do. I still hear her. I run back. Testing is here and now.

"Please, Janice, darling, they have to. It's necessary to know what's happening." I want to talk softly, but I'm shouting at her. Ordering. They are puncturing her spine with a blunt metal tube so they can scrape out tissue to examine. They hold her down. It's the last of the series of horrors, "procedures," as they call them here. Tests that involved the biopsy of one of her neck lumps, then another under her arm lumps. Dyes shot through her body. Needles sucking fluid from her lung. Blood test after blood test. Why don't they take it all at once? Her arms are black and blue. And at moments she is sure they are the Gestapo, the same nightmare, ever since her Bobby died in California.

I am gripping her cold, wet hand. Her naked back and thinning buttocks bespeak victim.

"Stop them," she begs. "They are torturing me!" Her words end in screams. They *are* torturing her. Even in the name of medicine and for good, it's torture.

"Oh, Melvin"—I summon spirits—"Mommy, Daddy, I didn't know how to help you. Help me help her."

"Perhaps you'd better go back to the hall," says the young doctor in charge. He still has pimples. The metal tube is only half pushed into her, and it's dangerous to move and jump. She can be crippled. "You don't," he adds, "seem to be too effective." I hate his damn pimples.

The young girl in the next bed with the kind mother and the face of an angel talks to me. "Go outside," she says. "I'll help her. I get one of those tests done every two weeks." Slipping from her sheets and wheeling her intravenous stand dripping four tubes through two needles into her right arm, she moves to Janice's naked side. She has leukemia.

In the hall a nurse's aide offers me orange juice. "You

look terrible," she tells me. "You'd better sit down." I do, right on the floor. The nurse runs for a chair. You should be made of tougher stuff, I reprimand myself. Stop this shit. And I stop.

"No, thank you. I don't need a chair. I am fine. Where's the telephone?" I go and call Big Steve.

"How's it going, babe?" he asks.

"It's going," I say, breathing smoke into the mouthpiece. "But I'm not sure how. Steve, the little girl in the room with Janice needs blood. She needs people to replace what she gets from the bank. I'm going to try to donate. If they'll take mine. Would you donate?"

"Oh, sure, babe. I have more than I need. I'll be there tomorrow. Just get her name and the information."

"Thank you," I say. "I've got to go back to Janice."

"See you at Margot's backgammon tournament?"

"Maybe." I hang up. Back in the room it's over. Janice's roommate is back in her own bed and staring at the ceiling.

"That was tough," the roommate says, looking at me. "I wish I hadn't seen it. I never quite knew what they did before."

"I don't know how to thank you," I say.

Fragile and sweet, she waves my thanks away, saying, "We have to help each other." She smiles. She will not be able to help anyone too much longer.

The late air bit at my face as I walked from Klingenstein down Madison Avenue to the Eighty-sixth Street apartment of my friend Dani. She liked an open house, and people were sitting around talking art and politics. Mostly writers with an occasional painter for color. Hearty and healthy, they welcomed me. I felt as if I'd just escaped from Hades, leaving my persimmon seeds behind me. I listened as they talked style. Jo Durden-Smith, the most intellectual of the group, said, "Barbara, why don't you read them that last chapter? She's quite adept for a new writer." He was proud of me since I'd joined the ranks. I had no voice to read. He did it for me, correcting some loose punctuation. I was not, it seemed, secure with my semicolons. But I did have a contract. And they loved the chapter he read them. It was sexy.

The next day I sat with our "chest man." At Sinai they

have "blood men" and "bone men" and "brain men" ad infinitum. The chest man was one of heavyset twins, robust. One was newly divorced. They both smoked constantly.

The married one lit my cigarette. I was perched cross-legged on a metal X-ray table. He paced before me. A lit box illuminated shots of my sister's organs. And he divided his attention between the box and my legs. He was liking them and I was letting him. Shades of Dr. Chow. Was I whipping myself up a new set of medical chums? No, now I had money to buy freedom. But it didn't hurt to be friendly.

"You see," he said, pointing at parts of the X rays, "this, and this, and look at that!" I looked at the spots, not knowing which ones were the murderers. "It's fifth-stage mixed cell." He paused for a reaction. "With Hodgkin's, that's as bad as you can get. Why did she wait so long?"

"She's afraid of doctors."

"Is she?"

"Yes. Me, too."

He coughed his dry smoker's cough. "You don't have to be afraid of me," he said.

"Don't I?"

He furtively patted at my knee. "No."

"You ought to quit smoking," I said, freeing my knee to slide off the table.

"Fifth-stage mixed cell," I repeated to Teresa in the hall. She had no idea what I was talking about, but she had every idea what I meant.

"She got one chance?" Teresa's eyes were childlike.

"A small one, yes."

"What you hold in paper bag?"

"Brandy. I am trying to raise my blood pressure so I can donate blood."

"Run around block," she suggested. I did.

The Colony restaurant, where my pal Margot had a backgammon tournament happening, steamed with anticipation. I wore my embroidered jeans, the ones I'd stitched while sunning myself on the Krupp yacht cruising the Mediterranean. Would I ever do that kind of thing again? Did I want to? I wished I looked better. Milling around was half my public. Oh, the hell with it. I decided on a second glass of wine. In the corner of the lounge sat a palm reader, her tarot cards at hand. Her client bent toward her, over the small round table, trying to get a handle on her future.

"Isn't that a good idea?" Margot was pleased I agreed. "People just love fortunes. And you know how impatient they get till things start rolling. What division are you playing, Barbara?"

"Intermediate, I guess." I wasn't up to it and was here only because she needed me. ("Please come. I've got to dress up the room," she'd insisted.) My wine tasted sour. I'd switch to juice.

Studying my sweating palms, the lady didn't have to be a Gypsy to know I was in trouble.

"There is death around you," she said, "sickness."

"Let's talk about love." I smiled. "I can use some."

"Oh, there is love in your life, too. Definitely."

From the bar an orphan-faced little guy was watching my every move. Totally transfixed. I'd seen him before at another of Margot's tournaments, and I'd noticed him always looking at me. I usually noticed who was really looking. Such attention is frequently sustenance. In a world of imperfect loving one sometimes accepted shabby substitution. I knew, for instance, that my London love took enormous pleasure in being seen out with me whenever he could swing it. Which was usually in New York. He puffed up when I was on his arm, sparkling for him, saying clever things. Trendy. Sexy. Then he, as well as I, liked to notice who was really looking. Such were the thoughts that had sent me over to this palm reader, who was hinting at my not being able to save my sister any more than I could have saved the rest.

"And be careful of blood," she was saying. "You almost died once yourself, didn't you? Look at that break. Be careful how you handle sharp objects and where you walk."

Behind her, through a crack in the draped window that turned noon into night, I watched the heavy snow falling. Soft and gentle and quiet. I was glad Janice had the window bed.

The crook of my arm, beneath its tape and gauze, started throbbing. I handed her ten dollars and made my getaway. Not so much money for a future, but ten was all I had left on me, plus the diet pill I'd promised Jo for his deadline. Deadlines are the "now" of a writer's existence. The pill wrapped in Kleenex was safe in my jeans coin pocket. The snow, however, might prove a problem. I'd need a cab to get me there, wait, then go on to Sutton Place, where my doorman would act as my banker. But at a better rate of interest.

"Play with someone for me," begged Margot, leading me to the bar. "He needs a partner, and I know he'll be thrilled if it's you." It was the orphan-faced little man. Working at a smile, he ordered my juice and suggested we start our game. I felt light-headed. The tournament was on. Players, flexing fingers in front of boards, looked tight and intense. I, on the other hand, was loose. I lead a loose life, I told myself as I carried my orange juice to the board. A loose-leaf life. A lease on a loose life. Loose as a goose. My goose was cooked.

Facing the short, silent man, I watched as he stood reverently waiting till I was seated. He was certainly polite. I hated his suit, and his puffed and blown-dry hair was almost embarrassing; but I liked his attempts at a smile. What he needed was a personal shopper. May I be personal, sir? Personally I hate loud plaids on small fellas. How about you? Jesus, my head was light.

"Are you all right?" he asked.

"I'm just fine," I said, then found myself sinking onto the checkers. Someone was covering my pips. It was me. Was I black or white? I must be black. It was getting too dark to see.

"Here, drink this." He had a cup of coffee to my lips.

"What time is it?"

"Please take my watch. You keep asking the time. I have others." His watch, a prosaic Omega, was slipped onto my wrist. Holding my hand, he patted it awkwardly. "Are you better now?"

"I gave some blood this morning. I have very low pressure." I felt silly saying all that, so I stopped.

"What can I do?"

"I need to deliver something and go home . . . I need a cab."

"I'll drive you."

"Don't you date Connie from California?" I asked while he scraped snow from his windshield and I studied the watch he had so quickly given me.

Actually I kind of remembered Connie's friends referring to him as "a mark" because he had bailed her out of a large gambling debt even as she barely gave him the time of day. They giggled over the sad poems of lost love he wrote to her. He was, I decided, old-fashioned, and walking to his car was somehow old-fashioned, too. So was waiting in a parking lot. It took me back to my father, Chulky, Buddy. Nobody I knew now kept a car in the city, unless he or she had a chauffeur.

"I used to go with Connie," he said, "but I think it's almost over." It was his longest sentence so far.

At my friend's I delivered my pill and told of the silent man who had given me his watch.

"How charming," said Jo.

"Almost," I agreed. "Anyway, he's standing at attention downstairs, waiting to drive me home. He is sort of like a little lost puppy."

"But still helpful in a snowstorm," suggested Jo.

On the following morning two dozen red roses were at my door. "Meeting you," the card said, "made me feel like a teardrop from heaven reuniting with the sea." Signed Jerry. The little guy from yesterday and as romantic as a Woody Allen hit man. I carried some roses through the snow to Mount Sinai to cheer Janice. What would have cheered me would be an international card from my man of chosen words. Not many flowers, but there used to be letters. I saved them all. Letters that started:

> We've been sitting on the runway for hours. . . . All the first-class gentlemen around me are drunk. I'm not. But sozzled perhaps. Sitting we sit . . . still there is the whiskey. Still you . . . and when next it will be, it will be you, still you . . .

and got to:

> Darling, I know you're home now. A place I know so privately. I know you're alone. What—don't I know. I mean we

know each other's facts. The fact that you sit alone now my darling. This fact. You are here: Beautiful girl. Beautiful girl. Beautiful girl. I'm happy and unhappy. So are you. Are we.

and ended up at:

But my other life is there as you know. It is there for so many years. How can one live? Just the way we do? What else? You are so patient with me.

> But I can't be other than I am in
> what it is that is for me.
> And you are for me.
> And she is for me.
> This fucking
> Joy and pain.

I don't know the answer . . . but I love you and I am in your body. . . .

It might be that flowers were better.

"Who is that strange guy you dragged up here?" Janice asked me breathily from her bed. "Jesus, he never said one word. And he doesn't look you in the eye either. Is he okay? He's like a frightened mouse. And that haircut!"

"He's a kind of Brooklyn guy named Jerry something or other, but his pals at the trading desks call him Weasel. He's supposed to be clever with money, though he doesn't have much right now. Anyway, he has a big silent crush on me."

"You can't have a big crush on him,'" said Janice, perplexed, "unless he is supertalented in bed or something. He seems so stunted."

"Actually he is so inept in bed that he touches my heart. I want to make it all better for him."

"Like a mommy, huh?" Janice decided. "Barbara, you better be careful of those frustrated maternal urges. They can get you to nurse a weasel at your breast."

"He is being kind," I rebutted quietly, thinking, Who else could I entertain in a cancer room but a semicatatonic anyway? "Don't worry," I added, "I'll fix him up."

Janice looked at me. "I saw a cartoon once," she mused, tiredly. "It showed a pretty girl duck cuddling up to a painted decoy male. And another duck comes along and says to it, 'What do you want with that thing? It's not real, it has no soul, it's only painted wood.' 'He'll change,' says the first duck." Janice smiled wearily. "Get it?" she asked.

I said yes, but years later I realize I'd missed her point.

It's X-ray time, and the old man is slipping from his wheelchair. Janice points in horror. She wants me to do something. He's on the floor, eyes shouting for help, mouth dribbling helplessly. I kneel next to him. What do I do now? Taking a thin, scarred hand, I stare into terror. Then the attendant is there. He is lifted and strapped back into the aluminum chair. "Heavier than you'd think," says the attendant, gold teeth flashing as he tightens straps to hold. Nothing will hold. The old man and I look at each other and know this.

I go back to my sister. Next to her, on a stretcher, an ancient woman moans. Scalp shining pink beneath a hairnet. She moans again. The neon is cruel to her as a porter pushes her up in line. We—my sister, the old woman, the old man—have been in that hall for almost three hours. That's how it is waiting around this vestibule to Cobalt Canyon. The last retreat of a failed species.

Three hours of children who look out from oxygen masks in confusion and doped despair. Of mouths whose teeth left next to beds gasp air through black holes. And most don't care anymore that their bony backsides show as they shift in their split gowns. Healthy ones in casts and splints stare away from the sick ones. The sick just stare. And there are smells. Urine bags hang off metal bars connected under soiled sheets to sad bodies and threaten to overflow. Fecal odors, gastric odors mix with medicine.

"Please," I hear myself say to passing attendants, "we've been here so long. She can't sit for so long." They have heard this song before.

"We are understaffed," they repeat. "We are doing the best we can."

"Any minute now," I soothe. God how I hate it.

"Oh, look at that little one there!" Janice cries. "Look at

that poor baby!" Don't look, I warn myself even as my eyes follow her direction.

"Three months premature," says its nurse. "Two pounds one ounce at birth. Something wrong with its lungs. I don't think it has much chance."

"Here I go." My sister sighs as at last they wheel her into Death Valley. I kick at cigarette butts on the floor and long to have one of my own. I'd better not leave, and I won't do it here, not right under the No Smoking signs. Not me.

The old woman suddenly vocalized in Yiddish. She wants me to understand something. I don't. She says more words that I don't understand. I wonder why my mother didn't teach us some Yiddish, for the sake of Sholom Aleichem, if not Grandma. She makes me think of my grandma, this old woman. Of Grandma in her old rooms, empty except for the one the Talmud scholar rented. He didn't speak English either. "We ought to move her someplace clean," my father said each visit. "Someplace she can handle, with an elevator."

"No." My mother would sigh. "She's afraid she'll have no one to talk to, Hymie. She says Papa died here, and she will, too. She says it's her home. And what's that in your hand, Babsie? Hymie, she's got a dollar again."

"Grandma made me, Mommy."

"She keeps giving the kids her money, Hymie. I can't stop her."

"It's all right, Rose. We'll give her some more."

"Why does she give us her money?"

"Because she can't tell you she loves you in English."

The porter comes for my old woman. And they are wheeling Janice back out. She can't hold her head up anymore.

"Get me away from here," Janice whispers. "They've ruined me. Get me out."

"They have all your charts. We can't just leave them here. It will complicate things."

"Get me out," she pleads.

"I must get your charts."

"Fuck my charts." She is crying now, and I start pushing, following the color-coded lines that lead back up to the

Klingenstein Medical Center. "My charts," she says softly, "will follow me to my grave."

We wait by an elevator that takes its time. An impatient visitor taps her high-heeled foot and drums at the box of candy she carries.

"Hospital elevators are hell, aren't they?" she comments.

"Only the anteroom to hell," I say. The visitor doesn't pursue the conversation.

Silent Jerry will be waiting to drive me home. He, too, will not pursue conversation, rather will offer me a cigarette as we sit wordlessly in his car. He offers cigarettes in lieu of comfort. Lighting mine is his best act of communication. Have you hugged an illiterate today? I'll take the cigarette.

So we sit in silence and breathe smoke at each other, which is not altogether his fault.

"I'm glad you got here," says the nurse outside my sister's door. "She's had a bad afternoon."

"Barbara, is that you? Good, good. I was going crazy," Janice says, tapping her head. "I didn't know where I was. Then it came back to me." Thin fingers curl around my own. "Janice has aristocratic hands like mine," Auntie H. is fond of saying. "She takes after our side. You, on the other hand, are the spit of your father."

"I brought you carrot juice and a sweet potato, steamed."

"Good, good. I tried to eat the egg they sent up, but the white was so gushy." A child's word for me to smile at.

"Just eat the yellow then," I say.

"It tastes funny." She rebels. "All their food tastes funny."

"It's the chemotherapy," I say. "They've started that now, too. Eat anyway."

"Try it sometime." She grimaces. "Look at my mouth, sores everywhere." Her breath is foul. I look and look away.

"I stink, don't I?"

"No, of course not."

"I do, I do."

I mash her potatoes up with sweet butter. "Change the channel," she says. "Maybe something good is on."

"Edith"—Archie Bunker sneers through the tube—
"stifle yourself." Janice laughs. I laugh with her.

"Doesn't Archie Bunker remind you a little of Daddy
sometimes?" she says, sitting up and sipping at the juice.
"His expressions, I mean, the New Yorkese."

"No, Daddy wasn't a bigot."

"But something in the style, the way he moves his
eyebrows." We stare at the set.

"Daddy was handsome, elegant." I am not loving the
comparison.

"But Bunker is sort of cute. I can't drink any more of
this."

"Drink it. I made it from organic carrots."

"It's making me gag." She pushes the juice away. "Why
do you speak as if Daddy was your own personal property?
You weren't an only child. I was there, too, and I say Archie
Bunker reminds me of him sometimes."

"Do I speak that way?"

"All the time."

"I'm sorry."

"You might have been his favorite, but he loved me, too,
didn't he?" China blue eyes question from hollow cheeks.
"Didn't he?"

"He adored you. He called you his *faygeleh.* That means
'pretty little bird.' "

"You do remember more than me." She had almost
accepted my olive branch, but not quite.

"I'm five years older," I say apologizing.

"And you got to visit more, when he was away, I mean.
Mommy always took you." No longer accusing, she just
wants to get her facts straighter.

"I was older, better behaved, easier to travel with. And
Mommy was so sick." I have made the connection.

"Poor Mommy." Janice sighs, closes her eyes, and lies
back on her bed. It's hard to realize Janice is not just part of
my history but is out there on her own. Her sadness and her
madness are hers, not mine. Her pain, her parents, her
sister, her child. We share the same facts, but our histories
are different.

"Did I tell you the one," I offer in desperation, "about

God calling the pope on his private phone and with great organ chords and harps announcing that He has good news and bad. That He, God, tired of holy wars, of hate in His name, has decided there will be only one religion.

" 'Ah,' says the pope, 'that is good news. But what, Majestic Father, is the bad news?'

" 'This call,' booms God, 'is from Salt Lake City.' "

It works. Janice giggles. "I never," she says, "understood about the Mormons anyway."

Sidney Siegal, Jerry's only confidant, whose apartment he'd been sharing this last year, was dead. And Jerry was in shock, enough to talk about his impoverished childhood and his mother, whom he could not forgive for dying when he was eight.

The only two things he'd ever spoken of before were how he'd worked for the local numbers racket at a very early age, till an uncle made him the family scandal. And how he'd cut the eye out of a *melanzona* (a black) in a Sand Street gang fight. I don't remember if he said he made him eat it or not. It doesn't matter; it was a lie. Told, obviously, for some sense of personal machismo or power. I should have found the fantasy revealing. But I didn't pay much attention. I did pay attention, however, when Jerry talked of his mother's funeral. How in the tradition of the very poor they'd laid her body out in the living room, where little Jerry slept. He continued, he said, to sleep there next to her coffin for days. No wonder he had difficulty looking at a live woman's body. Bit by bit, I got the impression of a chilling childhood.

My heart broke for him. He could come to live with me, and I'd try to make everything right for him. Perhaps, at least, I could save him from ulcers and asthma—certainly easier to deal with than cancer. And he was so much in love with me, sending so many roses and cards to say it by, that it just might work. It seemed the natural move. Of course, he had once cried for the love of Connie from California, hadn't he? But that was before. Yes, I'd fix everything, including the socks that still sagged at his ankles. I'd already done wonders for the rest of his wardrobe. So I removed the playwright's picture and let Jerry in.

"Are you sure of what you are doing?" A worldly friend questioned my commitment.

"No," I said, "but I'm trying to do good."

Now it is one of the new longer days of spring but still short on promise. Night's cold had barely moved enough to allow an afternoon's city sun to warm either heart or hands. Still, my sister was happy to be in the wheelchair, out in the real world. Out on a real path in Central Park, where frosty dog excrement and leftover leaves made way for crushed cans of beer and unexpected hints of green grass. *Grimy April,* and all that.

I pushed her hurriedly, having set up this outing with great difficulty. All human needs were difficult at Mount Sinai, Moses notwithstanding. But at last I'd wheeled her, wrapped and capped, into the slow-to-arrive visitor's elevator. Then down and out.

Out, the glass door swung behind us. Out, I ran her helter and scooted her skelter into the park. But it was cold. Was I doing something wrong? Forcing something, spring perhaps, pushing too hard for something that only hurt in the end.

Her wool ski cap slid over her thinning hair and transparent ears. Her head wobbled above shrunken shoulders and listed to one side. She was tipping over right in front of me. I stopped and steadied her.

"Are you all right?" She nodded. "You're sure?"

"Push me faster," she whispered, and I rushed her headlong down the path. She always liked moving fast. She had galloped her hired horses through Forest Park, like a Magyar. She had raced all the red lights along Queens Boulevard in her various cars. She was still rushing.

My breath stabbed my smoker's lungs. I had to stop pushing. Janice didn't mind; she was feeling sorry for a bag woman stumbling across the path in front of us. The woman, bent and busy, parked her stolen A&P shopping cart, stuffed with newspapers and plastic parcels, to look through a wire mesh garbage can. Unwrapping the crushed remnant of a sandwich and tearing off some bread, she threw it to a nearby squirrel; then she stored the rest carefully and selectively back in one of her plastic bags.

"She has a filing system," I joked to Janice, who had followed every move.

"It was sweet of her, though, wasn't it?" Janice said. "For the squirrel, I mean."

"It's too cold today," I said, giving up. "Let's go back." Janice allowed this.

"Maybe," I offered as I turned the chair around, "we can do it again. When it's sunnier." She turned her head for a last look at Central Park.

We returned to find Buddy from old times, standing inside the Klingenstein Medical Center doors. In glass-warmed sunshine, he looked for us. Janice smiled at him in pleased surprise. She hadn't known he was coming. I had. Buddy, now divorcing, had kept in touch. He reached a large, still graceful hand into a deep pocket and pulled out some money.

"Take this," he said gruffly. Years of cigarettes had cracked his voice. "You must need money."

I found it sweet and gratefully would not refuse money. Cancer costs.

" 'Take the Cash,' " I quoted, as I folded the bills into my purse, " 'and let the Credit go, Nor heed the rumble of a distant Drum!' " I smiled, waiting for him to respond.

"As usual," Buddy said, "you didn't get that quite right." Then, smiling his old Forest Hills smile back at me: "But close enough, anyway. I'm pleased that you still remember the *Rubáiyát* at all." It was good to have him there.

We were outside Janice's door. She had flirted with Buddy from under her ski cap. But his visit tired her, and it was medication time anyway, so we stepped into the hall while they hooked her to her chemicals.

"Can you go for something to eat?" he asked me.

And soon we were packed into his neat BMW, driving to the Shanghai Café. A place he used to take me, for those long-ago special treats. It was exactly the same. The Shanghai Café, epitome of cheap Chinese cuisine, was still a dump. Peeling Leatherette, cramped booths, and tired tables, but oh, the divine smells!

It was amazing to be there again. Especially with Buddy.

We fell into gluttony and a lot of "Do you remember?" How old would our child be now! If alive, he might have been dragged to Vietnam and killed there. Small comfort among the chopsticks. If my Uncle Dan hadn't forced the issue when Buddy wasn't ready, would we be married?

"Probably divorced by now," I suggested. He winced, and I was sorry. In the middle of divorce he was going through a hard time.

"What" he asked, "do you think about that news broad who shot herself right on TV after telling them they were about to see a first." I winced, and he was sorry he brought up that sore subject. On to others. His two sons were the raison d'être of his existence. Now *I* was sorry again that he'd brought up that subject. I wavered between tenderness toward an old love and irritation. Funny that should be there after so long.

"Do you think anyone still sits for hours in unheated cars, thrilled to talk of Shakespeare and Goethe and read poetry?" Buddy mused. He answered himself. "Not now. Not these kids I see on my sons' campus. All they give a damn about learning is what translates into their pockets."

"It makes them perfect for the coming age," I said. "Please notice they've stopped caring about social issues as well, and pass the hot sauce." He smiled and did. I'd always loved this hot sauce.

"Why should these kids care? The sixties seem to have been a failure." Buddy liked saying that. He had missed the sixties, stuck somewhere in between Scarsdale and the fur district. Oh, Buddy, my heart echoed. Yes I still felt for him. I still loved the eyes that smiled at me from behind his tragic fat.

We talked about the changes in our more usual world. Usual combinations of words followed one another. Teresa and the words "amazing," "still so young." The word "cancer" and the words "death" and "expected."

"Has expecting it ever made separation less painful or death less final?" I asked, protesting patness. His experience with death was limited, but he imagined not. "You'll find out," I said. Shit. I was being mean again. I, who had loved him so tenderly. And who but I would ever remember him as young, eager, and fresh?

I passed on the dessert. With a terrible sense of lateness, I picked up the package of won ton vegetable soup I was taking back to the hospital to tempt Janice and followed him out to the car. He'd drop me off, but would I mind if he didn't come up again? I wouldn't. It had helped me to hold his hand.

Janice's taste buds are not tempted. She can't get anything down. Pushing the cardboard container away, she says, "Don't be angry. My swallow won't swallow." She is missing her plants.

"I have these nice pots of greens"—she smiles—"and cactus and African violets in a standing planter. They all need different kinds of water."

She looks through the plastic vein dropping chemicals into her arms up to the bottle on the rolling stand and back to me.

"Teresa overfeeds them," she adds.

"They will be fine." I comfort her.

"You've never seen them, Barbara. They are very cute plants. I bet they'll be dead when I get home. We don't get good light in Long Beach like we got in Rego Park."

She is sweating some strange smell. I smile through it toward her. I repeat Indian mantras. I want to mend her with a cosmic thread and a spiritual needle.

"What about the healer Jan?" I inquire softly. "Do you want to see him again?" "He" is really "they" since the healer works with his wife.

"Why not?" she answers, and looks back up at chemicals dripping into her stick-thin arm. "Buddy sure got fat," she says. Then adds: "But I understand it."

I had a bewildering dream of Buddy that night. Buddy, babies, and a beauty parlor. I woke wanting Jerry and safe dullness. Odd that this Jerry of no words or vision had become the person I could best bear to be with.

Carrying a carrot juice and puréed vegetable breakfast

to the hospital, I anguished about not writing. I had a deadline and wanted to meet it.

But Janice was fighting her own deadlines, wouldn't eat the hospital breakfast. I couldn't blame her. But I started to be very grateful for Jerry. When he could, he carried this carrot juice up to Klingenstein for me, inevitably getting a 7:00 A.M. parking ticket before heading his car south to Wall Street. Wall Street had turned tough after '73, especially on little traders like him. He was in debt. But his kindness permitted me some morning hours, and I returned his kindness with whatever help I could give him. He was even starting to speak.

Last night's soup still sits on her rollaway bed stand. No one has cleaned yet. I'll see to it.

"If there is one thing Jews know about," Janice says to me, her eyes looking out of balance and her mouth pinched and dry, "if there's one thing, it's cheap Chinese, expensive jewelry, and the unfairness of who suffers in this world."

"Nick," I say, "knew all that stuff."

"Greeks aren't goys," says Janice. "They have almost been around as long as us."

She's right. I put the straw in the carrot juice and hold it so she can sip without sitting up. She obliges me for a moment or two, then gags and pushes the glass away.

"It's my fault," she says. Thinking ancient thoughts: "God is punishing me. I killed Bob, didn't I, so now he's killing me, isn't he? I mean," she goes on, "everything happens for a reason, doesn't it, suffering is educational, right, and I'm going to be a better person now that I have cancer, aren't I?" Somewhere mid-sentence, her tone had changed.

"Shut up, Janice," I say. "I can't take this kind of talk. Not right now. So stop it."

"Oh, you're strong, Barbara. You can take it. God only gives you what you can bear. Isn't that what your mystics are always saying?"

"So if I were weak," I ask her, "would God take away your cancer because I couldn't bear it? This is dumb damn talk. Stop it. The healers are coming this afternoon. And drink the goddamn juice I carted up here whether you can

swallow or not." She drinks the juice, slowly and mournfully. She drinks the juice.

Teresa had arrived, bringing Janice a beautiful lunch,
sweetly wrapped and carried all the way from Long Beach.
Involving two buses, the Long Island Railroad, the subway,
and a bit of a hike. We stood, she and I, on either side of
Janice's bed, willing her to eat. Janice did the best she could.
When the healers arrived, Teresa busied herself in Janice's
small almost-bathroom, then went to stare out the window,
her usual posture when she couldn't bear what was happening in the room. This stuff of candles and chanting and
laying on of hands confused her. But maybe it would help.
What did she know, anyway, except that life was too often
terrible?

The healer was young and blond and earnest. I'd found
him through my astrologist, who, looking at my sister's
chart, had clucked her tongue and offered little. "There are
so many critical dates here," she had said, her pencil and
ephemeris in hand. "So many dates where a soul might take
leave of the body. . . ." This was the healer's second visit.

"We can use your energy, too." The healer smiled at me.
"Come on, Barbara. Bring all that love and energy over
here, and do as I tell you." I hoped they were correct about
my energy. I'd never noticed such an abundance of it. It
seems to me I've spent my entire life tired. But I placed my
hands as he told me over her heart's center, about four
inches above the body, right where she said she had her
"dead spot."

"Visualize," said the healer, so pale, so earnest himself.

"Visualize," repeated his wife, who looked to be a fem-
inized version of himself.

"Visualize God's love pouring from your heart, my heart,
Sarah's heart, and Grandma's heart. Come here, Grandma,"
he called to Teresa, who obeyed him. "Come here and put
your hands over Janice's feet and visualize the love of the
ages, the love of all the saints, the love of all those people who
have passed into the beyond but who still care about Janice.
Feel their protective love pouring forth and showering her
with help. We will ease her pain," he chanted. "We will heal

her wounds; her blood will purify; her heart will calm itself; she will be bathed in that great cosmic ocean of all-powerful consciousness that is our creator, the Eternal."

A half hour later the candles were extinguished, the healer and his wife were gone, and Teresa and I stood alone, two sentinel figures, on either side of Janice's bed, hoping Someone had listened.

Janice lay still. Her eyes closed. She seemed to be breathing more calmly than before.

"Janice," I whispered, "are you all right?" Janice nodded, eyes still closed. "Janice," I persisted, "do you feel any better?" She nodded again and seemed to drift away to a more peaceful place than she had been for days.

"You think it helped her?" Teresa's eyes were questioning.

"It couldn't hurt her," I said.

It was nice for Teresa to see Janice look serene.

At home the puppy Jerry had just forced on me under protest was sleeping in the middle of my writing. Jerry was determined to mommify me. But my papers were a mess. That, I told myself, is what happens if your bed is your desk. I didn't chide the puppy. It had to be hard being a dog. Was I ever one in a past life? Did I beg God the generosity to open my universe? Just a little more. Did I complain dog style? Of course, that would have made me a Jewish dog. A funny idea, I wished for my playwright to share it with. It was hard, this current translating down of everything I said. But I suspected our secret life of letters was over, our play had run its course. I suppose I stopped being fun.

No, that was a cheap shot and not true. My playwright was better than that. It was just life. And I would miss him. I reminded myself again of asking God, like Oscar Wilde, to be spared physical pain and promising to handle the mental by myself. That was the deal I'd opted for. And so far I'd mostly gotten my wish.

So I warned, Don't complain, Barbara. But it was hard not to complain a little. It was a matter of blood.

Sisters

Auntie H. was lying on her own hospital bed only thirty blocks from Mount Sinai, complaining bitterly, "You don't care; nobody cares. I cared for you. I came to you kids every week, rain or shine. And it was wartime too. I came even though Eddie, my meal ticket, resented having his weekends loused up. I came. And here you brought me to this hospital three days ago, and this is your first visit since."

"I called, I spoke to your doctor."

She sniffled her nose at these feeble attempts. "Easy," she said, "you always look for the easy way. If I looked for the easy way, who knows what might have become of you?"

"It's hard with Janice and all. And working on my book."

"Yeah, you told me about your mistresses. Babsie, the authoress, ha. I could give you a real book to write. I should write a book."

"Why not?"

"Nobody cares."

"I care."

"Not as much as for that puppy. How dare you bring a puppy in here? They should kick you out. They will if I tell them." Fingering the buzzer pinned to her sheet, she reflected. "Your mother, my best sister, would have cared."

"I can't stay long anyway," I was too quick to say. "I hope your checkup turns out well. If only you would eat better."

"I knew it, you're running away."

"Finish the malted. If you would eat, Auntie H., you'd get your weight up."

"I hate malteds. I'm only sipping it so as not to offend you. Since you brought it. Actually I wish you'd finish it yourself."

"I had mine," I told her, and she sipped reluctantly while coughing.

"It's sticking in my throat. Why didn't you bring coffee flavored? I love coffee flavored."

"I thought you loved French vanilla."

"I don't."

"I'm sorry."

"Oh, it's all right. And leave if you have to. I see you want to."

"I don't want to, but I do have to. I'm meeting Janice's radiologist at one and—"

"Are you taking the puppy there, too?"

"It's so small, and no one sees it in my tote. It makes Janice happy."

"You're both crazy, and she really hates you. I know. Call me later." Slurping sounds signaled that she'd sipped everything. Did Janice really hate me? It didn't matter. I really loved her. As I reached the elevator, I could hear Hermosa's litany: "Nobody cares."

I apologized to my little dog on my aunt's behalf. "She can't help herself," I told it, stuffing it deep into my canvas tote. "She loved my mother, but she was often mean to her, too. I left my hand in the tote bag for her to nibble at and explained Hermosa's slaps. "She has allowed herself so little," my father often said. "It's hard for her to allow anyone else."

The first time we rode the elevator at Mount Sinai, when I'd shoved the little head deeper down my tote, it would not stay there. Up came a black nose and fuzzy ears. This head, they assured me, would turn elegant, but for now it was as ridiculous as curious.

"She's got a dog in there!" a female voice exclaimed as I exited.

"A stuffed toy," I had shouted back.

"Oh, I love her," squealed Janice, as the puppy did puppy things all across her bed. At the moment we were in private, and the nice rotating nurse dropped off her pills and pretended again, I'm not sure for whom, not to notice the moving bump under the quick-thrown covers.

"Oh, this is what you always needed. That Jerry is smarter than he looks. He'll get you with this puppy. He'll turn you right into Mommy." Would he? A shrink I'd been talking to told me Jerry really hated his "Mommy." I fingered a bandage on my wrist.

"What did you do to yourself now?" asked Janice. "Every other time you walk in here you've cut something else."

"This one's a burn."

"It's not your fault, you know," she said, looking down, "that I have Hodgkin's." And tickling the dog carefully, she added, "And I didn't get it just to aggravate you."

"It's so complicated, being sisters," I said.

"It is," she agreed, and started to cough. I lifted away the dog.

"Don't take her," she begged. But she kept coughing, so I did.

"Another time," I promised.

"She is so cute." She sighed. "Come early tomorrow."

I came early, and we walked the corridors. Teresa, Janice, and I. Janice was celebrating the shorty robe I brought her that matched her eyes and wearing Teresa's babushka for the occasion. She leaned heavily on my arm. Teresa supported her other side. I was surprised she was moving at all. But down the long hall we went, past the crazy black woman who sat outside her room babbling and chewing on her tubes, toward the elevators.

"I remember walking with Daddy," she mused. "Sometimes I'd sit right on his shoulders."

"You very delicate child," commented Teresa.

"Do you think," whispered Janice, "we can just keep on walking, right out of this damn hospital? Like real people. Remember," she pleaded, "how we went to the park."

"Not today," I said. "Today is not a good day for the park. And I haven't arranged it."

"Oh, please, let's get on an elevator and just go as far as the lobby. For the fun of it. I'm covered up." We went down. In the lobby, people pushed by her, and she panicked. We went back up. "You were right," she said. "This is not the day." Teresa looked upset.

One week later, and Janice, handing me the medical shears, said, "Cut it off. Just cut it all off."

"I'll just cut it short."

"No, off, all of it. I can't stand waiting for it to go. Cut it." What wanted to be a commanding shriek was only a rasp. Sometimes she could still shriek. The scissors were awkward for me. Clumsily I started to cut.

"Faster."

Taking large handfuls of her hair in my hand, I cut; some just fell as I touched. Around us scattered the once-treasured hair, thick and more lustrous than my own. I'd always envied it. Now it shrouded her gown and spilled to the floor.

"Is it gone?"

"Almost."

"Right to the scalp, dammit."

I went to the scalp. How beautiful my sister still was with her Nefertiti head and huge eyes. I'd envied their china blue, too.

"Get it out of my sight," she ordered, shaking it off her robe. A strand stuck to her skin. She couldn't get free of it. At last she did.

"I feel as if I should save some," I said.

"Dump it. It has nothing to do with us anymore. It's garbage, like the peelings off an apple." Taking some moist paper towels from her washroom, I swabbed up the floor around where she sat, crumpled to one side of the Leatherette seat. A fallen puppet.

"Get me back on the bed," she begged. "I'm exhausted."

"What did you do to your hair?" asked the nurse's aide who came to help me move her.

China blue eyes stared at her. "I got tired of watching it fall, clumps on the pillow," whispered my sister.

The aide stopped protesting. "It will be more comfortable this way now that summer's coming," said the nurse in that tone reserved for patients and the simpleminded. Janice just nodded.

"Actually she's really one of the nice ones," Janice admitted after the aide left. "I guess I must look scary."

"You look beautiful, just slightly science fiction. Very *Star Trek*."

"Let me see."

I lifted the top of the rolling red table. She stared in the mirror that lined its underside.

"No, not *Star Trek*. No, I'm a Dachau Dolly. A Belsen Beauty," she decided. And we both laughed in embarrassment because she was right. We laughed till her coughing stopped us.

"It will grow back," I said, ashamed.

"If," she whispered, "I can wait for it."

That night Jerry escorted me to a party that was to be "good" for me.

"You have to have some fun." Everyone agreed. So there I was flirting with a rather wordy man at this flashy party. And I was trying. I'd done a full makeup and wore a much too low-cut gown. Over this low-cut gown, I flashed my best lip-glossed smile. And now I was hating it, myself and the world and everyone at this damn party. I hated the damn talk.

"Venice is wonderful this time of year."

"So is Milan, the opera."

"Actually I prefer the tropics anytime."

"Do you?"

"Yes, bodies, sun, and sea."

"Pass me those hors d'oeuvres."

"What are they made of? It's not real caviar."

"Isn't it?"

"Lumpfish, I think. Much cheaper."

"Shame on the host."

"And the hostess."

"Don't you hate it when they serve onion dip?"

"That dried-out soup stuff. So unimaginative."

"I guess Middle America spends time reading Lipton soup packages."

The wordy man, nearer and louder, forced compliments on me. They sounded somewhat familiar.

"The first art," he bellowed in my ear, "a beautiful woman must master is how to deal with envy. The second is flattery. The third vanity." Waiting for my appreciation of his wit, he fingered one of my stray curls. Getting rather familiar, was he? Well, that did it.

"The fourth thing she learns," I said, "is making a quick getaway." I slipped past him and pushed through to the corner where Jerry stood, as usual, looking ill at ease. Mostly this posture of the lost soul somewhat embarrassed me. "Doesn't he talk?" I'd been asked too often. Right now it was fine.

"Feel this spot here," she whispers as I go to help her from the bed. Teresa is almost out of hearing, putting the towel away "for later." I feel where she directs. Under her rib cage on the left side.

"That spot is already gone," she says. "I don't even feel pain there anymore." Her eyes look simply into mine, and she waits for me to speak. Let me say the right thing. Please God, don't let me con her. I con.

"It may come back," I say, "when the chemicals do their work."

"It won't come back. It will just take the rest of me." "You know," she adds after I don't comment, "you know what I've been thinking about all morning? Salami. Real Jewish, like Daddy kept hanging in the kitchen." She smiles like a kid caught in the act. "Some vegetarian I am, huh?"

"Would you like salami?"

"Isaac Gellis, like Daddy got."

"I'll have to go downtown. It'll take an hour at least."

"Don't worry, I'll wait right here. And bring me a dill pickle, too." she says.

"Okay." I conspire. I am whispering, too. In case a passing natural hygenist might report us.

"And," she adds, "a knish, if you can manage, and Dr. Brown's cream soda." I rush away. I'll manage.

On my mission I remember my first vegetarian lecture. Still married to Nick.

I was to meet him later at the Harwyn Club, and I was, you might say, dressed to kill. On my head perched an expensive white-feathered spread-winged bird. I still own that hat stuffed and boxed in back of my closet. On my feet were black alligator pumps to match my alligator purse, which blended with my long kid gloves. And over my silk was an ankle-length mink. Breathless, I rushed to hear how to save my health before cocktails. After collecting the complimentary pencil at the door, that said BE KIND TO ANIMALS, DON'T EAT THEM! I sat in my seat and noisily arranged myself and finery to my comfort. At that moment a little old lady with unblinking eyes turned to look me up and down and stated loudly, "Some fancy vegetarian you are, kiddo!" After I'd blushed, I laughed. Because she had been absolutely right. Now I smuggled the stuff to Janice, who was actually salivating for it and actually managed to get most of the sandwich down.

What was the matter with Paulie? He veered into the room on a slant and went straight for his mother's container of apple juice. Picking it up, he sniffed, made a face, and set it back down. Then he looked in her silver water jug. Then he studied the oxygen tank to the left of her bed. Then he touched it. Then he took a straw from her stand, removed its paper wrapper, and started to blow into it. He hadn't said a word.

"What's the matter with Paulie?" I poked Teresa, whispering. She didn't answer. Instead, she did a stiff about-face away from him and me. She did not want to see. Paul's eyes were narrow and unfocused. His mouth was on crooked. He picked seriously at the hole in his jeans. Jesus, he was stoned! But on what? I took a shot. . . .

"Paulie." I moved next to where he started leaning on the foot of Janice's bed. My sister wasn't with us at the

moment. The day had turned bad, and they had medicated
her spirit away. But what was left of her flesh was there. . . .
Paul stared at it. He didn't respond to me. Was his spirit
away somewhere, searching for hers? I didn't think so. I
figured his spirit was finger-popping its way to a rock-
and-roll heaven. "Paulie, you have any extra?"

"What?"

"More of what it is you're high on. Acid?" He grinned
and nodded. He had been found out. Recognized. He sort
of liked it. I had his attention.

"I've got Black Dots," he admitted proudly. What the
hell were Black Dots? It was obvious I was no longer current. I covered myself with an encouraging smile. He pulled
a torn piece of blotting paper from his pocket and offered
it. It was marked with dark, inklike spots.

"You chew one." He was ready to show me. I took the
single spot he'd ripped from the rest and placed it in my
own jeans pocket. Then I patted the pocket theatrically. He
giggled. I wanted him to see me as on his side.

Trying to imagine what it must be for Paulie to see his
mother through psychedelic eyes, I was surprised he hadn't
rushed screaming down the hall. I didn't yet know of his
penchant for downs. Fearing he still might freak, I took his
arm. "Walk me," I said, "for a cigarette." We left Teresa
standing guard.

The lounge on Janice's floor was a dismal affair. Set
between parallel corridors and boundaried by dirty glass
panes, you crossed its smoky, littered borders only in desperation, to sit on its worn Naugahyde in defeat. I hated
being there. Ambulatory patients, sloppy in loose robes,
some rolling their racks of tubes along with them, sat smoking with relatives differentiated only by the suits and coats
and real shoes they wore. Shoes that walk pavements. They
hardly talked. Two television sets blared at odds with each
other. Sides were drawn, and groups settled in to stare at
one or another. Some were really watching TV. Most
weren't. Paul was. I wasn't.

"How do you feel?" I asked, pulling out a Benson &
Hedges. At Janice's bedside I could only chew on an empty
holder.

Paulie involved himself with the *I Love Lucy* rerun and didn't answer. Lucy in tramp costume bared her blacked-out front teeth to the camera. Paulie laughed. The plot allowed her to mug and move around like a demented clown. Paul loved it.

"When did you drop?" I asked at last, jerking at his arm.

"Huh! Oh, I don't remember. Around nine this morning, I guess. Look at that." Lucy was smashing around with a broom. I wanted to smash Paulie. I wanted to squash his silly grin away. How dare he have done this? I had enough to deal with. Fighting my wars and making my truces with this hospital. I had to get Janice's medication altered. I had to get food in her. I had to see that her bed was moved. Changed. I had to humble myself to sullen people who swept floors and emptied bedpans. Making nice to the night nurses, palling with the interns. I had to . . . well, now I had to smile my horrible hospital smile at him and ask, "How are you going to get back to Long Beach?"

He didn't answer. Perhaps Jerry would lend him a bed. What do you do with a freakout? Shades of Mexico and Millbrook. Had I forgotten?

"Yes," I promised Janice every time she asked, "yes, I'll take care of Paul for you."

"Promise?" she begged.

"Promise," I assured.

Would Paul come back tomorrow? I wanted to know. His mother longed to see him, but he stayed away more than Arturo. He nodded yes.

"Try to get here before two P.M. and without your Dot." For the first time he recognized my tone as unfriendly. It startled him. It startled me. I was getting mean here. I altered my reading.

"Please," I said more sweetly, and my smile was almost sincere. "Come earlier and come straight. Promise?" I sounded like Janice.

We are having a lucid day. We have gone from talking Watergate—"That Rabbi Korf says Nixon's bones are sticking out. He visits him a lot"—to history, then back to us.

"You'll be all alone, you know, after I'm gone. You'll be alone, with no one to understand."

"I'll have your Paulie."

"He won't understand. It's hard to get him to understand anything." She wants to complain more of Paul's failures but gives it up. No time now for that. And I'll have lots of time for that later.

"Take care of him," she says at last. "It helps me to know that. Even when I was mad at you, I would think how if anything happens, if I can't stand it anymore and die, my sister, Barbara, will take care of Paul. After all, you heard him get born. I called you from the bed he was born in."

"Long distance, very expensive."

"I was always free with the phone, Barbara." She pauses. "You should have had a baby, you know." Oh, dear, here we go again. Since the puppy she had sort of stopped.

"I know."

"You'd have been better than me. I always got so crazy so quick. I can do mean things."

"You are a good mother, Janice. And we all do mean things. Yesterday I slapped the little puppy for peeing on the bed. Can you imagine? I hated myself all night."

"Don't be upset. The puppy will forgive you. You'll see. What did you name her again? I keep forgetting."

"Snow Blossom, but I call her Shnubby."

"Shnubby is better. She's such a little baby."

"Let me rub this on your forehead."

"What is that? Water?"

"Yes. Baba's Muktananda bath water. He's an Indian holy man, and one of his devotees smuggled it to me. It's supposed to be healing."

She shakes her head but lets me do it.

"You are so funny sometimes, Barbara, with your holy men. But it's really sweet of you."

"Is it?"

"Yes, you are sweet, even when I hurt you. I know I hurt you." I am quiet, and she goes on. "But sometimes I hate you, and I don't always know why. Sometimes it's because you talk to everyone else more than to me. And you shouldn't. I know you better."

"You certainly know me longer."

"Longer and better."

"Yes. Better." I give in to her, and she lies back to enjoy her victory.

"One thing about being in the hospital with cancer," she says as I get ready to go, "is I don't have to pick up Hermosa. Now you do."

"Phew," Hermosa said loudly. "This car really stinks of cigarettes. Is that all you do, Jerry, smoke?" He hadn't greeted her properly. And herself just out of the hospital. Even if only for a checkup. She humpfed a lot and rearranged her seating to let me know that I had not done enough to get her comfortable. I pretended not to notice. We began driving down Lexington. Stopping and jerking our way through the worst of rush-hour traffic started to make me dizzy, and it made the puppy throw up.

"What's that I smell now?" Hermosa demanded from the back seat. "Do I smell vomit? Is that dog vomit I smell?"

Kleenex in hand, I started wiping green bile off the lap of my fur coat.

"Did you come to pick me up from a hospital with a sick dog? Are you crazy!"

"No, I didn't come with a sick dog. The dog is very young, and sometimes she reacts to cars."

"So I see, she reacted all over your new mink. If it were mine, I'd throw the damn dog right out the window."

"I'd as soon throw the coat out," I said, thinking: And you, too. She felt my thoughts. I felt hers back.

"See," I said, "it's all cleaned up. Here." I lifted the sour wad of tissues for her inspection.

"Disgusting," she said, grimacing. "And don't wave that filth in my face. The least you can do is throw that mess out the window."

Something primal in me balked. Slowly I decided to wipe up some more imaginary slime and study it.

"I don't litter," I pronounced. "You'll have to stop by a bin or wait till we get to the St. Moritz. I'm not just throwing it into the middle of the avenue." Self-righteous reproach formed my words. Maternal wrath added sting.

"Barbara, you are not to leave that filth by my hotel. Do you hear me, Barbara! What would my doorman think!"

"I hear you, and your doorman sees drunks vomit by your hotel every day." I blasted.

"He does not!" She blasted back. She would have loved to rap her knuckles across my skull the way she used to. But she couldn't anymore. Life was not fair. Rolling her anger into one last swallow, she said, "I at least always had respect for how I looked. I always did. I still take more care of my pitiful wardrobe than you do over all your finery."

"Your wardrobe is not pitiful. Auntie H.—" I wanted to make amends, but she ignored me to address Jerry.

"I was always a terrific dresser, you know. *I* would never walk around with messy hair and no makeup on like some people." I bowed under the weight of her "some people." Jerry, I knew, would like it if I fussed more the way his Brooklyn girls did or like Hermosa's ancient flowers of the Lower East Side.

"Not that I was a great beauty," Hermosa was saying. "God, we had real beauties in my day. They were prettier than paintings. But I was stylish and spicy and lots of fun. I was one of the boys, too!" Well, we had that in common.

Jerry didn't respond. She leaned forward to push an emphatic finger into his neck. "That doesn't mean they didn't think I was sexy. I was plenty sexy, dolly boy. Plenty. You wanted some grace, natural rhythm. That's what I had. I showed them sex, but nice, not like nowadays." Rubbing at the spot in his neck, Jerry shifted uncomfortably under his coat. That satisfied her that he was listening, and she continued. I folded a fresh Kleenex over Shnubby's bile and settled in for her story with contraband pleasure. She knew I loved her stories, but of course, she was not addressing me.

"In those days, when I would walk into Lindy's or Barbara's father's restaurant, when he had one, which, by the way, was a big hit, except that he gave the place to the customers, well, when I walked in, I'd get cheers. Everyone wanted me at their table because I could make them feel good. Men love a laugh; someone here should remember that. Especially Hymie loved to laugh. He loved my second husband, Al Klien, who was the funniest man in show business. Much funnier than Nat Burns. Of course, Nat was clever, and Gracie was cute and could act silly, which audiences loved; but Al Klien and his brother were real clowns. Then—" She suddenly stopped bragging. "Vaudeville died, and everything was radio." A long time passed.

"But you still stayed a great dresser." I then prompted her, out of loyalty.

"Yes," she acknowledged. Then another jab: "Of course, I had respect for myself. And so did your mother. My sister Rosie was neat as a pin. She gets that sloppy stuff," she then explained me to the world, "from Hymie, who didn't give a damn if his kids peed all over him."

We inched up on the St. Moritz. "Don't disturb your dog," she said as I moved to help her. "The doorman will do it." Once on the sidewalk she almost turned on her heel to follow her overnight case but stopped herself.

"Roll down that window, Babsie," she ordered, and awkwardly reached in. "Hand me those filthy Kleenex." I handed them over as neatly as I could. Pinching a clean corner and holding them at arm's length, she moved a step or two away from her hotel to drop them into a sewer. Moving back, she thrust her face at me. "Now, give me a nice kiss good-bye," she said, and I was happy to do it. She would repent of her distaste when my dog grew beautiful. She would even come to brag of its pedigree. Stopping strangers on the streets to tell them her niece Barbara, "who is like my daughter," owned the same breed, "only prettier."

A few weeks later Teresa came to the city to stay, sleeping her nights on a narrow hospital cot and spending her days offering limited but priceless comfort. I became even more grateful.

Teresa, wearing pale blue stretch slacks and an aquamarine pullover and white shoes, has adopted the hospital colors. Standing, with her back to the bed, she leans on the sill of the window separating her from the world of the well. She stares at the few sprigs of spring, impertinent enough to bloom on this sooty street of New York City but doesn't see them. The months have bled by. It is our second spring at Mount Sinai, May and one day to Janice's birthday. Is that what she's thinking about? I can't tell. My sister lies still, mouth open and stretched like a starved bird, her irises hidden under half-fluttering lids. She is sleeping, I think. I move slowly through the wedged-open door. Sleeping, thank God. I slide softly across the antiseptic linoleum to tap Teresa's shoulder and signal her to follow me into the hall. The hall is where we can talk. I can question. We can sigh. My sister's screams stop us. She is not sleeping. She is conscious and fighting with her life.

"Why are you in the hall?" she cries. We come back in. I sit by her bed and take one hand. She taps at her bald head with the other. "I can't talk," she says. "It's brutal. Brutal." We are quiet. She is dying. Nothing lives but dies. No blade of grass, no king, animal, or vegetable. Twenty questions to why and then no more. The mini-television that swings across her bed is savoring shots of refugees, Vietnamese sinking in the South China Sea. One, crowded off a swamped sampan, is severed by a shark. It's sudden. But the hovering helicopter's camera catches it and Telstars it right to us.

There is nothing sudden happening here. My sister's agony is slow. That's the thing of it. Ears ringing with morphine that will not hold. She cries, "Let me die."

"Hold out," I tell her over and over. The radiologist has promised another chance of remission. "Hold out." Am I lying to her? No, that is what he told me. But I don't believe it. A conspiracy of compassion. The television focuses on a baby in Biafra withering without food. The baby doesn't know what's happening. My sister knows. She, like me, has died of cancer before.

And she wants to die at home, "out in Long Beach," she begs me. It's all right with Mount Sinai. They understand; she is only a statistic.

Only how to handle her medication? "Paulie can do it for me," she pleads. So now Paul would be educated in shooting up, too. He doesn't want to.

"It's not hard," the technician explains, showing him

how to find the vein. And after all, a visiting nurse will come for several hours a day. It won't be that hard. He can do it.

It *is* that hard. He lives in horror. He misses too many veins. She is having too much pain. I get an emergency ambulance. She and the siren scream the long ride back.

We are not having any more lucid days. Only one lucid hour since we returned to find no room at the inn. One hour of agony while they arranged her a bed in a large supply closet. And there we are, amid bottles and bandages. One metal bed, one intravenous stand, one small table with one drawer, and one chair, on which I sit and watch. She now inhabits the hospital half world. She moans beneath her mindlessness. Surrounding her body, terminal pain still pulsates, but part of her has left. A writer writes, I tell myself. Stop staring, and write something. Write endings for your kept ladies. Write! I pull out the pad I almost always carry back unused, and out comes:

> my sister is running for her life
> the torture already felt
> the needle already realized
> the chemical tasted
> its smell is in the air
> running she trips
> and changes direction
> running she runs
> a skeleton horse
> in last year's race
> to what is she running

No, not for my book. I start again. This time I title and even try to punctuate. But I can't find my way back to my prose.

I write:

Lying Around

> I think I've stopped lying.
> I don't know when that happened, but it did
> Oh, I didn't lie maliciously, more protectively
> like the changing colors of birds or lizards.

I used to lie on rocks at Cap d'Antibes or on Capri
And blend right into my environment
Golden tan was awfully good for the Mediterranean
Especially in August

I used to dine at Chambord and Pavillon,
when New York had such places,
Remark upon the wine and the sauce
And make brilliant conversation to show
how goddamn smart I was
As well as pretty.
Of course I knew better.

I used to set my hair in huge plastic pipes
to soften its curl
I didn't want to look too Jewish, or ethnic either.
I used to boil my diamonds as well as my eggs.
I used to be funny but never too funny for the crowd.

And I used to paint roses on my cheeks
And I glowed with seeming health while
wasting into a shadow
At those times what I was after was erasing my mind
I wanted my brain numb. Or at least friendly.

Please notice I didn't say I've stopped lying entirely.
I can't always control it.
Nobody can
But when I can, I do. And that's certainly something
I still confuse lying and laying. Or do I?
I think I did last night. And here's how it went.

How do I love thee, let me count the lies.

Should I send this to my playwright what's his name?
Would he phone in a friendly critique? I decided not, not
judging by the papers (how had such a private man become
such a public scandal?). What pain for his wife. Never
through me. I was in too much awe. Now he was on to other
plays. Did I care? And what about Jerry?

When Janice moaned, I equated pain. No question about
it. God, spare me that kind, and I'll handle this on my own.

Pangs of guilt would follow this. And as always the big question: Why her and not me? I still drank and smoked, though I intended to stop. I ate badly, deprived myself of sleep, and yet, outside of this burning beneath my rib cage our chest men said was anxiety, I was healthy, healthy, healthy. Even if not sexy anymore. Oddly, I realized I owed some of this health to my sister and all those vegetables. To say nothing of the first fasting she'd forced on me after Nick and my attempt at suicide. "You must get clean," she had chanted. "You promised."

"I am clean," I had protested.

"Inside, you must get rid of the poisons. You must come and fast with me."

"All right." I'd given in at last, and she had rushed to make our travel plans. She had just met her Bobby and was strong with love.

"The first rule of fasting is never eat on an empty stomach," my sister had instructed seriously, while munching a handful of cashews and handing me a second grapefruit to peel.

The stewardess looked on in dismay. "Please fasten your safety belts," she warned. "We haven't even taken off yet."

Janice, ignoring her, dropped into my lap a cellophane bag stuffed with darkish lumps. "Try these. Honey ball dates; see, they're round and really sweet." I'd released my grip on the grapefruit and shoved the stickiness into my mouth.

"Delicious," I agreed. And Janice smiled smugly.

The stewardess was losing her official smile even before Janice's almond butter spilled on the seat, which was even before the cashews and grapefruit appeared. "Your safety belts," she insisted in a full glower that forced her breasts into war with her waistcoat. She tapped Janice's satchel with her oxygen mask and signaled it under the seat. Janice dropped her grapefruit and, in an act of compassion, buckled up. I pointed out my already secured belt and continued peeling. The stewardess sighed and moved on.

"Feast tonight," said Janice; "tomorrow we fast." Janice was having a wonderful time. A high priestess with convert in tow. She was going to lead me along the paths of health and righteous eating. Strange to me was this kid sister, stretching to full height, which at eighteen was two inches loftier than mine. She attributed that to my bad diet, smoking, and Nick. "He's stunted you," she pronounced. "He never lets you get enough sleep." How convenient to have Nick to blame everything on. Janice continued, "You could have kept growing until twenty-two or twenty-three. Even Melvin grew an inch the same year he died."

The stewardess marched along, buttocks doing battle with tailored blue serge; her tapered look wasn't quite working. Or perhaps it was. The men seated across the aisle seemed to enjoy watching flesh fight constriction.

"She looks," I commented, "a little like Marilyn Monroe."

"I don't like that look," said Janice, spitting out a seed with practiced precision. "It comes from white bread and candy and too many dairy products. Look at her eyeballs, the uneven color of her calves. She'll have varicose veins before she's thirty." I reluctantly confessed to eating a salami sandwich before the plane.

"I hope you enjoyed it," she said from deep into her cashews. "It will be your last."

By the time we reached Palm Beach, Janice had kindly advised the stewardess of the poisons rampant in red meat, the deadly rewards of refined sugar, and the dangers of hair dye. Handing her a tract on raw juice therapy and suggesting wheat germ for her circulation, she disembarked in triumph. The stewardess watched her descend in awe and gratitude. Nutrition wasn't much talked of in the fifties, and I remember considering, with awe myself, the blessings soon to be mine. The sweet breath and regular bowels were birthrights to be reclaimed. The various inflammations that had plagued me since St. Francis would be a thing of the past. I would no longer get dizzy rising from a chair or swoon on a street corner. I would lavish love on my liver and kindness on my kidneys and would help out my heart. Dr. Esser, a saint according to Janice, was going to guide me through.

"You see," Janice pronounced, "I will never die of cancer. And if you live right," she went on, "you won't either."

She stuffed me with proof and cashews. "The Hunzas survive to be over a hundred and fifty. They eat only natural foods and yogurts and take no drugs or liquor or smoke or anything."

"Maybe they don't live that long, but it just feels that way." My joke had fallen on deaf ears.

"I'm saving your life," she stated flatly.

And I said, "Thank you."

We'd awakened to an uncertain sort of day. I, Janice, and Bambi, the crippled puppy she had stored in with the baggage of the plane.

The Bedlington puppy lapped up some nut butter and cottage cheese. He was not fasting. I remembered the Russian film Melvin had once taken me to see on animal conditioning, where tamed vegetarian lions leaped in surprise and fear when confronting their first croaking frog. "Pavlov propaganda," I had argued.

The Bedlington dropped a pale little turd on some newspaper in the bathroom. My sister observed the turd's consistency before dumping it into the toilet. "Too much nut protein," she said.

Dr. Esser, glad to meet Janice's sister, considered my case. Asking about my life habits and my death habits, he decided I needed a twenty-one-day fast. "Twenty-one days on water! I'll starve!" I'd cried.

"That's the idea," explained Esser.

So for days we limped her dog around the mango trees or sat dangling our thinning limbs in the small blue pool, chewing ice instead of fat.

"If only I'd known this stuff when Melvin got sick," she sadly lamented, "I could have saved him." Finally I decided she absolutely could have saved him. And was converted into the perfect natural hygienist Janice herself always meant to be but somehow never quite was. Janice thrilled when we became sisters in the organic life.

"Remember," she said, "how Daddy wouldn't let us fast on Yom Kippur."

I remembered the argument. "Growing children need food, and you have nothing to atone for."

The protest: "All the other kids are fasting."

The decision: "Not my kids."
The appeal: "We will feel funny at temple."
The dismissal: "God will forgive you."
The realization: "But not the neighbors."
The conclusion: "God will forgive them, too."

Then it was over. My sister was dead. Early one sweet-scented July morning, her heart decided to give in and let her go.

Arturo, never well able to face the hospital while she was still in that body, was able, after the custom of his parentage, to dress and prepare that poor body by himself. "I am her husband," he insisted, not letting the undertaker touch her. He was also able to mourn out loud. Which I was not. I'd become a funeral director.

"No," I supported Arturo's intentions. "We don't want embalming. No more chemicals. . . . Yes, we are keeping the casket closed. . . . Yes, pine, the cheaper, the better for burning. . . . Of course, there will be a service. . . . Yes, with a rabbi." I will not send her to the oven without words.

And did I want flowers? As many as I could get. "Send flowers," I begged. Everyone did. Janice loved flowers.

Placing pictures from when she was beautiful among the bouquets that blanketed her was my last protest in her behalf. As I stood silently at her coffin, wanting to say good-bye, Hermosa, out of control, denied me the moment.

"Jews don't have flowers," she accused with anger. The friends I'd sent to call for and drive her to the viewing had come late. Keeping her waiting an hour in her lobby convinced her that obviously I was not doing things correctly. And as was her way, she competed with the corpse.

"I have no one now," she cried to one and all. "I supported her for years, and now she's left me. Why?" She questioned, "Why Janice? Why not Barbara?" Not sure that she wanted me to hear this, I did. But I was too numb to care. Besides, it was my very own question. It got worse.

The next morning, just before the funeral, the young rabbi, a total stranger, found himself confronted by one Auntie H. trimmed in black, except for naked legs, and wearing eyes that looked darkly on the other two aunts (Caplin sisters-in-law), who surprised us by coming.

"Is this what they show up for. After years of indifference!" she said, and refused to acknowledge them further. The problem was the rabbi who lumped "surviving aunts" together in his eulogy, releasing Hermosa's floodgates of ancient furies. She was not to forget his "insult" or mine of seating Teresa to the other side of Paulie on the first mourners' bench, leaving her to the lesser status of the bench behind. And she hadn't forgotten Paulie's crimes either. "He stole from me when I was in the hospital," she shouted across the chapel to her crony from Uncle Al's store. It took her a long time to forgive him anything. She finally began to soften when he was grown and handsome. And especially when he made the long drives to the out-of-the-way institution her own good sister's concerns locked her into. But during the hush of Janice's service her condemnation rang out loud and clear: "He made her sick, you know. He's a rotten kid."

The "rotten kid" was so dazed with despair he was hardly there. I sat holding his hand. Over his choked breaths I heard the words of the rabbi reading the small personal paragraphs I'd asked him to include. It started, "Her father called her *faygeleh*. It means 'little bird.'"

Hermosa punctuated his sentences with exclamation points, sighs, and loud mutters of "And her father would turn in his grave if he saw those two hypocrites sitting here." She pointed the Caplin "aunts" out to the rest of the mourners. And she certainly resented their partaking of the customary cold cuts and cakes and coffee I'd put out for those who had attended the services for Janice. I had done the best I knew how. Hermosa huddled in her corner of the crowd and concluded, "Janice is dead, and *they* are enjoying the party."

The day following the funeral Auntie H.'s "good sister" from deep New Jersey, who hadn't managed to make the funeral, rushed, complete with warring daughters and wary sons-in-law, to Hermosa's side. They helped her along to their lawyer where she altered her will, precluding little Paulie by name. Thus Hermosa took the first step that led her to lie on an institution floor dying from a fall no one even noticed. But before that she will have recanted. She will lean on my arm, telling nurses how I helped her "more than a real daughter." And I will hear her verbally instruct the New Jersey heirs to honor her wishes and make sure that Paul received the small legacy she wanted him to have, "for Janice's sake."

"Trust us," they said, even as they pulled her bankbooks from hospital-weary hands. In the end when informing Paul of his future gift, Hermosa warned him "not to waste, but save like I always did." It won't matter. They won't honor her wishes. . . .

Slumped in isolation at the New Jersey nursing home so convenient to this good sister, she sadly admitted, "They only come now when it's time to sign over my Social Security check." My poor Auntie H. was to die alone.

Did she have such premonitions then as we stood at the grave hole, holding the bronze box that was all that once was Janice? Hermosa had studied the embossed metal square in odd envy. "I want to be cremated, too," she suddenly stated flatly. And pointing to the one space remaining, next to my mother and above Janice, she added, "And I want that spot, by my sister Rose. I am entitled to it."

It was my place to give. I will see that she has it. And she will be hard to handle to the very end. She will manage to get her ashes misplaced by parcel post while being mailed back from New Jersey. "She's lost in transit," I cried until they finally tracked her down.

Here, standing firmly on her "spot," Auntie H. was busy explaining herself, to the regretful rabbi. "I am Hermosa," she made very clear. "That means beautiful, you know!"

When alone with Jerry, I made an announcement of my own. "We both are going to stop smoking," I said, "if it kills us!" I was determined to save someone.

He spent a lot of time pretending to me that he had stopped.

BOOK FIVE

A Case of Mistaken Identity

Something Borrowed, Something Blue

"**I**'m glad you like it," I said to Monti as he snapped his shears at the pretty Dali etching bought from the TV auction. "Jerry has become comfortable at auctions," I explained. "He's good at bidding."

"Glad to know he's comfortable with something," said Monti, moving me to the light of the garden. "Usually he just sits and stares. If anyone studied me the way he studies you, I'd think he was trying to steal my act."

"He loves me," I said.

"Does he know you once sat on a stage as part of a Dali happening?"

"I don't think I ever mentioned it."

"Does he know you used to play with Dali's leopard?"

"Why should he know that? I'd forgotten that."

"Just wondering if he really knows you?"

"We"—I bristled—"have been together for years."

"Most of which he stared through," said Monti.

I laughed, realizing I'd stopped trying to explain the staring. "What are you thinking?" I used to ask. He never had an answer.

"You," said Monti, looking around my walled garden of ancient trees and statues, "are having prewedding nerves." He started clipping at my dead ends, his own hair, gleaming like new-minted gold in the Florida sunshine.

"Adio," he suddenly said, "went completely bald,"

"Adio?"

"Adio," Monti repeated. "You remember Adio, Dali's beautiful protégé from the sixties. You remember, Barbara. The one with the face."

"That was Crazy Billie. That's what they called him on Brighton Beach, where I first saw him." Stumbling over groups of tan and wrinkled vegetarians, Brooklyn body builders, grandmas and babies, Crazy Billie had looked like a lost prince from the *Arabian Nights*. "Crazy Billie, sleeping under the boardwalk, eating leftovers from beach-browned bags. A worn winter coat, worn over nothing. And above that the face of an angel with masses of blue-black ringlets cascading over elegant ears. He wandered and smiled at everyone."

"It's all gone now," Monti said, making me stand so he could even my trim. "Adio's bald as a bat. And living with a new French wife on his vaultful of Dali sketches. Like that one. When he needs money, he unrolls a sketch, frames it, and sells it."

"What happened to his Mexican wife? The one who changed his name and was going to make him a movie star?"

"Well, they were sitting at dinner with some pals in Acapulco, and she kept asking Adio if he loved her. And he wouldn't answer, kept ignoring her. Then she pulled out a gun and shot her own face off. She died before they got her to the hospital."

I visualized her tight, tough little face. Thin lips stuck to a perennial cigarette. I also remembered a nice laugh. "They love their damn guns and grand gestures, the Mexicans," I said. "Such romantic primitives."

"Sit still," ordered Monti, wiping his shears and rising to his full, coordinated elegance. "I've got to rush. I'm going to see my new boss and explain that I'm a jewel to adorn his nightclub."

Monti Rock III né Joseph Martinez, Puerto Rican slum kid, had certainly pushed a crazy path through the world of fashion. By 1962 he was master of his own pavilion at Saks Fifth Avenue. And it was a grand salon in the classic sense. He "did" everybody who was worth looking at or worth knowing or wishing you did. I was always thrilled to be there.

The place had been noisy with yapping Yorkies, models, the avant-garde, bohemians, femmes fatales, entertaining ladies, business ladies, and lots of ladies who liked ladies. Under his dryers you could puff a joint or pop a pill in style and safety, if such was your wont, and among Monti's clientele it mostly was.

But Monti, wearying of off-camera miracles, yearned to be a star. "I've always been a legend in my own mind," he would say, and it was almost true. I had agreed to help him. So we waltzed the Fire Island sands to the beach house of Trude Heller, who ran a rock-and-roll joint in the Village. I decided he needed a new name and christened him Monti Rock III. He loved it.

Monti considered going from earning thousands a week doing hair to a few hundred doing rock-and-roll, the career move of his life. He's never been sorry about it. I, on the other hand, have been constantly guilty. Twenty years later, in my Florida garden, I still looked at him with wonder. Naming Monti, like saving the life of an Oriental, meant in some way I was forever responsible for him. And he, responsible for me. If it hadn't been for Monti, I might never have become the favorite "love goddess" of Tim Leary's hip new world. Monti, who reintroduced me to Van Wolf, and his assortment of sixties hallucinogenics.

Right now Monti was more het up with my coming wedding than I was. He wasn't sure about marriage, but weddings were truly important affairs. He, of course, would do my hair; but what was I wearing, and who was coming and should he get the local press to cover it? No! But why not? Jerry's sister, né brother, wasn't going to be there, was she?

"No, Jerry could never face that." Monti slid past the guests to question the one-man band I'd hired. A strolling trio would be more fun. My mind lingered on Jerry's closet sister. Poor thing. When the mystery calls started from this woman who wouldn't give her name but asked personal questions, I thought it was a random crank. The look on Jerry's tight little face told me it was more.

He told me of his brother's wearing their dead mother's clothes and the grief it had caused little Jerry in the Brooklyn Navy Yard neighborhood of his childhood. He wasn't ready for this reunion. But it seemed unavoidable, so I supported and cushioned him through it, more shocked by his deceit than by his sorry sister.

He sat in a total catatonic spasm as his sister described the many operations and hardships of her transformation. She made no secret of it. And wanted his sympathy for her ordeal. Under her red wig, her Adam's apple bobbed with emotion as she spoke of how they "line the new vagina with the skin of . . ." And how they "cut and sewed and sawed . . ." Jerry's poor eyes started rolling up. So I quickly moved the conversation toward the safety of her new job and her nice boyfriend, seated on my left. We got through it. After that Jerry kept contact on the phone in unseen safety. He said he did it regularly because if he didn't, she might suddenly show up somewhere, like at his office. I felt sad for this sister and sadder for Jerry. Anyway, she wasn't to be told about the wedding. He'd apologize later.

A psychologist told me this might explain Jerry's fear of water and other dark, moist places. I was to be patient. I was.

"You must buy your gown" were Monti's last words as, polishing the big glittering *M* that hung along with the huge amethyst cross I gave him, and lots of other gold across his hairy chest, he left me. *M*, I muse, is for Monti, for Marvelous, Money, Madness, Murder, Michael, Mexico. . . . What a mountain of memories Monti had dislodged. My God, how did I ever get here alive!

I remembered staying at Monti's apartment at the time of his debut, having sublet my own for my coming trip to Mexico. Monti needed a lot of support for this opening and insisted I room with him and delay leaving till *it* happened. Wanting to be a part of his adventure, I did. And found myself happily sitting in Monti's 1938 Packard, boasting a sequined placard reading it was autumn in New York. In fact, it was Thanksgiving, and despite my vegetarian ways, I had decided to give Monti, who was yearning for one, the biggest turkey, homemade cranberry sauce, apple-raisin stuffing, and candied yams Thanksgiving I could conceive.

That I'd never cooked such a thing till then didn't deter me. Laboring, I laid a table my grandmother and, indeed, a grandmother of the DAR would have been proud to look at. Monti was doing the inviting. I waited eagerly for our feast to commence. And I waited. Then they all arrived, four hours late for dinner: six faggots, two of what Michael would term "rough trade," and one black hooker, whose sex I could not determine. The "elegants" were dieting and didn't eat. The rough trade was and continued to be drunk. And the hooker was lifting makeup from my handbag. It was a night to remember. Later I was grateful no one ate, as I found I had amateurishly totally undercooked the bird.

What was making me think of that now? Was it this marriage stuff? Was it Monti?

No time to wonder. I was almost late for Jerry's plane.

It was always a point of honor for me to be on time for his plane. After circling the airport for parking, I took an illegal spot and raced to the gate. Raincoat over his shoulder, a smile on his face, Jerry ambled toward me. He wasn't the shrunken little man with the crumpled socks and frightened eyes anymore. I'd done that. He looked healthy and happy and alive. I rejoiced.

"Where's the car?" he said, embarrassed by display, and handed me the folded papers I'd asked him to bring from New York. "Love on a Winter's Afternoon," he'd titled it, years back when I'd wanted a testimonial of devotion.

As I pulled out of the illegal parking spot that raised his eyebrows, he seemed unsure of my driving acumen. I started skimming the twelve-page piece. Some phrases stopped my eye: ". . . a crisp afternoon, with a forecast for snow . . . on my way to a backgammon tournament . . . I'd lost interest . . . went to the bar . . . a beautiful, voluptuous lady floated by . . . I remembered her . . . God had heard my plea. Margot . . . approached me with Barbara . . . asked her if she would like a drink . . . orange juice . . . she told me of her sister who had cancer . . . she apologized about her appearance, but her beauty was in my eyes . . . told her about my life, my children . . . the California girl I was dating, whom she knew . . . gave me her phone number . . . should I send her flowers . . . thank her for her company . . . what would she think of me still married and cheating on both my wife and the California girl . . . my every thought was about this beautiful woman . . . decided I should call . . . in her apartment . . . finally experienced true love . . ."

"Why are you smiling?" he asked as we drove home.

The wedding day did not dawn well. Was it an omen? Hurricanelike winds swept fronds from the palms into the pool. Large mango and small orange leaves littered the lawn. Where was my perfect sunrise, the one I'd counted on for good fortune?

Beyond my garden wall I could hear Lucky as he bayed at no future at all, didn't need a moon. He lay in his hole, his chain heavy on his neck, and howled. Poor old Lucky (and what cynic thought to name him that!) fought his eight feet of chain twenty-four hours a day. Occasionally for a few minutes my neighbors so favored him as to set him loose to stretch his great dog legs and chase the winds of evening. Released, he knocked them over in delight and adoration. They would shout him away. No one wanted such a pest hill of fleas and mites swarming over them. Except, it seemed, me. When I was around for the freeing.

Then I suffered Lucky's great paws and nose till the worry of carrying fleas to my own pets finally overwhelmed me and I stood aside to watch him rush streets, crash hedges, and leap walls. Finally, bullied by the family he so loved, Lucky was back in his hole.

"He's an outside dog," they explained.

"Please, Lucky," I asked loudly, "give me a break today." And strangely enough, the baying stopped. That, at least, almost augured well.

In our bedroom, beneath embroidered sheets, Jerry lay sleeping. None of this was his concern. He would wake and drive off to take breakfast with my cousins, safely away from the combat zone of commands and action soon to be created here. This wedding seemed to be my own affair.

I continued to walk and worry. Should I marry beneath a fresh or naked sky or not? With the help of an astrologist, I'd set high noon for our vows, under an auspicious sun, on the Valentine's weekend of Florida's driest month. So much for astrologists. February '83 seemed the month of the Deluge. Behind glass doors Shnubby followed my movement with resentful eyes. Her rightful place was to pace alongside me, but it was too dirty out here for that just-groomed and gleaming creature. She, at least, would look as I intended. I considered my growing compulsiveness to do things right. It had, I decided, more to do with my mother and Jerry than me.

The two days of carefully planned prenuptial festivities flourished despite the weather. Except for Monti, who was growing tenser as the wedding grew closer. He was having "feelings" that I didn't want to hear. He might be right, but I didn't want to know. Besides, I had immediate concerns. Thinking back to the reception of my last literary agent at his bride's Scarsdale estate, I remembered wind whipping around a striped tent set upon slanty ground and rivers of water rushing between chairs, tables, and guests. I remembered how the waiters had skidded along plastic runners, their trays teetering and threatening to spill. Some did. And the cute old Jewish ladies, who'd linked arms to dance the hora, slipping in mud to land on their behinds. Giggles instead of applause. No good. It would be Plan B, which meant emptying the ground floor of all furniture and setting up indoors, and there was no time to lose.

"Watch the chandelier!"

"Careful with that couch! It's satin."

"Oh, dear!" A pane of glass from the Art Deco table was smashed. Never mind, never mind. When had my life become so loaded with things? Jerry's newfound money had made him the ultimate consumer, dragging me along. "Things are just things," my father had admonished. I didn't want to hear that either.

"Please, Paulie, help them remove that Oriental screen. No, I've changed my mind, leave it, it looks too nice. But move it farther back." Paulie obliged me. Not right yet. "Move it to the left." Paulie did. "Even more." That was good. I was satisfied. Beautiful, everything had to be beautiful. Okay, good. "Paulie, now go help with the tables."

Paulie was glad to help. He was about to experience the second happy ending of his entire life.

The first was only six months back, in that fearful courtroom, where who knows how many lives were shattered like my piece of Art Deco glass. It was all as terrifyingly predictable as the clinical case histories psychologists so delight in.

"He is going to serve time," said the local lawyer, who had handled his case before.

"He is going to do some time," informed all the important friends of friends, who were experts in such things.

"If we are fortunate and approach the judge carefully," offered the private counsel, who used to be prosecutor of Nassau, "we may hold it down to county jail and probation."

"He won't survive a penitentiary sentence," warned Jerry's pal with the state troopers. "He's too pretty and too innocent. But I think that's what he'll get."

No, I promised myself, my legal friends and relatives, that's not what he is going to get. No. No county time. No state time. No.

And so the ordeal started. Or did it? Hadn't it started back at Janice's bedside or even before that?

"Keep a strong emotional tie," advised a psychologist, "no matter what he does."

"What do you mean, no matter what he does? The kid is killing me." Christ, I sounded just like Janice. "I mean, he's so destructive. He does such shitty things. No matter how I explain—"

"He doesn't hear you. You are speaking another language."

"But I show him logically."

"He is not in reality." The shrink had tapped his pencil. "Logic won't work."

"Oh, God," I had repeated to my friend Phyllis, "he is not in reality, and logic doesn't work, and those psycho tests showed him suicidal. One test required an explanation of a drawing, of a violin resting on a table by an open window.

Do you know how Paulie explained it? He said the musician who had just been practicing put down the violin and jumped out the window."

"Paulie is a musician," Phyllis commented.

"That's right."

On the first Thanksgiving after Janice died, I'd held a Thanksgiving feast. I knew how to do it by then. It was to be a big one. Mostly for Paulie, partly for Jerry. "I've ordered a twenty-pound turkey. And I'm making fresh cranberry sauce, and I'm inviting a lot of friends who are bringing their own specialties, creamed onions and sweet-and-sour beets and mincemeat pies. So you invite some friends, too, Paulie. It will be nice."

He called the day before to tell me he'd invited two of his Long Beach bums: Dennis, an older solitary type, and Jeffrey, spoiled and fat and unloved. I disliked both, but said, "Swell, and please come early. I want you to help with the chestnuts."

This huge endeavor was going to tax my small city kitchen but I'd prethought it as best I could; a buffet would work. And the bird would be well and elegantly cooked.

"It's a quarter to one," I complained as Jerry opened bottles of wine and mixed bloody Marys. "I told Paulie to be here at twelve-thirty."

"So he's a little late. Relax."

"It's one o'clock." A little later: "It's one-thirty." Then the phone rang. And before picking it up, in an awful flash somehow I knew what I was going to hear, and I wasn't prepared.

"Aunt Barbara." Paul's voice came at me as out of a fog. "I'm in trouble."

"You are in jail?"

"Yes. How did you know?"

"What happened, Paul?"

"I was caught selling grass to a narcotics cop on the boardwalk. It was last night, late, and I was afraid to call you then, and well . . ."

I waited. He went on.

"And . . . well, there's no court today because of Thanksgiving. So they are going to keep me till tomorrow, when a lawyer or someone has to come and maybe bring bail. . . ."

I sat down on my bed, my head spinning. Emotional ties. "Listen, Paul," I asked as gently as I could, "have you had anything to eat?"

"They just brought me an American cheese sandwich and some milk. I guess I'll get some more later."

"Are you in a cell? Are there other people locked in with you?"

"No. They've got me alone in a room. Will you come tomorrow?"

"Yes," I said. "I'll be there, but where?"

"The Mineola Courthouse. They say to get here early."

"I'll be there early."

"Aunt Barbara. I'm really sorry."

So was I. Then my buzzer sounded and my first guests arrived.

The small dark hours make everything worse. Unsleeping, I'd waited for morning. Listening to the snoring to my right, I felt lonely, deafened, and detached. Sharing one bed didn't join Jerry and me; it almost mapped out our separate boundaries. Our blankets became barricades as we occupied our opposite ends. I clung to my end and thought of Janice, her Bobby and Paul.

I could see Paulie as an infant, sitting securely in his father's big hands. Bob, feeling his parenthood, talking happily of his baby's future. How cute they all were together. How much in love. I couldn't stay angry with any of them. Not for long. But what a bad Thanksgiving day I had just smiled my way through.

We waited in the corridor for court to come to session; only O'Reilly, the lawyer, was at home.

"It's a first offense," he said to soothe me. "And he's still a juvenile."

Uniformed guards with guns brought Paul in: stooped forward, his hands cuffed behind his back, and his hair uncombed. He was one of six.

Then came the judge. After all the "Hear, ye" and "right honorable," the calendar crawled along. The guards, bored, huddled next to the entrance of the prisoners' dock and rocked resignedly on their heels.

"When will he get to us?" I kept asking of O'Reilly.

"Have patience," said O'Reilly, adjusting his large bulk to our bench in the third row. I sat and craned my head to watch every move the judge made. What I wanted was a clue to what was coming. Then I was granted a small gift from God.

A defendant under immediate examination spoke very little English. His Hispanic forehead furrowed with lines of confusion.

"Where's the Spanish translator?" the judge kept asking. No one stepped forward. The judge was getting frustrated; the district attorney, agitated. Even the Legal Aid defense counsel, dulled by defending too many indigents, seemed desperate. "Have you found that translator yet?" the judge again demanded. Then asked, "Isn't there anyone in the court who can translate Spanish?" There was a long silence. Gathering what little of my wits were with me, I rose to my feet, and as charmingly as I could, I called, "I'm no translator, Your Honor, but I do speak a kind of Mexican street Spanish. If you like, I'll try to help." O'Reilly and Jerry seemed alarmed.

"Come right up here," called the judge. "We will take any help we can get."

Congratulating myself on a decision to put on makeup and to dress up, I moved past the wooden gate that separated bystanders and lawyers from the accused and the officials. Carefully I lent myself to the cause of the law and order. Then, demurely, returned to my seat. Two hours later, when it came time for Paul, the judge remembered.

"Who is here representing the defendant?" he asked. O'Reilly and I rose in unison.

"And who are you?" the judge asked me.

"His guardian and aunt," I said, quickly adding, "His mother died of cancer this summer."

"Approach the bench," the judge ordered. Paul shuffled forward, his eyes staring at the floor.

"Is this the first time you've been in trouble?" asked the judge almost gently. Paul nodded.

"If I remand you to your aunt's custody, will you promise to obey her and behave yourself?"

"Yes, Your Honor," said Paul.

"Then that's what I'll do. But if you are brought before me again, beware." We were released, till the next time.

The next time, I remembered while watching Paul wheel one of the wedding tables through the archway, was the next year.

And that year had seemed to go well. Paul was a senior at Long Beach High School, and I had looked forward to the milestone of graduation.

"Paulie behaving good," Teresa lied over the phone. And in truth, there were not as many unmentioned kick marks on her closet doors as there had been.

That he was medicating his anger down with drugs became evident after the fact, but for then "behaving good" was good enough for me. My book on American mistresses was coming out.

A generous review in *The New York Times* overwhelmed me. It was my baby. And the *Times* had recognized it as legitimate.

I carried a copy to the upstate ashram of Baba Muktananda, a unique being to whom I had turned for consolation when I heard that Master Kirpal Singh had passed on. For weeks I had been dreaming of Master Kirpal and would awake longing to throw myself on his mercy and restore my spiritual life. But it was too late. I'd never see that incredible face in this world again. I had needed to talk to someone saintly.

Paramahansa Muktananda, a Hindu Siddha called Baba, sat yogi style and studied me seriously as I listed all my failures. I said I hadn't seen Kirpal Singh in years, not wanting to act the hypocrite in light of my behavior. Could that behavior have affected him? Could a disciple's failures hurt the teacher? Muktananda had signaled me to be quiet. Through his translator he said, "All that is not your business. A great master knows his own mission. Your business is to use the gift he gave you. If you don't like your behavior, change it." And was I meditating?

"No, not really." He shook his head. That was the loss.

"Come and meditate with us," he offered. I did. He had given me blessed apples to bring to Janice's bedside, and when I needed it, he had given me a place to hide. So there I was again, standing on line at his door for a private moment, balancing a huge begonia plant in one hand, my book in the other.

"You aren't going to show Baba that book, are you?" an alarmed devotee demanded, pointing to the seductive picture of myself on its cover.

"Yes." I nodded, more bravely than I felt.

"What if he reprimands you?"

"Then I'll take it," I said. "Better to be abjured by a wise man than admired by a fool." I hadn't expected to find myself so sententiously protective. And could I really handle holy displeasure?

By the time it was my turn, I was shaking. Slowly I stepped into a serene incense-scented room, at the far end of which sat Baba. He rested in a wide rattan chair, a candle lit a picture of his Baba, and on his right was lovely Malti, his disciple and translator. Now I was called, how I'm not quite sure; my plant was at his feet and my tears were spilling across his vest. He patted me, allowing this flood, and my heart, dammed up for too long, cried itself clean.

When I came to myself, I was embarrassed. I had meant no indiscretion.

"It's all right," he said, smiling. "You have a pure heart, full of love." So I wiped my eyes and spoke of my parents, my brother, my sister. I told him I still hadn't become what I should be. I told him about my book. Taking it from my hand, he flipped its pages, looked at its cover, jiggled it a bit, and spoke.

"This is a serious and sincere book. These women, too, have hearts and souls, feel pain, give kindness, and want God's love. It's good that you wrote it." He stroked it with his hand, smiled, and handed it back to me, adding, "It is also good to see you again. Be more regular. It will make you happier."

Walking out, certainly happier than when I had walked in, I remembered my blessings and the words of my beautiful Master Sant Guru Kirpal Singh: "Love beautifies everything. When seen through the eyes of love, even the darkest thing appears beautiful. Every saint," he'd said, "has a past and every sinner a future."

While I anticipated a future, Paulie was adding to his past. Selling pot for his use and his friends was too lucrative to give up over one mistake. He'd know better than to sell to a narc again. He'd be careful, Aunt Barbara would never know, and he'd afford all those extras her frugality denied him. So when the next phone call came, that he and his pal Dennis, the beach bum, had been arrested with a suitcase full of Acapulco Gold, I was shocked. Another friend had "set them up" to get himself clear.

"That's how the narcs work," Paul's court-appointed lawyer explained to us later, when we retained him on a paying basis. He said we were lucky to keep it in Long Beach, where he was on home ground. Looking to our luck, we paid for a psychiatric study, a caseworker's report, as well as therapeutic counselors, people who would come to court on Paul's behalf and recommend leniency. And we found Father Ritter.

Father Bruce Ritter, founder of Covenant House, a refuge for runaway teenagers, *was* a blessing. He suggested Paul come and stay in his community for a while, to live not with the runaways but with the clerics, who worked with them. He even rented a piano and outside of the sisters' complaints about Paulie's racing around their halls in his Jockey shorts, it seemed a successful stay.

Father Ritter also convinced us all that Paul should undergo a wilderness experience called Outward Bound, where young people confront nature. The judge agreed that Outward Bound plus the cloistered cleric time, plus graduating from high school successfully, might add up to probation rather than internment. So I divided my time between promoting my book and concentrating full power on Paul. I visited his school, worked with him on his assignments, and even did three reports he owed, without him. My essay on Bach got only a B. My work on Bali and the Egyptians did a little better.

Something Borrowed, Something Blue

Paul wrote me from his rock in the wilderness during his solitary survival time. Here is some of it:

Dear Aunt Barbara,

How have you been. I've been fine. It's really beautiful up here although a lot of the time, I wish I never came. . . .

Two days later. I am writing you now from a rock in the woods. I am all alone out here, and I am all dirty too. . . . I've been thinking a lot about what it means to be a man and how to prove I am a man. . . . When I come back I'll show everyone I can be one. Even the judge . . . the fuck . . . I can't wait till I come back and start my life on the right foot. . . . There's nothing more to say, except I love you all.

Love
Paul

It sounded pretty good to me. He was thinking. That he wanted to change was evident. That he wasn't yet able, time would show.

However, at that trial the judge judged him reformed enough for probation. The local mental health clinic made time for him, and he swore he was a "new man." I, who believed, patted myself on the back and let go my death grip on his life.

Now I looked past Paul to the centerpiece I'd carefully done for this wedding. If Paul would move that last table a little to the left, I'd be happier.

"Paulie!" I shouted after him, to slow down his enthusiasm. "Watch what you're doing!"

"Sorry, Aunt Barbara." He gave me his best Jimmy Dean smile, bashful and brazen at the same time; then he widened it into a genuine grin. How good he looked, I thought, and how long it took him to get there. Years of caring, waiting, and prodding. Then came the Porsche.

Was it because Paulie's father had been a friend of Jimmy Dean, out of the same acting lineage? Was it because Paul himself had seen all of Dean's movies once too often? Was it that, like Jimmy, he truly wanted to burn up the road and end pain forever? Perhaps he just thought it was sexy to own one. Whatever it was, turned twenty-one, he wanted that Porsche. I had worked to preserve what little that was left of his mother's estate, and he took it, running to the used car dealer to buy the damn thing. Black, it had been mean and pointy. With everything wrong that could be. Nobody, especially Paulie, could have afforded that car.

In the foyer the one-man band was plugging in a thousand wires. He would be fine if he could just find another outlet. I pointed behind a pink-bowed potted palm. Good smells were coming from the kitchen. Shrimps and oysters started to adorn hills of ice. Champagne glasses glittered and waited. Jerry's pretty daughters had long gone to their grooming. They were world-class groomers. Teresa had brushed and put a bow on Shnubby's head. Noon was approaching, and I was a mess. I looked like a teamster. I declared Plan B accomplished and circled up the beribboned stairway I would descend in an hour, as a blushing bride. "Memories," I announced to my one-man band. "I will march down the stairs to '"Memories.'" Later I thought it an all-too-appropriate choice.

"You're gonna make a great bride, Babsie," Big Steve had said. I smiled as I thought of him and stepped into my bathroom. While the tub filled, I stared at my face in the narrow mirror.

Was that anxious face the face of a great bride? Why was I so anxious? Could it be that like Monti, I was having "feelings"? There were shadows under the eyes. I had covered them up with makeup, and under the wide-brimmed hat, I'd veiled and trimmed myself. I would look as fresh as a bride is supposed to look, and I hadn't even chipped my nails this morning. A good sign, I hoped. A bride should have beautiful hands to receive the ring. I checked out my nakedness, too thin perhaps, but shapely. While my waistline would do for Scarlett O'Hara, my thighs were showing some wobble. I'd better get back to swimming. I pulled at my face; no, I didn't need a lift yet, not yet.

What lines, what shadows had shaded my face the last day Paulie had in a court. That was only six months ago. A day that followed so many sleepless nights. Nights that started in prayers and ended in plots, schemes, and finally more prayers.

We had thought for good or bad it was settled. Paul's

local lawyer had dealt with the narcotics agents, part of a federal task force before I knew what happened. When they impounded that Porsche, with which Paul had couriered the "goods" and taken him away, Paul contacted his last lawyer. He got Paul released on a quick "deal" with the feds, which meant Paul, too, would join the long list of people forced to "cooperate." If you didn't "cooperate," a federal word, you faced a "federal prison."

It had been a frightening, ugly, and guilt-ridden experience for Paul. Yet strangely enough, it triggered his transformation. Suddenly he truly wanted to "be good, Aunt Barbara, I just want to be good." He voluntarily went again for a long stay at Father Ritter's, switching to a real therapist and quietly doing what had to be done. The "strong emotional tie" I'd hung on to had paid off. He became "good." And I had hope.

Since the trial was to be a formality, his lawyer didn't feel the need to be at Paul's pretrial hearing. Despite being assigned Nassau's toughest judge, the one they called "Put 'em away Ray," Paul was there on his own. But his "Hanging Honor" wasn't having any of Paul's "deal."

"No," he intoned. "I don't care about the DA's recommendation. You, young man, are going to be made an example of."

"Aunt Barbara"—Paul's phone voice was shaky—"Aunt Barbara, things didn't go well today." I listened, my chest growing rigid, and started the plotting and praying that had carried me the weeks to judgment day.

As I sponged my bride's body, I counted back to those terrible weeks, the first definitely being the worst. I was disoriented, and all good expectations expired for me with the thought of Paul being locked away in a prison, as my father had been. Paul might indeed die there. I'd seen those programs televised from Rahway prison. I'd met ex-jailbirds and heard the odds everyone gave me about Paul's chances. My closest legal counsel shook his balding head, saying he was pessimistic. His advice translated out that I'd better face facts and make my peace with the inevitable. I wasn't making my peace. Instead, I went to war. However, the news from the "front" continued discouraging.

"You know," one ex-inmate informed me, "drugs are highly available in state pens. If he doesn't go in as a junkie, he'll probably come out as one. If he comes out at all." I could visualize it. Paulie lying cold on a cement floor, his head against the ceramic toilet bowl, a needle up his vein. I could visualize it, but I'd spend my last breath to prevent it.

Not Paulie, I invoked God and the gurus, not my poor Paulie with his kind heart, sweet smile and talent. Don't let it happen.

By the second week, with the aid of Paul's lawyer, I had organized sympathetic case reports and enough letters to the judge to fill a tank: heartbreaking letters, beseeching letters, letters that told of Paul's past, letters that praised Paul's promise, letters that listed his last year's progress into health and positive behavior, letters that told of his good deeds and good influence on others. It was all somewhat true. "Truth or lies, everyone says the same stuff. The thing is," one lawyer advised, "to get the judge's attention and direct his mode of dispensing justice differently." It was important for Paul not to get chewed up by the legal machine. So I sent a long letter to Baba in India and kept praying to the oversoul of Kirpal Singh. "How to get the judge to see this as a case of a different sort, where hope is not lost?" I needed divine inspiration. And it came.

It came one sleepless night, as I stared at 3:00 A.M. television and yawned through one of those public messages that networks reluctantly run at those hours. A man was talking about a drug help hotline. He spoke of the ex-junkies who ran it and the amazing results they achieved where others had failed. Then followed a talk show, on which a social advocate spoke of the experimental new sentencing in certain courts, in which the offender is given time served out of prison in behalf of society.

Then I was wide-awake. That was it! Something to try for, not just this throwing ourselves on the mercy of jaundiced justice. If this judge was determined to sentence Paul to do time, couldn't we change the kind of time? Life time, not death time.

I called Paul's lawyer at the break of dawn. He agreed it could be a shot. The day of the trial I beautified myself as nicely as I could, but my eyes still looked like Anna Magnani's. In the car I went over my battle plans. I calculated how to seat the army of friendly witnesses I'd drafted to appear in Paul's behalf. Close like a Roman brigade. They would be well dressed. "I don't want to see any unshaved faces," I had shouted into telephones. "Teresa, I want you to wear the gray, not the black. That black is too deadly. . . . Paulie, you must wear that nice sports jacket, the tan one we just bought, and the beige shirt and the knitted tie, and I want your hair cut and groomed and your nails clean and your shoes shined." Like Cecil B. De Mille's, my directions were very clear.

In the front row I would seat Father Ritter, then Jerry, then myself, then Paul, and Teresa, and then the lady who ran the child center where Paul had done some recent volunteer work. Behind us came the rest of the battalion, the schoolteacher, the fireman, the man who ran the music studio, his piano professor, friends, mothers of friends, and most important, the man representing the Nassau drug clinic who would be happy and anxious to have Paul come work with him. Had I forgotten anybody, anything? I didn't think so. As prepared for combat as I could conceive of being, I closed my eyes and began repeating holy mantra.

The mantra sang through my blood, ran around my brain, breathed from my nostrils, burned in my breath. I started to feel as if I were going to levitate right off the seat.

The judge deftly dispensed other justice while skimming Paul's case history and the ton of material presented to him regarding our case. "Make sure you include everything you might ever want said," the ex-prosecutor of Nassau had advised as I sat in his office and a brand-new smashed-up car sat in his parking lot. Just licensed, I had hit a cement barricade on my way to that appointment.

"The appeals court," explained the ex-DA, "does not allow new evidence." So I threw in everything, including a chapter of this book.

All of them black, the other defendants being "dispensed" with at the rate of one every terrifying twenty minutes had families clustered crying about the courtroom.

The crying was almost more than I could bear. His Honor was oblivious of it. He kept rubbing his hands back and forth across his jaw and making little legal jokes to the coterie of clerks and newly moustached prosecutors camping about his bench. Through it all his eyes constantly lifted to relook at our brigade of supporters who sat seriously and silently and stared back at him. Each time (and that was every time) he sentenced one of these defeated young men to do time, my body jerked and my hand holding Paul's clenched like a vise. I tried to control it. I was scaring him.

My mantra rang louder in my ears. I watched the young mother with the two-year-old girl, who kept waving and calling, "Hi, Daddy," swoon as she heard the prosecutor say, "Unlicensed gun found in the glove compartment," and the judgment: "New trial denied. Eight to ten." The daddy was led away while his bewildered baby cried and his wife died, just a little. I, too, found myself growing dizzy. It was a strange dizziness; it was a dizziness drenched in white light. The light pulsated. I pulsated. Was I about to have, I worried, an out-of-the-body encounter of the worst kind? I might be dying, and more than a little. Oh, compassionate Kirpal Singh, I begged, oh, sweet Baba, oh, great souls, living and dead, help now. Daddy, help poor little Paulie, your only grandchild, who looks so much like you, who is our last, help him now.

The judge's eyes met mine in the pulsating white light. He pulled his eyes away. They returned. He pulled away again to turn out the light of another poor soul. A young man, whose father and mother, old and dark with too much wisdom of this world, waited on his words. Would anyone show them mercy? The white light receded. Their son would spend his next three and a half to ten years at the state penitentiary at Attica. America was sending their poor effort to jail. It seemed America's final solution to their problem. The guards who took him away were unmoved by it all. They had seen this part of the American dream die too often to respond.

I desperately divorced myself from it, too, allowing the white light to take over completely. Eventually the whole courtroom disappeared. Nothing existed except the white light, the judge, and me. Somewhere I heard the case of Paul Morris being announced, and the white light started to falter. I brought it back. This was the moment. Here it came, ready or not.

The judge looked almost as if he had lost a long tug-of-war. In a voice quite unlike the one he had used previously dispensing his justice, he explained how puzzled he was over this case. He said he had heard of this avant-garde kind of sentencing but didn't know much about it. He said he was impressed by the amount of material and the caring and "obviously solid citizens who showed up here today on behalf of this young man." He said his inclinations would normally be to send "this young man away" and give him time to "meditate on his wrongdoings." When I heard the word "meditate," I felt I was getting a sign, and I found myself resettling into my body. It was right then the judge finally made his decision.

"I'm going to give it a try," he said, smiling, to the surprise of the bureaucracy surrounding him. "I'm going to sentence you to work in the public's behalf, but God help you if you fail. God help you, Paul, if one of these urine tests I am ordering you to take every day comes back slightly suspicious. And God help you if you are late or miss one morning's work. Look to yourself," he warned, adding, "I'm not sure why I'm doing this, but you'd better be sure of what you're doing."

We left in a body, my army, not one of whom had even been asked to take the stand, but all of whom had done their work well. Behind us, the courtroom went into chaos. All those clusters of blacks who'd seen their friends or family taken from them, without a moment of judicial hesitation or compassion, went from stunned silent to cries of revolt. The white boy had gotten away with it.

Stepping out of my bathtub younger than when I stepped in, I thought with gratitude about my two saints who had not failed me. Above the sink my face shone back at me. I didn't look old after all. I looked, in fact, like a young lady of good fortune. Considering the luck I'd so often complained of not having, I decided I was loaded with it! Luck! Why I was lucky just to have known such beings. No matter what happened next.

People passed in and out of my bedroom, asking me how they looked.

"Beautiful," I said. "Love beautifies everything."

"That's right, Barbarosa," said a bright, bosomy woman with a loud laughing voice, adding, "That's what the master said." It was Astra Turk, who maintained Kirpal Singh's mission in Miami and had sent that letter to India two decades ago.

"Love, when it comes from the heart, is beautiful," she announced, seating herself next to my dressing table. Resplendent in white Punjab, silks, and jewels, she commanded, "Stop daydreaming, and finish your face, and someone get a towel to cover her gown. Don't waste time, Barbara, everyone's waiting, and you must be beautiful." Her final words were not just for me but for a hyper Monti, sailing in, workbox in hand ready to complain of his "feelings."

Seeing her changed his mind. Instead, he said, "I just left Peggy Hitchcock downstairs. It's been years. She looks great."

"Fix up Teresa," I asked of him, "and give her a little color." I was sorry Teresa's lovely granddaughter, Michele, the gift of her son, Michael, wasn't here to enjoy herself. It made me glad that Teresa's good stock continued.

"She'll look better than the queen mother," he assured me. And Teresa, proud and happy, held the dog while Monti did her. Monti put a bow on Shnubby as well. Forty-five years, I thought, watching her smile, of pure devotion. How loyally she'd stayed up late to see all the talk shows I did for my book, straining to understand what it was I said that was important enough to be on television. Some of the talk shows I did turned into surprises, the most startling of which I recalled as Monti combed, had happened here in Miami. I remembered sitting at another makeup mirror getting ready for it and worrying over my dog.

*　　*　　*

"I think I better leave Shnubby locked in my bedroom," I'd said at least three times to Margie, my Miami hostess, as I worked on my makeup.

In fact, I thought, taking in account Margie, other houseguests, I would take the key with me. No, there might be a fire. I'd leave the key in the door. I was almost getting used to my own preoccupations of forthcoming disasters. I had also become used to getting a touch nervous before an interview show. Adding another lick of mascara and wishing I had a better mirror, I looked out at the lights twinkling across Biscayne Bay. And changed my mind again. No, I'd take the key with me and feel easier.

"I am staying at home to listen." Margie sighed. Her huge house was haven to all, including clumps of chronic hippies left over from 1969. "The dog will be safe."

"I'm locking the door anyway," I said at last. And I did.

"Just," called Margie from her bedroom, office, and refuge from the live-ins, "be brilliant."

Once at the studio my nervousness turned nice. Something quick and bright happened to me on camera, even when it was radio. I sat happily opposite the host, smiled at the man in the booth, sipped my tea, and when the On Air sign lit up, I lit up as well.

The interview was proving to be terrific. The host, asking all the right questions, was as impressed as I myself by *The New York Times* review. And when it came time to "open it up" to calls from listeners, I was ready. The first call went right for jugular. It was an angry lady.

"Just who the hell does that Barbara Condos think she is?" The voice was shrill. "My daughter, who is a good woman, not some ex-tramp, is losing her husband. He's been keeping some bimbo for years. And he's divorcing my daughter for her. So how can she say these mistresses of hers don't break up homes? She probably broke up some herself."

Before I had a chance to respond, the host took another call. This voice, oddly familiar, seemed to echo from the back of my life, back home, to Ingram Street, Forest Hills.

"My name is Edith Donner," it said, "and I want to tell you I lived next door to Barbara and her family for years.

417

I watched her grow up. And nobody should call her names. She was the sweetest little girl; The whole block loved her. And her family, too. Fine Jewish people, they didn't deserve what happened. If your listeners knew what that little girl lived through, they'd forgive her anything. Not that she did anything. Can I speak to her?"

"Certainly," said the host.

"Barbara, dear, do you remember me, Mrs. Donner?"

"Of course I do, Mrs. Donner. How are you?"

"Well, not as good since Mr. Donner passed away—"

"I'm sorry."

"So I'm living down here now. I have a beautiful place, right on the ocean. You should come. I heard when you got married to that show business man. I was sorry to hear about the other thing, the hospital . . . I felt bad. [Pause] What happened with Melvin?"

"Melvin died a few years after Daddy."

"Oh, how that child suffered. That poor boy. We used to hear him, you know. The Shulmans on the other side and us. We used to hear him cry at night, 'I'm too young to die.' He was so scared. But tell me about Janice. I heard she married an actor?"

"Yes, and she had a son."

"Give her my love."

"She died, too, Mrs. Donner. Same disease."

"The same disease!" Mrs. Donner sounded as if she were crying, and I must have looked sad. The host became distracted. What was happening to his "sophisticated lady" show? He interrupted us.

"Mrs. Donner, why don't you leave your number with the operator and Barbara can get back to you after we're off? My board is all lit up. Thank you for calling." We stopped for a station break. And then he tried again. "Hello, this is *The Larry King Show*. I'm here with Barbara Condos, author of the hot, controversial book *Beautifully Kept*, a terrific lady ready to answer anything you ever wanted to know about mistresses in America." It was a brave try, but it failed.

"Is Barbara Condos Hymie Caplin's daughter?" the next

voice wanted to know. The host raised his eyebrows in question. And signaled me to answer.

"Yes," I said, "I am."

"Babsie?"

"Yes."

"I'm related to Gertie, your father's sister's kid."

I'd never heard of a Gertie. There had been talk of a sister who had died. Was that Gertie? The caller was still speaking.

"My name is Maxie. I remember when your dad brought his fighters here. You know Solly Krieger still lives here. He works the parking at Pumpernicks. And I think a couple of the brothers are down here, too. Izzy and Louie. That's all that's left, isn't it?"

"Yes, I think that's all." The host looked dismayed.

"So how you been?" Maxie wanted to chat. "How's your health? Are you pretty?"

The host looked anguished. He jumped in again. "She's in great health," he said, "and really looks great. Take my word." He switched to another call. There was the first woman again, the one with the daughter.

"This nice Jewish girl crap is making me sick!" she shrieked. "My daughter is a nice Jewish girl, not some damn gold digger. . . ." She went on till the host tuned her out. The very next call turned out to be Mrs. Donner in rebuttal. Determined to fight the good fight.

"Don't anyone call Babsie a gold digger. She was absolutely the most generous child I ever saw," started Mrs. Donner. She ended with "And, Barbara dear, I enjoyed your book very much. I told my girls to buy it. And don't forget to call me."

"I won't, Mrs. Donner."

"What," the host asked, covering his mike, "am I running here? *This Is Your Life?*" It seemed that he was.

The next five calls were also from friends. Or friends of friends. Or folks who knew Nick, or Martha, or Melodye. The technicians looked on in amused silence while the host and I struggled to center the show back on the book. The center didn't hold. It was, as hippies might say, a trip. And

I arrived back at Margie's stoned on the experience. "If you ask me," she said, "you sold more books than usual." Sitting on the floor of her bedroom, I listened to her review.

"It was fantastic," she said, curled in her bed, surrounded by books. "I never heard anything like that. And that Mrs. Donner, she was more protective of you than you are of that silly dog." She tapped her pencil and smiled through her glasses. "Tell me about your family sometime. You never mention them."

I finished my wedding lipstick the same moment Monti finished my hair. We smiled at each other. Satisfied, he raced off to witness my descent. Everyone followed him. Teresa, carrying Shnubby, was the last to go.

It was tense at the top of the stairs. Susan's older daughter, Berns, rushed over to me with her costume sapphire ring for "borrowed and blue." I slipped it on next to my real one. In my new sleeve was tucked Cousin Ellen's lace handkerchief. It had been her mother's. Little Sasha, my Gainsborough of a flower girl, stood at attention. Clutching her basket, she took her mother's last-minute instructions. "Stop on every stair," Susan told her, "and throw the rose petals." Please God, I prayed, don't let this all be a mistake.

The music started, and there went Sasha, seriously scattering her petals. Susan followed, head tilted, blue gown swaying gracefully. Stanley Peal, friend and acting father, waited a beat, then gave me a strong tennis arm to steady me.

"I'm fine," I whispered, but in fact, I was trembling. Rounding the top steps, I suddenly remembered Nick standing at the bottom of the grand marble staircase of the Hôtel de Paris, waiting and taking such pleasure in my appearance before those men of the moment who used to crowd Monte Carlo in season. I remembered his smile. For a moment Nick and Jerry were confused in my mind, and I lost my footing. Stanley discreetly stiffened his grasp on my elbow and saved me a stumble. Then I heard the welcoming "Aaah" of those anticipating the bride. No matter what, I sure knew how to descend a staircase. And no matter what, the groom sure looked like a man to marry. All I wanted to feel was love.

When it was over, when the sonnet had been read, when vows and rings had been exchanged, when Jerry had kissed me, when our crowd cheered as the one-man band burst into the victory theme from *Rocky* (I am my father's daughter, after all), and when we had feasted and finished Ralph's rocky road wedding cake and everybody was dancing, I said to Teresa, who was doing a Russian kazatskeh with the dog, "You know who I should have invited?"

"Who?"

"Mrs. Donner."

Epilogue: Return to the Ring—New York 1987

"That's it!" I shout, moving into the aisle of the stagnant aircraft now reeking with our overheated bodies after two hours on a ninety-nine-degree tarmac. When I move, my writing pads clatter to the floor. "That's it!" I'm on my knees, recovering pens and scattered paper, while in dead silence passengers shift heavy feet to accommodate me. I feel a stitch pop in the seat of my pants. Was my ass about to hang out just as I start my revolution? Never mind. I straighten, smile, and, waving my yellow pads, begin my crusade.

"I've drawn up a petition," I say, making what contact I can with the glazed eyes of those within hearing. To my surprise the eyes refocus, and yes, they are actually listening. And no, they're not reacting as if some crazy were in their midst. Which after eight blistering hours of delays would be more than they needed. Especially as it now seems we have been abandoned by our pilot out here on the strip. Compared with Jerry's, this abandonment will be the least I'd suffered in over a year. Never mind that, too. So I start to speak passionately to these frustrated people. I appeal. I assure them I will send copies to the airline and all governing agencies involved, as well as the board of health, *The New York Times* and Ronald Reagan. They listen to my script, which starts: "We, the passengers of horrible Flight 802 from Miami International to Kennedy, August 29, 1987, strongly protest" and finishes "and we want an apology and our money back."

"Well?" I ask. "What do you think?"

"I think I'll sign," says the lady to my left. Standing, she turns to her fellow passengers.

"I arrived from Key West at eight A.M.," she says quietly, "to connect with a flight that was canceled. I've been bumped from flight to flight all day, and I've got a new puppy locked in some compartment somewhere"—she stops for a breath—"I hope on this plane, who's been without even water." Looking around, she adds, "And nobody would help me get him out. I hope he's all right."

I hope he's alive. But I reassure the lady, as she sits to sign, that puppies are resilient and he's probably slept through it. She holds my hand for a moment as she gives me back my pen.

Reaching the next section, I begin my plea again, adding, "If you want to, you can write your own comments alongside."

Paragraphs start to appear to the right of the names. Long paragraphs of "you idiots. I've missed my boat to . . . . . . I've got people waiting at . . . this is no way to run an . . . Traveling with two small children . . ." Some passengers don't speak English, so others translate. They smile and wait to add their names, and I think of Teresa waiting for me at my apartment, guarding with her life my own two small pets. Sweet Teresa, how she sat in her corner of the limousine on that last ride to the country house. And how silent.

It had always been Teresa's pleasure on these trips to break into songs of her village. Some her mother might have sung, she translated for my amusement the lyrics, which mostly ended in death. Girls made mad by infidelity, soldiers who lied. Mothers who mourned.

"Does this chorus wind up with another slit throat?" I might ask, to make her laugh.

But this ride was different. Jerry wasn't driving. It was Anthony's Limousine Service, and I was crouched in the opposite corner, my head against cold glass. And she staring with eyes too sad to look at. It was holiday season, but I wasn't rehearsing guest lists or menus or worrying whether I'd made it Christmas enough for Jerry's Catholic heart. I just watched as Teresa's hands absently comforted Shnubby nestled in her lap. Teresa certainly hadn't wanted me to make this trip. She'd wanted me in bed, "where you belong." But I'd insisted on going to check the house, to snug the shrubbery safe from winter-mouthed deer, to test the fence that guarded the sleeping pool, and to set the heat for the plants. I was always burdened by this beauty under my protection and even more now as I would certainly have to sell it.

"For what," Teresa demanded, "you knock yourself so many years? So he could just go and leave you so sick? Maybe," she added, wincing at the jagged red line the surgeon had left over my heart, when he cut away the hungry new cancer, which Teresa thanked God was caught so quickly, "maybe he too cripple to love a wife." She could never have imagined that little "Jerushka," whom she'd preferred to see with a halo, could do that. "Not even visit the hospital."

"That mean Jerry," she stated to my friends, "he like a dead thing till Barbara make him alive." My friends, of course, agreed.

But I don't want to refeel those feelings. That world of pain I stepped into when that flat, otherwise engaged voice met my call, stating thinly how I wasn't to count on him for the surgery or anything else. He had "other plans."

The stewardess taps my arm. "They finally found us a pilot," she says. "So you better sit down for takeoff." I sit. I would rather remember other rides. Wet spring rides rushing to start my country garden. Lush summer rides of verdant air and fields of corn. Even that autumn ride to share Yom Kippur at my cousins' northern Westchester temple, when I was so happily forgiving.

"Jews on the move," I'd said as we stalled, "racing sundown."

Staring at the bumpers ahead, Jerry just blinked. "They're not doing so good," he said at last.

"Bums! Sunday drivers!" my father shouted at holiday cars that cut you off to slow to thirty miles an hour in the fast lane. Jerry, too, cursed other drivers, but his names were unrepeatable. That evening, however, he seemed to welcome the delay. Perhaps he'd been afraid of the Hebraic ritual to come. But I had been ready for it. It had been too long.

When the traffic finally moved, I'd talked Thanksgiving. "I've clipped cornstalks for my stack," I had told him, and went on to describe how I would decorate and what I would serve. He seemed to like that, to love the domesticity. Loved the rustic house with the big garden and tennis court. Loved racing across his own clay, not so bad for an uneducated kid from around the Brooklyn Navy Yard. And I'd been so proud. He was my accomplishment. Hadn't I transformed him, enlarged him? All, say the yogis, is illusion.

"Do I need a yarmulke?" Jerry suddenly asked.

"I don't think so," I said. "It's a reform temple."

But in my handbag, just in case, sheathed in a plastic Baggie, was the blue and white wool skullcap I'd crocheted while sitting by Janice's hospital bed. The volunteer lady wheeling her cart of games and needles had taught me in lieu of Janice.

"I'm not good at that stuff," Janice had apologized. So I'd jumped in, whether it was to help the volunteer lady, Janice, or me I hadn't been sure. Ah, Janice. Yom Kippur seemed to be starting, and something had lain crumpled on the side of the road.

Oh, God, I had silently begged, don't let it be anything that once was alive. No broken beauty. Nothing haphazardly smashed.

"A dead piece of tire," Jerry had said mechanically. He sure knew my terrors, if not my joys. I'd spent the rest of the ride counting off aunts, uncles, and cousins. Who was alive. Who was the best-looking. My parents, of course, and Melvin and Janice. Then Uncle Dan and Aunt Josie and sweet Jean and her husband, whom we were driving to see. And what about cute Cousin Ellen? And what about Uncle Izzy's kids, so strangely beautiful? Hermosa had the most style. But that was my mother's side. There was no doubt that Sadie was the ugliest. However, on the whole, we looked good at weddings and funerals.

So, I had wondered, could I finally forgive dead Aunt Sadie for being so cruel to the child that was once me. Could the child that still was me forgive the child that was her daughter Hilda? I'd met the adult Hilda a few years ago. When I saw her, somewhat sad-looking and as orphaned as myself, heir to an older sister's sudden death, my heart had opened to her. Could I forgive? Sure I could. That was easy. On the other side, there was Uncle Al, whose favorite child had committed suicide. And Aunt Ruthie, of the scheming daughters? Yes, a little harder, but why not? Uncle Louis? Well, that would be a toughie. Easier for me to forgive Senator McCarthy and the House Un-American Activities Committee for banning the folk-singing Weavers than Uncle Louis. Yet how very long ago all that was. And I had been so sure there would be no more of that kind of pain for me. I shiver beneath my thin airline blanket. They are finally blasting us with air-conditioning.

No, it couldn't have been easy to live with all these people who were in me, who still are me. The child, the adolescent, the saint, the sinner. How could he have liked them all? Had I? You have to be a good yogi for that. Now, I consider, I will have to forgive Jerry, too. But I'll let that go for a while.

That Yom Kippur the rabbi had sat with his head dropped forward, fingering the tassels of the prayer shawl draped over his shoulders. Jean had told me he'd lost a young son.

The cantor, choir, and organist had all been ready. All waiting for the holiest of all holy moments to descend and envelop us. I'd worried, Was Jerry feeling strange in his Catholicness? Stranger than I in my Jewishness? Then I had stopped worrying, to wait for God.

The next day my cousin had handed me my copy of

"The Book of Life" printed each year for yizkor, and I had searched out the names of:

Hyman Caplin
Rose Caplin
Melvin Caplin
Janice Caplin
Hannah Segal Klien
Harry Magid

held in sweet remembrance.

But that Yom Kippur night, while I had waited, I'd opened the maroon-bound text in my lap. And read the words translated in English:

THE GATES OF REMEMBRANCE
The New Prayer Book for
The Days of Awe

Central Conference of American Rabbis
published 5738 New York 1978

Turning to the Yom Kippur evening service on page 250, I had studied the written meditation:

KOL NIDRE

Kol Nidre is the prayer of people not free to make their own decisions, people forced to say what they do not mean. In repeating this prayer, we identify with the agony of all our forebears who had to say Yes when they meant No. Kol Nidre is also a confession. We are all transgressors, all exiled from the Highest we know, all in need of the healing of forgiveness and reconciliation. For what we have done, for what we may yet do, we ask pardon. For rash words, broken pledges, insincere assurances, and foolish promises, for these may we find forgiveness.

I am jolted into the present by the plane hitting an air pocket. "You'll have to buckle again," I say in Spanish to little Jose, one row up, five years old and frightened as he travels his first time north to be picked up by a relative he's never seen. They serve us stale pizza. I wish I had something tough and sweet to offer Jose. Hard candy like my father carried to comfort a kid. Instead we boo the pizza.

We also hiss the reluctant pilot in contemptuous relief when he finally arrives. He, who would rather be landing in

San Juan as he was scheduled, sneers back. He never speaks to us once during the flight. Not even to say, "Fasten your seat belts." I signal little Jose how to handle this cold slice of supper, which he somberly does, and sends me right back to the California Ristorante in Naples. Not Naples '58. Naples '87 on my way finally to seeing San Michele, the trip never finished the time of the count and Luciano. And it was right where it stood, three steps above the Via Lucia. But like everything else, somewhat changed. The California, adapting to a different Naples of car and noise pollution, had covered the terrace.

The trip had been meant to lift me from the occasional remains of what had been termed my "major clinical depression." Major clinical heartbreak was more to the point that winter which I had spent so sick and alone with sadness and terror. I'd become as a lost child again, standing by my mother's grave. The kitty, the Shnubby, and I wandered the rooms of the beautiful Florida villa where I had made my pretty wedding and wondered if I would have to sell that, too.

"Why not rent?" suggested a real estate friend. "Everyone does it." But everyone doesn't get Gypsies and a full-grown cougar named Rambo. And everyone doesn't receive a midnight call from Detective Joe Mathews of the Miami police explaining how the Tampa police had broken down my doors and windows, trying to nab this notorious tribe of clever con men and murderers they were trailing. But they missed.

"They said they were Hawaiian," I mumbled to the FBI agent as he showed me their mug shots and told me they were wanted in fourteen states. "The last Gypsies I've seen were on Broome Street visiting my grandma. I was only six." The FBI accepted my facts with understanding. They had heard this story before.

But in Anacapri, San Michele, the home of Axel Munthe's book still stood pristine, proud and welcoming. "The most beautiful house in the world," Uncle Charlie had said wistfully, trapped as he had been by the bay and his curfew. So I'd, sat again on the Via Lucia, shuttered behind brown panels and glass sheets, built to separate patrons from the street scene, realizing I missed the urchins. Acknowledging the changing years, I stopped trying to spot a familiar face. But another old familiar face sat along with me, chiding that though I'd escaped his embrace that bad winter, I'd better keep him in mind.

The seat belt sign is off, and I finish my petitions. By now I've inspired two volunteers to work the far aisles, and the passengers sign without hesitation. Great, they've given up being victims and are fighting back. And so, I suddenly realized, had I. I was out of my stupor, and I'd come out fighting. I hadn't survived not to learn something. And the truth is we change as we grow, and if we are lucky, we grow better. I'll make Teresa sing me a song when I get home, I decide, as with all my petition sheets signed, I am applauded back down the aisle. I will ask her to sing one about the betrayed wife who revenges herself on her worthless husband and goes on to find true romance. And I know she'll come up with a good one.

We are waiting for my luggage, I and this serious man and neighbor from former days who has gently returned to my life. The conveyor belt has yet to move. I smile into his fine face, which brings back my youth and yoga, but like a boxer who's gone a hard twelve rounds and is still standing at the final bell, I've nothing to say. He relieves me of my carryall and my cluster of pads and paper.

"A petition." I smile. We are interrupted by the lady of the dog, who kisses me.

"I want to thank you," she says. "I think you saved my life by listening. And I want you to know I'm not just waiting here helplessly. I am going right in there and get my puppy."

"Good for you," I say, with a voice hoarse from speechifying, as she marches right through the No Admittance doors. By the time the first piece of my luggage rolls onto the conveyor belt, half the passengers from Row 11 to Row 50 have stopped by to shake my hand, wish me well, and pay me assorted compliments. "You," they tell my handsome man, "are lucky to know such a wonderful woman."

"She rescued our sanity," says the man from the smoking section, with the large family, who wrote reams.

The stewardess pulling her portable luggage cart waves us down. "Here, she says, "is the name of the pilot and the flight they pulled him from. And here's a phone number you should call and tell about the petition. And give 'em hell!" She rushes off.

Baggage almost in hand, I see from the corner of my eye that a short, round woman has a family grip on little Jose and he is smiling at last. Ready to move, my lady of the dog reappears, clutching her puppy in her arms. "Thank you again," she says, then stops. "By the way, what's your name? Just in case you decide to run for president."

"Barbara Caplin," I hear myself say, "Hymie's daughter."